The Difference Makers

 **Sandra Waddock** is Professor of Management at Boston College's Carroll School of Management and Senior Research Fellow at BC's Center for Corporate Citizenship. She holds MBA and DBA degrees from Boston University and has published over 100 articles on corporate responsibility, corporate citizenship, and intersector collaboration in journals such as the *Academy of Management Journal, Academy of Management Executive, Strategic Management Journal,* the *Journal of Corporate Citizenship, Human Relations* and *Business and Society.* Author of *Leading Corporate Citizens* (McGraw-Hill, 2nd edn 2006), coeditor of *Unfolding Stakeholder Thinking* (Greenleaf Publishing, 2002, 2003), and *Learning to Talk* (Greenleaf Publishing, 2004), she is a founding faculty of the Leadership for Change Program, cofounder (with Steven Lydenberg and Brad Googins) of the Institute for Responsible Investment, initiated *Business Ethics'* 100 Best Corporate Citizens ranking with coauthor Samuel Graves and editor Marjorie Kelly, and edited the *Journal of Corporate Citizenship* from 2003 to 2004. She received the 2004 Sumner Marcus Award for Distinguished Service from the Social Issues in Management Division of the Academy of Management, and the 2005 Faculty Pioneer Award for External Impact by the Aspen Institute Business and Society Program and the World Resources Institute. She has been a visiting scholar at the Harvard Kennedy School of Government (2006–2007) and University of Virginia Darden Graduate School of Business (2000).

THE DIFFERENCE MAKERS

HOW SOCIAL AND INSTITUTIONAL ENTREPRENEURS CREATED THE CORPORATE RESPONSIBILITY MOVEMENT

Sandra Waddock

Greenleaf
PUBLISHING

2 0 0 8

In loving memory of my niece
Jessica Lee Peterson
(1977–2007)
Live well. Laugh often. Love much.

And for all the difference makers in this troubled world.

Published by Greenleaf Publishing Limited
Aizlewood's Mill
Nursery Street
Sheffield S3 8GG
UK
www.greenleaf-publishing.com

Printed in Great Britain on acid-free paper by
Antony Rowe Ltd, Chippenham, Wiltshire.

FSC
Mixed Sources
Product group from well-managed
forests and other controlled sources

Cert no. SGS-COC-2953
www.fsc.org
© 1996 Forest Stewardship Council

Cover by LaliAbril.com.

British Library Cataloguing in Publication Data:
    A catalogue record for this book is available from the British Library.

ISBN-13: 9781906093044

Contents

List of boxes 9

Foreword 11
James P. Walsh, Gerald and Esther Carey Professor of Business
Administration, Professor of Management and Organizations,
Professor of Strategy, Ross School of Business, University of Michigan

Acknowledgments 13

Introduction: creating a social movement 15
  The difference makers 16

1 Making a difference 19
  The difference makers 20
    In their own words 21
    A short history of accountability, responsibility, transparency,
    and the corporation 22
    Growing global inequity 24
    How the book is organized 25

2 Building a different future: an emerging corporate
  responsibility infrastructure 29
  Corporate responsibility from the inside: pressure from the outside 30
  Creating new pressures on corporations 32
  What have difference makers attempted to do? 32
  Principles, standards, and codes 33
    An emerging infrastructure of principles, standards, and codes 35
  Responsibility 36
  Accountability and responsibility assurance 41
    Responsibility assurance: verification, certification, monitoring,
    and enforcement 42
    Emerging infrastructure: verification, certification, monitoring,
    and enforcement 44
    Consultancies 45

Transparency 46
  Transparency and reporting 47
  Other mechanisms of transparency 48
Stakeholder engagement and dialogue 50
  Business and other associations 51
  Multi-sector coalitions 53
Questioning the system 55
  Alternative ways of measuring progress 55
  Journals and popular magazines 56
  Academic associations and interest groups 57

3 Early inklings: social pioneering for responsible investing

3 Early inklings:
social pioneering for responsible investing 59
  A framework for responsibility assurance infrastructure development 59
    Elements of a social movement 60
    A dialectical process of change 61
  Framing the problem: social pioneers 62
  Alice Tepper Marlin 63
    The seeds of social investing 65
    The Council on Economic Priorities (CEP) 67
  Joan Bavaria 69
    Trillium Asset Management (Franklin Research and Development) 71
  Timothy H. Smith 72
    Campaign GM 73
    Interfaith Center on Corporate Responsibility 75
    Expanding social agendas and multiple strategies 76
    Crafting a vision 78
  Amy Domini 81
    SRI gains shape 83
    The Domini Social Equity Fund and Domini 400 Social Index 84
  Roots of a changing vision about SRI 87

4 Emerging accountability structures 89
  Steven D. Lydenberg 90
    Rating America's Corporate Conscience 91
    KLD Research & Analytics 92
  Peter Kinder 93
    The continuing story of KLD and the Domini Social Index 94
  Steven D. Lydenberg and the Institute for Responsible Investment 99
  From the CEP to SAI: from shopping to labor standards 101
    Seeds of SAI 103
  Simon Zadek 106
    AccountAbility 109

James E. Post 114
    The infant formula controversy 115
    Public affairs and the environment 120
    Voice of the Faithful 121
    Accountability as an emerging issue 127

5 Emerging responsibility standards 129
    The next important breakthrough 130
        Joan Bavaria and Ceres 130
    Robert K. (Bob) Massie 133
        The evolution of Ceres and the founding of new institutions 137
    Robert H. (Bob) Dunn 138
        Levi Strauss 140
        The Fair Labor Association and other developments 142
    Steven B. (Steve) Young 145
        The Caux Round Table 146
    John Ruggie 156
        The UN Global Compact 157
    Georg Kell 160
        The Global Compact 161
    John Ruggie: broadening scope 168
        Millennium Development Goals 168
        Human rights 171

6 Transparency and common reporting 174
    John Elkington 175
        Going public once 178
        SustainAbility 180
        The demand for transparency and reporting consistency 186
    Allen White 187
        From Ceres to the Global Reporting Initiative 188
        The Global Reporting Initiative 194
        From code to transparency 195

7 Networking 197
    Laury Hammel 197
        Business for Social Responsibility
    Bob Dunn and the evolution of BSR 201
    Laury Hammel moves on 205
        Business and spirituality 205
        Engaging local networks 206
        Business Alliance for Local Living Economies 207
        Social Venture Network 211
    David Grayson 212
        Business in the Community 213
        International Business Leaders Forum 215
        Small Business Journey 216

Focus on multinationals 217
Bradley K. (Brad) Googins 217
Center for Work and Family 220
Moving to corporate citizenship 220
Boston College Center for Corporate Citizenship 222
Emerging professional networks – someone to consult to 222
Global action networks: a new approach to global governance 223
Steve Waddell 223
GAN-Net 226
A broad base of networks 228

8 Engagement and dialogue: changing the fundamentals 229
David Logan 230
Corporate Citizenship 235
Malcolm McIntosh 236
Corporate Citizenship Unit, University of Warwick 239
Journal of Corporate Citizenship 239
Applied Research Centre in Human Security, Coventry University 240
Jane Nelson 242
World Business Council for Sustainable Development 246
International Business Leaders Forum 248
Corporate Social Responsibility Initiative,
Harvard Kennedy School of Government 248
Judith Samuelson 250
The Ford Foundation's business-in-society approach 252
Aspen Institute Business and Society Program 256
EABIS: the European Academy of Business in Society 260
Tomorrow's dream: changing the nature of the corporation 261
Corporation 20/20 262

9 The vision thing 265
Obstacles to achieving the vision 265
The fundamental issues 266
Other obstacles 271
What needs to change: a better world 279
Decision-makers' hopes for system change 279
A better world? 295
What is this thing called making a difference? 296

References 297
Endnotes 302
Abbreviations and acronyms 311
Index of organizations 313

Boxes

2.1 Some key principles, standards, and codes for business 36

2.2 Major responsible investment institutions in the United States 38

2.3 Major stock indices with a social sustainability orientation 39

2.4 Major SRI professional organizations/associations 39

2.5 Major social research- and investment-oriented firms 40

2.6 Other organizations with responsible investment interests 40

2.7 Some verification, certification, monitoring, and enforcement organizations 44

2.8 Some major corporate responsibility consulting organizations 46

2.9 Standardized reporting 48

2.10 Corporate ratings and rankings 49

2.11 Watchdogs and activists 49

2.12 Sample business and other membership organizations 52

2.13 Major NGO/business, NGO networks, multi-sector engagement forums 54

2.14 Alternative ways of measuring quality of life/progress 56

2.15 Examples of magazines and journals related to business in society 56

2.16 Academic and academic-affiliated organizations 57

3.1 Trillium Asset Management mission statement 71

3.2 ICCR core values 75

4.1 Institute for Responsible Investment mission and goals 101

4.2 Social Accountability International 105

4.3 AccountAbility 109

5.1 The Ceres Principles 131

5.2 Fair Labor Association Workplace Code of Conduct 143

5.3 The Caux Round Table Principles for Business 148

5.4 The Caux Round Table Principles for Responsible Government . . 154

5.5 The Global Compact's Ten Principles 159

5.6 Principles for Responsible Investment 166

5.7 Principles for Responsible Management Education 167

5.8 The Millennium Development Goals 169

6.1 SustainAbility's Rules of Engagement 180

7.1 BALLE's Living Economy Principles 208

7.2 Social Venture Network's Mission 211

7.3 GANs: a definition 227

8.1 Applied Research Centre in Human Security 240

8.2 WBCSD objectives for members 247

8.3 Corporate Social Responsibility Initiative 249

8.4 Goals of the Beyond Grey Pinstripes program 258

8.5 Corporation 20/20 Principles of Corporate Redesign 263

Foreword

... it's easy to dream when you watch the river flow by. I guess everybody has beautiful dreams, or should have, but the real challenge is to find a way to give them practical meaning.

Georg Kell, p. 290

I look at CSR and I see a bunch of people trying to encourage companies to be good and to be nice. I'm all for that, but actually I think companies succeed because they are predatory, they are territorial, they are competitive ... It doesn't engage with the guts of the DNA of the business and that's where I think we ought to be operating.

John Elkington, p. 278

These two comments capture much of what this terrific book is all about. Many of us dream of a better world but only a few of us have the courage and fortitude to make it so. Sandra Waddock identified 23 remarkable people who stepped away from the bucolic riverbank to engage the predatory, territorial, and competitive world of the modern corporation. Their goal is to constrain the firm's excesses and harness its capabilities to leave the word a better place. Their stories inform and inspire.

I was reminded of Louis Pasteur's famous observation as I read this book: "Chance favors the prepared mind." Chance encounters in these folks' lives became serendipitous moments that sparked the creation of their influential initiatives and organizations. Not one of them tells the tale of a planned life that led them from point A to point B in a journey of transformation. Instead, they were all shaped by early life experiences that gave them a set of values and capabilities that, when combined with an astute observation of what is and what could be in the world, left them ready to seize these propitious moments. I was inspired by example after example of how a mindful awareness of one's values combines with dogged determination to create a life of purpose, meaning, and accomplishment.

This book is about more than a group of remarkable people. It is also about their work. I like to think that I am fairly aware of the corporate responsibility movement. But, even so, my head hurts when I try to keep track of the work of AccountAbility, the Aspen Institute's Business and Society Program, Boston College's Center for Corporate Citizenship, Business for Social Responsibility, the Caux Round Table, Ceres, Corporation 20/20, the Fair Labor Association, Human Rights Watch, the Institute for Responsible Investment, NetImpact, the United Nations Global Compact, the World Social Forum — and so many more. Sandra Waddock has done us all a great service by not just sharing the back-story of many of these initiatives but also by placing them in their historical context. Moreover, she tells us just who is doing what today in the areas of accountability, responsibility, and transparency. She has given us an invaluable mental map of this world.

And then there is the last chapter. She mined all of her interview notes to create a kind of conversation about where we are today and what tomorrow may hold. Reading the chapter, I felt like I was sitting in Sandra's living room listening to these people reflect on their current dreams and plans to "give them practical meaning." I wanted to jump in and offer my own ideas. This is the ultimate power of the book. This book is not just about these difference makers; it is about us. By sharing what others have done in such an accessible and even intimate way, she leaves us motivated to follow their lead.

Ultimately, this book is not just about 23 difference makers and us. It is about 24 difference makers and us. Sandra Waddock is a difference maker. She had the vision and perseverance to write this book. She gave us the mental map of the corporate responsibility movement. With her own history of incredible work in this area, she earned the respect and trust of these people. Without that trust, this book would not exist. And, finally, she had the wisdom to know that, by elevating and celebrating the work of others, she would inspire us all to get off that riverbank and engage the world. Unbeknownst to her, Sandra Waddock left us with yet another model of how one person's passions and unique gifts can leave the world a better place.

James P. Walsh
Gerald and Esther Carey Professor of Business Administration,
Professor of Management and Organizations,
Professor of Strategy,
Ross School of Business, University of Michigan
March 15, 2008

Acknowledgments

There are always so many people who need to be thanked at the end of a book project like this one. So much gratitude goes to all of the difference makers themselves, for their willingness to share their stories and insights with me, not to mention their hard work in trying to build a better world for all of us.

My thanks and gratitude go to Boston College's Carroll School of Management, which granted me a year's sabbatical to write this book, especially Dean Andy Boynton for his support. Thanks also to John Ruggie and Jane Nelson of the Mossavar-Rahmani Center for Business and Government at Harvard's Kennedy School of Government, who invited me to become a visiting scholar for the 2006–2007 academic year, giving me the freedom so the book could actually get written. That gift of that space and place to think and write, to be re-inspired, and to learn untold new things cannot be measured.

There are so many others to thank who have supported me in ways that they cannot even begin to know. My longtime colleague and coauthor on many articles Sam Graves, my colleagues within the Leadership for Change Program at Boston College, who inspired so much of the original thinking that led me to this path, including particularly Judy Clair and Bill Torbert, Charlie Derber, Paul Gray, Janice Jackson, Robert Leaver, Manuel Manga, Ken Mirvis, Joe Raelin, Rebecca Rowley, Eve Spangler, and Steve Waddell. And, of course, Theresa Mahan for her constant support, both while I was editor of the *Journal of Corporate Citizenship* and beyond.

My Boston College colleagues and those who work at the Boston College Center for Corporate Citizenship have also provided grounding in the realities of the world of corporate citizenship, and helped push many of these ideas along. My students, most recently doctoral students Jegoo Lee and Jennifer Leigh, but also the many MBA and undergraduate students taught over the years, always inspire new insights.

Of course, many colleagues in the business-in-society field and beyond are inspiration for so much intellectual stimulation and inspiration, especially Ed Freeman, Bill Frederick, Jim Post, Lee Preston, Malcolm McIntosh, Peter Senge, and

David Cooperrider — all in their own way difference makers on the academic front. I am particularly grateful to Jim Post, who long ago served as my dissertation advisor and for these many years as a good friend, for believing in me when I started on this career years ago and for always being there when I need advice, insight, or support. Jeanne Liedtka and Dawn Elm deserve mention for their years of personal and academic support and encouragement when we have our annual get-togethers at the Academy of Management annual meeting.

Books, of course, are not written in a vacuum, and there are always those friends and family members behind the scenes who play roles that cannot be overestimated. In my case, there are some who deserve special mention: my two oldest (well, ahem, longest-term) and dearest friends Pennie (Hunter) Sibley and Priscilla (Stewart) Osborne (they are listed in the order in which I met them, Pennie in fifth grade when we were but ten and Priscilla when we were freshmen in college), and Margaret Skinner, Laurie Pant, and Tish Schilling, who have been there in recent years.

These days I cannot leave out my musical buddies from my former folk band Cachet, Leslie Bryant, Judith Christianson, Roger Cleghorn, and Paul Beck, and all the folks in the Folk Song Society of Greater Boston, Summer Acoustic Music Week (both staff and campers, particularly Peg Espinola, my SAMW 'roomie'), and Mystic Chorale folks (including Harriet Hart, Jack Lynch, Donna Ferullo, and Dorothy Orzalud — and the rest . . . you know you who are), particularly founder and director Nick Page (who saw fit to give me a solo while this book was in production). Then there is Alan Rubin, musical buddy and special friend — I am grateful for all you give. You have all inspired so much of that other side of my life — the side that feeds the ability to continue to do academic work. As Kahlil Gibran reminds us, "Music is the language of spirit. It opens the secret of life giving peace, abolishing strife." It is this peace that the difference makers documented in this book seek, and that we need to find in our own ways. You have all helped me find it in my life.

Of course, there is the support and joy that I always get from family, my sister Eileen and her family, my brother Jim, and particularly my son Ben Wiegner, now an accomplished computer scientist. I am so proud and love you so much, Ben!

Finally, I want to thank John Stuart at Greenleaf for taking on this project and for being such a wonderful publisher, editor, and source of inspiration for the whole field of business in society, and Dean Bargh for his incredible production work.

This book — and the difference that I hope it can make in inspiring others to themselves become difference makers — is dedicated to my niece, Jessica Lee Peterson, who unexpectedly passed over during its writing just before her 30th birthday. Jessica's all too short life was one of giving to others through her work as a recreation therapist. She loved people of all ages, whatever their disabilities and problems, and had a true gift for helping them lead normal lives. We miss you, Jess.

Introduction
Creating a social movement

Let's call it a social movement. The "it" is the emerging corporate responsibility infrastructure, still relatively new and made up of evolving institutions working towards change from within the current economic system. The change these institutions are leveraging is holding companies, particularly large multinational companies, to be more accountable and responsible for their actions, impacts, and decisions. This corporate responsibility infrastructure has developed as part of a much wider movement for change being demanded from outside the system to counterbalance the growing global influence of corporations since globalization took root in the late 1970s. It is the inside-the-system counterpart to the antiglobalization activism by non-governmental organizations (NGOs) and others demanding greater accountability, responsibility, and transparency from corporations.[1]

The subjects of this book are "the difference makers" — the remarkable people who have built the corporate responsibility infrastructure. The aim is to examine their motivation, inspiration and how they see this rapidly evolving infrastructure evolving in the future. Their myriad stories are told largely in their own words and, taken as a whole, represent a unique perspective on the developments that have taken place around corporate responsibility in the past 20–25 years.

The individuals in this book were the pioneers, starting new organizations and institutions — often on a shoestring budget — to develop the social investment movement, corporate accountability standards, and codes of conduct and principles that aim to challenge the dominant credo that the maximization of shareholder wealth is the sole responsibility of the modern corporation.

The difference makers are social and institutional entrepreneurs. Their stories clearly demonstrate that the ideas, insights, and leadership actions of one individual can effect change. Each of these people saw in his or her own unique and individual way that there were (and still are) significant problems with the responsibility of the corporation and how environmental, social, and governance issues are perceived in the boardrooms of the world. Each has done his or her part to change things.

The difference makers

Who are the difference makers whose work and commitment are profiled in this book? They are:

- Joan Bavaria: founder and CEO, Trillium Asset Management; founder, Ceres, which supported the founding of the Global Reporting Initiative; founder, Investor Network on Climate Change

- Amy Domini: founder and CEO, Domini Social Funds; cofounder KLD Research & Analytics

- Robert Dunn: former executive director, Business for Social Responsibility; executive director, Synergos

- John Elkington: founder and chief entrepreneur, SustainAbility

- Bradley K. Googins: executive director, Boston College Center for Corporate Citizenship; founder, Center for Work and Family (now at Boston College)

- David Grayson, CBE: director, Business in the Community; director, Doughty Centre for Corporate Responsibility, and Doughty Chair of Corporate Responsibility, Cranfield University, UK

- Laury Hammel: CEO, Longfellow Clubs; founder, New England Business for Social Responsibility; founder, Business for Social Responsibility (BSR); cofounder, Business Alliances for Local Living Economies (BALLE)

- Georg Kell: executive head, United Nations Global Compact

- Peter Kinder: president and cofounder, KLD Research & Analytics

- David Logan: founder, The Corporate Citizenship Company (now Corporate Citizenship, part of Chime Communications)

- Steven D. Lydenberg: chief investment officer, Domini Social Funds; cofounder KLD Research & Analytics; founder, Institute for Responsible Investment

- Malcolm McIntosh: professor and director, Applied Research Centre in Human Security, Coventry University, UK; former director, Corporate Citizenship Unit, University of Warwick, UK; founder, *Journal of Corporate Citizenship*

- Robert K. Massie: cofounder, Global Reporting Initiative; former executive director, Ceres

- Jane Nelson: director, Corporate Social Responsibility Initiative, Mossavar-Rahmani Center for Business and Government, Harvard Kennedy School of Government; board member, International Business Leaders Forum

- James E. Post: professor of management, Boston University; former president, Voice of the Faithful

- John Ruggie: Evron and Jeane Kirkpatrick professor of international affairs, and director Mossavar-Rahmani Center for Business and Government, Harvard Kennedy School of Government; co-creator, United Nations Global Compact; principal drafter, Millennium Development Goals

- Judith Samuelson: executive director, Aspen Institute Business and Society Program

- Timothy H. Smith: senior vice president and director of socially responsible investing for Walden Asset Management, part of US Trust; former executive director, Interfaith Center on Corporate Responsibility; former president, Social Investment Forum

- Alice Tepper Marlin: CEO, Social Accountability International; founder, (former) Council on Economic Priorities

- Steve Waddell: chief information steward and cofounder, Global Action Network Net

- Allen White: vice president, Tellus Institute; cofounder, Global Reporting Initiative; cofounder, Corporation 20/20

- Steven B. Young: global executive director, Caux Round Table

- Simon Zadek: founder and CEO, AccountAbility

To all of these difference makers — and so many more whose work and inspiration could not be included — thank you. The world is a better place because of your work.

Sandra Waddock
Chestnut Hill, MA, USA
February 2008

The Difference Makers:

1. Alice Tepper Marlin
2. Allen White
3. Amy Domini
4. Bob Dunn
5. Bob Massie
6. Brad Googins
7. David Logan
8. David Grayson
9. Georg Kell
10. Jim Post
11. Jane Nelson
12. Joan Bavaria
13. John Ruggie
14. John Elkington
15. Judy Samuelson
16. Malcolm McIntosh
17. Laury Hammel
18. Peter Kinder
19. Simon Zadek
20. Steve Lydenberg
21. Steve Young
22. Steve Waddell
23. Tim Smith

1
Making a difference

Since the 1970s, public and civil society dissatisfaction with the global clout and power of corporations has generated a growing wave of new institutional mechanisms that attempt, in different ways, to create more accountable, responsible, and transparent corporations. Created in a context in which global corporations seem to be growing ever larger and more powerful and nation-states weakening, these institutional mechanisms have become part of a much larger social movement. This movement is attempting to develop a set of constraints on the modern corporation that stands in stark contrast to the dominant economic logic of maximizing shareholder wealth and growing the size and economic and social power of multinational corporations.

As the next chapter will discuss in more detail, these new institutions include business associations and alliances focused on sustainability, responsibility, and accountability, consultancies that help companies behave as good corporate citizens, responsible investment entities, social research organizations, social and environmental standards, monitoring, and reporting initiatives, and initiatives focused on incorporating social issues into management education. Together, they constitute an emerging infrastructure aimed at corporate responsibility, accountability, and transparency. These new institutions are based on the work of a number of pioneering individuals which this book refers to as the **difference makers.**

This emerging accountability infrastructure works from within but at the margins of the existing system. It has had the effect of increasing the pressures on companies from their stakeholders, a group that includes but goes way beyond shareholders, and attempts to get decision-makers to incorporate social and environmental criteria in the decision-making, strategies, practices, and purposes of the modern corporation. As such, the infrastructure created by the difference makers goes well beyond traditional economic thinking, which argues that the purpose of the firm is solely the maximization of shareholder wealth. These new institutions represent leverage points for change that may ultimately alter the focus and purpose of the firm as a whole so that it better responds to and meets broad societal and environmental needs — and not just the demands and interests of its shareholders. Understanding both the need for change — and the ways to effect those changes — underpins the vision that has inspired the difference makers, even if, as we will see in some cases, that vision itself evolved over time.

While no one would claim that stakeholder, social, and environmental criteria today claim as much dominance as economic wealth maximization for shareholders in most managers' thinking, there has been remarkable progress in advancing an alternative agenda and in creating this responsibility infrastructure, particularly since the late 1980s and the 1990s. So many new institutions have emerged, in fact, that we might call this move toward greater corporate responsibility a social movement.[2] This book tells the story of some of the key players and the institutional infrastructures they have built in the emergence of that social movement.

The difference makers

All of the people discussed in this book are leaders, but they are not leaders in the traditional sense. Their motivation has not been to make lots of money (though some have done reasonably well by global standards) or to gain prestige and power (though some have attained that status as well). They do not head up huge corporations, political institutions, or even non-governmental organizations (NGOs). Their individual roles have been to hope to do good in the world by focusing on a progressive view of the public good and by building new institutions of accountability, responsibility, and transparency for corporations and other institutions. They have been able to see or sense that a problem exists in the macrosystem that supports the world as we know it, and move to establish new institutions that create leverage for long-term change — institutions that create a demand for greater responsibility and accountability from corporations and large institutions. In that sense, the difference makers operate in a domain of what some scholars call institutional design, while they are simultaneously attempting to mobilize a social movement of responsibility assurance for large and powerful institutions.[3]

Modest by nature, most of these individuals would not claim kudos for their leadership or vision, yet they have developed new organizations and new ways of seeing the world that have had a definite and profound impact on the way that business is conducted today. They have, in short, made a difference in the world. Acting as social change agents, they have operated largely from inside the system, rather than as external activists and demonstrators, and along the way they have tapped into other existing networks, created new ones, and found ways of working with or dealing with conflicts in existing entities and networks.[4] These difference makers have effected change by understanding the current system and then creating new organizations and entities at its edges that have grown to constitute an emerging global responsibility assurance infrastructure.[5] They too are activists, but activists working thoughtfully and incrementally within the system.

By understanding and appreciating how businesses operate and what their imperatives are, they have had the foresight to set up institutions that create new pressures for accountability, responsibility, and transparency — and perhaps ultimately for system change. For, as Peter Senge points out in *The Fifth Discipline*, Archimedes said, "Give me a lever long enough and I can change the world." Large-scale systems change when appropriate levers can be found. This book is the story of some of the individuals who have found such levers, and of the institutions that they have created to effect positive change in the world.

There are several driving questions behind this book. How does this type of long-term, inside-out social change happen? What is the role of individuals in creating a social movement like this one? Do these individuals arrive on the scene with fully developed visions of the changes they hope to inspire, or do these visions evolve over time? What, indeed, are the visions behind the changes that have been developed? Are there unifying driving forces in the backgrounds of those individuals who have led these initiatives that sets them apart, or are they disparate human beings who happened upon their leadership opportunities and somehow took advantage of them? I will explore these questions and many other nuances of the leadership exhibited by the difference makers in ensuing chapters, but first I will explore the need for change and look at the wealth of new corporate accountability and responsibility institutions that have sprung up since the 1980s, many of them considerably more recently.

In their own words

It is not often that we have the opportunity to hear from the founders and early pioneers of a social movement about how it grew and evolved, and how the institutions that form the core of that social movement were created and developed over time. But that is exactly what this book attempts to do: to tell the stories of these social and institutional entrepreneurs using their own points of view and, where feasible, their own words, supplemented by archival and web-based information about the organizations they founded or developed. But, before moving to the stories of individual difference makers, we need to understand the larger context in which their changes took place.

A short history of accountability, responsibility, transparency, and the corporation

The sense of unease about corporate power and the potential abuse of that power by the privileged individuals who control it is hardly new, though it has grown precipitously during the current wave of globalization.[6]

Concern about corporate responsibility was deeply embedded in the very charters that companies were originally granted in the United States, reflecting early distrust of the amassing of power and wealth into the hands of the few. Early charters required that incorporation papers be granted only as long as companies were benefiting society or fulfilling some sort of public purpose.[7] One can look back even further to the governmental powers of the Dutch East India Company granted by its charter, which allowed the company to monopolize trade with the East Indies, maintain armed forces, establish colonies, make war, peace, and treaties, and even coin money.[8] Deep concerns about profit mongering were raised by the tulip mania that gripped Holland in 1636–37 and destroyed many investors, and by the South Sea Bubble of 1720, which ruined many British investors through unbridled speculation and general fraud.[9]

Demands for greater corporate accountability and responsibility can be traced back as far as the muckrakers of the early 20th century. For example, Ida Tarbell's muckraking story about Standard Oil, published in 1904, and Upton Sinclair's novel about the meat-packing industry, *The Jungle* (first published in serial form in 1905), created somewhat of a sensation. Similarly, the publication of Rachel Carson's *Silent Spring* in 1962 focused new attention on the environment and the potentially harmful role of chemical companies. The then fledgling environmental movement galvanized public concern, which eventually resulted in the establishment of the Environmental Protection Agency in the United States in 1970. Ralph Nader's 1965 publication *Unsafe at Any Speed* created a wholly new wave of consumer activism that has resulted in automobile safety legislation, occupational safety and health legislation, environmental legislation, and freedom of information legislation. Jeremy Rifkin's 1977 critique of the budding biotechnology industry *Who Should Play God?* focused public attention on the ethical, moral, and social issues associated with DNA research.

Coming closer to our times, much of the developed world seems to have lived by a political slogan of the 1990s since the early 1980s — "It's the economy, stupid": the economy and only the economy. Broader societal interests were largely shunted aside in favor of profits and growth for large corporations and those who run them. This emphasis prompted Robert Reich, the then US president Bill Clinton's secretary of labor, to ask the question: "Do you want to live in an economy or a society?" Still, the mantra of corporations has been to maximize shareholder wealth since the early 1980s when the Reagan–Thatcher revolution shaped a new rhetoric around corporations and the fiduciary duty of executives and boards, and focused them single-mindedly on shareholders to the exclusion of other stakeholders. Nearly three-quarters of US states have enacted stakeholder legislation since about 1980 in efforts to protect workers, communities, and customers from the ravages of unbridled capitalism, but shareholder primacy still largely reigns in financial and some other circles. Simultaneously, globalization has accelerated. The World Trade Organization has fostered global free trade with the elimination of many so-called trade barriers that might protect local economies as a prerequisite for participation in the global economy.[10]

Despite the fact that there is actually no *legal* obligation for corporations to maximize shareholder wealth written into US law, many people believe that this obligation exists, confusing fiduciary duty to run the company well for the benefit of shareholders with a need to maximize shareholder wealth.[11] Fiduciary duties to shareholders and attention to corporate profits are also enshrined in global trade agreements fostered by the Bretton Woods organizations – the World Trade Organization, the World Bank, and the International Monetary Fund, which favor developed nations and their multinational corporations above other interests.[12]

The forces of globalization have further emphasized the creation of wealth, particularly for multinational corporations and those who lead them. Multinational corporations have steadily gained in size and power in the last part of the 20th and first part of the 21st centuries and today are among the world's most dominant and powerful institutions, in some cases surpassing the clout of governments. Although one can question the logic of assessing power by revenues, one study by the US Institute of Policy Studies in 2000 suggests that by that assessment 51 of the world's largest revenue-generating entities (e.g., through income or taxes) are corporations rather than countries.[13]

Globalization stands accused of many crimes, such as the erosion of democracy, the destruction of native industries in developing nations and the creation of massive debts. In addition, critics charge that current global practices generate negative social impacts ranging from loss of domestic jobs in developed nations as they are outsourced to sweatshops in low-wage developing countries, to ecological havoc as natural resources are overused, forests are destroyed, and agribusiness moves quickly to manmade fertilizers, genetically modified crops, and pesticides that destroy the health of the soil.

The forces of globalization have reshaped the social contract between workers and employers and left many communities in developed countries wondering how they will cope with reduced employment bases and fewer headquarters compa-nies, which have tended to provide significant local community support, especially in the United States. At the same time, developing nations are coping with the global race to the bottom[14] for ever-lower wages, working conditions and environ-mental protection. National sovereignty is eroded and excessive debt incurred. Meanwhile, the lack of trust in large corporations has grown precipitously since the scandals of the early years of the 21st century in companies such as Enron, which suggest that corruption, fraud, and other forms of corporate and general institu-tional malfeasance are more common than anyone might have wished to believe.

The stage is set for a worldwide drama of rich against poor and developed against developing nations.

■ Growing global inequity

Although there have always been poor people in the world, the current round of globalization has created vast chasms of inequity in the world's distribution of wealth. These inequities are further compounded by the revolution in global com-munications technologies, which shows the world's poor how their counterparts in the richer nations live their lives. A 2006 study by the World Institute for Develop-ment Economics Research (WIDER) of the United Nations University placed these inequities in stark relief on a global level, finding that the richest 2% of the world's population owned more than half of global household wealth and the richest 10% accounted for 85% of the world's total.[15] The WIDER study further showed that North America with 6% of global population has 34% of the world's wealth. North America, Europe, and high-income Asia–Pacific nations control 90% of the world's wealth. Other results show similar concentrations of wealth in developed nations, for instance, the 24 Organization for Economic Cooperation and Development (OECD) countries, with about 15% of the world's population, control nearly 64% of the world's wealth and almost 54% of the world's income (measured as gross domes-tic product).

The same study also focused on inequities within different nations, with equally dramatic findings. One disquieting set of figures indicates that the top 1% of the US population shared nearly 33% of the world's wealth (nearly 35% when the Forbes 400 richest families are added in). The top 10% in the United States control 69.8% of that nation's wealth, while in China, the top 10% control about 41.4%. Finally, the study estimated that the an individual needed an annual income of only about $2,200 to belong to the top half of the world's wealth distribution, while the price tag for entry into the top 1% (consisting of some million people) was over $500,000 per person, with the inequities expected to have increased since the original data were collected in 2000.[16]

Given these numbers, it is small wonder that anticorporate activists criticize the growing gap between rich and poor in the United States, and between the Northern and Southern countries. Meanwhile, compensation for chief executive officers (CEOs) soars well above anything comparable to worker wages (one recent estimate pegged CEO compensation in 2004 at 431 times that of the average worker in the United States, down from the all-time high in 2001 of 525–1 but still astronomical). While activists decry the lack of decent jobs for the many millions who need work in developing nations, big businesses continue to push for greater productivity and automation, further reducing job availability and creating excesses and imbalances between supply and demand. Simultaneously, labor and human rights abuses, sweatshops, child labor, abusive managers, and generally poor working conditions are still rampant in many global companies' supply chains.

Under such conditions, the demands for corporate accountability, responsibility, and transparency and the corporate abuses of power that have triggered these demands have been fertile ground for the emergence of a social movement for change led by the difference makers.

■ How the book is organized

Largely through the lens of the ideas, insights, and words of the difference makers themselves, *The Difference Makers* demonstrates how people from a wide variety of backgrounds and interests converged on a similar set of ideas aimed at making the world a better place by creating pressures in the existing system that countermand a shareholder-only philosophy and emphasis business's impacts on stakeholders, society, and nature. The book also focuses on the infrastructure-building process and the realities of working with scarce resources, the need for a long-term perspective on accomplishing one's goals when social and system change is involved, and the capacity to find critical leverage points that effect that change.

The Difference Makers first provides an overview of the global context in which the pioneers we examine perceived a need to change the way things work with respect to business in society: that is, the need for "Making a difference" (Chapter 1). Set in the context of increasing globalization and accompanying concern about the impacts of globalization, and beginning as many social movements do with a few individuals and fewer resources, the difference makers initiated — from inside the system — changes that could be leveraged for long-term societal benefit. In the course of establishing these changes, over a period of about 30 years, they (and, of course, others) have built a substantive infrastructure that provides new leverage points to pressure businesses to behave in ways more compatible with society's needs, as we will see in "Building a different future: an emerging corporate responsibility infrastructure" (Chapter 2). These first two chapters provide a general overview of the context for the work of the difference makers and Chapter 2 illustrates quite dramatically the extent of the changes that have taken place and the infrastructure that has already been built.

The next six chapters tell the stories of some of the pioneering individuals who have been central to the initiation, growth, and development of this infrastructure. Their stories, told as much as possible in their own words, demonstrate not only the entrepreneurial initiatives that difference makers have taken, but also the motivations and hopes behind the establishment of different institutions. Chapter 3, "Early inklings: social pioneering for responsible investing," focuses on the early days of the now burgeoning infrastructure, which really got started through the lens of social and environmental investing. The pioneering work of **Alice Tepper Marlin**, founder of the Council on Economic Priorities, and later Social Accountability International (SAI), **Joan Bavaria**, founder of Ceres, and Franklin Research and Development (now Trillium), and later the Social Investment Forum, and **Tim Smith**, first executive director of the Interfaith Center on Corporate Responsibility, and at the time of writing at Walden Asset Management and president of the Social Investment Forum, provided core elements of the institutional framework on which the responsible investment movement has been built. Another pioneer, Amy Domini, also played a crucial role as cofounder of KLD Research & Analytics and Domini Social Funds.

Accountability is the theme of Chapter 4, "Emerging accountability structures," as the difference makers shift from a direct focus on socially responsible investing toward creating the beginnings of a new accountability infrastructure. **Steve Lydenberg**, one of the founders of KLD Research & Analytics, and later the Institute for Responsible Investment, now at Domini Social Funds, gained his entry into this arena working with Alice Tepper Marlin at the Council on Economic Priorities. Amy Domini, already discussed in Chapter 3, and **Peter Kinder**, CEO of KLD Research & Analytics, together created the Domini Social 400 Index to track against more traditional indices such as the Dow Jones Industrial Average. This chapter weaves together the stories of these three social entrepreneurs as they built KLD and branched out into other related ventures. The chapter then circles back to Alice Tepper Marlin, who in the 1990s founded SAI when it became clear that accountability standards were needed for companies with long global supply chains. The chapter then focuses on the work of **Simon Zadek**, founder of the UK's AccountAbility, the Institute for Social and Ethical Accountability, an organization that sets standards and provides assessment tools for a broad array of corporate activities. Finally, Chapter 4 looks at the work of **Jim Post**, professor of management and public policy at Boston University, who did early research on the impact of infant formula in developing nations and worked with the Nestlé Audit Commission to help develop a breakthrough auditing and accountability approach for the company.

Chapter 5 focuses on "Emerging responsibility standards" through the eyes of several difference makers involved in important early initiatives aimed at setting new and more aspirational performance standards for companies: Joan Bavaria, and her seminal work with Ceres, who ultimately hired **Bob Massie** as executive director. Massie later went on to work with **Allen White** to cofound the Global Reporting Initiative. Another of the difference makers, **Bob Dunn** worked within Levi Strauss to develop and implement one of the first, if not *the* first, company codes of conduct to deal with the global supply chain issues that have attracted so much activist pressure. The chapter also focuses on **Steven Young**, the executive director of the Caux Round Table, a group that has promulgated a global set of principles that are based on the ethical ideals of human dignity and the Japanese principle of *kyosei* or living together. Perhaps one of the most important initiatives to emerge around corporate responsibility and corporate citizenship is the UN Global Compact, which at the time of writing claims nearly 5,000 corporate signatories. Developed in a speech given by then UN Secretary-General Kofi Annan in 1999, the Global Compact was the brainchild of difference maker **John Ruggie**, now a professor at the Harvard Kennedy School of Government and director of the Mossavar-Rahmani Center for Business and Government there, as well as special assistant to the UN secretary-general on human rights, and **Georg Kell**, who has been executive head of the Global Compact since its inception.

Transparency is the key theme of Chapter 6, "Transparency and common reporting." The chapter emphasizes the work of the United Kingdom's **John Elkington**, founder of SustainAbility, one of the earliest consulting firms in the corporate responsibility arena, and one that has been unafraid to deal openly with some of the more serious issues facing companies. The chapter next moves to the work of **Allen White**, vice president at Boston's Tellus Institute, and cofounder with Bob Massie of the Global Reporting Initiative, an effort to provide a common reporting framework for companies so that transparency along environmental, social, and governance (ESG) dimensions becomes feasible and comparable across companies. White also later founded (with Marjorie Kelly) a new effort aimed at corporate redesign called Corporation 20/20.

As the field of related initiatives began to develop, networking among the like-minded individuals who were establishing these new institutions became important, so Chapter 7, "Networking," focuses on this topic. First discussed is **Laury Hammel**, who was the original founder of New England Businesses for Social Responsibility, and later Business for Social Responsibility (BSR). Hammel, who is CEO of Longfellow Clubs, a local group of health and recreation facilities, went on to found the Spirituality in Business Conference, which has been held annually for nearly ten years, and the Business Alliance for Local Living Economies. **Bob Dunn** later took over as Executive Director of BSR and moved the association towards an emphasis on global corporations. Another networker of note is **David Grayson**, a director of the UK's Business in the Community, who has worked extensively with the Prince's Youth Business Trust, the International Business Leaders Forum, and the Small Business Consortium. **Brad Googins**, executive director of the Boston College Center for Corporate Citizenship, has evolved the Center from an emphasis on the functional area of corporate community relations to the broader arena of corporate citizenship in his tenure, after having founded the Center for Work and Family earlier in his career. The final difference maker in this chapter is **Steve Waddell**, co-lead steward of Global Action Network Net (GAN-Net), who is focused on understanding how a new approach to global governance can emerge from the relationships that are now beginning to emerge among institutions in different sectors — government, business, and non-governmental organizations.

Chapter 8 covers "Engagement and dialogue: changing the fundamentals," focusing on the ways in which some of the difference makers are now explicitly trying to change the system. The chapter focuses on entrepreneurs such as **David Logan**, who founded The Corporate Citizenship Company to help companies better contend with the new societal expectations that are being placed on them, and **Malcolm McIntosh**, who was the first hired director of the Corporate Citizenship Unit at the University of Warwick and at the time of writing is professor and director of the Applied Research Centre in Human Security at Coventry University, the first transdisciplinary center of its kind in the UK, having founded the *Journal of Corporate Citizenship* along the way. **Jane Nelson** is senior fellow and director of the Corporate Social Responsibility Initiative at the Kennedy School of Government, Harvard University, but has also worked extensively with the International Business Leaders Forum (IBLF) and the United Nations on issues of global peace and business, emerging economies, and poverty and business, and is a leading spokesperson on these issues. **Judy Samuelson** is founder of the Aspen Institute's Business and Society Program, which has as its goal integrating ecological and societal issues into management education programs to better prepare tomorrow's leaders. The final part of this chapter looks to the future, focusing on Allen White's vision for Corporation 20/20, an effort noted above, to generate interest in redesigning the function and purposes of the corporation to incorporate environmental and social considerations.

Chapter 9, "The vision thing," attempts to synthesize the visions that have been behind the work of the difference makers over the years. It focuses first on the obstacles to change, before moving on to a more positive vision going forward, developing a sensibility that all of the difference makers, though very different in their approaches and in the institutions they have founded, seem to share. The goal, for all of them, is a better world for all of us.

2

Building a different future

An emerging corporate responsibility infrastructure[17]

The rapid evolution of the infrastructure associated with corporate responsibility represents a process of significant social and institutional change, although necessarily the end result of these changes is still in flux. Indeed, it is a social movement, and it is one that has been created in no small measure by the work of the difference makers. As used here, the terms *corporate responsibility* and *corporate citizenship* mean the impacts that a company's strategies and operating practices have on society, its stakeholders, and the natural environment, and are distinguished from *corporate social responsibility*, which encompasses those activities that companies undertake to directly benefit society.[18]

This chapter outlines the amazingly rapid development of infrastructure and institution building that has taken place in the last couple of decades of the 20th century and early part of the 21st. The term *institutions*, as used here, means organizations, associations, or forums that create norms and standards, pressures and processes, or what some scholars call "institutional arrangements" that establish pressures for the regulation of behavior of other social actors — in this case, mainly corporations.[19] What difference makers have done, I will argue, is to establish wholly new institutional arrangements, fostered by the new infrastructure.

These institutional arrangements have created pressures, forces, norms, and dynamics to push corporations in the direction of greater accountability, responsibility, and transparency. They are intended, in some respects, to cope with the dominant and powerful position that corporations, particularly multinationals, have assumed in the world and provide countervailing pressures to the profit-seeking and wealth-maximization motives built into the current corporate design.[20] The new dynamics created by these institutional arrangements are attempting to shift the context in which businesses operate from one dominated solely by economic logic to one that operates dialectically to create new emphasis on other imperatives, particularly social, environmental, sustainability, and governance imperatives that complement economic pressures on firms.

The difference makers discussed in this book did not establish all of the now-existing responsibility assurance institutions alone, but, as will be demonstrated, they were all key actors in creating the beginnings of a relatively new and still emerging responsibility assurance infrastructure and even newer efforts to reshape the fundamental structure of the system so that there is better balance between profit-making enterprises and societal interests or the public good. The responsibility assurance infrastructure attempts to hold corporations accountable, responsible, and transparent with respect to their social, stakeholder, and environmental impacts.

In many respects, this emerging infrastructure is complementary to other initiatives that surround and support it, which have also evolved rapidly during the same period. The growth of NGO and activist anticorporate and antiglobalization activities in this period has been phenomenal, as are efforts to create local and regionalized economies. Taken together, the whole infrastructure can be said to focus on a process of system change attempting to reorient corporations toward social, stakeholder, and environmental as well as economic purposes. Let's now look at the landscape in which the difference makers have been operating.

■ Corporate responsibility from the inside: pressure from the outside

Many companies, particularly large, branded, and highly visible companies, have now started to take their wider responsibilities more seriously, arguably as part of their response to growing pressure for greater responsibility. Many companies have expressed significant and growing interest in issues of corporate responsibility. This growing corporate concern for wider societal responsibilities began to become apparent from the mid-1990s, evidenced by the findings of a regular KPMG study of the US *Fortune* 250 firms. That study found that broadly defined sustainability reporting has been increasing substantially since 1993 (when KPMG initiated the survey), and that by 2005 more than half of the top 250 *Fortune* 500 companies had issued stand-alone sustainability reports, and that 33% of the top 100 companies in 16 countries had issued such reports. The figure stands at nearly two-thirds (64%) if companies that include responsibility issues in their annual reports are included.[21] This substantial change clearly reflects companies' recognition of the mounting pressures for such reporting and the growing demands for transparency about their social and environmental impacts.

But sustainability reports alone are only part of the changed picture for large companies and, increasingly, for smaller ones as well. Citing the need to protect their reputations, a desire to contribute to society and be "good corporate citizens," or an ethical belief that "it's the right thing to do," many large corporations have begun implementing significant programs related to a broad definition of corporate citizenship/responsibility. Some of these initiatives (and some companies' definitions of corporate citizenship) are, of course, restricted to narrowly defined criteria of corporate social responsibility and simply involve corporate philanthropy, volunteering, and community relations – and even public relations – programs (which causes some critical observers to claim that much corporate social responsibility is nothing more than window dressing designed to disguise the real and sometimes negative impacts of companies' business models).

Other companies, however, go considerably beyond the narrow definition of corporate *social* responsibility. These companies are engaged in managing their corporate responsibilities (citizenship) explicitly. My collaborator Charles Bodwell and I have elsewhere called the management approaches that companies use to manage stakeholder, governance, and ecological responsibilities "total responsibility management" or TRM (following the labeling that was already popularized as total quality management, TQM).[22]

TRM approaches have three main elements: inspiration, integration, and improvement and innovation. **Inspiration** means developing a vision that explicitly includes responsibilities of the firm, underpinned by values that are alive in the company, and processes of stakeholder engagement to get input on issues and concerns, as well as potential opportunities that might be facing the company. **Integration** involves integrating the vision, values, and what has been learned from stakeholder engagement into corporate strategies, human resource practices (since employees will have to implement the company's practices), and other key management systems as well, including communications systems, reward systems, marketing and customer relationship systems, and so on. **Improvement and innovation** involves development of indicators or measurements to assess progress, transparency and accountability for results, and mechanisms and practices that build new innovations and improvements into existing systems when problems are found.

■ Creating new pressures on corporations

One of the reasons for this surge in interest in corporate responsibility for many companies, particularly the large and highly visible, is that reputation has become a crucial element of branding that has been time-consuming and costly to develop, yet increasingly easy to lose if key stakeholders such as customers or investors lose trust in the brand. Brands and reputation have become particularly important because large portions of shareholder wealth now reside not in tangible assets but in intangibles such as reputation. Thus, partly as a response to growing distrust of large companies by the general public, and in part a recognition of the embeddedness[23] of business in society (i.e., not separate from society), many multinational businesses have voluntarily initiated programs such as public–private partnerships, multi-sector collaborations and dialogues, philanthropy, volunteerism, and other forms of corporate community relations.

Implicit in these responses is an acknowledgement of the pressures that the emerging infrastructure around corporate responsibility has placed on companies to change how they implement their business models, not just to get them to "do good for society." Much of the evolving internal responsibility infrastructure deals not simply with philanthropic activities of firms but with the broader set of corporate responsibilities that all companies have. The focus is on how companies' business models affect stakeholders, the natural environment, and societies. Many initiatives have been voluntarily developed by businesses themselves, including internal responsibility management processes, sustainability and environmental management initiatives, stakeholder engagement practices, development of codes of conduct, and progressive human-resources, customer-relationship, and issue-management processes, to name a few; albeit some of these came about as responses to external stakeholder pressures. Other initiatives have been developed by coalitions of businesses within the same or different industry sectors, which are attempting to bring greater responsibility, transparency, and accountability to businesses, and work with companies to develop practices that suit local conditions.

■ What have difference makers attempted to do?

The difference makers are part of a substantially larger group of people who have tried to establish a new infrastructure that ensures that companies are **responsible**, **accountable**, and **transparent** with respect to the impacts on societies, stakeholders, and the natural environment. In many cases, the difference makers have actually pioneered new organizations and entities to push the demand for greater corporate responsibility forward. They have developed **research and measurement**

tools that track companies' performance in a variety of areas, created **standards** and ensured that once companies have committed to standards they are actually implementing or living up to those standards. They have evolved processes, particularly processes of **engagement and dialogue**, both within the business context and in broader multi-stakeholder contexts. Ultimately, as the problems of globalization and sustainability have shown themselves to be relatively intractable to the leverage that these institutions have created, some difference makers have begun **questioning the system** and whether it adequately serves the needs of future generations and **proposing alternatives**. Necessarily, these themes are overlapping and the institutional infrastructure that has evolved frequently works on many of them simultaneously, so any categorization is more illustrative than definitive.

The broader infrastructure in which the difference makers are working implicitly or explicitly recognizes the important role that businesses play in building healthy societies by providing needed goods and services. Combined, the initiatives noted in the boxes below, and many similar initiatives not mentioned, represent a relatively extensive emerging institutional infrastructure around corporate responsibility. (I would note that there is also a mandatory regulatory structure evolving, largely at this point around disclosure; however, this discussion does not deal with that development.)

In the rest of this chapter, I will draw attention to the particular difference makers who played roles in developing specific institutions and provide an overview of the emerging responsibility assurance infrastructure. The analysis is organized around several important purposes associated with different types of infrastructure: responsibility; accountability and responsibility assurance; transparency; engagement and dialogue; principles, standards, and codes; and questioning the system. The following discussion focuses on these elements, with the constant proviso that many entities in the infrastructure operate with many of these purposes in mind, and others have evolved their focus over time to encompass broader or different purposes. Still, these purposes seem a reasonable way to think about how the corporate responsibility field has organized itself over time. I will begin each section below by defining the concepts and then very briefly look at some of the institutions that constitute that subfield.

■ Principles, standards, and codes

One of the foundational aspects of the emerging responsibility assurance system involves the development of standards, principles, codes of conduct, and guidelines that establish a normative framework for company practices and behaviors. Although codes of conduct have been around in businesses for a long time, early codes were driven largely by compliance and were in part fostered by scandals that created public distrust over corporate practices. For example, there were numerous internal company codes of conduct developed in US firms in the 1980s following a wave of defense industry scandals and the passage of the Foreign Corrupt Practices Act. Many companies hired ethics officers to ensure compliance with this act and introduced standards, frequently relatively narrowly defined, around issues such as bribery and corruption.

By the mid-1990s, a new wave of concerns about corporate practices had begun to emerge from the practice of outsourcing manufacturing, assembly, and other production functions to developing nations. Wholly new issues faced companies as they attempted to deal with long supply chains and supplier organizations that were not actually owned by the multinational corporations that used them, but whose practices began tainting products distributed in the developed world. The advent of easy-to-use global communications technology, and particularly the Internet, fueled the capacity of activists to bring attention to labor, human rights, wage, and environmental practices in these supply chains and caught many companies off guard, setting off a new round of code-of-conduct development.

These newer codes, however, were broader in nature and dealt not only with what was going on in the multinational corporation but increasingly throughout the whole supply chain. The wave of principles, codes, and standards that began to emerge in the early 1990s thus followed public concern about issues related to supply chain management, specifically labor practices in developing countries. In addition, the 1990s witnessed numerous sets of principles developed outside companies that companies were increasingly expected to adhere to in order to retain what came to be called their license to operate. By one count conducted by the International Labour Organization (ILO) in the early 2000s, there were more than 400 principles and standards, including company codes, in existence, and the number has continued to grow since that time.

Principles can be defined as basic truths or essences, with the implication of rules or standards of behavior, norms of practice and behavior, and something that is fundamental to a way of being in the world. Principles thus are foundational elements in determining the "rules of the game" or the parameters and limits that govern individual and, in the case of corporations, company behavior in any given situation. Principles attempt to provide guidance as to what kinds of behavior are and are not acceptable.

Standards encompass principles in that they are agreed principles of protocol. Standards, that is, are specifications, often generated by a group of interested parties, which establish how things are to be done in given circumstances and conditions (e.g., industries or practices). Standards are generally agreed on to establish normalized ways of operating or practicing to ensure that other more foundational principles are taken into consideration, quality levels are met, or performance is achieved. In other words, standards are formalized expectations about behavior and practice typically established by a group that assumes some authority over the subject matter of the standard. In technical and scientific situations, standards are developed to ensure consistency, interoperability, and quality. In more behavioral settings, standards such as codes of conduct provide a floor of action below which it is unacceptable to go.

Codes of conduct, as relevant in the responsibility assurance domain, are typically generated voluntarily either by individual organizations or by associations of organizations rather than by governmental authorities, but are considered binding on members of the group or organization that generates them. Codes of conduct define the guidelines that the organizations (or individuals) are to follow to meet stakeholders' and society's expectations. The key for some observers is that codes of conduct, where generated by individual organizations or associations, are not mandated but are voluntary with implementation generally left to the organization that has adopted the code.

An emerging infrastructure of principles, standards, and codes

Since the early 1990s, possibly beginning with Levi Strauss's supplier code of conduct, there has been an explosion of internal company codes of conduct, principles, and standards relating to business activities. For example, the advent of the Global Sullivan Principles in 1999 (originally the Sullivan Principles launched in 1977), which primarily dealt with South Africa and apartheid in the 1980s, signaled growing attention on how businesses conducted their business models. The more generally oriented Caux Round Table Principles, promulgated in 1988, attempted to foster better overall business ethics and responsibility. Broader in scope than earlier codes of conduct, which tended to focus on issues related to bribery and corruption, the new sets of principles in many respects expand companies' explicit responsibilities to issues such as those included in perhaps the best-known set of principles: the UN Global Compact's Ten Principles — human rights, labor rights, environment, and anticorruption.

The Global Compact was originally launched in July 2000 by the UN Secretary-General Kofi Annan and by 2008 had nearly 5,000 participants, including over 3,700 businesses. The Global Compact also launched the Principles for Responsible Investment in 2006. Other sets of principles have somewhat different focuses. For example, the Ceres Principles emphasize sustainability, while the Equator Principles focus on standards specifically aimed at the financial industry. Many of these codes are internal to companies; however, some developed by business associations or multi-stakeholder coalitions have gained prominence. Box 2.1 lists some of the most well-known business-related principles.

Box 2.1 **Some key principles, standards, and codes for business**

- Caux Round Table Principles for Business (launched 1994)
  (www.cauxroundtable.org/principles.html)
- Ceres Principles (launched as Valdez Principles, 1989) (www.ceres.org)
- Equator Principles (financial services) (launched 2006)
  (www.equator-principles.com)
- Global Sullivan Principles (launched 1999, from Sullivan Principles launched
  in 1977) (www.thesullivanfoundation.org/gsp)
- OECD Guidelines for Multinational Enterprises (agreed 1975, revised 2000)
  (www.oecd.org/department/0,2688,en_2649_34889_1_1_1_1_1,00.html)
- Principles for Responsible Investment (launched April 2006) (www.unpri.org)
- Private Voluntary Organization (PVO) Standards (2006) (for NGOs,
  Interaction) (www.interaction.org/pvostandards/index.html)
- Tripartite Declaration of Principles Concerning Multinational Enterprises
  (launched 2000) (www.ilo.org/public/english/standards/norm/sources/
  mne.htm)
- UN Global Compact Principles (launched 2000)
  (www.unglobalcompact.org)

Responsibility

The concept of responsibility involves recognition that social forces bind both individuals and companies to certain obligations and duties, which can be moral, civic, legal, or socially demanded. Responsibility also implies a proper sphere of activities, suggesting some limits beyond which responsibilities do not go, and carries with it a form of trustworthiness or answerability for one's actions. Given this breadth and the dynamic nature of society, it is not surprising that there has been difficulty in defining corporate responsibilities because, as society itself changes, its demands on and expectations from companies are also likely to change.

Corporate responsibility is defined here as the ways in which companies' vision, values, and business models (ways of adding value) affect societies, stakeholders, and the natural environment, which is the same way I define corporate citizenship, so these terms will be used interchangeably.[24] There are, however, almost as many definitions as there are writers about corporate responsibility, and a good deal of confusion about whether corporate responsibility is the same thing as corporate *social* responsibility, which we defined in Chapter 1 as the ways in which companies act to explicitly benefit society.

A sampling of definitions will give some sense of the scope of issues encompassed by the notion of corporate responsibility, corporate citizenship, and corporate social responsibility, as well as an evolving consensus about what is actually covered by the term. Corporate social responsibility (CSR), in fact, is sometimes defined in much the same way as we have defined corporate responsibility/citizenship. For example, the Boston College Center for Corporate Citizenship (CCC) says, "Corporate citizenship is the business strategy that shapes the values underpinning a company's mission and the choices made each day by its executives, managers, and employees as they engage with society." The CCC further identifies four principles that define the essence of corporate citizenship: minimize harm, maximize benefit, be accountable and responsive to key stakeholders, and support strong financial results.

The US association Business for Social Responsibility (BSR) defines CSR as "achieving commercial success in ways that honor ethical values and respect people, communities, and the natural environment." BSR claims that CSR means addressing the legal, ethical, commercial, and other expectations society has for business, and making decisions that fairly balance the claims of all key stakeholders.

Along similar lines, the UK Institute of Chartered Accountants notes that while there is no commonly accepted definition, corporate responsibility is "about how firms manage their businesses to bring an overall positive impact socially, environmentally and economically, whilst at the same time maximising value for their shareholders."[25]

There are other definitions, but the general thrust is clear: corporate responsibility (citizenship) encompasses the responsibilities engendered by the firm in the course of doing business. These responsibilities arise because large corporations are recognized as powerful forces playing a critical role in fostering healthy societies because of the jobs and infrastructure of goods and services they provide. They are not separate entities from society; hence companies, like individuals, are subject to the social forces that create norms and expectations. In this age of instantaneous global communication, the power of corporations and their business models has become apparent, along with the need for companies to respond to external pressures demanded by societal actors and stakeholders. The forces for corporate responsibility increase daily.

The socially responsible investing (SRI) movement has been built in some ways to counteract the growing power of corporations and the powerful global institutions that support them. These global institutions, the World Trade Organization, the World Bank, and the International Monetary Fund, foster investor capitalism, globalization, and free trade and, antiglobalization activists would argue, dominate the world through force, money, and power in ways that preserve the status quo for the elite at the expense of the less well off.[26] Anticorporate and antiglobalization activism and SRI have grown alongside the growing influence of these global institutions. Working from inside the system through activist investors, SRI leaders have attempted to foster more responsible practices and policies inside companies, brought social and environmental issues related to corporate behaviors to investor and public attention, and created a plethora of new organizations and institutions designed to pressure companies into better behavior and practices. For example, there are now numerous responsible investment institutions that invest money for individuals and organizations that wish to either proactively engage companies on their ecological, social, and governance practices or to avoid companies whose practices are unacceptable to them. Box 2.2 lists some of these institutions.

Box 2.2 **Major responsible investment institutions in the United States**

- CalPERS
- Calvert
- Citizens Global
- Domini Social Funds
- Dreyfus
- Green Century
- Parnassus
- Pax World
- Smith Barney
- Trillium
- Walden Asset Management

Note: In June 2006, the Social Investment Forum's website listed nearly 100 different "socially responsible mutual funds" from these and other firms. Numerous others exist in Europe and elsewhere in the world.

Accompanying the development of socially responsible investors has been the emergence of stock-market indices that trace the performance of companies considered to be more responsible (Box 2.3 gives a sample). The pioneering SRI stock index was the Domini Social Index (DSI), launched in 1991. As SRI grew, so did related professional organizations and associations (Box 2.4). In addition, following the lead of the first social research organization that provided social, ecological, and other stakeholder information, including social screens to investors, now called KLD Research & Analytics, other social entrepreneurs have developed independent social research organizations in numerous countries around the world (Box

Box 2.3 **Major stock indices with a social sustainability orientation**

- Domini 400 Social Index (United States)
- Dow Jones Sustainability Index (United States)
- FTSE4Good (United Kingdom)
- SRI Index (Johannesburg, South Africa)
- Calvert Social Index (United States)
- Kemper SNS/Smaller Europe Social Responsible Investment Index (Leuven, Belgium)
- OWW Responsibility Malaysia SRI Index (Malaysia)

Box 2.4 **Major SRI professional organizations/associations**

- European Social Investment Forum (Eurosif, Addressing Sustainability Through Financial Markets) (www.eurosif.org)
- Social Investment Forum (SIF) (www.socialinvest.org)
- Social Investment Research Analyst Network (SIRAN) (www.siran.org)
- SRI in the Rockies Conference (sriintherockies.com)
- UK Social Investment Forum (www.uksif.org)

2.5), and a network that links the major such research entities, Sustainable Investment Research International Ltd. (SiRi Company).

In addition to investment and research entities, numerous other organizations and networks with interests in SRI have emerged as the impact of SRI has become clearer (see Box 2.6 for a sample of such organizations). For example, perhaps the earliest and still most active shareholder activist organization is the Interfaith Center on Corporate Responsibility (ICCR), which annually submits about 200 shareholder resolutions on social, ecological, and other matters of interest. More recently developed, the Institute for Responsible Investment (IRI), housed in the Boston College Center for Corporate Citizenship serves as an organizer and think-tank for progressive interests around investing. The Social Investment Forum (SIF) serves as the major professional organization in the United States for social investment professionals.

Box 2.5 **Major social research- and investment-oriented firms**

- Analistas Internacionales en Sostenibilidad SA, Spain (www.ais.com.es)
- Avanzi SRI Research, Italy (www.avanzi-sri.org)
- Centre Info SA, Switzerland (www.centreinfo.ch)
- Dutch Sustainability Research BV, Netherlands (www.dsresearch.nl)
- GES Investment Services AB, Sweden (www.ges-invest.com)
- Innovest Strategic Value Advisors (www.innovestgroup.com)
- Jantzi Research Inc., Canada (www.jantziresearch.com) (publishes Canadian Social Investment Database, see www.jantziresearch.com/index.asp?section=2&level_2=3)
- KAYEMA Investment Research & Analysis, Israel (www.kayema.com)
- KLD Research & Analytics, United States (www.kld.com) (publishes Socrates database)
- Pensions & Investment Research Consultants Ltd., United Kingdom (www.pirc.co.uk)
- Scoris GmbH, Germany (www.scoris.de)
- Sustainable Investment Research International Ltd. (SiRi Company) (network of 11 research organizations) (www.siricompany.com)
- Sustainable Investment Research Institute Pty. Ltd., Australia (www.siris.com.au)

Box 2.6 **Other organizations with responsible investment interests**

- Co-op America (www.coopamerica.org)
- Council for Responsible Public Investment (www.publicinvestment.org)
- Fair Pension (United Kingdom) (www.fairpensions.org.uk)
- Good Money (www.goodmoney.com)
- Institute for Responsible Investment (www.bcccc.net/responsibleinvestment)
- Institutional Shareholder Services (Environmental, Social, Governance) (www.issproxy.com/institutional/esg/index.jsp)
- Interfaith Center on Corporate Responsibility (www.iccr.org)
- Responsible Wealth (www.responsiblewealth.org)
- Risk Metrics Group (riskmetrics.com)[27]
- Social Venture Network (www.svn.org)
- SocialFunds.com (www.socialfunds.com)

As can easily be noted from the lists in Boxes 2.1–2.6, a major set of new institutions has arisen to support the SRI industry — and push for corresponding changes in companies' relationships to at least one segment of their investors. Indeed, the major US-based SRI professional association, the SIF's 2007 *Report on Social Responsible Investing Trends in the United States* finds, using a broad measure of SRI, that one in ten investment dollars is now invested using some sort of responsible investment strategy, up from one in nine dollars in the 2007 study — or a total of $2.71 trillion. Increasingly, companies ignore this segment of the investor market at their peril.

■ Accountability and responsibility assurance

Accountability is a concept related to responsibility, but with a key different connotation. Accountability implies an obligation or willingness not only to take responsibility for one's actions, but *also* to explain and answer for the outcomes and impacts of those actions to others, particularly to others in some authority relationship. The very word *accountability* suggests the important differentiation from responsibility: being accountable means being "called to account" for one's actions and needing to accept whatever consequences might result from those actions. In this sense of needing to accept the consequences that result from one's actions, accountability is clearly a more stringent and demanding concept than responsibility.

While dictionary definitions indicate that accountability implies either an obligation or willingness to answer for one's actions, the notion of corporate accountability attempts to ensure that companies recognize the obligations that they have undertaken to answer for their actions, in part resulting from the social contract that society in the form of governments has issued as a corporate charter. The growing demand for accountability from corporations has arisen because of past abuses of power, misuse of resources and fraudulent or ethical lapses, which have created distrust of corporations among many stakeholders in society. These calls for greater accountability were certainly fueled by the scandals in the first years of the 21st century, which hit major corporations such as Enron and WorldCom in the United States as well as elsewhere around the world and arguably resulted from an overemphasis on short-term profit maximization, combined with greed on the part of corporate leaders and managers.

There are significant implications of the notion of corporate accountability that go beyond simply recognizing corporate responsibilities. One of the implications is that the willingness to accept responsibility for outcomes means that both good and bad, or expected and unexpected, results must be acknowledged and dealt with. Accountability further implies that, when mistakes are made, as they inevitably will be, or when actions have negative impacts, the consequences of those mistakes will be handled in satisfactory ways, particularly with respect to those affected by the mistakes. Accountability also implies an authority structure that can enforce corporations to mitigate negative impacts and hold them liable for actions and outcomes. Accountability is therefore not an entirely popular concept with many corporations.

In management theory, a distinction is often made between responsibility and accountability in that a manager can delegate responsibility for getting something done to a subordinate, but remains accountable for the outcome because of the supervisory role that management performs. Similarly, while states, provinces, or nation-states have granted corporations the license to produce goods and provide services through corporate charters, at least in theory, incorporated companies remain accountable to the authority of that state and, in a democracy, ultimately to the people who elect public officials. In management systems, accountability often necessitates the development of systems of responsibility and authority for actions so that they can be traced back within the system to those who authorized or undertook certain actions. In a broader societal context, it has been more difficult to hold corporations accountable for their actions and impacts, particularly as they have expanded globally and are frequently beyond the reach of any single local government or other authority. Hence, difference makers have worked to create new, pressure-based accountability structures and standards that can begin this crucial task of fostering greater corporate accountability.

Another important implication of accountability is that one will honor the obligations, commitments, and requirements to which one has committed. Applied to the corporation, this means that, for example, if a company signs up to a code of conduct or establishes an internal code, the company will actually live up to those commitments. In turn, then, accountability means that the impacts and outcomes of actions, decisions, and practices in companies have to be visible – transparent – to those who would hold the company accountable. Hence, the next concept, *transparency*, has grown in popularity simultaneously with that of accountability. There are several key aspects of creating a responsibility assurance infrastructure that holds companies accountable: verification, certification, monitoring, and enforcement, which we will now discuss.

Responsibility assurance: verification, certification, monitoring, and enforcement

Accountability seeks to hold companies to account for their actions, while assurance means freedom from doubt with an implication that what is assured is credible and believable, even to skeptics. Assurance, then, gives a certain level of confidence that the reality that underlies any rhetoric, in this case about corporate responsibility, is as it seems to be. Assurance, as a system for giving confidence that responsibility measures taken by companies are real, is today composed of a number of elements: verification, certification, monitoring, and enforcement.

As calls for corporate accountability have grown, so has a system of new entities that work in the general domain of responsibility assurance. These organizations deal with issues of verification, certification, monitoring, and enforcement (often as combined functions, which is why they are considered together here). One of the key aspects of the emerging responsibility assurance infrastructure is that it is largely — at least to date — voluntary, rather than mandated. Hence the credibility of statements about responsibility, accountability, and transparency as manifested particularly in sustainability reports, and principles, standards, and codes, rests to a great extent on whether one can be assured that what is stated or seen is in fact accurate.

Verification indicates that there is a review process that involves checking, inspecting, and otherwise testing whether, for example, the requirements of a set of principles or a code of conduct are being met. Verification, then, attests to the truth of statements and practices.

Certification, which is typically undertaken by a third party (typically an external auditor, rather than the company itself), aims to ensure credibility. It is a statement that requirements have been met, standards lived up to, or codes of conduct actually implemented. Often applied to labor standards and renewable resources today, third-party certification provides a degree of credibility to a company's statements about its performance in a given domain that would not otherwise be present.

Monitoring means that someone is observing a process or system on a regular or intermittent basis to assess whether standards, codes, principles, and the like are being met. Monitoring processes typically mean that someone, often but not always a third party, gathers relevant data on a system and evaluates it to determine whether or not stated requirements are being complied with. With respect to responsibility assurance, monitoring most often takes place with respect to labor, human rights, and environmental practices in the supply chains of multinational corporations, although monitoring can be undertaken in virtually any situation where standards have been committed to and compliance is expected.

Enforcement typically implies that a legal mandate needs to be met and that some authority has the power to insure that any requirements are complied with and, if they are not, impose sanctions. Enforcement is typically more associated with the law, regulation, and courts than with the voluntary responsibility assurance approach that has emerged to date; however, some new laws, particularly on disclosure, have been passed in various countries in recent years. Companies that have evolved corporate responsibility practices voluntarily have largely done so in order to avert mandatory measures that could lead to enforcement.

Emerging infrastructure: verification, certification, monitoring, and enforcement

Accompanying the development of new sets of principles and demands for business-oriented transparency has been a burgeoning consulting industry that fosters a number of different aims with respect to corporate responsibility: standard setting (frequently within industries, but sometimes across the board); helping companies improve various types of stakeholder relationship and practice; and external verification, monitoring, and certification of those practices. Some of these enterprises are non-profit organizations, such as the UK's AccountAbility, which has developed the AA1000 standards to help businesses improve overall corporate responsibility, and SAI, which focuses on labor issues with its SA8000 standards. Most standard-setting and accrediting agencies are NGOs (e.g., Transfair, Rugmark International). Box 2.7 lists some of these new entities.

Box 2.7 **Some verification, certification, monitoring, and enforcement organizations**

- AccountAbility (www.accountability.org.uk)
- Ceres (ceres.org)
- Fair Labor Association (www.fairlabor.org)
- Fair Trade Labeling Organization (www.fairtrade.net)
- Forest Stewardship Council (www.fscus.org)
- Institute for Global Ethics (www.globalethics.org)
- ISO Strategic Advisory Group on Corporate Social Responsibility of ISO (developing corporate responsibility standards, due 2008) (isotc.iso.org/livelink/livelink/fetch/2000/2122/830949/3934883/3935096/home.html) (see also www.iso.org)
- Rugmark International (www.rugmark.net)
- Social Accountability International (www.sa-intl.org)
- Transfair (www.transfairusa.org)
- Transparency International (www.transparency.org)
- Verité (verite.org)

There are several developments that warrant specific attention. For example, in 2003, AccountAbility launched the first-ever responsibility assurance standard, the AA1000 Assurance Standard (AA1000AS) in an effort to create a credible means of verifying the information reporting in companies' sustainability, social, and environmental reports or so-called triple-bottom-line reports. In 2004, the International Organization for Standardization (ISO) began development of an international set of guidelines on corporate responsibility, ISO 26000, which are due for launch in 2009. ISO initially created quality standards that became core elements of quality assurance in many large companies around the world, and then environmental standards. Its move into the corporate responsibility arena highlights the seriousness of efforts to try to quantify, measure, and standardize approaches to managing responsibilities in companies. Another type of institution, the Voice of the Faithful (VOTF) network, is attempting to bring dialogue, transparency, and greater accountability to the Catholic Church in the wake of the pedophilia scandals of the early 2000s.

Consultancies

Accompanying the emergent responsibility assurance system is an entire and relatively new industry of consultants (see Box 2.8) that has developed since about 1995, with a few pioneers, such as The Corporate Citizenship Company and SmithOBrien, starting a little earlier. Many of the same organizations that verify or accredit practices will also help companies to improve their performance. Companies such as The Corporate Citizenship Company, SmithOBrien, SustainAbility, and Sustainable Value Partners are for-profit consultants that, like many of the large accounting firms, have developed practices geared toward helping companies improve their responsibility performance in one way or another. Some consulting practices revolve around sustainability and environmental matters, while others focus on labor practices or are more general in scope, encompassing many different corporate activities. Indeed, a new association (and related magazine) called *The CRO: Corporate Responsibility Officer*, formed from *Business Ethics* magazine, began in 2006 and claimed that some 500 different organizations were by then focused on helping companies implement their corporate responsibilities more comprehensively: for example, through compliance, supply chain management, environmental management, and related functionally oriented practices. The UK alone has over 50 consultancies that offer corporate social responsibility consulting.[28] Further evidence of the development of responsibility infrastructure is that the newsletter *Ethical Performance*[29] listed in its 2007 Professional Services Directory[30] some 443 organizations in 49 different categories ranging from consultants to academic institutions, from research and rating groups to auditors.

Box 2.8 **Some major corporate responsibility consulting organizations**

- Corporate Citizenship (www.corporate-citizenship.co.uk)
- CSR Global: Ethics and Corporate Responsibility Consulting (www.csrglobal.com/index.htm)
- Deloitte & Touche, Corporate Governance and Accountability (www.deloitte.com/dtt/section_node/0,1042,sid%253D5601,00.html)
- Interpraxis (www.interpraxis.com)
- PricewaterhouseCoopers (www.pwc.com/sustainability)
- SmithOBrien (www.smithobrien.com)
- SustainAbility (www.sustainability.com)
- Sustainable Value Partners (www.sustainablevaluepartners.com)
- Utopies (www.utopies.com)

◾ Transparency

Transparency, as used with respect to companies, implies openness, communication, and accountability (see above), metaphorically extending the definitions of clarity and capacity to see through something or let light shine through implied by its usage in the physical sciences. The concept of transparency as applied to management practices was first used with respect to governmental processes that were opened up to more democratic input: for example, by opening up meetings and proceedings to the general public. Transparency, applied to corporate responsibility today, means that information about a company, mostly, of course, non-proprietary information about social, environmental, and stakeholder impacts, is open and available to interested or affected stakeholders.

Authors Don Tapscott and David Ticoll have argued in *The Naked Corporation* that the Internet age has made companies, and particularly their misdealings and bad behaviors, considerably more transparent today than in the past. Because of the Internet, transparency, at least in part, means that an activist in India can notice that a beverage company is using too much local water and broadcast that information globally, or that an NGO investigating sweatshop conditions in Indonesia can raise the hackles of antisweatshop crusaders around the world, creating an international boycott of a company's products. But transparency also reflects a company's willingness to be open about its social, environmental, and governance practices and impacts and has come about largely because of external demands for greater openness and more information.

Companies have responded to pressures for greater transparency in a variety of ways. Corporate transparency is perhaps most evident in the rapid growth in publication of social, triple-bottom-line (social, environmental, and economic), and sustainability reports. Companies frequently detail their social programs, volunteering activities, environmental management systems, multi-sector collaborations and engagement (see below), and philanthropic activities as a means of establishing their good practice of corporate citizenship and attempting to be open to external stakeholders. Some companies, however, have recognized that many NGOs and particularly activist customers and investors are interested not just in their so-called do-good activities, but more importantly the way that companies develop and implement their business models, corporate strategies, and practices. Hence, some social, environmental or sustainability reports (Gap's reports are good examples) go far beyond detailing social programs and discuss important internal matters such as supply chain management practices (e.g., Sainsbury's), sustainability initiatives (e.g., Interface), and other matters related to the business model (e.g., BP).

Corporate sustainability, social, and environmental reports (which will be called sustainability reports henceforth as a shorthand designation) are a major step toward transparency, as is engagement with stakeholders, which we discuss next. But, despite the progress that has been made, and the ever-growing numbers of companies issuing such reports, problems remain. Unless they are following a standardized format such as the model produced by the Global Reporting Initiative (which will be discussed later on in more depth), companies are still largely free to say what they want, when they want, and how they want in their sustainability reports. Thus, the content, scope, quality comparability, and focus of sustainability reports vary widely and the degree of openness is still largely dependent on the company's willingness to be transparent. Some of the initiatives taken by difference makers are working on exactly this issue.

Transparency and reporting

An important element of responsibility assurance is to encourage standardized reporting of corporate responsibility, sustainability, and social and ethical impacts and practices along the lines of generally accepted accounting principles. The leading organization doing this type of work is the Global Reporting Initiative (GRI), which is developing a common framework for sustainability reporting that will allow cross-company and sectoral comparisons based on a common standard. Begun in the late 1990s, the GRI is a multi-stakeholder coalition that includes thousands of experts from businesses, NGOs, and other types of organization from around the world. As of 2006, some 1,000 companies were formally using the GRI framework to report on issues related to sustainability, and many others were using it informally or partially. The GRI, along with other standardized reporting systems, is noted in Box 2.9.

Box 2.9 **Standardized reporting**

- Global Reporting Initiative (www.globalreporting.org)
- AccountAbility (AA 1000) (www.accountability21.net)
- Social Accountability International (www.sa-intl.org)

Other mechanisms of transparency

Another aspect of transparency – and one that companies arguably pay considerable attention to – has been the growth of ratings and rankings of companies' social and environmental performance in many different dimensions. Box 2.10 lists some of the more prominent corporate rankings that deal with issues in the social and environmental domain. Ratings and rankings related to business and society have been around since *Fortune* magazine launched America's Most Admired Companies ranking in 1983, but numbers have multiplied in recent years, with *Fortune* itself adding rankings on the Global Most Admired Companies and Best Companies to Work For. Other rankings and ratings highlighting best practices and best performance include the *Business Ethics* Best 100 Corporate Citizens ranking, the Business in the Community Corporate Responsibility Index, and the World's Most Respected Companies rating by PricewaterhouseCoopers and the *Financial Times*. So important has it become to be well placed in these rankings that the Reputation Institute offers stakeholder surveys of companies and maintains a "list of lists" of rankings that is available only to members. Further, the Reputation Institute has documented in published research the relationship between corporate brand, financial results, and customer reactions to companies' reputations.[31]

The final development that has generated greater transparency has been the growth of watchdog NGOs and activist organizations that target corporate behaviors in particular. The listing in Box 2.11 notes some of the more notable of these watchdogs, but does not even begin to list the company-specific activist organizations and associated websites, which are numerous and frequently oriented toward creating transparency around the largest and most powerful corporations and their practices. Some of these watchdog and activist groups focus on raising awareness of corporate actions, sometimes with a broad scope and other times on specific issues. For example the Corporate Accountability Project, Corporate Predators, and Corporate Watch focus on corporate behavior in general. On the other hand, organiza-

Box 2.10 **Corporate ratings and rankings**

- 50 Best Companies for Minorities (*Fortune*)
- 100 Best Companies to Work For (*Fortune*)
- 100 Best Companies for Working Mothers (www.workingmother.com)
- Best 100 Corporate Citizens (*CRO*) (www.thecro.com)
- America's Most Admired Companies (*Fortune*) (money.cnn.com/magazines/fortune)
- Global Most Admired Companies (*Fortune*) (money.cnn.com/magazines/fortune)
- Hispanic Corporate 100 (www.hispaniconline.com/buss&finn/corp100-2005.html)
- Inner City 100 (www.theinnercity100.org)
- Most Valuable Brands (Interbrand) (www.interbrand.com/surveys.asp)
- Business in the Community CR Index (www.bitc.org.uk/what_we_do/cr_index)
- Top 30 Companies for Executive Women (www.nafe.com)
- Global 100 Most Sustainable Corporations in the World (Innovest, World Economic Forum, 2007) (www.global100.org)

Box 2.11 **Watchdogs and activists**

- Corporate Accountability Project (www.corporations.org)
- Corporate Accountability International (formerly INFACT) (www.stopcorporateabuse.org/cms/index.cfm?group_id=1000)
- Corporate Predators (www.corporatepredators.org)
- Corporate Watch (www.corpwatch.org)
- Global Exchange (www.globalexchange.org)
- Human Rights Watch (www.hrw.org)
- Human Rights Advocates (www.humanrightsadvocates.org)
- The Multinational Monitor (political) (multinationalmonitor.org)
- Sweatshop Watch (sweatshopwatch.org)

tions such as Human Rights Watch and Human Rights Advocates are explicitly designed to look at human rights abuses, and Sweatshop Watch emphasizes issues related to sweatshop conditions, particularly in the supply chains of multinational corporations.

Stakeholder engagement and dialogue

Stakeholder engagement by corporations became a popular term in the late 1990s, as the Internet exploded and companies' actions, decisions, and outcomes gained greater global visibility, particularly with NGOs. Stakeholder engagement means that the company openly involves itself in conversation or other communication with stakeholders such as activists, NGOs, customers, regular and dissident investors, suppliers and distributors, employees and trade unions, relevant government officials, legislators and regulators, the media, and others as appropriate to the situation and issue. Most simply, stakeholder engagement is the interaction that a company has with its stakeholders: that is, those affected by or able to affect the company and its operations.[32]

Typical of many initiatives that foster corporate engagement with stakeholders is an emphasis on dialogue: that is, conversations that are open-ended and subject to multiple points of view – engaged, rather than one-way conversations. Account-Ability issued the AA1000 Stakeholder Engagement Standard (AA1000SES). This standard identifies three important categories of stakeholder engagement: thinking and planning (identifying stakeholders and material issues, defining an engagement strategy, and developing a plan); preparing and engaging (figuring out how to engage so that understanding and mutual learning occur); and responding and measuring (implementing results from the engagement in the organization and then assessing performance).[33]

More broadly, corporate engagement can mean company involvement in multi-sector dialogues and partnerships that aim to cope with both broad or specific social or environmental problems, issues of sustainability, and development of tools and standards. Some types of engagement focus on developing new business opportunities; others are useful for building important relationships and establishing a basis of trust with non-corporate actors. BSR lists numerous rationales for corporate engagement: assuring the company's license to operate; reducing costs; building markets; strengthening shareholder value; improving market access; protecting against negative consumer actions; increasing organizational effectiveness; enhancing two-way conversations; bridging cultural gaps; developing a culture of innovation and learning; and simplifying conflict resolution.[34]

Corporate engagement in society and with stakeholders today takes a number of forms, many of which are based on dialogue or conversation across sector boundaries, although some forms of engagement occur within them. According to William Isaacs, who has worked and written extensively about dialogue, dialogue involves the free flow of meaning, and "is a unique form of conversation with potential to improve collective inquiry processes, to produce coordinated action among collectives, and to bring about genuine social change."[35] This meaning of dialogue goes much beyond typical dictionary definitions of dialogue as a conversation between two or more people, because it is focused on the learning that occurs when those people in dialogue are open to new ideas and willing to learn from the conversation itself. It is this sense of stakeholder engagement focused on dialogue that has evolved as part of the responsibility assurance agenda.

Business and other associations

Partially in self-defense of reputation and partially in an effort to advance the cause of corporate citizenship because it is considered to be the right thing to do, a number of business membership organizations have emerged around these topics, as well as other institutions that are more difficult to classify. As noted above, the Center for Corporate Citizenship at Boston College, while academically affiliated, is primarily a business membership organization (which evolved out of the Center for Corporate Community Relations, a more functionally specific professional organization). The other major US business membership organization, focused now on large corporations, is BSR, while Ceres and Global Environmental Management Initiative (GEMI) focus specifically on the environment.

Business membership organizations are not limited to the United States. Europe has emerged as a clear leader. In the United Kingdom, the major business organizations focused on general issues of business in society are Business in the Community (BITC) and the International Business Leaders Forum (IBLF). In continental Europe, CSR Europe and the World Business Council for Sustainable Development draw together global leaders on business in society from the business community.

BITC is a British membership organization counting as its members over 700 of Britain's leading business organizations. It considers itself a "unique movement of . . . companies committed to improving their positive impact on society."[36] Similar mission statements could be found for most of the associations listed in Box 2.12 While the drive to be more accountable and responsible for bettering the world may be limited to top-management levels in many large multinationals or to the rhetoric that some call window-dressing, the rapid emergence of these numerous business associations on related topics highlights the concern in executive suites about the pressures that companies, particularly large and visible companies, are facing today and their proactive moves to respond.

Box 2.12 **Sample business and other membership organizations**

- Association of Sustainability Practitioners (ww.asp-online.org)
- US Chamber of Commerce Business Civic Leadership Center (www.uschamber.com/bclc)
- Business for Social Responsibility (www.bsr.org)
- Business in the Community (www.bitc.org.uk)
- Canadian Business for Social Responsibility (www.cbsr.ca)
- Caux Round Table (www.cauxroundtable.org)
- Center for Corporate Citizenship at Boston College (www.bcccc.net)
- Ceres (www.ceres.org)
- CSR Europe (www.csreurope.org)
- Fundación Empresa y Sociedad (www.empresaysociedad.org)
- Ethics Resource Center (www.ethics.org)
- Global Environmental Management Initiative (www.gemi.org)
- International Business Leaders Forum (www.iblf.net)
- New Economics Foundation (www.instituteforphilanthropy.org.uk)
- World Business Council for Sustainable Development (www.wbcsd.org)
- World Council for Corporate Governance (www.wcfcg.net)

Other associations

- Dubai Ethics Resource Center (www.dubai-ethics.ae/derc)
- Global Ethic Foundation (www.weltethos.org)
- Green Reporting Forum (Japan, awards, no website available)
- International Center for Trade and Sustainable Development (www.ictsd.org)

Not only do many companies engage with NGOs on specific company-related issues, but numerous new networks have also emerged. Some of these networks are business-only and include dialogues on issues related to topics as broad as general corporate responsibility, sustainability, and environment. Some have developed standards that have been adopted by businesses, while others foster dialogues, share information and tools, and provide a reasonably safe forum for discussing topics related to business in society. Some of the business forums and their stated purposes are:

- The World Business Council for Sustainable Development (www.wbcsd. org) focuses on business's common interested in sustainable development though economic growth, ecological balance, and social progress

- The World Council for Corporate Governance (www.wcfcg.net) attempts to galvanize good corporate governance practices globally

- Business in the Community (www.bitc.org.uk) tries to translate corporate values and commitments into management practice

- Caux Round Table (www.cauxroundtable.org) is attempting to develop what it calls moral capitalism

- Boston College Center for Corporate Citizenship (www.bcccc.net) focuses on improving companies' ability to leverage corporate citizenship for the benefit of society

- Ceres (Investors and Environmentalists for Sustainable Prosperity) (www.ceres.org) works with companies to address sustainability challenges

- Business for Social Responsibility (www.bsr.org) works to translate corporate vision and values into management practice

- The Global Environmental Management Initiative (www.gemi.org) helps companies improve environmental health and safety performance, corporate citizenship and shareholder value

- The International Business Leaders Forum (www.iblf.org) promotes responsible business leadership and partnerships for international development

- CSR Europe (www.csreurope.org) helps companies integrate corporate social responsibility into the way they do business every day

A partial list of networks where business can engage with stakeholders is provided in Box 2.13.

Multi-sector coalitions

Multi-sector groups work collaboratively though dialogue and action, to shape the public space for the public good rather than profit. Steve Waddell calls such groups global action networks (GANs). They are relatively new types of entities. Among the issues that some of the GANs to date have been working on are

- Corruption
- Provision of water

Box 2.13 **Major NGO/business, NGO networks, multi-sector engagement forums**

- Business and Human Rights Resource Center (www.business-humanrights.org)
- Corporation 20/20 (www.corporation2020.org)
- Instituto Ethos Empresas e Responsibilidade Social (Ethos Institute for Business and Social Responsibility) (www.ethos.org.br)
- Ethical Trading Initiative (www.ethicaltrade.org)
- European Partners for the Environment (www.epe.be)
- GAN-Net (Global Action Network Net) (www.gan-net.net)
- *Making Waves* magazine: The Centre for Community Enterprise (Canada) (www.cedworks.com/waves.html)
- Responsible Business Initiative (www.rbipk.org)
- Tamarack: The Social Economy (Canada) (tamarackcommunity.ca/g3s10_M4C2.html)
- UN Millennium Development Goals (www.un.org/millenniumgoals)
- World Economic Forum (www.weforum.org)
- World Social Forum (www.forumsocialmundial.org.br)

- Climate change
- Corporate reporting and performance standards
- Corporate performance
- Sustainable fishing
- Sustainable forestry
- Youth employment
- Nutrition
- HIV/Aids, tuberculosis, and malaria
- Microenterprise

■ Questioning the system

The most recent evolution of the corporate responsibility movement has seen a number of initiatives spring up that question the very structure of the current economic–social nexus and attempt to develop new visions of the role of the corporation in the 21st century. Some of these attempt to create leverage for system change by arguing that the idea that companies are responsible only to one stakeholder — the shareholder — is fundamentally wrong. Rather, broader, multiple-stakeholder and multiple-bottom-line conceptions of responsibility are being developed. Issues of long-term environmental sustainability form the foundation for much of this thinking, which argues that current consumption, population, and social patterns are inherently not sustainable over the long term and that very different ways of living are necessary for the planet to be able to sustain human life.

Some of these initiatives, such as the UN Global Compact and the UN Millennium Goals represent consensus views about important social issues in the world that deserve attention from many sectors. Others, like the networks listed by GAN-Net[37] are coalitions of different types of actors pushing for deep change in society around important issues such as water resources, ethical trading, forest stewardship, and climate change. Others such as Corporation 20/20 fundamentally question the nature, purposes, and roles of the corporation and attempt to develop new definitions. Still others focus on specific types of desired changes: for example, the Aspen Institute's Business and Society Program, which is attempting to change management education through a variety of mechanisms.

Alternative ways of measuring progress

The current economic system, which emphasizes free trade, based on neoliberalism[38] has focused some people's attention on developing alternative ways of measuring quality of life. A notable example is the UN's Millennium Goals, which focus on improving life for those people most disadvantaged by the current system. The group Redefining Progress has developed a "Genuine Progress Indicator," which attempts to measure progress in terms that go well beyond traditional measures of gross domestic product. The social fund Calvert has worked with futurist Hazel Henderson to develop the Calvert–Henderson Quality of Life Indicators (see Box 2.14). The Millennium Goals have received widespread attention, but neither of the others has yet come close to substituting for traditional measures of gross domestic product. On the other hand, they represent an alternative to viewing every aspect of life purely in financial terms and the beginning of a new conversation about what is truly important in life.

Box 2.14 **Alternative ways of measuring quality of life/progress**

- Calvert–Henderson Quality of Life Indicators (www.calvert-henderson.com)
- Redefining Progress Genuine Progress Indicator (www.rprogress.org)
- UN Millennium Goals (www.un.org/millenniumgoals)

Journals and popular magazines

There have, of course, been a couple of academic journals devoted to business in society and ethics issues that have been around for quite a few years, but the availability of information and analysis about corporate responsibility issues has exploded since the 1990s. There are now numerous popular journals and online magazines devoted to these topics, as well as several academic journals that allow publishing opportunities for researchers on these subjects, most of which began in the 1980s or later (see Box 2.15).

Box 2.15 **Examples of magazines and journals related to business in society**

Popular press and online magazines

- *Business Respect* (www.mallenbaker.net/csr)
- *CSRwire* (www.csrwire.com)
- *CRO* (*Corporate Responsibility Officer*, formerly *Business Ethics*) (www.thecro.com)
- *Ethical Corporation* (www.ethicalcorp.com)
- *GreenBiz.com* (www.greenbiz.com)
- *Sustainable Business* (www.sustainablebusiness.com)

Academic journals

- *Business and Society*
- *Business and Society Review*
- *Business Ethics Quarterly*
- *Greener Management International*
- *Journal of Business Ethics*
- *Journal of Corporate Citizenship*
- *Organization and Environment*

Academic associations and interest groups

Finally, a number of other important academically oriented associations have evolved that are putting pressures on current approaches to management education, including the European Business Ethics Network, the European Academy of Business in Society, and the CSR Academy, which in 2005 developed the first CSR competency framework for managers to help managers integrate CSR into their companies. There are also management education programs beginning to emerge with curriculum specifically dedicated to business in society issues (see Box 2.16).

Box 2.16 **Academic and academic-affiliated organizations**

- Ashridge Center for Business and Society (United Kingdom) (www.ashridge.org.uk)
- Aspen Institute Business in Society Program (including www.caseplace.org)
- Bainbridge Graduate Institute (www.bgiedu.org)
- Center for Corporate Citizenship at Boston College (www.bcccc.net)
- Centre for Corporate Citizenship, University of South Africa (www.unisa.ac.za/Default.asp?Cmd=ViewContent&ContentID=18145)
- Corporate Citizenship Research Unit at Deakin University (Australia) (www.deakin.edu.au/arts/ccr)
- Corporate Citizenship Unit at the University of Warwick (United Kingdom) (www2.warwick.ac.uk/fac/soc/wbs/research/ccu)
- Corporate Social Responsibility Initiative, Kennedy School of Government, Harvard University (www.ksg.harvard.edu/cbg/CSRI/about.htm)
- CSR Academy (www.csracademy.org.uk)
- European Academy of Business in Society (www.eabis.org)
- European Business Ethics Network (www.eben-net.org)
- International Association for Business in Society (www.iabs.net)
- Net Impact (student organization, founded 1993, now over 10,000 members) (www.netimpact.org)
- Organizations and the Natural Environment, Division of the Academy of Management (one.aomonline.org)
- Social Issues in Management, Division of the Academy of Management (sim.aomonline.org)
- Society for Business Ethics (www.societyforbusinessethics.org)
- Sustainable Enterprise Academy, York University (United Kingdom) (www.sustainableenterpriseacademy.com/SSB-Extra/sea.nsf/docs/SEA)

Difference makers and others evolved this emerging infrastructure around corporate responsibility to pressure companies to change how they implement their business models, not just to encourage them to "do good" for society. The new infrastructure focuses directly on the business models companies employ and the impacts that those companies have on societies, and is no longer simply evaluating philanthropic efforts. The institutions described represent, in a sense, countervailing forces to the current dominance and power of (particularly large, multinational) firms and are attempting to change the system by operating at the margins. The next chapters will go directly to the words and actions of some of the difference makers and explore the story of how this infrastructure came together.

3

Early inklings
Social pioneering for responsible investing

As we begin this journey into the development of the responsibility assurance infrastructure, it is helpful to have a guiding framework. Institutional theorists have provided a developmental framework that illustrates, in general terms, how institution building happens and social movement theorists have described how social movements, such as the responsibility assurance infrastructure we are looking at, evolve. Below, I will briefly describe the core elements of this framework, which will guide the subsequent analysis of how difference makers built a responsibility assurance infrastructure.

A framework for responsibility assurance infrastructure development

The responsibility assurance infrastructure described in Chapter 2 can be characterized as a part of a social movement intended to create a world in which corporate interests are balanced against human, societal, and environmental interests. Social movements, according to sociologists Doug McAdam, John McCarthy, and Mayer Zald,[39] have three core elements: framing processes, political opportunity structures, and mobilizing structures, which will be discussed below. Difference makers, as we shall see, used all three elements to construct the responsibility assurance infrastructure. In addition, we shall view the development of the responsibility assurance infrastructure through the lens of what theorists Hargrave and Van de Ven have called a collective action theory of change.[40]

Elements of a social movement

Framing processes indicate that there is a debate or conversation going on between parties with different views. In responsibility assurance, that debate exists between the proponents of the neoclassical economic model (e.g., the late Milton Friedman whose famous *New York Times* headline in 1970 proclaimed "the social responsibility of business is to increase its profits"), free trade, and globalization, and individuals who believe that corporations should serve a broader public purpose. In the early stages of the development of the responsibility assurance infrastructure, the focus of activity was largely on the development of social investing strategies. For traditional investors, responsibility is simply assumed to mean wealth maximization within the constraints of the law. As things have evolved, the debate has centered more explicitly on what the purpose of the firm is — and, importantly, what it should be. What early proponents of social investment realized, however, was that, for some investors, factors other than wealth maximization were also important. As we shall see, this recognition triggered new framings about how investors might invest with social purposes in mind.

  Opportunity structures are the established order in the existing political, social, and institutional environment facing the movement, where gaps and opportunities that can be tapped by the right social entrepreneur may exist. Typically applied to the political domain, this concept of political opportunity structures suggests that social movements face existing political arrangements that can either enhance or inhibit mobilization of resources around the relevant movement. In the case of the responsibility assurance infrastructure, the surrounding opportunity structures were more associated with business as usual, within companies, in the investment community, and with respect to social expectations from companies. Thus, what has had to be mobilized for the movement to go forward has involved the shifting of, for example, investors' expectations about company performance, standards, accountability and transparency mechanisms, opportunities for dialogue and engagement between companies and other social actors, and related items. Basically, change makers find the places in existing systems where gaps exist or leverage for change can be implemented and find ways of tapping into these opportunities. For example, the financial investment community has traditionally made investments solely on expected financial performance criteria. Before the social investment movement could gain a foothold and begin to establish traction, therefore, new mechanisms or institutional arrangements[41] had to be invented, such as criteria for systematically evaluating companies along social, environmental, and related dimensions, many of which were identified in the last chapter.

Mobilizing structures involve the use or creation of networks of interested parties, including individuals and organizations, some of which are newly created to tap into the opportunities identified by social entrepreneurs, to move the social movement's agenda forward. Mobilizing structures in the political domain might be activist organizations, protest groups, or, in recent years, use of the Internet to foment action on a cause. Of course, all of these vehicles have been used by various groups in the antiglobalization and anticorporate movements, but we shall see that difference makers created their own mobilization structures via linkages with each other in trade and professional associations, networks of forward-looking businesses, and other types of alliance.

A dialectical process of change

The elements of framing, opportunity structures, and mobilizing structures can be found in all types of social movements. Institutional theorists, however, argue that the building of a set of institutional arrangements such as the responsibility assurance infrastructure is a specific form of institutional change called collective action, even though it is generally begun piecemeal by individuals.[42] According to Hargrave and Van de Ven, here is how social movements evolve under this collective-action model of change. The social movement is initiated by a few individuals — social or institutional entrepreneurs — who perceive that change is needed, but don't necessarily have the resources, power, or legitimacy themselves to create that change by themselves. In essence, they are beginning the framing process by articulating the need for change or new ways of doing things.

Typically these social entrepreneurs then build a grassroots network to create coalitions for change. This process of network building is that of creating mobilizing structures — enough interested parties to foster some sort of movement, and the initiation of new institutional arrangements that can spark change. In the case of the difference makers, they built new organizations that either mobilized the resources of interested individuals, either in the investment community for the social investment community or in the corporate community for the evolution of standards, accountability, transparency, engagement, and implementation, or created new pressures on companies for greater responsibility.

The next thing that social entrepreneurs typically do to create a social movement through collective action is to ally themselves with others who have similar or complementary interests and resources. This is a process of creating political opportunity structures, institutional arrangements that advocate for change by filling in gaps in the existing system, fostering new ideas and ways of thinking about the system, and bringing in new allies that then form other institutions. We shall see that, as the responsibility assurance movement began to develop, new professional associations and other ways of linking and informing interested parties also began to evolve, generated in part by difference makers. Hargrave and Van de Ven note that opposing groups also mobilize during this phase to counteract the new pressures they are experiencing.

After a while, different groups with varying points of view become involved in the process and create a plethora of different activities that are all linked to each other but that eventually become overwhelming and confusing, and need to be rationalized. When the social movement is effective, the leaders work through that process of rationalization so that the most effective organizations and institutional arrangements are the ones that survive, and they can draw in other actors. A scan of the abundant new institutions (or institutional arrangements) that have emerged since the early 1980s around responsibility assurance overviewed in Chapter 2 suggests that this phase may well have been reached.

Of course, since this process is dialectical, it is not under the control of any one individual or organization and is subject to further evolution and changes as the process continues. Social development, and in this case the development of the responsibility infrastructure, is a never-ending process.

In this and later chapters we will see how difference makers used this social movement process to develop the responsibility infrastructure that exists today and which is still rapidly evolving. We begin with the framing process by social pioneers.

▓ Framing the problem: social pioneers

The story of the evolution of the responsibility assurance infrastructure can best be told through the stories of individual difference makers, who served as social pioneers and institutional entrepreneurs along the way. Telling the story this way will also, perhaps, allow some insight into what it takes to be a difference maker.

Some of our difference makers can be classified as social pioneers. Social pioneers are those individuals who lead or prepare the way for others to follow. Pioneers frequently initiate change, establish types of organizations that may not have existed before, and take chances that others cannot envision. Social pioneers take these steps because they see or sense a gap that others may not see or may see but not know what to do about. Often, they also envision opportunity in that gap. Many of the difference makers served this role as pioneers, and simultaneously see an opportunity to achieve – or at least move toward achieving – some deeply felt personal purpose or goal, often one that reaches well beyond themselves. Frequently this goal or purpose has little to do with economic gain and may appear to the difference maker as offering the chance to improve the world in some way. The story begins with creating a new understanding of corporate responsibility, largely through evolving the social investment movement and, to a large extent, this story will be told through the words of the difference makers themselves.

Alice Tepper Marlin

No one, of course, can say where what we're calling the responsibility assurance movement began or exactly how it has evolved. But one possible starting point is with difference maker Alice Tepper Marlin, who founded an organization called the Council on Economic Priorities (CEP) in 1969. She was its CEO for 33 years until the CEP spun off the labor standards organization, Social Accountability International (SAI), where at the time of writing she continues to serve as president and CEO. CEP was perhaps the pioneer institutional arrangement in the current development of the social investment field, originating at a time when only a few religious investors were doing any screening of investments to ensure that their investment goals did not collide with important values. There were few systematic approaches to so-called socially responsible investing at the time. Earlier some religiously oriented or values-driven investors chose not to invest in companies producing products that contradicted their values (e.g., the Quakers did not want to invest in companies that produced military equipment), but any screening on those grounds had been unsystematically implemented. Alice Tepper Marlin was working for the then Wall Street firm of Burnham & Company and was asked put together a "peace portfolio" of firms that had little or no involvement with the war in Vietnam.

A graduate of Wellesley College, Tepper Marlin, recounts the history.

> It was at Wellesley that I decided on this particular avenue. I had long wanted to do some kind of public service work but enrolled in college expecting that I'd be a doctor. I was in pre-med and was very influenced by a sociology course on the cycle of poverty and how one breaks it. It was the year that Daniel Moynihan[43] released a study finding a high degree of correlation between family structure and race and income levels and saying you should break the cycle of poverty by changing family structure. And I did my first piece of professional research with Census Bureau Data and refuted that and found a stronger relationship with poverty in general than with race or cycles in family structure. It was really related to female-headed households.
>
> I decided that the most effective and timely way to break into the cycle of poverty was not through what was usually worked on at the time, which was integrating education or housing. Not because either of those weren't good

to do, but because they took a very long time. I thought that it was urgent to move faster and that that could be done by making jobs and capital available in minority communities and communities caught in the cycle of poverty. So I switched to economics in order to get the skills to do that. When I graduated I discovered that I really needed business experience, not just an economics degree. So that's why I went to work on Wall Street. I was very fortunate to get a job as a securities analyst and a labor economist. At the time there were only six women analysts on all of Wall Street in New York. Fewer in Boston: only two or three.

Working as an analyst on Wall Street from 1966 to 1968 provided the base for Tepper Marlin's move to found the CEP in 1969. As she notes,

[The Wall Street job] wasn't an easy position to leave but I had gone [to Wall Street] in order to get the background to address poverty and discrimination issues. Also I was active in my spare time on the war in Vietnam. I had tied the war into a fairly major paper I did for the investment firm Burnham & Co. on the acceleration and rise of wage rates based on the effect of the Vietnam War and the draft on men who had worked in prime blue-collar jobs. I felt that it was the war's effect in either drafting people or encouraging people to stay in school or leave the country or making themselves ineligible for the job that was reducing the labor pool in that key age group. That was the reason for the acceleration in wage rates.

For the paper I looked at which sectors could best offset [the acceleration in wage rates] through productivity gains or passing on prices and which would have created a labor squeeze — a profit margin squeeze. That got quite a lot of publicity. It was written up in the *Wall Street Journal* and some other places. Because of that our firm got an inquiry from a religious institution to ask if we'd invest their funds, but not invest in companies that were supplying weapons to the war in Vietnam. [The company] gave that account to me. I got quite interested then in the leverage that investors could have with business decision-making, partly because I actually did a fair amount of civil rights work as well as antiwar work in my spare time, evenings after work, and on weekends.

So I compared the impact of my volunteering with the leverage I had when I talked to companies as a securities analyst for a major firm and felt that I had far more leverage and could make far more change from a position in the investment community than as an individual, even though it wouldn't have been the only thing I'd be doing as an analyst. All of that led both to the fund and to getting to know the folks who were working on social proxy issue changes, early on.

Here we see the core insight that shifted Tepper Marlin's framing of the situation and, ultimately, her way of making a difference. From working as an activist from outside the financial institutions, she shifted to understanding that there was considerable leverage to be gained by working from the inside out, but with different goals and different criteria than traditional investment houses used. Her position as one of the pioneering women in a financial analyst position gave her understanding, leverage, and insight that were an important underpinning for her later work. In 1969, Tepper Marlin left Wall Street to found CEP. CEP was a non-profit public-interest organization focused on researching corporate social responsibility and clearly a pioneer in this field.

At the time, the field of social investing was nascent. Certain religious investors had attempted to invest with their consciences by not investing in companies that contributed to war or produced tobacco or alcohol. We will see these avoidance principles come up again much later as firms such as KLD evolved formal "screens" to help investors screen out companies engaged in certain activities. For example, investment in companies doing business in South Africa became a major screen for some investors and an important trigger point for the development phase of social investment. The seeds of these later developments were being planted throughout the 1970s into the 1980s by the CEP and related organizations.

Tepper Marlin's pioneering spirit and approach to difference making sprang from a passion for dealing with issues of justice and poverty generated in her undergraduate days, a willingness to learn what was needed to provide the foundation for that work, and, of course, the happy circumstance of landing a job on Wall Street at a time when few women were able to do that and being given the investment work for the values-sensitive religious institutions. The rather dramatic insight that came from this experience was the discovery of how investors' interests in issues beyond economic returns could be leveraged in ways that traditional poverty work could not necessarily match. As well, these early opportunities resulted in new contacts with others who were interested in similar issues, some of whom, such as Joan Bavaria and Tim Smith, are discussed in this book, thus establishing an early coalition of individuals interested in similar issues.

The seeds of social investing

Although the exact origins of social investing are unclear, the terminology apparently became popular during the late 1960s under the influence of a number of religious organizations and the Ford Foundation, which announced in 1967 that social investments would become part of its philanthropic program.[44] The Ford Foundation focused some of its contributions on what would today be called economic development — for instance, minority housing and businesses — and others on conservation projects, which today we might term sustainability. All of these projects were viewed as having inherently higher costs and risks, and probably lower yields than returns on traditional investment.[45] These approaches formed the nexus of today's community investment sector of the social investment field.

During these early days and even into the late 1980s, however, there were no real systematic approaches to selecting or de-selecting companies. That is where social pioneers such as Alice Tepper Marlin, and later Steve Lydenberg, who worked with the CEP in the late 1970s and early 1980s, had an impact. Ultimately, Lydenberg, who with difference makers Amy Domini and Peter Kinder cofounded what is now KLD Research & Analytics in 1990, gained skills in assessing company performance along social dimensions of interest to concerned investors. KLD became the first independent social research organization focused on providing information to the investment community. As data gradually became more available and pressures for better data mounted, certain investors, including some institutional investors such as pension funds and mutual funds, began investing at least some portion of their investments along social lines.

Severyn Bruyn, a sociologist, was one of the earliest scholars to study social investing. According to Bruyn, early adopters mostly had one or two individuals research social criteria for some portion of investments. These early entrants included the Dreyfus Third Century Fund, US Trust in Boston (where difference maker Tim Smith heads the Walden Asset Management group at the time of writing), the Teachers Insurance and Annuity Association and College Retirement Equities Fund, Shearson American Express, Drexel Burnham Lambert, Traveler's Corporation, the Calvert Social Investment Fund, Franklin Research in Boston (where difference maker Joan Bavaria began her work in this domain), the New Alternative Fund, the Pax World Fund, and the Pioneer Fund.[46]

To show how rapidly things have evolved since the late 1980s, when Bruyn wrote his seminal book, *The Field of Social Investing*, published in 1987, he could state categorically:

> Investment analysts are interested in developing systemic studies of social criteria to determine their reliability and validity. They are also interested in evaluating the social impact of their investments on investees and evaluating their own efforts on a larger scale of values. There is no systemic theory guiding these separate efforts to utilize social criteria for investments, and almost no empirical research on the issues. The problems in the field have yet to be clarified and formulated for systematic criticism. Indeed, there is need for developing a social science of investment that can track and study these new financial interests.[47]

The Council on Economic Priorities (CEP)

Although it can hardly be claimed that all of the problems that Bruyn identified have been resolved, what is clear from the sketch of developments in the social investing field provided in Chapter 2 is that much has changed and that a great deal of development has occurred. Things have changed because some of the difference makers we discuss here took the necessary steps and established the organizations needed to accomplish many of these tasks. Establishing CEP was one important step toward creating institutions that could systematically evaluate company performance along social criteria, even if early efforts were mainly focused on screening out behaviors and practices that some investors wished to avoid.

Evidence of some of these new institutional arrangements is noted by Tepper Marlin as she recounts CEP's own evolution,

> There are a couple of other important streams [in CEP's development that need to be mentioned]. One is that we began the America's Corporate Conscience Awards to focus more on the positive. Originally they were awarded in the United States, and eventually internationally, for best-practice examples, to give lots of credit to those companies. Also we began to team up with magazines on some of the corporate best lists. The first one we did was with *Working Woman* on best places for women to work. The one that had the biggest impact is the series at *Fortune* magazine on best places for women and best places for minorities. *Fortune* is still running those as are a bunch of other magazines.
>
> [CEP] built its revenue streams very slowly. We charged for providing the research to the investment community but, in the early days, there were very few clients and they didn't pay very much. We got advances on books and we sold membership. All of which was relatively small-scale and we were mostly funded by project grants and individual contributions from individuals who were members of our board (some of those were major). Then when our book *Shopping for a Better World* took off we grew enormously and very rapidly. I don't mean that we grew to be enormous, but our size must have doubled within a couple of years, through book sales and membership recruitment through the books. The books had membership forms in them, and because we got so much publicity people became members.

Shopping for a Better World

As Tepper Marlin remembers it, several things began to happen that furthered the development of the work of the CEP:

> One stream was in the mid-1980s. We had just started paying attention to it right around the time *Rating America's Corporate Conscience* [CEP's 1986

publication, the first-ever book to rate brand-name companies, of which the lead author was difference maker Steve Lydenberg] came out. That was how limited we were by only evaluating US companies. Because it was not so much an investment community issue, as soon as *Rating America's Corporate Conscience* came out, we began to address consumers. We were aware how many very popular consumer products were made by non-US companies, particularly Japanese and some European at that time.

So we began to think about how could we rate consumer products — companies that made consumer products but weren't US companies. Our entire methodology was based around data available in the US, around US cultural norms, and around US law. We had very complicated rating systems with the criteria and indicators and weightings, and so on. But they were very nationally focused. We became aware of two limitations in trying to study companies abroad. One, it was almost impossible to get data. Two, the comparisons with US companies didn't work very well because of legal and cultural differences.

These issues with the data had further developmental impacts on the emerging understanding of how to rate companies on criteria about which customers and investors might care, but which were not conveniently presented in financial statements. Tepper Marlin continues,

So we began to build a network of organizations in other countries that did similar research. A few of them already existed and a number of them were formed, modeled on CEP right after the consumer guide came out. Because *Shopping for a Better World* got to be so popular, there was lots of coverage around the world, not just in the US. Other organizations thought about it and said, "We'd like to do that." Or people said, "We'd like to start an organization to do that." So, in several countries, new organizations were formed modeled on CEP, particularly focused on the shopping guide.

Here we see the beginnings of the creation of necessary mobilizing structures to tap the emerging opportunities that CEP had uncovered. As will be detailed in Chapter 4, new recognition that the work of CEP needed to shift eventually resulted in the creation of yet another institution by Tepper Marlin and her associates, SAI, a leading labor standards and accrediting organization. Meanwhile, others were beginning similar journeys of discovery, framing, and institution building. We turn next to Joan Bavaria.

▪ Joan Bavaria

Bavaria is founder and president of the social investment firm Trillium Asset Management (founded as Franklin Research and Development), founder of the Coalition for Environmentally Responsible Economies (Ceres), and founder of the Social Investment Forum (SIF). She played a critical role in the founding of the Global Reporting Initiative (GRI), and, more recently, was one of the founders of the Investor Network on Climate Risk.

About the time that Alice Tepper Marlin was wondering whether to leave her Wall Street analyst's job and establish the CEP, Joan Bavaria was looking for a way to support her two young boys. A divorced artist, Bavaria had come to Boston in the late 1960s from a rural part of Massachusetts to attend the Massachusetts College of Art and

> tried to earn a living doing art, but it wasn't secure. One of my kids got really sick with scarlet fever over the Christmas holidays and ended up in Children's Hospital. It scared me . . . and that's when I walked into the Bank of Boston to get a job, and ended up in the trust department, and, well, art would have to be an avocation. And life evolved from there.

Happy chance, perhaps, but within about 18 months Bavaria found herself managing trust accounts. She was, like Alice Tepper Marlin, a pioneering woman in a man's world. She says,

> I was partly lucky in being able to do that. They figured out that women were cheaper and did a good job. So I did. I was promoted to investment officer and started managing a portfolio. But even back then people would ask questions. One woman in particular inherited a fair amount of money and wanted to know what percent of the world's wealth [was doing good] because she was feeling guilty about the money. With all these prodding questions I was getting from clients, I began asking questions about the investment policies at the bank. I won't say horrible things about the Bank of Boston, which became the Bank of America [after having been absorbed by Fleet Bank] but they weren't terribly enlightened.

Unlike some of the difference makers, Bavaria did not always see herself as an activist, though she always had a deep concern about and commitment to the natural environment. But she remembers how her "radicalization" came about.

> At a time when there were 54 people performing as investment professionals, only four of them were women and at least one of those was an officer. We all had the lowest salaries and they didn't even think about that. They didn't talk about it. In other words, it was a typical situation. Women simply worked cheaper. I had two kids I was raising so I didn't lead in [trying to change the

situation] or the turnaround, but I did help, and by the time I was out of there the bank had changed its policy.

But this was not the turning point for Bavaria's activism.

> I remember that moment. Basically, because I was working long hours, I had very little time to do much with my own life. Like, for instance, I wouldn't have exercise time and I really valued that. So I had some friends who at that time were running Joy of Movement [an early fitness organization]. I talked them into working with me to open up an exercise program in Boston during lunch hour. We managed to get a space in the new building [that Bank of Boston was moving into], a little bit of space on the 13th floor because they hadn't filled it yet. So we ran an exercise program, which was very robust.
>
> Then they wanted the 13th floor for other uses, so we petitioned and wrote a paper, and went all the way up to the president asking for space in another part of the building. But they said no. We had coverage on every major TV station in Boston. The next step was to petition the personnel department for permission to send notices around about the program, but the proposed flyer came back rejected because the logo of the Joy of Movement was thought to be too suggestive. I sat there at my desk and somebody came up to me and said, "What in God's name are you going to do?" I was stunned. I just sat there and said to myself, "This is not radical stuff." Ultimately, we didn't get this place that we wanted.

As it turned out, instead of the bank providing an opportunity for all employees to join a health club, only officers were given that privilege — and Bavaria's perspective became much more radicalized as she witnessed first-hand the differential treatment of workers and officers.

In 1975 Bavaria was headhunted out of the then Bank of Boston and became an investment advisor at Franklin Management, an investment house, also in Boston, where she was responsible for managing individual portfolios. Between listening to clients' questions about possibilities for investing their money in more environmentally responsible ways and her own deep concern for the environment, Bavaria found herself trying to think through how what would today be called SRI could be done in more systematic ways. She notes that the questions that investors were raising in those early days were different than they are today. For example, fast-food giant McDonald's at the time was under considerable pressure for its environmental impacts, and, by the early 1980s, the apartheid regime in South Africa had gained the attention of activist investors and become the focal point of much of the early action and ultimate growth of SRI. The seeds of what was to become the responsible investment movement were being sown.

In 1982 Bavaria founded the company now known as Trillium Asset Management (then called Franklin Research and Development) as a vehicle for taking the kinds of questions her clients were asking about their investments and putting them into practice through an SRI strategy. Having been radicalized by her experience in the bank and by listening carefully to clients' concerns, she was open to new and different considerations in the practice of investment management: practices that encompassed social and environmental, as well as financial, criteria. Today, as it has always been, Trillium is a leader in the social investment world, and an employee and majority woman-owned firm "guided by a belief that investing can return a profit to the investor, while also promoting social and economic justice."[48]

Trillium Asset Management (Franklin Research and Development)

The name shift from Franklin to Trillium, which occurred in the early 2000s, reflected the importance of the triple-bottom-line approach that weaves together three elements of: sustainability, ecology, or a healthy environment; equity or social justice; and economy or healthy commerce,[49] which the investment firm has always focused on. The name may have shifted but Trillium's mission remains fundamentally unchanged and clearly reflects the values that Bavaria's long-term commitment to the environment and radicalized sensibility brought to the organization.

The mission statement (see Box 3.1) states that "Trillium Asset Management will be the leader in investing to achieve financial gain, social equity, and environmental sustainability," or what difference maker John Elkington coined as "the triple bottom line."

Box 3.1 **Trillium Asset Management mission statement**

Trillium Asset Management will be the leader in investing to achieve financial gain, social equity, and environmental sustainability.

To bring this vision to life, we seek to:

- Provide superior products and services that fulfill the financial, social, and ecological goals of individual and institutional investors
- Explore and develop all possible means of social progress offered by the capital markets, and educate other concerned investors in their use
- Create a work environment that encourages personal development and growth, and in which ownership, responsibilities, and rewards are broadly shared
- Support other persons and organizations working to build a just society and a better world[50]

It is possible to see in Trillium's mission statement some of the characteristics that institutional entrepreneurs — difference makers — use to move their visions forward. First is the recognition that new innovations will be needed to create markets that focus on social progress as well as financial wealth — and that this will be done by focusing not just on one but on multiple bottom lines. Second is the recognition that one organization alone cannot achieve the vision and that others must be encouraged to "own" the processes and practices of the organization, which involves the very ownership structure of the firm. Third is the recognition that alliances with similarly concerned others, both individual and organizational, need to be formed to ensure that the vision of a better world moves forward.

Thus, it is perhaps not surprising that in 1984 Bavaria recognized the need for people working in the field of social investment to have a place where they could come together regularly to discuss their work, and founded the professional association the Social Investment Forum. Today the Social Investment Forum, whose president at the time of writing is Tim Smith, is the largest trade association in social investment, with counterparts in the United Kingdom, Europe (Eurosif), and France.

Meanwhile, in those early days, another aspect of social investment — activist shareholders exerting direct pressures on companies — was beginning to gain importance.

■ Timothy H. Smith

Timothy H. (Tim) Smith became known for the nearly 30 years (from 1971 to 2000) that he worked with the Interfaith Center on Corporate Responsibility (ICCR), serving for most of that time as ICCR's executive director, where he became a global leader in the 1980s' drive to persuade companies to divest from South Africa. At the time of writing, he is senior vice president and director of socially responsible investing for Walden Asset Management, a division of United States Trust. He also serves as president of the Social Investment Forum, the largest SRI industry association.

Smith's activist roots came early, as he recounts,

> Way back, I went to the University of Toronto. One of the things that I got involved with was the whole issue of South Africa. When I graduated, I went on a program called Crossroads Africa. We went to Kenya, and other groups went throughout Africa, working with Canadian and American self-help projects. It was just very eye-opening. I had never traveled like this to other countries, so going to Kenya and helping on projects there for two months was very revelatory.

Then I came back not to Canada, but to Union Theological Seminary [in Schenectady, New York], though I wasn't sure of my goal. I wanted to look at religion and consider whether the ministry was an option for me, but I wasn't committed to it. At that point, of course, there was the whole expectation of going back to Canada. When I went to Union, we all had to do field work, and one of the opportunities for me was to work with a group called the Southern Africa Committee, a university Christian group. That was in 1966. They became very involved with a campaign to end bank loans in South Africa to the government. It was again very revelatory, in that we had information that had not been exposed before about who was lending money, and could make a pretty clear case that the government was supporting the apartheid system. We had banks scratch their heads and say, "Well, that's not the way we make loans."

It was a fascinating insight into how companies thought about corporate responsibility, so I continued to work in South Africa with the United Church of Christ as a fieldwork student. Then when I graduated, I began to work with both of them, the United Church of Christ and the Southern Africa Committee, both on a half-time basis. The work we were focusing on involved the role of banks and companies in South Africa, which was a major issue, then other religious groups started to get interested in this issue and wanted to work together. Thus, the Interfaith Center on Corporate Responsibility was born and I became its first program director. I was present at the creation, so to speak. And also, for example, I was present at the first stockholders' meeting of General Motors where the South Africa issue was raised by the Episcopal Church. That was the first shareholder resolution on this issue that had ever been filed! We helped a little on that one and then with some other companies, and then my work became working with other people [within ICCR], but as a staff person.

Campaign GM

Shareholder meetings at General Motors (GM) became, unwittingly and unwillingly on management's part, a core strategy for activists to engage with and pressure corporations to change. The first notable shareholder protest occurred in 1970, through a strategy called Campaign GM, when the very first socially oriented shareholder resolution was submitted. Campaign GM was one of the seminal triggers in creating understanding that pressures for corporate reform could be brought about through shareholders – activist shareholders in this case – submitting shareholder resolutions for consideration by the board of directors at the annual meeting. The core insight was similar to those insights that Tepper Marlin and Bavaria had also had: leverage could be gained by working within the system but using criteria that went well beyond simple financial criteria for investments or, in this case, to pressure companies by using the mechanisms of the proxy vote.[51]

The 1960s, of course, were a time of social ferment and dissatisfaction with the established powers in the United States. Campaign GM grew directly out of this ferment, and General Motors was by no means the only target of this activist group. Other companies, including United Aircraft Corporation (now UTC), American Telephone and Telegraph (now AT&T), Columbia Broadcasting System (CBS), General Electric, Union Carbide, Gulf Oil, Commonwealth Edison, and Honeywell, were also subjected to shareholder protests at their annual meetings. The Campaign GM strategy of shareholder activism using a shareholder proxy resolution was, however, perhaps the most sophisticated of the protests. The shareholder resolution was formally submitted by a group that owned only 12 GM shares, known as the Project on Corporate Responsibility.[52]

According to Donald Schwartz, who was counsel to Campaign GM, two proposals were the focus of the activists' campaign. The first asked the company to amend the bylaws so that three more individuals — and, importantly, a more diverse group of individuals — could be added to the board of directors.[53] The intent was to increase the diversity of the board without necessarily challenging the status of current directors. The second proposal sought to create a Shareholders Committee for Corporate Responsibility, which would have served as a forum for assessing the company's (and other corporations') role in society and addressing social issues, and would have included representation from the GM board of directors, the United Auto Workers, and Campaign GM. The idea was that this new committee would conduct a social audit of GM.[54]

Of course, like virtually all of the early shareholder resolutions, Campaign GM served more to alert management to the concerns of activist shareholders than to actually change the company's behavior since, particularly in those early days, few shareholders actually voted against management for resolutions submitted by activists. The costs of an activist group generating sufficient votes for the resolution to pass without it being included in management's prospectus were prohibitive and the process unwieldy. Still, with consumer activist Ralph Nader in the lead, Campaign GM fought to get the resolution on the general proxy statement, and the Securities and Exchange Commission concurred. Campaign GM generated widespread publicity and thereby public interest, particularly because the resolutions became tied to the first-ever national celebration of Earth Day in 1970. Although the resolutions received only a minimal percentage of shareholder votes (less than 3% of votes cast and about 7% of shareholders voting), Campaign GM nonetheless served as a bellwether for future shareholder campaigns that would be initiated by the newly formed ICCR.[55]

Interfaith Center on Corporate Responsibility

It was in the context of all these protests and new thinking about ways to influence corporate practices through shareholder resolutions that ICCR was born in 1971. ICCR is today an association of 275 faith-based institutional investors from a wide variety of denominations and religious communities. ICCR represents religious organizations and communities, pension funds, endowments, hospital corporations, economic development funds, asset management companies, colleges, unions, and publishing companies estimated to encompass a portfolio of some US$110 billion in 2007. ICCR submits more than 200 shareholder resolutions each year that demand various changes in governance, social, and environmental practices.[56]

Tim Smith notes,

> ICCR was very functional in that these religious groups were all facing the same issues. They had clear statements on an issue like South Africa or the environment or equal employment opportunity, and yet they had never taken those social statements and put them on the same table as their investments or financial decision-making. So people needed each other to think through these issues and also to engage companies on them. Companies didn't have any experience with us and we didn't have much experience with companies. It was all a brand-new ball game. So ICCR was initially formed by six Protestant denominations that decided they wanted to work together, and I was the (only) staff person, aged 26. I was the program person and they partnered with a research center called the Corporate Information Center that was part of the National Council of Churches. A guy named Frank White was the head of it. So they had a number of staff people working on research on corporate responsibility.

Today ICCR has a clearly articulated set of core values and a broad but focused set of issues on which it submits resolutions (see Box 3.2).

Box 3.2 **ICCR core values**

Our core values are:

- Faith-based: Faith guides and shapes our priorities for action
- Justice: We challenge ourselves and corporations to accountability for right relationships with all of creation
- Integrity: We are striving to be credible practitioners of the values we set forth
- Inclusive: We welcome diversity as we covenant to work together[57]

The priorities of ICCR, as stated in 2008, include: eliminating sweatshops and corporate involvement in human rights abuses; reversing global warming; halting the proliferation of genetically modified foods until safety is proven; making capital available for all on an equal-opportunity basis; working to make retailers of violent video games more accountable; making pharmaceuticals and healthcare safe, available, and affordable to all; seeking more reasonable executive pay; seeking more accountable corporate governance structures; and stopping the use of depleted-uranium weapons.[58]

Clearly, ICCR's agenda has significantly expanded from the early days of focusing much of its energy on issues related to apartheid in South Africa. As Smith notes,

> ICCR's work really expanded based on the initial work on South Africa. They also had a focus on the whole issue of strip mining in Puerto Rico, questions of discrimination and employment, and of the course the Vietnam War was a big issue: the whole issue of people owning Dow Chemical stock and the ethics of owning stock in the company that made napalm.

Also, of course, the apartheid regime in South Africa collapsed in the wake of many, many protests in South Africa and, probably not entirely incidentally, pressures from the emergent social investment movement.

Expanding social agendas and multiple strategies

The expansion of ICCR's agenda is symptomatic of the shifts that we begin to see as we scan across the developments in the more general responsibility assurance infrastructure over the years, particularly recently, and highlights one of the realities that has consistently confronted practitioners such as Smith, Bavaria, and Tepper Marlin who work in this arena: issues related to business in society, corporate power, and social needs change as society itself changes and new problems emerge.

The ground is constantly shifting, as Smith himself points out about the early days of ICCR:

> How would you discover an issue? Sometimes an issue came from the social side of a church because they'd already been speaking about it, so they didn't have to start from scratch, for example, with South Africa or with napalm. Those issues were easy connections to make. We don't think napalm is a good thing — oh, Dow Chemical makes napalm, and we currently own shares in it.
>
> The harder question is: what do you do? Some people, as you can imagine, said, "We should divest." But not everyone said that. Others said, "Let's engage the company. Let's put pressure on them."
>
> How did ICCR resolve that tension? We did both. Some people said, look, I'm not going to engage a tobacco company or an alcohol company or a

major weapons company, because we're not going to change them. We're
not going to move them. So [the investment community used] a screen [i.e.
investors "screened out" companies that produced these products from their
portfolios]. It was the second stage of screening, because for decades some
churches had been screening, for example, for tobacco, but this was more
formal. A second set of screens, where social issues beyond the major project
of the company were being addressed. Some people might have seen them
as divergent strategies because there was a big fight in the South Africa
movement about whether people should divest and sell their stock or use
their shares to influence. But in a way both of them were two approaches to
the same issue of trying to say this is a company that has significant problems
and we're going to address it — and here's how. Our members in ICCR were
using both strategies. We had resolutions and then some people would later
move on to divestment. Our members in the heat of the South Africa debate
had different strategies. Half of them had divestment strategies and the others had shareholder actions, and some had selected actions or divestments.
Some would focus on the significant players in SA.

Smith became well known, some might even argue legendary, for his work on
South Africa. The work that he did with ICCR to challenge the roles that banks and
companies were playing in South Africa was in no small measure critical in the
eventual divestment of many companies from active involvement in South Africa
and the ultimate fall of the apartheid regime. Along the way Smith became involved
with the Reverend Leon Sullivan, author of the Sullivan Principles, the first set of
principles guiding the behavior of companies in abusive regimes (now known as
the Global Sullivan Principles).[59] Reverend Sullivan was invited onto GM's board as
the South Africa controversy grew. When ICCR released secret documents that
showed that GM was supporting the apartheid regime by selling cars and trucks to
it and then filed a shareholder resolution proposing that GM stop these practices,
Reverend Sullivan publicly stated in the proxy resolution that he supported the
ICCR resolution. Sullivan continued to endorse his principles for ten years, until,
finally acknowledging that they were not working, in 1987, he turned in favor of economic sanctions, much as ICCR and other activists had been proposing.[60]

Smith reflects,

I was at ICCR for 30 years, working on specific issues and the issues more
generally for about 35 years. My role was to be involved in the program
which was to help coordinate the strategies, whether it was a public hearing
that we were having or issuing a report — the same kinds of thing we do
today, filing a shareholder resolution, having people go to a stockholders'
meeting, announcing a divestment in Citibank because a number of religious
groups had said they weren't going to do business with Citibank any more so

they were yanking their bank accounts. Publicizing all that in the press. Networking with other people. Working a little on the legislative issues.

Along the way Smith also became involved in another major controversy of the
late 1970s and early 1980s: the Nestlé boycott. In 1977 ICCR founded INFACT (Infant
Formula Action Committee) and organized a boycott against Nestlé because of its
aggressive marketing of infant formula in developing countries. Smith presented
ICCR's position and data to the Nestlé Audit Commission, an independent body
established to monitor that company's compliance with the World Health Organization (WHO) international code of conduct (on which difference maker Jim Post
served).

In 2000, Smith left ICCR for Walden Asset Management, where he still works at
the time of writing. As he thinks about the job change, he reflects,

> I decided to step down partly because I'd been on a phone call with a Roman
> Catholic sister who was 75; and we were chatting away and she made some
> casual comment, "Oh I'm in the middle of my five-year plan now." I thought,
> "I don't have a five-minute plan, I'm so busy," and I stopped and said, "In ten
> years, do I want to be here, doing this job the best I can, raising more money,
> doing the kind of work that was becoming much more administrative, or
> would I like to get my hands back into the issues again?" So I said, "No, I
> really need to segue out of this position."
>
> So I did something which a couple of years later would have been either
> impossible or very stupid. I said I would step down and start looking for a
> job, where most people would look for a job first. I just felt so uncomfortable
> quietly looking for a job and then announcing to ICCR, which I'd helped cre-
> ate, "I'm giving you a month's notice." So I was able to give significant notice
> and they were able to do a transition — and they did it well. During that time
> I was lucky that Walden reached out and asked if I wanted to work here. I'd
> been debating at that point about whether to work as an independent con-
> sultant assisting people like Domini or Calvert or work as staff somewhere. I'd
> worked with Walden before because they'd been associate members of
> ICCR, so I knew how good they were and what they stood for. I'm now senior
> vice president and director of socially responsive (that's their term) investing.
> When I was there I got elected to the board of Social Investment Forum, the
> trade association, and am now the president.[61]

Crafting a vision

As with many of the difference makers, Tim Smith found that his vision of being
part of building a better world emerged gradually. He reflects,

I think the vision does emerge. I don't think you have some sort of perfect vision and then walk in to try to make it happen. Certainly on issues like South Africa, you had a vision of a free and independent South Africa, with Nelson Mandela out of jail. On issues like the environment, you had a vision of people acting in respectful ways to the environment rather than exploiting it. So in ICCR that meant you wound up with very issue-specific visions. We did have goals and objectives; we did planning that way every year. We'd make a plan and evaluate it. All of that had to be done, but it wasn't just the leadership. The people who were there, their faith perspective was central to who they were. They had a passion for social justice and a commitment to action, to try to act in the world to bring about change, and an understanding of the need to bring about social and economic justice.

People might say things differently. A pension board might say something differently than the Adrian Sisters or the Episcopal Church, but they were all moving in the same direction. That was sort of amazing. We didn't have people who saw the world in entirely different ways. The initial tension was between people within the church or within ICCR who were very critical of the capitalist system and those who had a stake in it but were very concerned about it. Chastising the global economy, or saying, "Well, the global economy exists, how are we going to impact it?"

So I think in the earlier years I might have been more systemically critical than I am now. Now I'm part of the system, and I was then too. But whether it's the social investment or religious investment community, it's a tightrope we walk, because you know the systemic issues and you know the global justice issues. At ICCR there were people not just with global mind-sets but working globally. They were missionaries, they had partners around the world who were talking about the global debt, or oppression in South Africa, or what was happening to the environment in their area. Well, if you wanted to take those people seriously, or really be their partners, you had to listen; you couldn't say, "Well, that's very nice," and go about your business. So your agenda was partially formed by the people who knew what they were doing and seeing.

As with many of the institutions that have evolved as part of the responsibility assurance infrastructure, ICCR's work with shareholder resolutions was formed on a contested field, with parties with different ideas and interests coming together. While they might not have reached an absolute consensus about strategies and approaches, there does seem to have been, as Smith's words reflect, a coherent sense of direction and similar perspectives on how to move the progressive agenda of improving corporate behaviors forward.

Similarly, the vision that has evolved has a future dimension, for it is really about constructing a world that the religious investors behind ICCR and Smith himself want to live in. As Smith explains,

> You look at the systemic issues, the challenges we are facing globally, whether it's climate change, or water, or the huge gap in income between the rich and poor. It's both a description and a vision because the description leads to [the conclusion that] this is unacceptable. Well, fine, what are you going to do about it? So the vision is to try to create a more just and sustainable global economy and society.
>
> That's said in very abstract terms, but it very quickly becomes a reality as you work on each of these issues, be it climate change, or world debt, or sweatshops. It has a human face; it's not just a theological abstract. You only need to look in the *maquiladoras*[62] or the factories in the sweatshops of Indonesia, where we source our shoes and computers, and clothing and toy companies. You see the face of the Chinese girl who's working in that plant or the Mexican man who's working in the *maquila*, who are making pretty close to poverty wages as they're making a product for us that then gets sold for profit here. So you see the global economy not simply through an academic concept but through people.

Smith notes, as he thinks broadly about why people became activists around these issues in the first place,

> The base for many religious investors was the struggle and suffering of people and solidarity with them. Social investors would use somewhat different terms. There's an interesting bifurcation in the social investment community between mutual funds and money managers who are deeply passionate about the issues, and then big pension funds who are doing it more out of prudence. But whether you're watching the climate-change clock tick, or you're watching world debt help shred the lives of many people in the third world, or you're watching sweatshops and what role they play, they are about people and about our environment, not just an abstract idea.

Smith, like Bavaria and Tepper Marlin, was one of the true pioneers of the early social investment movement as we know it today. Another individual, Amy Domini, also played a critical role.

Amy Domini

There is one more social pioneer whose work needs to be discussed in the context of the emergence of SRI and that is Amy Domini, founder and CEO of Domini Social Investments, which publishes the Domini Social Index (DSI), and cofounder with Peter Kinder and Steve Lydenberg of the social research firm KLD Research & Analytics (see Chapter 4). By 2007, Domini Social Investments, which focuses exclusively on SRI, was managing US$1.8 billion for socially conscious investors and institutions. KLD had long since become an entirely separate entity doing social research on companies and producing the DSI, which will be discussed in the next chapter in more detail. Like Tepper Marlin and Bavaria, Domini, in her current position as private trustee and portfolio manager at the firm of Loring, Wolcott & Coolidge, found herself listening to clients' concerns about where the money they were investing was going — and whether those investments aligned with their values.

As she discusses the two positions she simultaneously holds, CEO of Domini Social Investments and private trustee at Loring, Wolcott & Coolidge, Domini explains,

> We serve individuals, not as a corporate trustee, so it's an old-fashioned model. My particular client base [consists of] people who agree with me on the importance of integrating social and ethical criteria into the investment decision-making process. And I've been here [at Loring, Wolcott & Coolidge] since 1987. It's been structurally a good place for me to operate out of. Now there are two other trustees who say half or so of their business is also that kind of a client base. I'm better known as a founder and managing principal or CEO of Domini Social Investments, a mutual fund company. It has four basic products, although they're distributed through different means: a domestic equity product; a European equity product; a bond product; and a money-market product. And those are all offered to the public in a highly regulated fashion, because the fund industry is highly regulated. The office is based in New York, where I spend a day or two a week. Pretty much you never know what you're doing at any minute, or which hat you're wearing.

Domini came from a large extended family with deep roots in American society on her mother's side; as she points out, she had "seven or eight Mayflower ancestors" and some 24 cousins that played together on weekends. Her mother had gone to Europe after World War II, married an Italian "kid off the streets," whom she brought home to the United States with her. The result of the mix was that the family did not fit well into either Italian–American groups or the high society on her mother's side, but was deeply exposed to both cultures. Domini reflects,

> I grew up in the era where everybody went to church on Sunday. Then everybody got very concerned about civil rights, and then about the Vietnam War, and we had the flower-power generation coming through. I was certainly influenced by all of the things that were going on from the time I was, say, 13 until 30. And I dropped out of college. I didn't want to be in school — I don't think I ever got above C+ in any grade — but finally finished up at Boston University [in 1973]. A girlfriend asked me what I was going to do after college. So I said, "I don't know, what are you going to do?" She said, "I'm going to learn to type." So I said, "Good idea," and we signed up for typing classes.

Despite learning to type, Domini still had trouble finding a job but, with her grandfather's assistance, ultimately got a position doing photocopying in the stock brokerage firm Tucker Anthony, where he worked. After a series of promotions, she was made secretary to the CEO and in 1975 convinced her colleagues that she should be allowed to take the licensing exam to enter sales and, having passed the test, that she should actually be in sales.

Domini was apparently the first female to hold a sales position in the firm, which came as a surprise to her. As she recalls,

> A couple or three years later, I was introduced by a senior person at the firm as the first female sales person at the firm. I don't know whether that's true or not. It certainly hadn't occurred to me until he said it. But I couldn't actually think of another woman who was in sales at the time. There were plenty of secretaries who also had a couple of clients or who had that license, but nobody who was only in sales that I could recall. So that shows how oblivious I was to feminist actions back then. It was the blooming of feminism and I was oblivious to it.

Like Tepper Marlin and Bavaria in analyst positions, and Smith with the religious investors, Domini found herself listening to clients' concerns and becoming open to the idea of aligning values with investment practices. She recounts her insights at the time:

> As a broker, and maybe it is somewhat of female trait, I listened, and customers would say, "I'm very opposed to the war. I wouldn't want to buy machines for war," or, "I'm a birder, and these people spray the trees and kill the songbirds. I wouldn't want to buy them." I don't know when, but at a certain point I heard it. To build up a client base, once I got to Harvard Square [in Cambridge, MA, where Domini lives] I started offering classes on the ABCs of investing and advanced investing through the Cambridge Center for Adult Education. So I put a new course description in the Cambridge adult education book called ethical investing and people signed up. Then I realized I had a real thing there.

SRI gains shape

As her client base grew, Domini began to become more knowledgeable about the possibilities associated with SRI. Then in 1984, with Peter Kinder, Domini wrote a book called *Ethical Investing*, which, combined with her willingness to teach and give public talks, cemented her reputation as a leader in the SRI field. New SRI networks had begun to evolve, based partly on the work of Joan Bavaria, who in 1984 established the Social Investment Forum, creating a formal professional network of individuals interested in SRI and exposing Domini and others to ideas and approaches to the field. As she puts it,

> Through that network, I was introduced to broader ideas to the one I had known about, which was pretty exclusively, "I don't want to own that." The broader ideas were, "I want to own something, I want to be involved in direct dialogue with corporations through my shareholder rights, and I want to support community-development financial institutions."

Indeed, these three broader ideas form the nexus that SRI as a movement still emphasizes today: screening for company behaviors and products, engagement with companies through shareholder activism, and investment in community and economic development.

Domini recounts,

> The book was published in 1984, and 1983 to 1986 were key years for the American debate over the role of US corporations doing business in South Africa. 1986 was the crescendo year of divestment — two hundred billion dollars divested from portfolios. That meant that every small endowment library board was looking for an expert to come talk about it and I had just written the book. So suddenly I was that expert.

Two concerns soon became evident to Domini: the need for better data on how companies actually performed along social and environmental dimensions, and the need to track performance to answer the questions that the financial community consistently raised about what the trade-offs — if any — were for financial investing.

We need better data

The ICCR was active in the shareholder engagement aspect of SRI, but there were numerous other issues associated with investing money into socially screened companies, since at the time there were no systematic methodologies for assessing companies. Domini tells the story of how several developments took place.

> I kept hearing essentially two big complaints or concerns. One was, "What is this squishy field called SRI or ethical investing? *Whose* ethics are at work

here?" The basic questions were How do you do it? Isn't it too hard? Where does the line get drawn? Yet we already had Calvert Funds, Pax World Fund, Trillium Asset Management [then Franklin Research and Development] investing along social criteria. There were already newsletters: *Good Money* was being published, and Trillium and US Trust had their newsletters. US Trust of Boston had their business. We all knew what we were talking about. So there was a definition; it was not just perfectly explained to the world."

We need to track performance

Domini continues,

The other big concern was, "How much is it going to cost?" As I thought through these things, the idea began to form that really what was needed was an index of our own. By 1987, I started really fooling around with whether or not [there could be an SRI] alternative to the Standard & Poor's index, which probably still is today the mountain in terms of indexes, the premiere index. Certainly at that time, it was the benchmark.

An SRI index built on solid, consistently gathered data that was as objective as feasible in the "squishy" domain of social, environmental, and what today we call stakeholder performance could potentially answer the question about financial trade-offs for social investing, at least over the long run. At the time, however, neither the data nor an adequate tracking mechanism existed anywhere. SRI was being done in a number of places, but not with the degree of systematic rigor that would satisfy many in the financial community.[63]

The Domini Social Equity Fund and Domini 400 Social Index

The two questions haunting Domini ultimately bore fruit — and some answers — in the form of the Domini Social Equity Fund, which uses a related index, the Domini 400 Social Index (DSI), now owned by KLD Research & Analytics in Boston, to inform investment decisions. KLD itself was founded to generate the systematically and rigorously gathered data that was needed, and was cofounded by Domini with Peter Kinder and Steve Lydenberg. KLD launched its first ratings in 1990 (for more on KLD, see Chapter 4).

The Domini Social Equity Fund was not the first socially screened fund; as has already been mentioned it was preceded by the Pioneer Fund, Pax World Fund, the Dreyfus Third Century Fund, Franklin (now Trillium), and the Calvert Social Investment Fund. What Domini brought to bear on the questions about the quality of SRI data and the performance of SRI investments was a different understanding of how to go about dealing with these questions from concerned investors, who also wanted to ensure solid returns on their investments. She says,

We could use the Standard & Poor's methodology to create an index of our own, using the kind of criteria that we *did* have in place as an industry, and that would address both of those concerns. To create the index, you'd have to define the terms. Eventually we'd know how much SRI would cost. Those seemed like valuable tools. By 1989 the formation of a company called Domini & Company was registered with the SEC [Securities and Exchange Commission] to provide social research and that rapidly became Kinder, Lydenberg & Domini, which is now known as KLD Research & Analytics. In May,1990 the DSI was launched along with the Domini Social Equities Fund.

Domini's instincts were honed by the socially concerned investor community with whom she had been working for years by this point, and she instinctively knew that an index alone would not prove the performance case for the DSI.

I had a feeling that a theory in a box would only go so far and that live money would be important to the argument. So I tried to get every major mutual fund company to offer a product based on that index but nobody wanted in. So, pretty naively, I just said, "All right, I'll launch it. I'll open my doors." By that point I had joined Loring, Wolcott & Coolidge in 1987. The senior partner there, Lawrence Coolidge, said, "I'll put $600,000 into this to get you started." Not into the management, but actually into the portfolio to buy $600,000 worth of shares. I was too naive to know that I needed at least a hundred million dollars, so $600,000 sounded like plenty to me.

The rest, as they say, is history, as Domini recalls,

We got that fund up and running. By 1997 it had grown up; the fund had enough in assets under management to have some budget to be able to support itself. Prior to that, I was writing checks when we needed a prospectus written. There wasn't enough cash flow generated in those early days, so I never quit my day job and I was able to subsidize this mutual fund and KLD. By 1997 we felt the mutual fund was going to succeed and should stand on its own feet and should be separated from KLD.

Along with developing the Domini Social Equity Fund and contracting out the administration of the Fund (and simultaneously developing KLD), Domini was trying hard to sell the DSI to an investment house, but kept hitting obstacles along the way. She remembers,

I went to [a major investment house] — I had a handshake with head of marketing. I went to a bunch of companies that are now out of business, like Drexel Burnham. The story was always the same. The head of marketing loved it, went upstairs to sell it, and they killed it.

New products evolve

The Domini Social Equity Fund was the first of the products that Domini Social Investments issued, but over the years the company has evolved a series of other financial products that reflect the breadth of the traditional financial services company and provide insight into the maturing of SRI. Domini remembers,

> The first *new* product after the equity fund was a relationship with the South Shore Bank of Chicago that we called the Domini Money Market Account. I had felt that if people think the market is going to go down, they're going to have to sell the fund and go away. We needed a money market account, so they could sell the funds but stay with the social investing criteria. But it turns out that money market funds are very, very expensive; you need billions of dollars to break even and make money. I had a lunch with the man who is still the CEO at Investors Financial [Kevin J. Sheehan], which is a Boston-based firm and was and is the custodian in the Domini Equity Fund. He said, "Why don't you just pick one of these community development banks and raise deposits for them?" I thought, "Well, that's not a mutual fund." But, as it turns out, you actually could do that. It does mean it's hard to distribute because I'm not listed anywhere. You know, there's no listing for the Domini Money Market account on mutual fund money market lists or on bank money market lists. So you have to find it the hard way, but it does work. We have raised $55 to $60 million in assets for Shore Bank and for their lending through that mechanism.

By 2007, Domini Social Investments was working in collaboration with Wellington Management and had a whole portfolio of funds, all invested with social and environmental criteria in mind. At the time of writing, Domini Social Investments has four actively managed portfolios: the Domini Social Equity Fund, the Domini European Social Equity Fund, the Domini PacAsia Social Equity Fund, and the Domini EuroPacific Social Equity Fund. The latter three funds were added in 2005 to give the company's investors a global reach in its investment strategies and are a graphic illustration of just how far social investing has come in a relatively short period of time. In addition, the company also has two innovative investment vehicles focused on the economic development elements of SRI: the Domini Social Bond Fund and the Domini Money Market Account.

▉ Roots of a changing vision about SRI

Like some of the other difference makers, Amy Domini is motivated by a desire to see a more equitable world, but one that has evolved and changed as she herself learned and grew. She notes,

> I was very motivated by a deep sense of injustice in the world. That [this injustice] was just plain wrong and [those who created it] had to be exposed and accountability had to be brought to bear. I had a background that had given me unique insights into interconnectedness that could be made between, say, faith groups or community organizers and the halls of power through finance and I had an obligation to bring that social capital to bear on these deep injustices.

She explains some of the shift in her thinking that has taken place as her vision and events in the field have matured,

> Even though the world seems to be accelerating and spinning out of control and is absolutely horrible, for some reason, in recent years, I have had a new motivation of hope that seems to be working. When I started, pretty much I had to define things for people all the time. The most educated people would say, "Oh you mean like South Africa?" [whenever SRI was mentioned]. Every conversation was ten minutes about what SRI was. Now there are 2,000 companies globally publishing CSR reports every year. CSR is on most corporate web pages. You can certainly read about it in most major newspapers in some form or another most every day. It's very much mainstream — and I don't think that it would have entered the vocabulary had it not been for social investors. I just don't think that corporations were going that way.

Part of what has happened, as Domini notes, is that a wholly new vocabulary and structures related to SRI have evolved since she, Alice Tepper Marlin, Tim Smith, and Joan Bavaria began their work in the 1970s and 1980s, making the idea of responsible investment much more current and mainstream. Some of the early seeds of social investing discussed in this chapter were planted long before these difference makers got in on the act, but the institutional framework that has emerged was kickstarted as they began establishing new ways of thinking — and acting — on the sense that the world needed to be made a better place. Domini points out,

> Entering the vocabulary might be a whole different kettle of fish from changing the course of human events. But you do first have to define some terms and I feel a sense that it's working. Look at the explosion of interest in the conventional investment management arena in microcredit. We wouldn't have heard of microcredit [for which Muhammad Yunus, founder of

Grameen Bank, won the Nobel Peace Prize in 2006] if it weren't for my field. That was entirely a support system that social investors put into place.

Recounting some of the shifts she has observed, Domini comments,

> Recently I'd say that hope has entered into it. I feel something is happening out there. There have been these oddball alternative things in the world that probably are completely independent of social investing, but that led to many of the same conclusions. And one in particular is the Slow Food movement in Italy. This movement is a response to the opening of McDonald's at the foot of the Spanish Steps in Rome and it is basically saying, "Fast food is not the greatest food on the planet and we Italians stand for slow food." I participated in their conference in the fall in northern Italy one year. I think 140,000 people came through that conference. It's sort of a trade fair, but if there's a traditional cheese that can only be made once every six years when the full moon coincides with the first clover bloom, that cheese is available at that slow food festival and goes for $75 a pound to some special restaurant that made its reputation on having things like that available. This meant that, for instance, in the Tuscany region where orchards have been abandoned for 50 or 60 years, families are now starting to grow their special organic olive oil again and selling it to all the restaurants in Tuscany. It's high-end but it is creating organic support for heritage animals, back to the local economy, sustainability — things that social investors also are saying are important to the future of the planet. So I see there are new trends out there.

Joan Bavaria echoes thoughts about the progress that SRI has made, and points toward obstacles that still exist:

> I think it's natural in capitalism that companies don't want to be messed with. They don't want extra costs. Their effort is always to keep down the costs. It's just part of the mandate. And they would say that's a moral mandate, to make money for investors. So even though you will find companies in the short term pragmatically going along with [accountability measures and reporting], there's always going to be this energy of resistance.

The SRI movement provided the seeds of another segment of the emerging responsibility assurance movement, that of different types of accountability structure that go way beyond fiduciary responsibility. We will begin looking at those developments in the next chapter.

4

Emerging accountability structures

The work of Alice Tepper Marlin, Joan Bavaria, Tim Smith, and Amy Domini described in the last chapter signaled the emergence of SRI, a cornerstone of responsibility assurance as it has evolved over time. But, as became clear, other types of institutional arrangement and new organizations were also beginning to evolve, and those arrangements focused on somewhat different aspects of the infrastructure, even as SRI continued to evolve. We can think of the early institution building around social investing as focused on highlighting and framing different aspects of corporate responsibility though the lens of the investor. With that as backdrop, we might think of this next phase of emergence as beginning to create a conversation around issues of corporate and institutional accountability, a theme that began to emerge by the mid-1980s into the 1990s.

In this chapter, we will explore the emergence of various efforts that focused on the early phases of developing a new emphasis on corporate accountability. Some initiatives emphasized accountability by creating new data that could be used to assess companies; others developed standards for accountability with respect to how corporations engaged with stakeholders and managed labor practices. We will see even more of that type of development in the next chapter, where we will look at the development phase of this social movement, and particularly the establishment of standards of practice.

As SRI evolved, the needs of socially responsible investors for systematic data beyond financial indicators became clear. In addition, it was obvious that new systems that could actually assess how well companies were doing, not just financially but also along the other lines considered important to social investors, were needed. Thus, by the 1980s and into the 1990s, the skeleton of an accountability framework started to grow. In this chapter we will go back to the evolving work of some of the social pioneers already discussed along with others as we also begin exploring new work begun by others in building an accountability infrastructure. The overall story becomes more complex and interwoven as time goes on, with more difference makers getting involved, some with new initiatives, and some continuing and elaborating existing initiatives.

▇ Steven D. Lydenberg

Steven D. (Steve) Lydenberg is chief investment officer at Domini Social Investments, and cofounder (with Amy Domini and Peter Kinder) of KLD Research & Analytics in Boston, and of the Institute for Responsible Investment (IRI) (with Brad Googins and the author) at Boston College's Center for Corporate Citizenship. Lydenberg did not start out with the idea of working in the social investment arena. Over time, however, through his involvement in SRI, initially through his work first with the CEP and ultimately with KLD, Lydenberg developed into a world-class expert and thought leader. He is particularly focused on measuring social, stakeholder, environmental, and governance aspects of corporate performance, and using SRI as a mechanism to push for better standards of corporate practice.

As with many of the difference makers, Lydenberg's work and vision developed over time. He recalls,

> I set out in life to be a playwright and backed into this field through the research door, starting in the mid-1970s when I went down to New York to see if I could get some of my plays put on. I knocked on the doors of a variety of organizations that I thought would be interesting to work for, doing something more than waiting on tables, which is what everyone else was doing. The first place that happened to have a job was the CEP [started by Alice Tepper Marlin, discussed in Chapter 3]. The job was opening the mail and filling orders. CEP just happened to be the only place probably in the world at that time that was doing research and rating on environmental and social issues. So I got into the research after about a year there and did the

research for about 12 years from 1975 to 1987. The last of my projects was *Rating America's Corporate Conscience,* which was the first attempt then by pretty much anybody to assemble social and environmental information aimed at consumers for use in making purchasing decisions.

Rating America's Corporate Conscience

Rating America's Corporate Conscience was a pioneering book. It was the first time anyone had attempted to systematically gather information about the responsibility of well-known companies and publish it widely. The book was part of the CEP's legacy of, as Robert Heilbruner put it, "naming names and supporting findings with painstaking research."[64] It provided systematic data on the performance of companies across multiple dimensions associated with corporate responsibility, including the company's percentage of women and minority directors and officers, its percentage of after-tax contribution to charities, its social disclosure, its involvement in South Africa, the percentage of its business associated with military contracting and nuclear weapons, and the dollar amount of political-action-committee contributions, along with the percentage allocated to Democrats and Republicans. Focused predominantly on consumer goods companies, *Rating America's Corporate Conscience* covered four categories of company: food product companies; health and personal care product companies; airline, automobiles, hotel, and oil companies; and appliance and household product companies. As noted in Chapter 3, the book morphed into a short consumer guide called *Shopping for a Better World,*[65] which shoppers could easily carry around with them to check purchases.

As the first effort to systematically rate companies, *Rating America's Corporate Conscience* obviously had its limitations, first in its emphasis on consumer-oriented companies to the exclusion of other types of companies, and secondly in the scope of data, which was primarily focused on issues that were already foremost in the minds of social investors. Further, the book covered only 130 companies in total, although for some of those companies it covered specific products as well as the company as a whole. The philosophy behind the ratings was that the users of the guide, and later the shopping guide, *Shopping for a Better World*, could make their own decisions about what issues and values were important to them. Notably, this philosophy is still core to the SRI world today, which provides a far broader range of data to investors than simply financial information and then provides mechanisms for investors to choose to implement their own values in their investment decisions.

The impact of *Rating America's Corporate Conscience*, however, was important, since it paved the way for future developments and at least two other key institutions in the evolving corporate accountability arena. One of these institutions was SAI, which was founded by Alice Tepper Marlin as the shortcomings of the CEP's

approaches, discussed in Chapter 3, became more obvious. The other was KLD
Research & Analytics, which was cofounded by Amy Domini, Peter Kinder, and,
bringing his expertise on social ratings, Steve Lydenberg. Since KLD was founded
earlier than SAI, we will take a look at the evolution of KLD through the eyes of all
three founders first, then at how SAI evolved out of the CEP.

KLD Research & Analytics

The company that is now KLD Research & Analytics was originally founded as
Kinder, Lydenberg & Domini by the three difference makers. Lydenberg left the
CEP in 1987, shortly after *Rating America's Corporate Conscience* came out, and went to
work with Joan Bavaria's company Trillium Asset Management, then called
Franklin Research and Development, where he came into contact with Amy
Domini, who at the time was married to Peter Kinder.

Amy Domini recounts her perspective on how KLD originated,

> I had a day job at Loring, Wolcott & Coolidge, and I had recognition that
> there were these two barriers to getting involved in social investing. One was
> defining it and another was tracking the cost. At Loring, Wolcott & Coolidge I
> was spending a lot of time doing corporate accountability research and it
> probably was duplicative of what was going on at Trillium and at US Trust
> [and other social investment firms]. They also had stock-picking roles: did
> they want to own that company? But [I knew] that a research product that
> was designed for all of us who had more or less the same standards in place
> could be of value to the entire industry. So I typed up a double-page social
> audit on a company, just as a sample, and took it around to people, and
> asked "If this were available would you buy it?" I got enough of a sense that
> they would that it seemed we could start, say, with the largest 50 companies
> and then move beyond that. There was enough interest at that point that it
> seemed like a fair bet for Peter Kinder, who was my husband, to quit his day
> job and take on this research product full-time. So [the early KLD] essentially
> lived in our house and we had piles and piles of annual reports around the
> house and proxy statements and things of that nature. And I would go home
> at night and contribute to that effort.
>
> I also brought home stacks of brokerage reports, and sometimes they
> would be helpful in the social audit process, too. That went on — really, that
> business lived at [Domini's home] for five years. I think we had six or seven
> employees before we finally felt safe moving into rented space in Harvard
> Square [in Cambridge, MA]. Steve Lydenberg had joined us. About a year
> into [developing the project], I had a conversation with a friend [about]
> angel capital, and he put in $200,000, which convinced Steve that he could
> join us, that we were fiscally sustainable enough between us.

Peter Kinder

Peter Kinder has been the president of KLD since it was cofounded in 1988, and was cofounder and principal of Domini Social Investments from 1997–2000, when the two entities split apart. A 1968 graduate of Princeton University, Kinder attended law school at Ohio State, and migrated east from his birthplace in the Appalachian region of Ohio. As he tells the story,

> While I was in law school, I started working for the state of Ohio, working on strip mining regulation and it went from there. After seven years in state service, I burned out and decided to move to Boston and find something to do. I went to work for a foundation for a couple of years. I had a friend who worked at the education school at Harvard, and one night he started complaining about how he had this unbelievable project and a writer who couldn't put subject and verb together. So he throws this thing on the table and it's a seminar on cross-cultural exchange between the Muslim world and the West. Now on this subject, I know nothing, *nada*, but I picked the thing up and it was clear that whoever wrote it, his first language was not English. It was the worst writing I'd ever seen in my life. Flipping through it, I said, "'I can do this . . . how much does it pay?" He quoted a number that today sounds derisory, but then was big money. So I said, "I'll start tomorrow," and went into my job and quit, and the next morning went to work as a freelance writer.
>
> It was a great project. It was one of the foundations of this firm [KLD] because it taught me to look at every exchange as a cross-cultural exchange. When you look at interactions between corporations, what you're looking at is microcultures. It also meant coming to understand that "Muslim–Arab world" was a misnomer, and that the range of peoples, backgrounds, and religious disputes are every bit as complex as what we have in the US. It was a fantastic experience. Also, I was the only American, white, Ivy League-educated person on the team. The rest had backgrounds that were truly global. That was a huge eye-opener. This was in June of 1979, and it finished in 1980.

About this time, Domini and Kinder met each other, and Domini exposed Kinder for the first time to the idea of social investing. Skeptical hardly describes his initial attitude,

> I thought [SRI] was total nonsense. I thought if you don't like a company, sell it. If you can't sell it, sue the bastards. It was a typical attitude, and certainly that had been my experience in the attorney general's office. I had a very jaundiced view of corporations, coming from strip mining and steel companies country, so SRI really didn't make any sense for me.

Still, the pair wrote *Ethical Investing*, a pioneering book in the field, and met difference maker Joan Bavaria as she began some of her networking outreach. Kinder, who is an omnivorous reader, began reading business magazines and learning more about corporations from, as he notes, the periphery.

The continuing story of KLD and the Domini Social Index

Kinder continues the story of KLD:

> I'd always been interested in corporate accountability. It wasn't till [Amy Domini] started working with ICCR that I really got it. As soon as I began to see what ICCR was doing, I understood instantly what this meant — it was just lobbying. All of a sudden I knew exactly what I was dealing with and understood the potential of it.

During this period, he was working as a freelance writer and lawyer and serving as the "at home" parent to the couple's two boys. A family crisis, combined with Domini's suggestion, came together around the creation of the incipient KLD, as he recalls,

> The way the company [KLD] actually got started was interesting. In March of 1988, my mother was diagnosed with a very rare form of cancer, which is known only among people who have smoked or worked with asbestos, neither of which she had ever done. It was terminal, and my father was not dealing with it well. Amy suggested that I quit the law job I was working at, and try to help out. She had this project she was really interested in working on and that was [to create] an index, rating companies. Could we do that? So the foundation for the firm was really laid in hospital waiting rooms in Columbus and going through these stacks of annual reports and 10Ks.[66] I'm sure the hospital staff still remembers me. Every morning there'd be another box of these bloody corporate reports.

Amy Domini describes the concept behind the research that KLD has done since its inception,

> Peter and I had developed a prototype of the index and had hired a third party to do back-testing on it, and felt that the index was a really powerful efficacy tool. But when Steve [Lydenberg] joined up, it really became his vision that was the driver to the [Domini Social 400 Index]. Steve applied a discipline to it that was iterated in a point-by-point assessment: that is, when you're looking at the environment, you check these five things. That was quite a blueprint for auditing. These were things that were systematically available. You didn't have to get the answer from the company; it was in the proxy statement. Those things were quantifiable. They were either yes or no

or they were a number kind of answer. How many women sit on the board? And they were in some way significant.

Steve Lydenberg interprets the founding of KLD in this way,

> KLD's stated mission was to reduce the barriers to social investing and its strategy to do that was to develop products that were systematic and could serve the mainstream financial community. In social investing up to 1990, the research had been done sporadically and anecdotally by money managers who were either choosing not to invest in certain companies — alcohol and tobacco — or to invest in certain companies: Herman Miller, at that time, as was Digital Equipment, and various other companies high on the list of social investors. But there was at that time no systematic research available and no systematic way of testing the effect of social investing on a given universe. So we set out to create the tools that would allow institutional investors to systemically evaluate holdings, for screening and evaluative performance attribution purposes.
>
> From [CEP] I was interested in the financial community at this point. I went to Franklin Research and Development, which is now Trillium, which at that time was the first money management firm in the US that was solely devoted to managing socially screened accounts, and was there for two and a half years and left there in 1990 to join Peter Kinder and Amy Domini to form KLD. So we started KLD basically in the back of Peter and Amy's house in 1990 and in 2001 I moved from KLD, where I was research director, to Domini Social Investments, where I am now chief financial officer.

Peter Kinder has a related recollection with a focus on the performance question:

> In the mid- to late 1980s, the big knock on social investing was that you couldn't invest according to your principles without giving up performance, and in every single presentation that Amy would make to a client, that question would come up. So she'd been talking about "How do you gauge what this give-back is?" We were assuming there was a give-back, and that, if we could identify how much it was, we could deal with it, but there were no numbers. The only thing out there was the Boston Safe Index, which was a South Africa-free index, and all it was, was the S&P [Standard & Poor's] with a bunch of companies knocked out. So Amy had the idea of putting together an index, and trying to do an SRI S&P 500. I didn't see why that would be so hard. She said, "It'll take about nine months." Well, it took 26. Off by a little bit.

It was Steve Lydenberg's knowledge about how to systematically rate companies on social criteria, however, that proved essential to KLD's ultimate success, as Domini points out:

That was where Steve Lydenberg's vision was particularly at work. For instance, even though he had done a great deal of work at the CEP, corporate lobbying [was not included in KLD's database]. We lived in 1990 in a far less partisan world, and he did not feel that whether somebody lobbied Republicans or Democrats was significant to a social audit. So it was not included in the social audit and the evaluation of the company. Today, I think lobbying has become much more of an issue and I think KLD is in fact beginning to look at lobbying dollars as telling a story about a corporation. But that rigor has become the template globally for corporate accountability audits. Not that everybody has the same points available. Each culture has their own disclosure and transparency, but that there will be across-the-board standards I think grew out of KLD.

That all-important understanding of how the research should be conducted came from Lydenberg's research at CEP. Lydenberg explains,

When I started working at CEP in 1975, I began to get interested in the business community. The stories that were associated with proxy voting, the ballot question campaigns that I did some research on, intrigued me. All of these were great stories about business in society and got me really interested in that, and trying to put those stories together into a coherent whole was the exercise of *Rating America's Corporate Conscience,* the brainchild of Sean Strub [third author on the book with Lydenberg and Alice Tepper Marlin], who made the crucial connection to the publisher. CEP had tried to do something like that in the late 1970s. [The original effort] was basically a compilation of the research that they'd done to date, and it wasn't aimed at consumers, and it was pretty sporadic and not particularly successful. *Rating America's Corporate Conscience* became *Shopping for a Better World* because [*Rating America's Corporate Conscience*] was a big heavy book that you couldn't take to the supermarket, so they started publishing a series of guides that you could slip inside your pocket.

In a sense, for Lydenberg, the transition from Franklin to KLD made the best use of his knowledge about ratings and fitted with his own emerging vision of what was needed to tell more than simply the financial story about companies. He notes,

The vision [for KLD] was to mainstream social investing, to provide enough data for the traditional investment community to make good decisions. What was missing was a way of screening systemically for a large universe of stocks, and in order to do that you needed to do some basic research on all the stocks in those universes, and our contribution was to evolve a consistent methodology for looking at each of them. Prior to 1990, if you were a social investor, all you knew about Philip Morris and all you needed to know about

Philip Morris (now Altria), was that it was involved in tobacco. That was the end of the story. We went to considerable effort to do the research on minorities, community, and environment, where they had some strong stories to tell. We looked at the same set of issues for all the companies so that you could compare them, and so you could track companies longitudinally from one year to another. So this was the first attempt to be systematic. [SRI] went from anecdotal to systematic.

An opportunity structure

Here in the story of the emergence of KLD, we see the founders sensing a gap in the market — the missing data that concerned investors could use. This gap is what institutional theorists call an opportunity structure. KLD filled that gap, and thereby created a new mobilizing structure. Lydenberg now details his assessment of how and why this new mobilizing structure worked and how it came into being.

In 1989, Amy was no longer with Franklin, she was with Loring, Wolcott & Coolidge. She and Peter were putting together this index. I kept in touch with her, and she would tell me about the index. I would say, "Oh that sounds interesting; did you think of this, that?" She said, "No" and they'd try those things. These conversations went on until finally one day she said, "Look, if you're so interested, maybe you'd like to come and join us." Not ever having founded a company before, having no idea what I was getting into, I said yes.

It really was an interesting exercise in creating a tool that would be useful to the broader social investment world. On the theoretical side, there was a great deal of criticism in the 1980s of social investing. Huge battles were being fought in the public arena over the appropriateness of screening on South Africa. Generally speaking, in the 20 years since it started to evolve in its modern form from the 1970s to about 1990, SRI had gone a very short distance. It still was treated with a great deal of suspicion at best and dismissed as something that was inappropriate and not something that one could do and exercise one's fiduciary duties. So there was a much larger issue that Amy, Peter, and I saw, which was how to legitimize SRI as a profession — and you just can't have a profession without the basic tools. KLD was our first attempt to say, OK, here are some of the most basic tools you need to have — consistent data, consistent methodology.

He reflects on the development of this new mechanism.

It was interesting what a powerful choice it was to focus on an index, because indexes within the traditional financial world stand for certain asset classes, certain investment styles. By creating an index for the first time, it

> was creating a *definition* of what social investment looked like. Throughout the 1990s, whenever anyone wrote an article on social investing, they would put a chart of the Domini Index vs the S&P index in that story, simply because it stood for social investing. [The DSI] became a symbol — it made an attempt, I think successfully, at capturing at least one definition of what social investing is.

In fact, the data provided not only a platform for already socially concerned investors to make more rigorously defined investment decisions, but also an important benchmark for Wall Street analysts generally, even when they were not (and despite growing investor interest in SRI, most are still not) interested in responsible investing. The data also became the basis for several other indices, including for seven years the Best 100 Corporate Citizens ranking published in *Business Ethics* magazine,[67] as well as considerable academic research. But those developments came much later.

Happy accident

It almost didn't happen, as Peter Kinder remembers:

> This firm [KLD] was never set up to do research. The reason we got into the research business was that we launched the index, and the first reaction wasn't, "Wow, what a great idea!" Or "What a great index!" It was: "How in the world can you justify choosing those companies and not these?" And thank God that was the reaction, because we didn't really start making money on the index for five or six years. But, because people were outraged, we had to actually produce something that justified why we were making these choices. We were careful from day one, even more so after Steve came on board, to keep copies (in fact, we still have them) of the annual reports from which we made our decisions. They used to be in the ground floor of our house in Cambridge in 45 cabinets. So we were really meticulous in keeping that stuff, but we had no intention of writing or producing these commentaries.

The transition for KLD to being a research firm rather than an index-producing firm was almost happenstance, as Kinder notes,

> We've now indulged in more conversation about that transition than we did at the time. The reason was pure necessity. We had had an initial angel investor, who put in [seed money] and that's what guaranteed Steve's salary for two years. The concept of "let's do research" was pure and simple: we needed the money. We could sell the research, but we could not sell the index.

Growth and elaboration

Today, KLD[68] has, according to Kinder, "230 research clients of which 200 are money managers and institutional investors and the other 30 are academic institutions." Its Socrates (SOCial RATE-ingS) database is the accepted standard for companies in the United States, and it has also been used extensively in academic research. As noted, KLD effectively spun off DSI in 1998. Although the research still links the companies, they are independent of each other, with KLD focused solely on research and Domini Social Funds managing its family of screened funds.

While initially KLD rated only the Standard & Poor's 500 companies, plus about another 140 or so smaller companies that appeared in the DSI, today the company focuses on the entire Russell 3,000 companies. In addition to the Domini 400 Social Index, KLD offers an entire family of indices, including the KLD Broad Market Social Index, the KLD Dividend Achievers Social Index, the KLD Global Climate 100 Index, the KLD Large Cap Social Index, and the KLD Select Social Index. As a measure of just how much institutionalization has taken place since its early days, KLD also offers compliance and consulting services to clients, and participates internationally in Sustainable Investment Research International (SiRi Company),[69] a group of eleven leading SRI research enterprises on three continents each of which is the top such organization in its country. KLD was the pioneer research institution in this group, and, although cultural differences exist and result in slightly different data, SiRi Company is able to provide common data on many global companies.

KLD effectively broke new ground when it established its research system, and its model has been imitated and adapted to conditions around the world, in the kind of institutional development that typifies a social movement. Although the job of mainstreaming SRI is hardly finished, the field has clearly come a long way from its early days, and, as we shall see, numerous other initiatives have grown up around the issue of corporate responsibility. Other important developments took place in wholly new areas of accountability, as we shall see as we continue the story of Alice Tepper Marlin and the CEP's morphing into SAI below. But before we move on to SAI we will take a quick look at the next stage in Lydenberg's career, the Institute for Responsible Investment.

■ Steve Lydenberg and the Institute for Responsible Investment

Steve Lydenberg left KLD in 2001 to join Domini Social Funds full-time as the chief investment officer. He recalls his thinking at that time:

Starting in the mid-1990s it became apparent that social investing was actually going to survive. I can remember in the early 1990s wondering whether, after the South Africa issue is resolved, will there be anyone still interested in social investment. A lot of it grew out of what was going on in Europe. For a variety of reasons a lot of European governments became interested in what was going on in social responsibility and drove and continue to drive the interest and momentum behind it. That was filtering in gradually, and at a certain point I felt it was going to survive as a movement, it wasn't going to go away, and we actually had a chance to be effective.

Lydenberg chuckles as he think about this transition,

In a certain sense, I'd been doing this so long — this was now 25 years — that I'd gotten used being a lone voice in the desert so the idea of being effective, again, it took me a long time to realize that was a real possibility. So I looked around and said, '"We've got data now, we've got the practical side of this thing, but what we lack is any kind of theoretical framework that goes with social investing." In the end, I think I believe in the dictum that it takes a theory to beat a theory. Just being a practical movement that a lot of people are interested in isn't enough to make it survive and thrive; you need some sort of theoretical framework. I also felt that I'd been doing this long enough that I had a kind of overview ability. So when I left KLD and went to Domini, part of the deal was that, half-time, I'd be able to do some theoretical thinking and writing.

When I say "theoretical," I mean it more in the framing than the academic sense. We have a lot of data, but what's the framework that the data is operating in? What's the theory behind how that data can make change? So that was a lot of my purpose for going over to Domini — it was easier to clear space in the Domini side of the business. That in turn led me to some writing, which in turn led me to the realization that as a movement we lack not only theory but the embodiment of that theory. We didn't have think-tanks, certifying or standard-setting organizations. We had the flesh but in a sense were without the skeleton of the movement. I am hoping the IRI will serve as a catalyst for development of the kinds of institution and thinking that we all recognize within the social investment movement that we need, but we don't have time in the day or the clear space to sit down with colleagues and talk about these things and think about how to move them forward. So that's the purpose of the IRI [see Box 4.1].

Box 4.1 **Institute for Responsible Investment mission and goals**

The Institute for Responsible Investment (IRI) is housed within the Boston College Center for Corporate Citizenship (see difference maker Brad Googins, Chapter 7). IRI offers convenings, research, and outreach activism that promotes responsible investing. It works on research about responsible investment practices, companies, investors, and governmental organizations attempting to serve as a think-tank for the long-term wealth creation that benefits both shareholders and society.

The mission statement is: "The Institute for Responsible Investment (IRI) seeks to catalyze thought leadership and action to promote the generation of long-term, values-driven wealth creation through the discipline of responsible investment."[70]

As an institute embedded within an academic institution, IRI undertakes and supports research on issues related to social investing (recent projects have included a study of the uses of non-financial information by financial analysts and research on investments in small and medium-sized enterprises). IRI also serves as a convener on important topics related to social investing, including mergers and acquisitions, responsible property investment, and building the infrastructure of responsible investing, to name a few related topics.

IRI's goals are stated as follows:

- To deepen the discipline of responsible investment through the development of disciplinary standards, the enhancement of practical tools, and the expansion of disciplinary infrastructure

- To broaden the scope and effectiveness of responsible investment through ongoing research and communication strategies that address the power and potential of long-term wealth creation

- To expand the access to and impact of responsible investing by laying the groundwork for the development of new products, analytical tools, and investment techniques[71]

From the CEP to SAI: from shopping to labor standards

The work of the CEP, established by Alice Tepper Marlin, continued and new networks began to form in other nations based on common interests. But this trend highlighted the need for a new source of data, that from developing nations, which did not exist in any coherent form in the mid-1990s when the seeds of SAI were growing.

Alice Tepper Marlin relates how the insight about the data gap evolved:

> There were some pre-existing organizations similar to CEP in other countries that had grown up, like we had, originally around social investing. We formed a little association and we began to meet regularly. For a few years we included foreign-based companies based on our collegial organizations' ratings of them. So we would have Japanese-, Benelux-, UK-, German-, Italian-, Swiss-headquartered companies in our books. There would be a note saying what we're rating here is not a direct comparison between their performance and the US companies. It's an indication, according to reputable research organizations in those countries, about how those companies perform relative to other companies in their country. So that was not *totally* satisfactory, but actually was *quite* satisfactory in terms of increasing the coverage we could have of developed countries. It was, however, totally unsatisfactory in terms of being able to get information from the developing world, because there weren't equivalent organizations and there weren't resources or enough interest to form them. In countries where they did start, and actually India was one of the examples, it was *so* difficult for them to get access to data that they really couldn't do what we were doing. The need for the developing-country information came to a head when we published a book called *Student Shopping for a Better World*.

As the globalization of business and outsourcing became both more common and more complex, the seeds of the organization that replaced CEP, SAI, which focuses on labor standards, began to form. Tepper Marlin notes,

> When *Student Shopping for a Better World* was published, we were very, very uneasy about this book. Because it was focused on students, we were looking at some sectors where globalization was most extreme at that time, because we had to look at things students bought. For food and personal products, which is what the earlier *Shopping for a Better World* had concentrated on, [the issue of globalization] wasn't as extreme.
>
> But here suddenly we were doing clothing, shoes, sneakers, and sporting goods. Most of the companies we were rating don't manufacture anything anymore. They're design and marketing companies or retailers. When we evaluated their employment practices and their environmental practices, we were basically looking at their white-collar operations. We were *missing entirely* the largest number of people who worked for them in a broader sense, the people who worked to actually make the goods that they sell, and we were missing the environmental impact. We had no way to get that data,

because you're talking about very large numbers of firms in countries where we couldn't find local research groups, or get access to data.

Seeds of SAI

Tepper Marlin continues,

> The public campaigns around these [sweatshop and labor standards] issues had begun. There was a total disconnect between our ratings and how the products were actually made. Now it's hard to remember. [I can] remember the days before that huge paradigm shift, when if you went back to the 1980s and anytime previously, *nobody* expected that companies were responsible for the employment and environmental impacts of factories or farms that they neither owned nor managed. Then it was perfectly acceptable to say "We just buy these things."

"But at that time that assumption was being clearly challenged," she notes, pointing toward a new logic that companies should be responsible for the goods that bore their brand name, whether they owned and operated the facilities that made them or not. She continues,

> So you had a point where an executive of Reebok stood up and said, "When a customer calls our 800 number and complains that the sole got detached from the top of our running shoe, we don't say, 'Gee, we're not responsible for that. Some factory in Korea is. Take your complaint to them! It has nothing to do with Reebok. We just bought the shoe.' Well, we would never think of doing that about the quality of our product or the safety of our product. We now realize that we cannot do that either for the employment practices or the environmental impacts of how those products are made." That was a real watershed.

In the morphing of the CEP into what is now SAI, we can see a genuine social entrepreneurial process, with Tepper Marlin building the network of individuals surrounding her, sensing a gap, and ultimately a new opportunity and creating an appropriate mobilizing structure. Ultimately, it became clear that what CEP had been doing, and what was needed in the new environment that globalization was creating were quite different. As Tepper Marlin recounts,

> So we began thinking and meeting on that. In 1991 we gave America's Corporate Conscience Award to Levi Strauss for their first code of conduct.[73] We got very, very excited about that idea. So we started in 1991 or 1992 to convene a working group of companies that were interested in developing codes like Levi's. We brought in experts. We did some technical work for them.

In a very short period of time, we had one of those great epiphanies where you succeed in your original goal. All of those companies adopted codes of conduct, and in the next few years hundreds more did. But the unanticipated side-effect was we had assumed that everybody's codes would look about the same. But even the dozen companies in the working group all came out with vastly different codes even though they all looked at the same model, Levi Strauss. We all looked at the ILO [labor] recommendations. We all had drafts from our technical people. Then they took it back to their companies and it went through legal and it went through marketing, and it went through various different internal processes. They came back so different that they weren't comparable one to another and we felt that everybody would be confused. Consumers wouldn't know which codes were good ones and which weren't.

Codes and monitoring: a new gap

It was the recognition of this gap — and attendant need on the part of socially concerned *consumers*, as opposed to investors — that the idea for SAI came into being. According to Tepper Marlin,

Fairly soon we realized that some of these places were buying from the same factories, so having multiple codes of conduct was confusing for the factories. We began to ask, "Well, how do you get compliance to these codes?" because it was clear that just asking the company to sign an internally generated document to say that they're compliant didn't mean much. So we were all talking about monitoring.

As the subject of monitoring compliance with codes of conducts in the factories crystallized, other issues also began to take shape, particularly the need for a coherent and systematic set of standards applied across the board. Tepper Marlin tells the story of how this awareness grew:

We began to address this problem. One: how do we get a more universal system where the standard is the same, the code is the same for everybody? Two: how do we share monitoring so you avoid duplication of audits, to lessen the burden on the factories and to lessen the cost for the retailers, and enable the money to be spent to get good-quality audits rather than a lot of cheap short ones. We came across the ISO system and we thought that that was a really good model [with changes to reflect different content] based on what the environmental community's reaction to ISO 14000, the environmental standard, had been.

ISO[73] is the world's foremost promulgator of quality and environmental standards. It develops standards that are meant to apply globally, originally around the quality of products, extended to environmental management systems, and, expected in 2010, to developing the ISO 26000 guidelines for social responsibility. ISO's standards are voluntarily adopted by companies, but are dominant enough that considerable demand for them exists on a global level. Having assessed the ISO's approaches, Tepper Marlin and her collaborators moved forward, as she recounts:

> We made a few changes. There needed to be performance elements in the same standard as management systems. We began to look at the model and decided we needed to set up a standard-setting organization and an accreditation agency. This was clearly international, and it needed to be established as an international organization, not as a national one. Then we took it to the

---

Box 4.2 **Social Accountability International**

SAI today is perhaps the leading organization that promotes standards for human rights for workers in global supply chains, working particularly through its voluntary SA8000 labor standards. SAI has a simply stated mission: "SAI promotes human rights for workers around the world."[74] SAI, which is a non-profit organization, works collaboratively with a variety of stakeholders, including companies, NGOs, labor and trade unions, and global network of auditing groups that have co-evolved with SAI and are known as certification bodies that ensure that the SA8000 standards promulgated by SAI are actually being adhered to in supply chain companies.

As with the rest of the responsibility assurance system that has emerged to date, the SA8000 standards, which are based on the ILO conventions for workplace rights, are voluntary approaches to managing workers responsibly. Part of the work is an effort to improve working conditions globally, with the underlying objective of demonstrating the business case that being more responsible is good business. SA8000 works through focusing at the factory level to ensure compliance with ILO and SA8000 standards and also emphasizes continual improvement. The system, although voluntary, includes independent expert verification and public reporting of compliance by SAI's partner certification bodies, an important element in any kind of voluntary system that is to have credibility with critical outsiders. The pressures that allow SAI to have credibility and effectiveness include those that come from concerned consumers and investors. SAI also allies with other bodies that can provide training for workers, managers, auditors, and others.

> board and it approved first setting this [entity] up as a separate project of CEP, and then very soon just spinning it off to being independent. So we set it up as an institution in 1996, did a business plan, and incorporated in 1997.

SAI is a very different type of organization than the CEP (see Box 4.2 for a description of SAI's mission). According to Tepper Marlin,

> SAI's mission is to improve the social and environmental practices and policies of companies, but in a much more focused way and on an international basis. We were a global agency to begin with, with three main mechanisms — three main strategies — for doing this. The first was to set international, social, and environmental standards. The second was to accredit qualified auditing organizations to ascertain whether there was compliance and certify facilities that were compliant. The third was capacity building by providing training and technical assistance to facilities all around the world that wanted to implement the standard either themselves or in their supply chains.

With the emergence of SAI, we see an evolution of the responsibility assurance social movement from emergence to development. Further, while CEP was morphing into SAI, by the mid-1990s other developments were beginning to occur in different arenas of SRI fueled by the efforts of other difference makers. One of the most notable of those was an organization in the United Kingdom called AccountAbility, which has been attempting a similar project to SAI's, with a slightly different and broader lens.

■ Simon Zadek

Simon Zadek was the driving force behind the founding of AccountAbility, served as its first chairman of the board, and currently serves as the CEO and executive director. By the time he founded AccountAbility, Zadek was already well known for his work as the development director of a leading think-tank in the UK, the New Economics Foundation, and had served as the founding chair of the Ethical Trading Initiative. His work with AccountAbility also led him to play a key role in the development of the Global Reporting Initiative, the brainchild of difference makers Allen White and Bob Massie with Joan Bavaria's support, which will be discussed in Chapter 6. In addition, Zadek has held several other appointments, including senior fellow, Corporate Social Responsibility Initiative of the Center for Business and Government at Harvard University's Kennedy School of Government, and 'professor extraordinaire' at the University of South Africa's School of Management Sciences. In 2003, he was named one the World Economic Forum's "Global Leaders for Tomorrow."

Zadek holds a PhD in economics and political science from the University of London and published his dissertation, demonstrating his long-standing passion for making a difference, as *An Economics of Utopia*. Zadek recounts his early history:

> Back in the '70s and late '80s, when I finished my first degree in economics, I spent three years working as an economic planner for the government of St. Lucia in the Caribbean. There I got my first taste of the broader development agenda and practice. The country had just been made independent from British colonial rule and was trying to find its way in a complicated world. It was a country comprising 130,000 people and had a seat on the UN, which is always a strange combination. I came back to the UK, did a master's and joined what was then Coopers & Lybrand at their management consultant group, doing development work in two places: one in East Africa particularly in Tanzania at what was then the height of economic collapse around '84, '85; and, secondly, doing work in my own country in the UK. I was more or less dealing with the fallout of [British Prime Minister] Thatcher's aggressive economic strategies that were busy closing down shipyards, mining towns, and communities.
>
> So I found myself doing development at both ends, if you like, in developing countries and in [developed] countries that were quickly unraveling, of which the UK was one. In 1985 I left Coopers & Lybrand to start up my own consultancy along with a few other people, working mainly in the development space that I'd been working with Coopers & Lybrand and previously in Tanzania, mainly working for development agencies on economic regeneration, stimulation, rehabilitation, and the fate of Tanzania. The name of the organization was Maendeleo Consultants, which is Swahili for "development." They're based in London and based in Gaborone in Botswana. I did that for three or four years, and did a lot of interesting work, again working at both ends of the pipeline. We were working, as an example, in Northern Ireland and Scotland, and on the other hand in Sri Lanka, South Africa, and elsewhere. It was all an interesting blend of economic development work, management consultancy, and increasingly helping large NGOs manage complex evolutionary processes.

Foreshadowing his current work with AccountAbility, Zadek continues,

> There was a lot of social metrics work, all of which was to serve a purpose later on. In 1992 I joined the New Economics Foundation (NEF), an alternative economic think-tank based in the UK that was originally created in 1984. I went into NEF with a mandate to build and run a program on value-based organizations, arguing that an alternative economics needed a different way of thinking about large-scale organizations. Then I spent a couple of years

looking in depth at a number of large NGOs around the world that had been around for 25 years or more, and tracking their evolution from their outsetting values through to their more corporatist styles later on.

All of this preliminary work set the stage for Zadek's role as AccountAbility's CEO, because, like Lydenberg somewhat earlier, he too began to understand the new types of metrics that were needed to build a responsibility assurance infrastructure. As Zadek recalls,

> NEF had got stuck in a very '60s cooperative way of thinking about little organizations and little communities which was not helpful in the world of transnational corporations. So I built a program of research, out of which came a bunch of tools to look at the relationship between values, accountability, organizational processes, and performance. We were looking exclusively at NGOs, very large NGOs. One of the tools that came out of that work was social auditing, which then got picked up by companies like The Body Shop and Ben & Jerry's. They became the first publicly listed companies to use systematic social audit procedures, drawn from the work of NEF, strangely enough. Our work on corporate accountability exploded and suddenly became quite a big story. We were shifted from what was a relatively small marginal organization into becoming quite a large, complex organization at the centre of a lot of the emerging work around corporate accountability.

Certainly, as we have seen with other difference makers, circumstance and luck played into the skill set and knowledge base that Zadek had developed. Like the other difference makers, he recognized the opportunities in existing gaps — and the need to create new mobilizing structures: i.e., new institutions. . He provides insight:

> I guess all of that, as always, is just one big bunch of luck. One just happens to be in the right place at the right time, doing stuff that catches fire in the right way. Then, because part of our strategy within NEF was to create new organizations that we felt were fit for purpose in the emerging work that we were involved in, we built a series of organizations that included, in particular, AccountAbility. We designed, with other people, the organization based around our perception of what would be needed in the corporate accountability field over the next 10–15 years. We also founded the Ethical Trading Initiative (ETI), which I chaired for several years. That was kind of the European equivalent of the Fair Labor Association, but multi-sector rather than only textiles, and in some ways dealing with a somewhat more complex agenda and approach than the fairly tactical compliance-based approach the FLA was taking.

Continuing the evolution of NEF's efforts, Zadek notes,

> We chaired the Jubilee 2000 Global Debt Campaign (with the aim of writing off third-world debt) and a number of other things. We were somehow at a sort of hub. That happens to organizations occasionally. So we found ourselves in a very interesting place just at the time that the then shiny new Blair government was coming in, in '97. In their early years they were highly supportive of the kind of work that NEF and others had been promoting for years. So that gave us an enormous boost and powered us forward financially, in terms of political patronage, in terms of business engagement, and in terms of the international protocol that our work got.

Clearly, there was a political opportunity structure embedded in the congruence between the needs and interests of the early days of UK Prime Minister Tony Blair's administration and the work that NEF had already been doing that allowed for the development of not just AccountAbility but also the ETI and the Jubilee 2000 Global Debt Campaign. Zadek and his colleagues took full advantage of that opportunity to create the new mobilizing structures of these institutions. In the years since their founding, particularly AccountAbility and the ETI have made considerable impact on the formation of the responsibility assurance infrastructure.

AccountAbility

The Institute of Ethical and Social AccountAbility, better known as AccountAbility, was established in 1995 to promote accountability for sustainable development by bringing together business, civil society, and public-sector organizations globally (see Box 4.3).

Box 4.3 **AccountAbility**

AccountAbility, the Institute of Social and Ethical AccountAbility,[75] founded in 1995, considers itself to be the leading international non-profit institute that brings together leaders from business, civil society, and governmental organizations globally with the explicit purpose of promoting "accountability innovations that advance responsible business practices, and the broader accountability of civil society and public organizations." As of 2007, AccountAbility had 350 members from businesses, NGOs, and research organizations and published the AA1000 series of Sustainability Assurance and Stakeholder Engagement Standards, which were the first of their type to be issued. These principles-based standards, which can be used by any type of organization anywhere in the world, are intended to help organizations improve their sustainability performance.

The proliferation of activities that AccountAbility is engaged in at the time of writing attests in no small measure to the ways in which its activities have enhanced the development of the field and in part to the rapid institutionalization of responsibility assurance. For example, in addition to promulgating the AA1000 standards, AccountAbility also pioneered the Partnership, Governance, and Accountability Framework, which is focused on helping entities engaged in partnership activities improve the effectiveness and success of the partnership, particularly with respect to governance and accountability. In 2006, AccountAbility, in collaboration with the European Policy Centre, INSEAD, and ESADE (two leading European business schools), issued a first-ever framework for assessing whether companies can build competitive advantage through reshaping markets to reward responsible goods and services. Drawing on the perspectives of stakeholders in multiple sectors and focused on European companies, the framework highlights not just the potential of such strategies, but also their difficulties.

Highlighting another of the initiatives that suggest that the responsibility assurance movement has moved into the development stage, AccountAbility has gotten into the rankings business. It issues an annual Global Accountability Rating, focused on the world's 50 largest corporations as measured by *Fortune* magazine (with CSR Network), plus another ten large companies, so that there would be at least ten companies from each of several sectors: automotive; computer, electronics, and telecommunications; energy and utilities; financial services; and petroleum refining. AccountAbility also convenes the Multi-Fiber Agreement (MFA) Forum, an international alliance of businesses, development agencies, NGOs, and labor organizations which focuses on supply chain issues, and with the Boston College Center for Corporate Citizenship cofounded and convenes the Global Leadership Network, which is a global network of leading businesses who are attempting to align their business strategies with corporate responsibility and developing relevant tools and benchmarking practices.

Zadek reflects on AccountAbility's fundamental purpose,

> AccountAbility was created to change GAAP, the generally accepted accounting principles [to which companies' financial statements must adhere], because we took a view that standards come and go, only GAAP remains, reinforced by the brute power of the key professions, notably, the financial audit profession. If we didn't change GAAP, then all would be for naught. So we took a view that changing GAAP meant a different way of thinking about accounting and auditing. It represented a qualitative shift. Change in GAAP required that we sought to reform the standards bodies that ultimately were responsible for stewarding standards into the future. So AccountAbility was created both to create methods and to represent a different way of thinking about standards organizations. Multi-stakeholder, open source co-design processes, non-proprietary, open access to the results. You know, a very dif-

ferent way of thinking about what standards processes were about and how one built them.

With its pioneering standards-setting emphasis on GAAP, AccountAbility explicitly recognized the power not just of standards, but also of the methodologies that support them. As Zadek points out, the Global Reporting Initiative (see Chapter 6), founded by Allen White and Bob Massie with support from Joan Bavaria and others, including AccountAbility and Zadek, "not only emulated but refined in a lot of ways as it came through."

AccountAbility actually stood for a far bigger vision than simply changing accounting standards, however, as Zadek points out:

> The *vision* behind AccountAbility was far broader and was to promote approaches to accountability that supported sustainable development. The pathway that it took in the first generation of its work was around standards. In the last four or five years, it has both pursued its standards agenda *and* significantly advanced other parts of its work, notably our work on partnerships, our work on competitiveness, more and more public policy work and so on.

Zadek details how some of the shifts described briefly above came into being:

> For the first five or six years, we focused almost exclusively on standards. Post-2002, which is when I came in, in an executive role for the first time as chief executive, we began to open up to the broader agenda but underpinned the vision of AccountAbility. [The vision] was that accountability and changes in accountability are prerequisites for advances in any significant social, ethical, environmental, or economic directions, adding up to whatever you want to call it — corporate responsibility or sustainability, or whatever language one happens to use.

Underlying all of this development was a theory of how change happens in the world, and how a social movement like the one in which AccountAbility was playing such a central role comes into being. Zadek elaborates,

> It was a theory about how policy worked, which had to do with the central role of accountability and a theory of change. How we could influence change, which was rooted probably to begin with primarily in standards, but over time different ways of leveraging change: ideas influencing practice, influencing standards, and influencing the framework of rules, regulation, and public policy. Ideas were the furthest upstream. You gradually moved downstream. Ideas, the way in which leadership organizations put them into practice, the way in which standards begin to systematize and formalize good-practice standards [represented] a sort of visionary change. [Ulti-

mately, the vision moved to] the way in which the rules of the game, frameworks, and public policy regulation were beginning to systematize private standards.

Reflecting back to his PhD work on utopian societies, Zadek comments,

So the PhD is about the limitations of economic theory and the proposition that utopian fiction and theory tells us more about socioeconomics than economic theory does because fiction is almost inherently systemic. People describe systems, not in theory or in concepts, but in narrative. What I went on then to argue or question was: what would happen if the way economies, market, and economic theory worked was rooted not in a condition of scarcity, but in a condition of dialogue? If economic decision-making was not about decisions concerning the allocation of scarce resources, which is definitionally the way modern economics is framed, but was built around a different proposition of both how decisions were made and what decisions were being made about.

This questioning led directly to some of Zadek's work at NEF and ultimately AccountAbility, and shows how deeply the roots of a different way of thinking about the world go in this difference maker. He comments,

I think when you look at the social auditing framework that we promoted in NEF and the AA1000 standards, and many of the things that I've been involved in, in the last ten years, it is all an expression of that PhD. It's an expression of the view that the heartland issue is process, in old '70s terms, the heartland view is democracy, that slightly funny old word if you remember it. That we were all in the business of reinventing democracy in a transnational globalized world and that AA1000 is a piece of that kit, because at its heart it's a project about the rights of people impacted to have a say over how such institutions make decisions.

So I'm not a localizer. I don't really believe in the localization project. I try to avoid falling into the trap of corporatism, but find myself hovering dangerously near it. I guess I'm convinced that there is a golden thread of accountability running through sane societies, sane and civilized societies. AccountAbility is profoundly about civilizing power. Not getting rid of it but civilizing it. I'm more interested in how processes of change can drive effectively new models of people's participation in emerging political institutions, and my focus on the business community is because I think it is the most important political institution to emerge in the last century, and therefore [the business community] needs to be politicized. [Businesses] need to be made accountable through political processes, not only through regulatory processes — to direct participation, a direct model for democracy. Because we can't separate out the wealth of nations and the theory of moral sentiments. That classical separation will not be part of our future and we have to face that and deal with it.

Of course, Zadek recognizes that this thinking is retrospective — making sense of what has happened by looking back on it as if it had been planned. He comments,

> To some extent this is a retrofit, because I think like many organizations one doesn't start off with the package, *one evolves the package* [emphasis added]. So we've distilled and distilled and distilled our understanding of what we're doing and why we're doing it, and where accountability fits into the architecture. Now, looking back, I can describe something that we wouldn't have described in 1995, because we weren't ready to think about it in those terms. So it depends which end of the telescope you really want to focus on, but if we're focusing on what I know now and what we have become, AccountAbility is not merely a compliance phenomenon. It's not merely a regulatory phenomenon, but it's the *driver of change*. It's the driver of organizational performance. It's what I've called elsewhere society's answer to the second rule of thermodynamics. It's the thing that moves things on. You push it, it moves. Instead of seeing accountability as something that was primarily to prevent something happening, which is how historically particularly some civil society organizations were seeing it, we saw it as the driver of performance and therefore as the phenomenon that needed to be innovated and evolved if one wanted to change the way organizations and systems performed. That was our take on accountability, as a DNA aspect of societies. In the same way that the right would see markets as a sort of DNA phenomenon of a society, we would see accountability in a similar light.

The initiatives that Simon Zadek has been involved with over the years fit well with his personal philosophy and fundamental interests, even as far as questioning the very nature of how a social movement like the responsibility assurance movement gains momentum. He comments,

> Somewhere the important question to me became — since we don't dig holes, we don't make food, we don't make medicine, we don't build houses, we don't even make money, all we do is take ideas and package them in lots of different ways, into standards, into academic pieces, into raging polemic, into whatever — why do some of [these ideas] catch fire and others not? One is dealing with a process that is obviously not the countervailing power [nor the dominating power], because this is not a revolution, and yet is obviously not merely an expression of dominant power. In other words, [an institution like AccountAbility is] somewhere mediating between countervailing power

and dominating power. How does one know really what's going on? Which is, you know, the thing — if it doesn't keep us awake at night it bloody well should do.

■ James E. Post

Back across the Atlantic, another difference maker, working in an entirely different context, mainly as an academic, was pushing forward a different type of accountability agenda, beginning by raising awareness in the academic community of the very issues with which the other difference makers already discussed were dealing on a day-to-day basis.

James E. (Jim) Post is not a typical difference maker in this study, as he is an academic rather than a practitioner, but he is an academic whose work from the start has consistently crossed the line into studying and influencing practice. As professor of management and public policy at Boston University's School of Management, he has produced some of the seminal writing on corporate responsibility, notably his 1975 book with Lee Preston entitled *Private Management and Public Policy*, and more recently his 2002 book *Redefining the Corporation* with coauthors Lee Preston and Sybille Sachs, along with his more recent work as president of the lay group that has been demanding accountability and transparency from the Catholic Church in the wake of pedophilia scandals in Boston and elsewhere. Post is also included because his late 1970s' work studying infant formula sales and distribution in developing nations, particularly by Nestlé, and his later participation on the Nestlé Audit Commission, forged new territory for corporate accountability — by holding Nestlé and other infant formula manufacturers responsible for the impacts of their business practices, rather than just focusing on the corporate *social* responsibility activities of firms. He later worked for two years for the business association The Conference Board as research director, and also with others pioneered a case-based focus on environmental management in the 1980s, before many others were paying attention to issues of sustainability in management education.

Trained as a lawyer (Villanova University, PA), with a PhD in management (State University of New York at Buffalo), Post had just graduated from law school during the Watergate era of the early 1970s in the United States. His interests in accountability, whether individual, political, or corporate, came early, as he relates:

> At first [Watergate] was just the burglary story and then it was the cover-up story and then it was the taping story. And, for a young lawyer at that time, Watergate was like a kick in the stomach, because everything that we had learned in law school about the role of the legal system and the role of

lawyers and the kind of ethical responsibilities lawyers had, all that was just cast into great doubt by the behavior of a *lot* of lawyers in the Nixon White House and by Richard Nixon himself, who was such a well-educated and successful lawyer. It made the whole notion of legal ethics look ridiculous at that time. It was also, I guess, my study of constitutional law that gave me a really special sense of how extraordinary it was to have the impeachment proceedings going on. Looking back on it, I know that it was in that period that my hard thinking about issues of accountability in organizational institutional systems began to take some shape.

Post joined Boston University for the 1974–75 academic year, finishing up his dissertation, which was ultimately published as a book called *Corporate Behavior and Social Change*, as well as the more conceptual book *Private Management and Public Policy* mentioned above. He points to the origins of some of his ideas about the intersection between public and private management:

It was [in this period] that I first used the terminology of reactive, proactive, interactive patterns of response [between companies and society or the public-policy process]. So we go from the principle of public responsibility in the first book, to the application in risk and response, and then to this looking at patterns of behavior. It was all about organizations and institutional behavior and trying to figure out what made that all work.

The infant formula controversy

As his conceptualization about the roles of businesses in society an the interaction between businesses and the public-policy process developed, Post began a long-term engagement with the practicalities of some problematic business practices. He comments,

After *Corporate Behavior and Social Change* came out, I moved into a period of time when I was doing a lot of practical stuff, because by then the infant formula issue had come to my attention. It was a place to study and apply the notions of industry self-regulation [developed in the dissertation work]. From about 1976, 1977, on through the 1980s, I had a lot of very hands-on involvement with [the infant formula controversy] including my years at the Nestlé Audit Commission. But, even before the audit commission, I had done projects for the Rockefeller Foundation in Latin America. We were involved in a big project at USAID, which sponsored a three-million-dollar, four-country study. And so my public policy/practical management bent was really a complement to what these other medical and public health people were doing.

The infant formula controversy was of long standing and had come to public attention during the 1960s. It became a major public controversy during the mid- to late 1970s, resulting in a long-term boycott of food giant Nestlé, which was accused of some of the most egregious practices, and, ultimately, the formation of the Nestlé Audit Commission, which was to monitor the company's infant formula sales practices during the 1980s until it was disbanded. The central issue was the use of manufactured infant formula as opposed to breast milk in developing nations, where mothers could ill afford to purchase it, where sanitary conditions did not support its safe use, and where little refrigeration existed. These issues were brought to public attention as early as 1966 by the WHO.[76]

Although use of infant formula to feed babies was quite safe in developed nations, that was not the case in less-developed countries. Many babies that were fed on infant formula, which was frequently mixed in unsanitary conditions, not refrigerated properly because no facilities were available, diluted too much and with impure water, developed severe diarrhea and many died from malnutrition or dehydration. The problem that Post, a management scholar, focused on was that mothers were often adopting the use of infant formula rather than more nutritious, safe, and available breast milk because of the infant formula industry's promotional practices. Frequently, companies sent a "milk nurse," a saleswoman dressed in a white uniform, when new mothers were still in the hospital. These "milk nurses," paid for by the infant formula companies, handed out free samples and urged mothers to adopt the more "modern" practice of using the formula rather than breast milk. By the time that mothers had taken their babies home and used up the free supply of milk, their own breast milk had dried up and they were essentially forced to purchase formula, which for many was financially impossible. As Post later pointed out in some of his cases and writings, this first-world product, while perfectly safe in its intended use, was quite literally unsafe in "third world" settings, where it was misused. The controversy resulted in round after round of lawsuits and countersuits, controversial publications, boycotts, and ultimately a negotiated settlement.

By the mid-1970s, the infant formula controversy was at its height, because of sev- eral widely circulated publications, the most controversial of which was titled *The Baby Killer*,[77] which targeted Nestlé's sales and distribution practices in developing countries and brought the issue to public attention. Post had become one of a very few management scholars focused on the business practices — and lack of account- ability for the consequences associated with those practices — that had created the problem in the first place. Some religious investors presciently used the same proxy voting mechanism used so effectively later in the South Africa divestment controversy to attempt to change corporate practices around the sale and distribu- tion of infant formula in developing nations. Numerous activist groups and the WHO became involved in trying to change the practices, which began to draw the attention of companies trying to preserve their right to sell the formula.

Post vividly remembers the period and the surrounding controversy, as well as his involvement in trying to uncover the facts from a management perspective:

> I worked with some great people and we traveled to some very, very interesting places in the third world [to do research]. That was actually the first time I had ever traveled to third-world countries. I saw things there that had a very powerful influence. So the Nestlé Audit Commission worked. I went onto the commission in 1984, which was when the Nestlé boycott came to a negotiated end by creating the commission. I had worked with WHO [which submitted a resolution to the UN that was finally passed by all voting members except, ironically, the United States] on shaping and writing the code of conduct before that. We thought that the commission would be in service for maybe three years or so. It turned out that it went from 1984 to 1991 or 1993, when we finally wrapped it up. We were looking for an exit strategy at that time. I remember that I had actually worked closely with Senator [Edmund] Muskie directly in writing up a kind of a blueprint for how we were going to get out of the business of being this audit commission.

Auditing Nestlé

Tim Smith was also involved, on the activist side of the infant formula controversy, and remembers presenting the opinion of concerned investors to members of the Nestlé Audit Commission,

> Yes, I think at ICCR some of the significant things were when the work became not simply raising the right issue, protesting from outside the gate or boardroom, but when we actually began to have an impact, whether it was on South Africa or changing a company's policies on the environment or encouraging them to disclose information on diversity. Or the baby formula debate, which was very intense. There was a sense that companies needed to not follow Western marketing and promotion practices for a product that could be — was being — used improperly. In the end the success story was multiple: companies changed because of the pressures being put on them, and also the UN, UNICEF and WHO passed a code of conduct. So these were international standards, and we could say, "We're not just saying this to Nestlé or American Home Products or other companies. This is what the international standards are, and you're still not following them." We'd do some monitoring of that kind of thing.
>
> The infant formula campaign was an example of a campaign where the engagement was long-term and intense. There was dialogue. There were shareholder resolutions. There was a boycott of Nestlé. There was a lot of public education and postcard campaigns. These companies were really put

under significant public pressure because of the campaign. Gradually, the rules of the road changed. The companies had to change their behavior. What was acceptable ten years before, when you put advertisements on a big billboard in Nigeria about your formula being the best for babies, now, if you sold a can of formula, you had to say that breastfeeding was best for babies and why that was so. So the campaign led to dozens of changes in promotions and policies.

The Nestlé Audit Commission certainly represented one of the first times that a company had been subjected to externally motivated and independent audits of its business practices; in that sense, it was a watershed for the responsibility assurance movement, showing what could be accomplished with sufficient external pressure. As with other elements of the institutional infrastructure around responsibility assurance, the Nestlé Audit Commission came about because of external pressures on the company by NGOs and activists, along with international bodies such as WHO, UNICEF, and other UN agencies.

As the Nestlé Audit Commission began to wind down its work, Jim Post shifted his scholarly attention to "thinking through what the changing relationship was between business and society in that era. We were a little ahead of the popular embracing of the notion of corporate citizenship." With his early work on infant formula, public affairs management, stakeholder theory, and work on environmental management by companies, Post pioneered a number of issues for management scholars. In a sense, these experiences created a confluence that has shaped his perspective on what it is to be an academic — or, better, what it ought to be to be an academic in today's troubled world.

Post reflects on his own purpose and career as he thinks about the ways that many young scholars are dealing with their careers today,

> What I see today as an academic who is closer to the end of his career than the beginning is that there are an awful lot of young faculty members trying to game the system by writing x number of articles in journals that somebody ranks as an A or B, or whatever. What I don't see often enough manifested in ways that I think would be more rewarding to people, but also more productive, are people focusing on important problems. It's hard for me to believe that there are so many talented people working on such mediocre, minor problems when there are such big problems in the world that need to be addressed. That concerns me, and I'm not sure if I'm ready to jump on that horse and talk about it in more public forums, but it's sad to see all this human talent being frittered away. It's not just that it's normal science in the way that Kuhn[78] writes about it, but it's that the problems are not really life-altering problems of people. So I look at these intelligent capable young scholars and say, "Work on something that matters."

The work that Post did with the infant formula issue, early 1980s research on public affairs management, the natural environment in the late 1980s, corporate citizenship and stakeholder theory in the 1990s, and ultimately the Voice of the Faithful, shaped and sharpened his critique of academia. As he states,

Some people would say, "Infant formula, ha!" I would say, "No, walk into a hospital in one of these developing countries, like Colombia, and look at what they called the drip ward": platforms where you had 50 babies, all with IV drips in their heads. They called it the drip ward because all the babies have chronic diarrhea. In one ward in a hospital in Bogotá, those 50 babies were all there because they were being formula-fed by mothers who didn't realize that there were mixing instructions and pure water requirements, and all the rest of that. They expected that of those 50 babies, probably 40 of them would die. So you look at situations like that and you say, there are things we can do, marketing regulations, by way of institutional accountability that can make a difference. That can mean something to the lives and prospects of those children.

I guess that the infant formula case was a tremendous learning experience for me, but it also really hardened my view of the importance of accountability and the pressures of the legal system and the activist community. The Nestlé boycott was my first really big experience with street-level activism. I was never a leader in the boycott, but I played a different kind of role because I was an academic and I had this academic, pointy-headed perspective on things. The people who were running the boycott were incredibly smart, probably smarter than I was, but they knew that they needed some academics to speak on these issues. I offered them a perspective that was valuable to the way that the accountability movement was shaping up. So that was a very important and satisfying experience to be part of that.

When I was sitting with the WHO in Geneva as part of this consultative process, drafting an international code of conduct, I had that sort of moment when you pinch yourself and say, "Am I really here? Am I really doing this?" There was an extraordinary sense of being involved in this process. I also found it ironic that, in this great amphitheater looking out over beautiful Lake Geneva, we were talking about drafting this code of conduct that would guarantee that mothers would be safe to be able to breastfeed their babies without commercial interference. Who was it who was talking about mothers breastfeeding their babies? It was mostly men, and it was mostly men from the industrialized countries of Europe and North America. I thought there was something ironic in that as well. It was also an introduction to a world of international relations that I had known nothing about before, and, for me, the most interesting example of what happens when you're part of that club

> happened about nine months after we had finished the code consultation process.

Post continues,

> I got an invitation to go to Sicily for another WHO consultation. And this invitation was for a snazzy-looking meeting. It was a meeting to work on developing a code for the rights of the mentally ill, and I thought, "Why me? I don't qualify either as a patient or as a provider of services to the mentally ill. I don't have any experience in that world." So I contacted the people, and the answer was, "Well, you were on the WHO list, and it's the wise persons list." And they may have been teasing about it, but there was a list of people who had been identified as experts who could be counted on to bring good judgment to these kinds of issues. I didn't go, so I guess I'm no longer on the wise persons list. But it was sort of a revealing opportunity, and insight into the way another important part of the world really works.

Public affairs and the environment

Post was also one of the pioneers of the study of public affairs management in business schools in the early 1980s, when he and colleagues at Boston University undertook the first-ever surveys of public affairs offices. He was among the first in the management disciplines to turn attention toward business's relationship to the natural environment through work in the late 1980s with Alfred Marcus and Rogene Buchholz, which resulted in numerous pioneering cases and the first environmental management textbook. He worked for The Conference Board in New York, for two years, in 1995–96, a period that proved fruitful in terms of advancing his thinking and understanding of critical issues of corporate accountability and governance, as he recalls:

> The Conference Board was actually a very conceptual period of time in my thinking, because it was a chance to work with independent contractors as well as their staff, who did do work on corporate citizenship. So we were thinking through what the changing relationship was between business and society in that era and we were a little ahead of the popular embracing of the notion of corporate citizenship.

By the late 1990s, Post was working with Preston and Sachs on the stakeholder ideas that were to become the book *Redefining the Corporation*, work that continued for several years under the auspices of a Sloan Foundation grant, with Max Clarkson, professor at the University of Toronto and founder of the Center for Corporate Social Performance and Management, and Thomas Donaldson of the Wharton School (of business) at the University of Pennsylvania. In the early 2000s, all of this past work converged for Post, a practicing Catholic, when the pedophilia scandals in the Catholic Church broke in Boston. He became deeply immersed in the very practical and hands-on lay efforts to reform the Catholic Church and make it both more accountable and transparent through his cofounding and service as the first president of the lay reform group Voice of the Faithful (VOTF), while continuing in his position at Boston University.

Voice of the Faithful

The work with VOTF helped Post to see how accountability in theory could be put into practice through a mechanism much like the one that Peter Kinder had recognized social proxy resolutions to be: grassroots activism. Post recounts the story of the formation of VOTF and his role as its president.

> What happened starting in 2002 with the clergy sex-abuse scandal in the Catholic Church is a whole new chapter. I went to a Catholic undergraduate school, St. Bonaventure, and then a Catholic law school, Villanova, which could have been anywhere, but it was a Catholic law school. But in my career, being a Catholic academic or a Catholic professional didn't ever have any special significance, except that there was a time in the late 1980s when I really thought hard about the Pastoral Letter on the economy developed by American bishops ["Economic Justice for All," 1986]. It served to raise the consciousness, the awareness of people about the economic justice issues in a booming economy, that there were distributive issues and also the productive issue like the side-effects or externalities of pollution and so forth.

The questioning raised by the bishops' Pastoral Letter resonated with much of Post's earlier work, as he related:

> I remember I was really thinking about the role of the Church as an institutional actor in society, being a voice around these justice issues. That issue didn't become widely discussed until the mid-1990s. But the notion of environmental justice problems and the poor communities that are downwind from industrial plants and that get the effluents in the water, and so forth — those were issues you couldn't avoid thinking about if you were doing the environmental stuff. The bishops' Pastoral Letter was a kind of reference point for me in thinking about the Catholic contribution to the business-and-society area, along with my friendship with Jerry Cavanaugh [another business-in-society scholar, who is a Jesuit priest].

Post had suffered a life-changing heart attack in 1984, which ostensibly slowed the frenetic pace of his life, but not its fundamental purpose: to bring accountability to large institutions, both public and private. He describes the origin of VOTF in 2002 as another such experience:

It was a Sunday morning, and I know exactly the date. It was January 6, and cold, clear, not snowy. I came down to the kitchen, went outside to get the newspaper, and got a cup of coffee and sat down and opened the newspaper. On the front page was the story of the forthcoming trial of John Gagen, a Catholic priest who has now been defrocked, but at the time he had been a Catholic priest for over 30 years. He had been accused of molesting, at the time it was more than 100 (it turned out to be 130), children in different parishes around the Archdiocese of Boston. And on the front page the story continued on that Gagen's behavior was known and protected by a series of pastors, auxiliary bishops, and the Cardinal of Boston himself, Cardinal Bernard Law.

The *Boston Globe* spotlight team had discovered from documents in the deposition and documents that had been made available in preparation for Gagen's criminal trial, that there was this paper trail of information about Gagen. I read the whole story and [this] was just like Watergate. I felt the same kind of kick-in-the-stomach pain as I read the story, because it was a disgusting breakdown of institutional responsibility. Here you had leaders and supervisors who protected a perpetrator who was committing some of the most awful kinds of crimes at least that I can imagine. My wife Jeannette was deeply shocked as well, and we talked about it, and we went over to church later on in the morning, over to St. John the Evangeline, and as we were walking in the former pastor then retired was walking out, and he was kind of muttering to himself, basically saying, "so terrible, so terrible." As we didn't know what he was talking about we said something flippant like, "Don't worry, Father John, we'll all pull together," but he was talking about the same thing we were talking about, which was the story in the paper.

In the days that followed, the *Globe* continued to run stories and the picture got larger and more complete. It sent a shock wave throughout the Boston community, certainly throughout the Catholic community. Because this was just the antithesis of what I think many Catholics are, or think of themselves as. They tend to be family-oriented people; many come from large families, with kids, brothers, sisters, and so forth. This idea that someone who had been as trusted as a priest could have been abusing someone in this way was horrible and really disconcerting to our sense of what it means to be a Catholic. Then on top of it you have this cover-up, which was like gasoline on this already hotly burning fire.

A confluence of the right people, the right priest at their church, and the outrage created by the scandal resulted in a desire for people to find a forum in which to talk to each other, according to Post:

> We had a pastor who was approached by Jim Muller, who turned out to be a very important person in the story of how VOTF emerged. There was a sense that we needed to have some coming together about this. The community needed to talk about this in some way. St. John's is a pretty affluent community of well-educated, professional people, and the idea that this was happening and not being able to do anything about it was, well, "No!" People know how to get things done. So we asked Father Tom Powers for the ability to use a function room in the basement of the church for a meeting. He thought about it for a day or two and then he came back with a different proposal, and he said, "Why don't we do this? After mass, we'll hold a listening session, we'll have an open discussion about this." The only caveat that he put on this was that although he'd be happy to attend, [there] had to be a lay facilitator.

Over the next five weeks, the listening sessions continued to be held and over 600 people ultimately attended them, and the organizers decided that a meeting should be held on a Monday evening to accommodate people who could not stay late after church services. Post recalls the sequence of events:

> We didn't know how many people would turn up on Monday night because it seemed like we had already captured a lot of people and the meeting was held, and at first there were only about 20 people there, and then there were 30, then 40, then 60, and there were about 100 people there that first night, and we didn't have enough chairs. But we noticed that some of the people who were there were the same people who had been involved in the conversations just the day before. They didn't want the conversation to end, and they wanted to keep talking about it. So we put the chairs in a semi-circle and we had two facilitators, Jim [Muller] and a woman named Peggy Thorp, and a lot of our leadership was done with a man and a woman at all of these events.

It turned out that people needed to talk and the convening was providing a forum for both speaking and listening that was unique and powerful. The crowds continued to grow throughout March and April, outgrowing several halls, until 700–800 people were in attendance at meetings. The first meetings were highly emotionally charged, both with anger and sadness over the extent of the damage that pedophile priests had done to children over the years. But, true to Post's leanings with respect to accountability, he soon recognized that new questions underlay the abuses. The working groups began to form circles around different questions: basic definitional issues, health- and mental-health-related issues, communication with children about the issue, outreach to those who had been abused, and, ultimately, organizational and financial accountability questions that had always been at the core of Post's work: What is the organizational responsibility and the organizational structure of the Church? Who's responsible for what? Different working groups formed around these different questions, did research and framing between sessions, and reporting back the following week, and a structure for what was to be VOTF began to emerge. In addition, because the church that Post attended was in the wealthy suburb of Wellesley, many of the parishioners were highly skilled professionals who could take on tasks and knew how to get things done effectively and efficiently. Another of the cofounders of VOTF was Jim Muller, a cardiologist, who had won a Nobel Peace Prize in 1985 for his work as one of the founders of International Physicians for the Prevention of Nuclear War. Post remembers Muller's contributions:

> Jim [Muller] is really an extraordinary organizer and a visionary person, and he had a vision that this could be the beginnings of a movement of Catholic lay people. He was an amateur political scientist and so he had theories about what could happen, which were exciting because they were an exciting vision, but mostly it was that we were organizing and shaping things.

As VOTF grew and became more formalized, the group established clear goals for the enterprise. Post states,

> Our goals ended up streamlined into three goals: to support survivors of abuse, to support priests of integrity, because we recognized that the bad guys were a small percent of the total population of priests — at least that's what we had reason to believe and that's what the evidence at the time suggested. The third goal was to shape structural change in the governance of the Church. That was a direct outcome of my belief that structure shapes strategy. If you don't change the structures that produce the problem, then you're not going to introduce a lasting result no matter whatever else you do. So the focus was on survivors, priests, and long-term change. Our mission was really to focus on the role of the laity in the governance and guidance of the Church.

VOTF then organized itself to push for the ousting of Cardinal Bernard Law, who had been in charge when the abuse took place and was widely seen to have been involved in covering up the abuses for many years. Law was holding a public meeting in Boston, and members of VOTF got 12 tickets and planned their strategy. Although Post could not himself attend, he recalls,

> I was part of figuring out who was going and what they were going to say. We had to have a statement, and we needed to write down what we were going to say. Our first formal statement, our first declaration of who we are, what we're about, what we want to have happen, began with the words "We are the Church." Then it went on to say who we are, where we come from, what we're concerned about, what we think has to happen. That was the first thing. The second thing was, we knew that there was going to be time limit on how long each person was going to have to speak, and our statement was

too long to be read in that time, so [we decided:] We'll send up several people, and the first one will speak, the second one will continue, and the third one will continue that. So we worked out who would be the speakers. The third thing was we were meeting at the home of one of our members here in Wellesley and we were brainstorming all of this stuff, and there were maybe a dozen of us, and it came to the end of the meeting, and one of the women said, "And wear red on Saturday, don't forget to wear red."

Using the type of grassroots activist methodology that protesters against globalization might have used in places like Seattle in 1999, when the World Trade Organization's meeting was closed down, the Wellesley contingent proceeded to act. Post states,

Come Saturday morning, I dropped Jeannette off at the church where people were assembling. The women had red dresses, they had red sweaters, everybody was wearing something red, and the men were wearing red ties. It turned out that during the day there was a lot of attempted manipulation by the bishop and the cardinal's staff, but we did get our statements read, and all of our folks sat together in the front row of one section. The media was not allowed into hall, but afterward the media was outside and they talked to us. They said that others had said, "Talk to the women in red, the people from Wellesley": they really had their act together. The next day when the *Globe* story ran, there it was about the Wellesley women in red. They didn't mention the men with their red ties [chuckle]. These were wonderfully talented and competent and professional people, so their voices carried well, the articulation was right. Everything worked.

The organization grew from 37 supporters in March 2002 to over 25,000 by early 2007, with chapters in 40 of the United States and in 21 other countries and more than 150 affiliates. As VOTF grew, it gathered public and media attention, which the organization attempted to leverage into meetings with the cardinal and a focus particularly on the work of gaining some lay input into Church affairs, and greater financial and structural transparency. Although VOTF is a church-related entity, the issues of transparency, accountability, and responsibility are strikingly similar to those that larger corporations faced in the economic domain during the early days of the responsibility assurance movement. What VOTF offers is an insight into how a group of people not considered part of the traditional hierarchy can begin to use grassroots methods to foster more openness, greater dialogue, and, ultimately, they hoped, structural change. With the Church, such change toward greater transparency and openness is clearly a long-term proposition, as it has been in many instances with companies.

Post details some of the events that have resulted in minor changes, even though he would probably be the first to admit that the Church today has not significantly changed structurally. Public pressure, some of it coming from the intense publicity that VOTF itself was generating, ultimately resulted in Cardinal Law's resignation. Post is cognizant of the bigger set of interests and ideals involved in any movement such as VOTF and also of the organizational issues associated with short-term success:

> We had about 19,000 members at the time that Cardinal Law resigned. Rather than decline, which is what we feared, we actually found that in 2003 our organization grew. We grew to having more than 25,000 members, which told us something — that it wasn't just Boston, it was all around the country [that the problems in the Church and strong feelings among the laity existed]. People saw VOTF as a vehicle or a force for change in the Church — for a larger set of reforms in the Church. What we've come to find is that there are a tremendous number of Catholics, of the 60 million Catholics in this country, who want structural change, structural reform.
>
> Many of the priests, who were heroes by speaking out in 2002, really pointed out that the problem was the clerical culture. The insularity of that culture was a root cause of what happened. If it hadn't been for the clerical culture some pedophilia might have happened, but it would have been disclosed, it would have been revealed, and there wouldn't have been the cover-up and the concealment and the deception that all went with it. All of that was rationalized by bishop after bishop, and even the cardinals as they dealt with these cases. VOTF became a mechanism for effecting larger change in the Catholic Church. Every time we've done the numbers we've been able to document over 35,000 people who are connected to us in some kind of membership way. We don't have dues; we don't have formal membership steps that have to be taken, other than to register on our website. There are always a changing number of people.

Post takes some lessons from the work of VOTF that are relevant for the broader responsibility assurance movement as well. First, he discusses organizational issues:

> What I see in terms of our membership is that it's like three concentric circles. You've got the hardcore group, who are willing to do lots of work. And that is about 25,000–30,000 people. There's a second group of people who are supporters, and they could be donors; they are more passive, but they are clearly supporters. We've estimated that number but don't have any hard way of confirming it. Then there's a third group, which are ordinary Catholics, who share the broad objects of cleaning up the mess. We know from public opinion polling of Catholics all across the country that *that's* a very large number. That when it comes to things like financial accountability,

that the public opinion polls, which we don't have any influence over, show consistently 80, 85, 90% of all Catholics want greater financial accountability in the Church. So VOTF is a voice for all three of those groups or some people in all three of those groups.

It is this realization that VOTF carries the weight of public opinion within the Church, much as the responsibility movement carries a great deal of popular sentiment, that gives impetus to such initiatives. Post continues,

> I think VOTF's being perceived as a voice for the laity has led us to the practical strategy. People keep saying, "What's your strategy?" I'm a strategy guy. I should know what that is. It's been hard to really define it. But we've gotten it to where I think we have two prongs to the strategy. The first is our strategy is to be a clear and reasoned voice about issues in the Church for the laity. The second thing is to be a catalyst for change at the parish and diocese level. And that is to help the formation of local groups of Catholics. When you look at the church closings issue in Boston [instituted in the wake of the scandal as a cost-saving measure], and you look at the vigils that have taken place, and the occupation of parishes, a lot of the people involved in that — the core group — are people who were early participants in VOTF. There's a movement of activism among lay Catholics. Not just in Boston, but in other places as well. At one point we had over 200 affiliate groups around the country. Now we've cut back some of those and consolidated it to get more critical mass, but there's a lot of activity by a lot of people.

Accountability as an emerging issue

Looking back across the issues he has dealt with over his career, Post reflects,

> Certainly one thread that runs through it all is resistance to change. Every one of these institutions has been enormously resistant to change, and so change has to be brought about with a combination of reason and pressure, some internal and some external. I don't think people get change in institutions without some combination of those things. The other thing is that in all of those other experiences there were cultural factors that created exaggerated pathologies. In Nestlé, to be a good Nestlé man you had to have a certain kind of behavior. It looks an awful lot like the fraternity mind-set of the ordained priests in the Catholic Church. In some of the companies that we studied in the environmental areas, some of the engineering mind-sets and the economic mind-sets were, again, as rigid as the kind of mental models that people had in the Church or had at Nestlé.
>
> So I think the important thread for me has been this resistance to change and understanding how you use a combination of carrots and sticks to create

the incentives and the pressures that will move things forward. If I think about Nestlé and the Catholic Church and I'll say the electric utility companies, the cultures have developed a series of structures, systems, and understandings around people that all serve to reinforce a dominant model of how things ought to work. Each instance really involved breaking through those barriers to get at the cultural things themselves. Nestlé did eventually do some internal change process management that helped them to effect that culture. The electric utilities did the same around environmental issues. I believe the Church will do the same in time as well, because it's already happening.

Post draws other lessons from his experiences that provide insight into the responsibility assurance infrastructure, and provide some guidance for future difference makers as well:

For me, the real question is: how do you take your values and translate that into actions? Actions in the face of obvious needs to create a world that is better than the one that we're looking at. Whether that's kids in the drip ward in Bogotá, or whether it's an institution that's abused children and protected the perpetrator, the real test has been: how do you take your values and translate that into action?

At the end of the day I tell people that the value of your degree isn't the first job that you're going to get or even the career you'll build. We hope you will have great jobs and build wonderful careers. But the real value of the degree is that when the time comes and if some issue that really matters to you is there, you're going to have the confidence to say, "This one matters. I can do something about it." That to me is what this whole story is about. I had no idea on that Sunday morning that this problem with the Catholic Church was going to appear. It was there. It needed something. Step by step you do what you can do. If you *do* that, that really does take your values and translates them into action. And it gives a purpose to something. The costs are there. They're real. They drive a lot of other things out of your life but what *really* matters is being able to look in the mirror and say, "Did I stand up for something that really mattered?"

5

Emerging responsibility standards

As we have seen, the early participants in SRI helped to frame some of the issues that activists and interested social investors were raising so that they would be accessible to the general investing public. Social movement theorists call this the framing process. SRI-supporting institutions such as the ones discussed in Chapter 4 then emerged, tapping into what are called opportunity structures where they saw gaps between what is desired (by some actors) and current practice. Thus, as antiglobalization and anticorporate activism began growing in the 1990s, new standards of practice also began to evolve, broadening the sense of what it was companies — particularly multinational companies — must do to be considered responsible.

Standards represent another aspect of framing where opportunities exist and the institutions that have been built to support these standards represent new mobilizing structures: that is, new institutions that can push in the direction of meeting new expectations for corporate behavior. We have already seen the evolution of SAI out of the CEP, which is certainly one new standard. Another important breakthrough was the establishment of what became the Ceres Principles by difference maker Joan Bavaria and her collaborators, including eventual Ceres director Bob Massie.

■ The next important breakthrough

Joan Bavaria and Ceres

Joan Bavaria has been involved in building the institutional infrastructure around corporate responsibility and accountability in a number of important ways that touch on multiple aspects of the emerging infrastructure. In addition to being one of the pioneers of formalized social investing through her work with Trillium, discussed in Chapter 3, she also became involved early on with the establishment of new standards and expectations for businesses through her work in developing the Ceres organization and its Ceres Principles. Ceres, founded as the Coalition for Environmentally Responsible Economies, is today a US-based network of investors, environmental organizations, and public-interest groups that works with corporations and investors on issues of environmental sustainability, including global climate change. The mission of Ceres is "Integrating sustainability into capital markets for the health of the planet and its people."[79]

Ceres built its reputation on a set of environmental principles originally promulgated in 1989 as the Valdez Principles shortly after the *Exxon Valdez* oil tanker ran aground in Alaska, spilling millions of gallons of oil and devastating a large tract of previously pristine shoreline. As Bavaria points out, however, the framing of these principles had actually begun about a year before the tanker spill: "*Valdez* hadn't happened when we started. *Valdez* happened in the spring of '89. I actually started working on the principles in 1988. So a lot of people think we [published the principles] because of *Valdez* but it's not so."

Bavaria founded Ceres and served as its founding chair from 1989 to 2001. She recalls,

> That was the year of the [*Exxon*] *Valdez* spill, and there was a lot of unanimous feeling on the part of the people about trying to deal with environmental concerns. I was put on a committee from the beginning to try to envision how would we go after Exxon and help them with more responsible investment or help them with their environmental approach. But [this development] was a direct result of Trillium's goals of networking and creating links between various kinds of people. You might not think these goals and groups were compatible or should be naturally. But they did have something in common around environmental capital and the goal of conducting social audits. So Ceres was begun really reluctantly. It was very difficult.

The Ceres Principles were originally launched as the Valdez Principles with the aim of immediately gathering public attention. They became the Ceres Principles several years later, Bavaria remembers, as a participant pointed out the negative connotation of the *Valdez* oil spill, saying, "You wouldn't name the Audubon Society the 'Dead Bird Society,' would you?"

Many people volunteered their time to get the organization up and running until the idea of creating a set of principles for companies around environmental matters arose. Bavaria comments on the rapidity of the evolution of Ceres and companies signing on:

> We thought it would probably take 50 years to actually achieve what Ceres wanted to achieve. It was just something for the distant future, but what has been true of Ceres and all of this stuff is that very often you get a momentum going and you almost can't stop it.

Ceres: principles and process

Today more than 50 companies have signed on to the Ceres Principles, a still modest number. Ceres participation includes a requirement that companies publicly and transparently report about their environmental management programs and outcomes. As Ceres itself notes, the voluntary principles push companies considerably beyond legal requirements toward much more of a sustainability agenda (see Box 5.1). The principles were developed at a time when few companies thought seriously about such voluntary participation in aspirational standards.

Box 5.1 **The Ceres Principles**

Protection of the biosphere

We will reduce and make continual progress toward eliminating the release of any substance that may cause environmental damage to the air, water, or the earth or its inhabitants. We will safeguard all habitats affected by our operations and will protect open spaces and wilderness, while preserving biodiversity.

Sustainable use of natural resources

We will make sustainable use of renewable natural resources, such as water, soils, and forests. We will conserve non-renewable natural resources through efficient use and careful planning.

Reduction and disposal of wastes

We will reduce and where possible eliminate waste through source reduction and recycling. All waste will be handled and disposed of through safe and responsible methods. *(continued over)*

Energy conservation

We will conserve energy and improve the energy efficiency of our internal operations and of the goods and services we sell. We will make every effort to use environmentally safe and sustainable energy sources.

Risk reduction

We will strive to minimize the environmental, health, and safety risks to our employees and the communities in which we operate through safe technologies, facilities, and operating procedures, and by being prepared for emergencies.

Safe products and services

We will reduce and where possible eliminate the use, manufacture, or sale of products and services that cause environmental damage or health or safety hazards. We will inform our customers of the environmental impacts of our products or services and try to correct unsafe use.

Environmental restoration

We will promptly and responsibly correct conditions we have caused that endanger health, safety, or the environment. To the extent feasible, we will redress injuries we have caused to persons or damage we have caused to the environment and will restore the environment.

Informing the public

We will inform in a timely manner everyone who may be affected by conditions caused by our company that might endanger health, safety, or the environment. We will regularly seek advice and counsel through dialogue with persons in communities near our facilities. We will not take any action against employees for reporting dangerous incidents or conditions to management or to appropriate authorities.

Management commitment

We will implement these Principles and sustain a process that ensures that the Board of Directors and Chief Executive Officer are fully informed about pertinent environmental issues and are fully responsible for environmental policy. In selecting our Board of Directors, we will consider demonstrated environmental commitment as a factor.

Audits and reports

We will conduct an annual self-evaluation of our progress in implementing these Principles. We will support the timely creation of generally accepted environmental audit procedures. We will annually complete the Ceres Report, which will be made available to the public.[80]

Bavaria, of course, was not the sole prime mover. As Ceres became more established, Bob Massie joined as executive director and provided wholly new insights and perspectives that ultimately led to the launch (with Allen White; see Chapter 6) of the Global Reporting Initiative. But the early part of Massie's story provides some relevant context for the emergence of important new institutions in this field as well as for Ceres itself.

◼ Robert K. (Bob) Massie

The *Harvard Business School* (from which he received a doctorate in business administration in 1989) *Bulletin* profiled Robert Kinloch (Bob) Massie by opening,

> Will the real Robert Kinloch Massie (DBA '89) please stand up? *Priest. Politician. University lecturer. Medical marvel. Social activist. Prize-winning historian. Environmentalist. Executive.* While Bob Massie is justified in rising to acknowledge any of these appellations, the ability to get to his feet at all may rank among his greatest achievements. The simple acts of standing and walking represent triumph for Massie, as does the fact that he is even alive today. Fittingly, his life's work is all about "standing up," as he forcefully advocates higher standards of corporate responsibility and social justice in the conduct of capitalism.[81]

Through his multiple roles as a researcher on South Africa's apartheid regime, his leadership of Ceres, where he complemented the work of founder and CEO Joan Bavaria as executive director from 1996, and as one of the cofounders of the Global Reporting Initiative (among other things), Bob Massie has made a major impact on the responsibility assurance infrastructure over the years. But it has not been an easy path. Massie is also an Episcopal priest, having attended Yale Divinity School after graduating from Princeton. Massie relates some of his early history:

> I was born in 1956, the eldest of three children. My father was a writer,[82] starting off at *Newsweek* magazine, a book reviewer. My parents had both gone to college. My mother was the first one of her generation to go to college. So we were starting out not with very much, but lots of hopes. Very quickly our lives were shaped by discovery that I had severe classical hemophilia, which is a bleeding disorder that mostly causes internal joint bleeding. There was no real way to control that [bleeding] when I was a child. As a result I had lots of bleedings into my joints that would eventually deprive me of the ability to walk when I was five and was not able to walk without leg braces until I was 12.

When he was 12, his parents moved to France for four years, where his medical costs, including the very expensive clotting factor that he needed to keep the hemophilia under control, were completely covered, and where Massie was exposed not only to a different culture, but also to other influences that would shape his career.

Massie attended Princeton after graduating from high school early and spending a year as an intern in Washington. His early experiences of being "different" because of his illness colored his attitudes toward people and the world as well as important decisions in his life. He recalls the reason for the choice of Princeton,

> I had not intended to go there because my father had gone to Yale and other family members had gone to Yale, although it's not a long family association. But Yale was too hard to get around physically. I was having a lot of trouble walking and Yale was in a city. Princeton made a huge, huge pitch to make it easy for me to get around campus. So I benefited from Princeton's commitment to diversity, and not just abstract commitment, but a very real and physical investment that allowed me to get around on campus on a cart. They put in electric outlets in places so I could charge my cart. So I went to Princeton and one of the things that happened to me there was that I got somewhat radicalized. I became very concerned about the question of university investments. I didn't presume that I understood everything about it, just felt that there's an important set of issues here that isn't really being taught but which is important and how can I find out more about this? I got very involved in an effort to get rid of the discriminatory eating clubs at Princeton, and essentially became trained as a political activist. I actually came back from France quite conservative. Having been over there during the Vietnam War, I was tired of listening to French criticism, which I felt was correct but excessive, over the top. So it was an interesting transition for me to move from being a more conservative young man to a more progressive one during that period in college.

Added to his interest in social investing on graduation were several other factors that have contributed to Massie's ability to make a difference. He recounts the story:

> Most people who knew me thought I would go to law school. I thought maybe I'd go into politics some day. But between my junior and senior year in college, I had a very profound reawakening of my religious faith, really what can be described as a conversion experience. I had grown up in an Episcopal Church. My great-grandfather was an Episcopal priest and missionary, and there'd been some respect for this, but not a lot of super energy about it. But I had a very deep experience of the reality of the love and forgiveness of God. How that changed me was that I felt I didn't have to hide the parts of myself that I didn't like, and I could allow myself to love more

boldly and care more deeply, and that these things weren't shameful things, they were appropriate things. That freed me to become even more of an activist.

An activist was what Massie became, but not without another health crisis that occurred shortly after he entered Yale Divinity School in 1978.

Around Thanksgiving, I became unbelievably sick with an undiagnosable ill-ness that landed me in the hospital for two or three weeks, and we learned many years later that this was the initial onset of my HIV infection. But at the time nobody had heard of HIV. So I went to Yale Divinity School, but got ill and had to withdraw in my spring term, which was a real sense of failure. Now I went back to live with my parents. I had withdrawn because of the undiagnosed and apparently undiagnosable illness, which, of course, people began to think — I began to think — maybe it was some sort of psychological or psychosomatic thing, since nobody could figure out what it is.

The HIV infection, which came from a tainted infusion of the clotting factor that kept Massie's hemophilia in control, caused him to take a year off — a year spent working in Washington for Ralph Nader and Mark Green,[83] and, as he notes,

I worked on corporate responsibility issues, and got more deeply engaged in some of the questions of substance that I later worked on. But it's always been done out of a sense that these weren't purely political questions. They were fundamental questions about how human beings should live. They were ethical questions. They were moral questions. They were questions that religious institutions should not only engage with but lead.

Struggling with his infection, Massie explains,

We discovered in '84 that I had the virus, and I was already married at that time, so that was a big thing. Then, many years after that, we discovered that my viral load was zero, and in fact the strange story is that I have had HIV for almost 30 years, with a viral load of essentially zero, with no drugs. So we learned I had HIV, which was troubling; then I learned that the HIV didn't seem to be affecting me, which was miraculous and inexplicable. Then I learned I had hepatitis C.

Hepatitis C is another bloodborne disease caused by the infusions, which today is destroying Massie's liver and has caused him to take a leave of absence from Ceres, while he awaits, he hopes, a new liver.

Despite all these tribulations, Massie's life of activism has had a direct influence on the corporate responsibility infrastructure. He had become interested in South Africa as a 16-year-old during his stay in France after seeing an early showing of the movie *The Last Grave of Dimbaza*. The movie provided a crucial insight, as Massie notes,

> It was a *huge* eye-opener for me. I had never heard of South Africa, and I just could not imagine that this place actually existed, and that people were systematically brutalized and oppressed because of their skin color. I thought we had gotten past that. You know, I was a young man, and to me the civil rights movement, which was less than ten years old, was long in the past for me — and resolved.

After completing his divinity degree at Yale, he earned a doctorate in business administration from the Harvard Business School, writing his thesis and ultimately an award-winning book called *Loosing the Bonds: The United States and South Africa in the Apartheid Years* on the history of US relations with South Africa. He researched and wrote the book in South Africa and, after returning, unsuccessfully ran for office in Massachusetts, and ultimately joined Ceres. He says,

> Joan Bavaria came along and said, "We're looking for somebody like you: somebody who knows about shareholder activism and who understands all the parties, and parts of our coalition — the investor side, the business side. You have business school training. You know the religious activists. You are a good public speaker, and we'd like you to be the director of Ceres."
>
> So I said, "Well, that sounds good. Do you have any money to hire an executive director?" They said, "We don't actually have any money." Anyway, we worked out a deal that, if they could raise one year's salary, I'd consider it. They came back a few months later and said, "Good news! We raised part of your salary." I asked how much, and they said, "We have six months of your salary. Now don't you want to come?" It was crazy, but I said yes, and started in April of 1996.

Massie's perspective on Ceres highlights some of the obstacles that the still-fledgling organization had to overcome when he joined it,

> There's a whole dimension to how Ceres was created and what it did. One of the things was that we continued to sign companies up, although at a very slow rate, to endorse the Ceres Principles, and one of the things that it did was that it allowed us into a much deeper relationship with some of these companies. I think they got a lot out of it, but we certainly got a lot out of understanding the real-time pressures that managers face, and it was like a constant online focus group for us to test some of these ideas. Some of our most sophisticated and energetic advocates for some of the things we were doing came out of companies, because they would say, "No, no, this is what we need and we think this is possible."
>
> It's counterintuitive, but very often some of the companies that we worked with gave us the backbone or energy when we didn't think something was possible. They'd say, "It's never going to happen in my company unless

someone from the outside does this, this, and this. I can tell you that we actually favor it." I'd say, "What? You're a company, and we're us." At one point Ceres had gotten to the point where we felt we had such good relationships with companies that we felt we should vote corporate representatives onto the board. The NGOs and investors were totally into this. I didn't have a particularly strong view. I wasn't the chair of the board, though my view counted somewhat, but I withheld judgment on it to hear what the discussion was. I was amazed to hear that people were so gung-ho, until we went around to the corporate participants who were there, and they were *unanimously* opposed to it.

The reasons were also counterintuitive to what might have passed for the common wisdom, but suggest some of the maturation of the field, as Massie illustrates:

They said, "The benefit we get from Ceres both internally and externally is that we know that Ceres' judgments are not being influenced by whoever happens to be in the room from the corporate community. We can tell outside parties that we're engaging in good faith with this group, which is not run by companies. So that gives us a certain element of credibility. Since we're working hard for it, we don't want to lose [credibility] because one or two of us get on the board. Secondly, we feel we have enough access to you, and we know what you're doing, and we don't want to dilute the energy and direction that you have. So actually, none of us want to be elected to the board." So it was really one of those moments where you go, "Well, who would have thought of that?"

As Massie points out,

When Ceres was started the idea that investors could work with environmentalists, with business, to set an affirmative ethic, well, that was brand new. But, since 1989, lots of other groups have stepped into that space, whether it was BSR, or any number of other groups, like Environmental Defense, picking up activities that were specifically related to business. The whole idea that business was anathema was beginning to switch to "Everybody's got to have some kind of relationship with businesses."

The evolution of Ceres and the founding of new institutions

Joan Bavaria's energy and her ability to build consensus among a diverse array of people has always served her well. Ceres has been able to develop a number of important new initiatives over the years, some of which will be discussed in later chapters as part of the work of developing new institutions. For example, in 1999, Ceres launched the Global Reporting Initiative, which has become a key actor in developing a generally accepted set of reporting principles as part of the move to demand more transparency and disclosure from companies (see Chapter 6), and similarly spearheaded initiatives by companies such as Nike to disclose information on their supplier companies. Bavaria was also behind the founding of the Social Investment Forum and the more recently established Investor Network on Climate Risk.

Ceres was one of the early entrants into the corporate responsibility standards arena, but by no means the only important one. The Global Sullivan Principles already existed, as did numerous UN-promulgated standards. A wave of business scandals in the 1980s had generated numerous company-based codes of conduct focused mostly around compliance with anticorruption laws in US companies. But a new wave of codes with a far broader mandate was on the way. The early leader in this new trend was Levi Strauss with its code of conduct for its suppliers. That code made important advances and, as Alice Tepper Marlin noted in the last chapter, actually paved the way for SAI to develop in the first place. As also noted in the last chapter, the founding of SAI was strongly influenced by Levi Strauss's initiation of a code of conduct that applied throughout its supply chain. One person who was deeply immersed in developing the Levi Strauss code was difference maker Bob Dunn.

Bavaria is somewhat stunned by the rapid evolution of SRI and related institutions, noting,

> We thought it would probably take 50 years to actually achieve what Ceres and social investors wanted to achieve. It was just something for the distant future. But what has been true of Ceres and all of this stuff is that very often when you get a momentum going you almost can't stop it. One way or another you get going. Ceres announced the principles, and embedded in that announcement was the idea of reporting for companies. We had real disbelievers. Companies were saying they couldn't ever do this kind of reporting. Now there are 700 companies worldwide that are using the GRI criteria.

■ Robert H. (Bob) Dunn

Bob Dunn was chairman, president, and chief executive officer of Business for Social Responsibility (BSR) during its early days as a national organization. Prior to that, Dunn was vice president for corporate affairs at Levi Strauss & Co., where he played a leadership role in the development of the company's ground-breaking global code of conduct, as well as programs addressing Aids, community economic development, and racial discrimination. At the time of writing, Dunn serves as president and CEO of the Synergos Institute and as a member of its board of directors. In this chapter, we will look at how Dunn's early career led to the evolution of the Levi Strauss code of conduct, and pay more attention to his work with BSR in Chapter 7.

The stage was set for Dunn's leadership on an ethics code early on, as he relates in talking about his childhood:

> I was greatly influenced by family and particularly, I would say, one of my grandfathers, a very thoughtful, earnest, and ethical man who liked to engage me in conversation when I was a young boy. And I think also very much by each of my parents. They led a life of struggle, and so it was always possible to see what the consequences were of people working hard and somehow never catching the break they needed to provide them with the comfort and opportunity that they richly deserved. My father was a very gentle person with a highly developed sense of moral and ethical values. I think sometimes he was willing to adhere to them even if it interfered with his capacity to move along in the world of commerce. My mom was a registered nurse, a very compassionate and caring person who divided her career between the care of children and the care of elders. So at various times of growing up I had a chance to be close to kids who were seriously ill and also have a look at end-of-life experiences and how we provided for them. I think all of that was mixed together inside of me and made me sensitive to the civil rights struggles of the 1960s at a time when I was a college student and a law student.

A graduate of Brown University and Vanderbilt Law School, Dunn became immersed in and deeply influenced by the civil rights movement while studying law at Vanderbilt. He recalls,

> Through a set of serendipitous circumstances I chose to attend law school at Vanderbilt University. One of the circumstances was the offer of a very substantial scholarship, because I was pretty heavily in debt from my college education and wanted to avoid making that situation even worse by going to law school. I was in Nashville, Tennessee, at Vanderbilt from 1965 to 1968. I arrived and people were blocking the primary traffic artery in Nashville to try to force the racial integration issue onto one of the last hold-outs in the fast-food industry, an entity called Morrison's Cafeterias. I have no idea if they still exist. So I became involved in the law students' civil rights research council. It was a time when there were so-called race riots in Nashville. Martin Luther King was assassinated in Memphis while I was in Nashville, and there were armored personnel carriers rolling down the streets, and I was part of

> marches at the time, [part of] a whole range of activities. It seemed as
> though the civil rights struggle was a defining issue of our time, and I thought
> that if I spent at least a couple of years in the South that maybe it would help
> give me a clearer understanding of what the obstacles were to making
> progress in civil rights.

As with many of the difference makers, circumstances, in this case a family
tragedy, intervened to change the course of Dunn's life toward work on corporate
responsibility,

> I had intended to go into the Peace Corps after law school and was accepted,
> and then my sister was killed in a car accident during the last semester of law
> school, and it was a devastating blow to the family. I felt it made it inappro-
> priate for me to be going to be a legal advisor to the Micronesian islands.

Returning to his home state of Connecticut to take and pass the bar exam, while
spending time with his family, Dunn received a fortuitous phone call from Wesleyan University to be assistant dean and faculty member, a position that satisfied
his interests in civil rights because Wesleyan was a leader in creating a diverse student body at a time when tensions about civil rights were still high, and, as he notes,

> I had a colleague who was African-American, and the two of us spent a lot of
> our time trying to help create an environment of communication and trust
> and civility within the university. That often meant that I would work with a
> lot of white students and I would work with a lot of African-American stu-
> dents and we would try to find ways for groups to come together.

After a couple of years, Dunn left that position and went to work for the newly
elected governor of Wisconsin, Patrick J. Lucey. Within a year he had become executive secretary to the governor. Once again, Dunn's negotiating skills, which had
helped at Wesleyan, were called into play when he got involved in negotiating a settlement between a utility company and a Native American tribe that had earlier on
been precluded from participation in the development of a dam. When the governor was asked in the late 1970s by President Carter to become ambassador to Mexico, Dunn went to Mexico for two years as the ambassador's special assistant, which
was followed by an invitation to join the Carter White House team, and, ultimately,
the transition team when Carter left office.

Levi Strauss

In 1981, Dunn was recruited to work for Levi Strauss. Dunn recalls,

> Initially I was there to manage the communications function, and then over
> time the portfolio essentially became external relations, government rela-
> tions, the foundation, and community affairs, and, for a brief time, investor

relations. Early on it became obvious that the way that I could be most helpful to the company, and certainly an engagement that was of great importance to the family that owned the company, would be to focus attention on
issues of ethics and corporate responsibility, so that became my informal
portfolio. I attracted great people, who led all of the functions reporting in to
me, and began working on issues like a global code of conduct for the company, creating a global environmental council for the company, being one of
a cohort who looked at issues of work and family, helping to design a new
ethics training program for management and employees working on the
company's use of its resources for community investments. Levi's was really
moving forward with an initiative on HIV and Aids and one on racism, and
doing a lot of work on community economic development. The company
was prepared to innovate and play a leadership role, and there was a chance
to work with lots of other companies and to engage stakeholders, although it
wasn't called that at the time.

We see that the issues that Dunn worked on at Levi Strauss were initially the traditional corporate *social* responsibility issues — having to do largely with the charitable activities of the company. But, as the portfolio of activities grew, Dunn pushed
toward corporate responsibility — issues that deeply affected how the company
operated its business model: for example, issues relating to the work environment
for employees with obvious differences and engaging with stakeholders well
before the term became popular. Then came a critical innovation that had to do
with fundamental business practices. As Dunn comments,

We looked at some very big decisions, like the company's role in doing business in China. We spoke to government officials, NGOs and human rights
activists, and suppliers and customers and academics. What was obvious to
me, and to the chairman and CEO as well, was that paying attention to such
issues was how I could really make a contribution [to the company] and that
I was never going to be the kind of person who ought to be leading a business and focusing on trying to improve gross profit margins by a nickel on
tee-shirts or pants. So it was a pretty exciting time and after a while it
became apparent that, despite what I could do at Levi's, if there wasn't a way
to affect other companies, we would be just a blip, and that we wouldn't
really be using the resources of the private sector in ways that were not only
good for business but also good for society.

Levi Strauss pioneers a global code of conduct for suppliers

Dunn and others in the company began to raise concerns about the working conditions of factory workers in developing nations, who were producing the goods

that Levi Strauss sold in the late 1980s. Of course, external activism was already focusing on poor global labor standards and bad working conditions, so in some respects, the company had begun to feel this heat. Under Dunn's guidance, a working group at Levi Strauss began putting together what became the first-ever supplier code of conduct. The goal was to ensure that workers in all of the factories from which Levi Strauss sourced were being treated fairly and with dignity and had good working conditions. By 1991, Levi Strauss had issued its pioneering Global Sourcing and Operating Guidelines, which included both Country Assessment Guidelines and Business Partner Terms of Engagement.[84]

The Country Assessment Guidelines determined whether a country in which Levi Strauss wanted to place operations maintained suitable standards for health and safety, human rights, and the legal system, and its political, economic, and social environment. Importantly, for the emergence of other codes and standards that came later, Levi's guidelines also developed specific "terms of engagement" for all of the contractors and suppliers who manufactured or finished products for the company. The Business Partner Terms of Engagement detailed explicit expectations about ethical standards, legal requirements, environmental standards, and community involvement and improvement. Critically, the code outlined strict employment standards for suppliers, including forbidding child labor (for workers under 15 or under the compulsory school age, whichever is higher), no use of prison or forced labor, no corporal punishment, appropriate work hours (no more than 60 hours per week on a regular basis), and meeting local minimum wage requirements. In addition, the code demanded that suppliers permit freedom of association (e.g., to create unions), avoid discrimination, and provide a healthy and safe work environment. The company regularly evaluates its suppliers to ensure compliance with the code. Since 1991 the code has evolved and the Guidelines are the cornerstone of a three-level approach to responsible global sourcing that addresses core issues at factory, community, and government levels.

The Fair Labor Association and other developments

Despite early skepticism about the value of the code, in the years since 1991 many multinational corporations in the apparel industry have followed Levi Strauss's example and established codes and guidelines that apply to their own supply chains. In addition, many large and therefore visible multinationals, particularly those with supply chains to manage, have established codes of conduct that apply not only to their own operations, but also to their suppliers.

Other companies have also taken important initiatives of their own that moved both accountability and transparency forward and set a new bar for competitors that wished to convey an image of corporate responsibility. For example, in 1995 clothing giant Gap Inc., which owns Gap, Old Navy, and Banana Republic, under heavy fire from activists for its supply chain practices, was the first retailer to agree to external monitoring of its factories. Although some critics charge that Gap has not fully enforced the needed changes, nonetheless, this agreement paved the way for other companies not only to implement a code of conduct, as Levi Strauss did, but be held accountable to it by external groups. This innovation highlighted the need for organizations such as SAI to develop so that trained, independent auditors could implement the evaluation and monitoring of factories in developing nations, and so that globally acceptable standards could be developed outside the purview of any one company.

Today, it would be unusual to find a branded clothing retailer or almost any other brand-name company that sources from developing nations not to have a code of conduct that applies to its factories and covers issues of human and labor rights, and, frequently, the natural environment as well. Of course, the situation with non-brand-name companies is somewhat different since they have much less visibility. Nonetheless, footwear companies such as Nike, Reebok, and Adidas have faced similar issues to clothing retailers, and athletic and other equipment manufacturers have followed suit, responding with codes and, sometimes, monitoring, auditing, and even external certification. At the time of writing, 20 major companies have joined an industry association called the Fair Labor Association (FLA) and committed to rigorous workplace-standards implementation programs.[85] The FLA was formed in 1999 in response to the growing criticisms surrounding global sourcing practices, and as a way for companies to monitor themselves (and as a result has received some criticism from NGOs). The FLA and its members focus explicitly on ensuring that labor rights are upheld in developing nations. Standards are high. Joining the FLA means adopting its code of conduct (see Box 5.2) and implementing a comprehensive compliance program throughout the company's supply chain, a program that includes required independent audits conducted by external agencies. Although the FLA is sometimes criticized because it is company-driven rather than an independent regulatory body, it and similar entities represent an advance in determining what global standards around labor ought to be.

Box 5.2 **Fair Labor Association Workplace Code of Conduct**

Forced labor. There shall not be any use of forced labor, whether in the form of prison labor, indentured labor, bonded labor or otherwise.

Child labor. No person shall be employed at an age younger than 15 (or 14 where the law of the country of manufacture allows) or younger than the age for completing compulsory education in the country of manufacture where such age is higher than 15. *(continued over)*

Harassment or abuse. Every employee shall be treated with respect and dignity. No employee shall be subject to any physical, sexual, psychological or verbal harassment or abuse.

Non-discrimination. No person shall be subject to any discrimination in employment, including hiring, salary, benefits, advancement, discipline, termination or retirement, on the basis of gender, race, religion, age, disability, sexual orientation, nationality, political opinion, or social or ethnic origin.

Health and safety. Employers shall provide a safe and healthy working environment to prevent accidents and injury to health arising out of, linked with, or occurring in the course of work or as a result of the operation of employer facilities.

Freedom of association and collective bargaining. Employers shall recognize and respect the right of employees to freedom of association and collective bargaining.

Wages and benefits. Employers recognize that wages are essential to meeting employees' basic needs. Employers shall pay employees, as a floor, at least the minimum wage required by local law or the prevailing industry wage, whichever is higher, and shall provide legally mandated benefits.

Hours of work. Except in extraordinary business circumstances, employees shall (i) not be required to work more than the lesser of (a) 48 hours per week and 12 hours overtime or (b) the limits on regular and overtime hours allowed by the law of the country of manufacture or, where the laws of such country do not limit the hours of work, the regular work week in such country plus 12 hours overtime and (ii) be entitled to at least one day off in every seven day period.

Overtime compensation. In addition to their compensation for regular hours of work, employees shall be compensated for overtime hours at such premium rate as is legally required in the country of manufacture or, in those countries where such laws do not exist, at a rate at least equal to their regular hourly compensation rate.

Any Company that determines to adopt the Workplace Code of Conduct shall, in addition to complying with all applicable laws of the country of manufacture, comply with and support the Workplace Code of Conduct in accordance with [a set of] Principles of Monitoring and shall apply the higher standard in cases of differences or conflicts. Any Company that determines to adopt the Workplace Code of Conduct also shall require its licensees and contractors and, in the case of a retailer, its suppliers to comply with applicable local laws and with this Code in accordance with the Principles of Monitoring and to apply the higher standard in cases of differences or conflicts.[86]

Another example of relatively early momentum with respect to company codes of conduct is associated with agricultural production and purchasing, notably coffee, also as a response to external activism. Starbucks had come under significant pressure from US Labor Education in the Americas Project (LEAP) in 1995 for its purchasing policies. Starbucks stood accused of not paying fair prices for its coffee (although the company would claim that it always paid premium prices). Initially, Starbucks issued a "Framework for a Code of Conduct" in 1995, which stated that Starbucks would purchase from coffee producers who paid laborers a fair wage and respected fundamental rights. LEAP accused Starbucks of stalling when, after two years, the company had yet to produce a code, and by 1997 the company had agreed to develop one.[87] Starbuck's innovative Sourcing Guidelines, first issued in 2001 and revised in 2004, are now complemented by a Supplier Code of Conduct, first issued in 2003.[88] These guidelines focus on what Starbucks calls Coffee and Farmer Equity Practices, and are aimed at ensuring that specific indicators related to product quality, economic accountability and transparency, social responsibility, and environmental responsibility are met.

Of course, none of these companies' guidelines and codes of conduct assures perfection, since all have enormous supply chains in multiple countries. Indeed, since issuing their codes, virtually all of the companies have encountered criticism from activists and NGOs still concerned about their labor practices. But these few examples (which could be greatly expanded) highlight the progress that has been made since 1991 when Bob Dunn shepherded the very first company code of conduct. Prior to that development, labor standards in multinationals' supply chains were simply not on the corporate agenda. Within 17 years, it has become all but impossible for brand-name companies not to have a code, partly because of company leadership on the issue and in no small measure because of the ongoing activism directed against poor labor practices in developing countries.

While all of this development was going on inside companies, various coalitions were developing general sets of standards and principles that could be applied to any company. The next sections will discuss the Caux Round Table's principles (Steve Young), and what is probably today's most notable set of principles: the UN Global Compact principles (John Ruggie and Georg Kell).

◼ Steven B. (Steve) Young

Steve Young is global executive director of the Caux Round Table, which is a coalition of business leaders who want to build what they call moral capitalism and sustainable and socially responsible prosperity as the foundation for a fair, free, and transparent global society. A lawyer by training, Young was previously dean of the

Hamline University School of Law and assistant dean at Harvard Law School. Son of the ambassador to Thailand during the Kennedy presidency, he attended high school in Thailand then went on to Harvard College and Harvard Law School. In a varied career Young has, among other things, worked to open the United States to Vietnamese refugees during the mid-1970s, discovered (in 1966) the bronze-age site of Ban Chiang in northeast Thailand, now a UNESCO world heritage site, taught law and Vietnamese history, and written extensively on a range of topics including ethics, jurisprudence, the law of negligence, fiduciary theory, the status of refugees, Chinese moral and political theory, Vietnamese history, and the cultures and politics of Thailand and Vietnam.

Young gives a short summary of how he came to be at the Caux Round Table:

> I was brought back to Harvard Law School [after graduating] by then dean Al Sachs as the first sort of dean of students, which then led to another odd experience out of the blue. That was to be named dean of the Hamline University School of Law in St. Paul, Minnesota. Our family has been East Coast for generations, but we've now lived in Minnesota longer than anywhere else. So I moved out to Minnesota in 1981. After I stepped down as dean, I was in [law] practice, consultation, various things, and then a friend of mine who described himself as a recovering lawyer, Mike Olson, had been involved in the Caux Round Table through the Moral Re-Armament Network, out of which Caux Round Table came.

The Caux Round Table

Young recounts the early history of the Caux Round Table:

> The man who founded the Caux Round Table, Frederick (Frits) Phillips, was as a young man influenced by Frank Buchman [one of the founders of Alcoholics Anonymous and the Moral Re-Armament Network] before World War II. Phillips was interned during World War II. Then Phillips worked with the moral re-armament process until reconciliation between the French and the Germans, right after World War II. His notion was that in business and management the same overall philosophy/approach should apply. In other words, individual people in business, and especially business leaders, need to morally arm themselves to confront, to use Christian terminology, the wiles and snares of mammon and temptation. [This thinking] leads to a sense of right-mindedness and high aspirations, which then leads to a whole series of difficulties, because talk is cheap. What do you do? When you're running a company and you have customers and markets and this and that, and demands and failures and setbacks . . . So what do you do in the real world? This has been the challenge of the Caux Round Table.

The Caux Principles

The Caux Round Table,[89] was founded in 1986 by Frederick Phillips, then president of Phillips Electronics, together with Olivier Giscard d'Estaing, former vice-chairman of INSEAD, and initially focused on reducing trade tension. Urged by Ryuzaburo Kaku, then chairman of Canon, Inc., the Caux group of company leaders began to focus on global corporate responsibility, particularly as it influenced peace and security. This focus emerged out of a series of dialogues and conversations in 1994, and the evolution of an earlier set of principles called the Minnesota Principles into the Caux Principles. The Caux Principles ask businesses to use basic ethical principles in their business decisions. Today, of course, as we saw in Chapter 2, there are numerous sets of principles intended to help businesses behave more responsibility, but the Caux Principles were among the first to be directed at businesses generally, and, particularly, to have emerged from conversations by an international group of business leaders from Europe, the United States, and Japan.

The Caux Principles for Business, like others that have emerged since they were first promulgated in 1994 and presented to the UN in 1995, are aspirational. They are founded on a belief that business has a crucial role to play in successful societies. They are based on two ethical ideals: human dignity and the Japanese principle of *kyosei* or living together. Building on stakeholder thinking,[90] the Caux Principles take a "beyond shareholder to stakeholders" perspective. In addition, the principles also deal with the role of businesses in contributing to economic and social justice and development via the innovations that they can bring, developing a spirit of trust that goes beyond simple compliance with the law, respect for rules, multilateral trade, the natural environment, and avoidance of illicit operations. The Caux Principles also articulate specific ideals around a group of what we can call primary stakeholders: customers, employees, owners/investors, suppliers, communities, and even competitors (see Box 5.3).

Steve Young became involved with the Caux Round Table, as he recalls,

> [around] 1998–99. In 2000 the then chair of the Caux Round Table was Win Wallin [Chairman Emeritus, Medtronics, Inc.], because Caux has some Minnesota roots. Mike Olson was the staff person, and he deserves a lot of credit for facilitating the writing of the Caux Round Table Principles for Business between 1992 and 1994. Win wanted to take this notion of principled action and commitment to the issues of globalization of the late 1990s. [A key question was]: How does business, private business, capitalism respond to the imbalances in the world, where some people are very wealthy and many people are very poor?

Box 5.3 **The Caux Round Table Principles for Business**

Introduction

The Caux Round Table believes that the world business community should play an important role in improving economic and social conditions. As a statement of aspirations, this document aims to express a world standard against which business behavior can be measured. We seek to begin a process that identifies shared values, reconciles differing values, and thereby develops a shared perspective on business behavior acceptable to and honored by all.

These principles are rooted in two basic ethical ideals: *kyosei* and human dignity. The Japanese concept of *kyosei* means living and working together for the common good enabling cooperation and mutual prosperity to coexist with healthy and fair competition. Human dignity refers to the sacredness or value of each person as an end, not simply as a means to the fulfillment of others' purposes or even majority prescription.

The general principles in section 2 seek to clarify the spirit of *kyosei* and human dignity, while the specific stakeholder principles in section 3 are concerned with their practical application.

In its language and form, the document owes a substantial debt to the Minnesota Principles, a statement of business behavior developed by the Minnesota Center for Corporate Responsibility. The Center hosted and chaired the drafting committee, which included Japanese, European, and US representatives.

Business behavior can affect relationships among nations and the prosperity and well-being of us all. Business is often the first contact between nations and, by the way in which it causes social and economic changes, has a significant impact on the level of fear or confidence felt by people worldwide. Members of the Caux Round Table place their first emphasis on putting one's own house in order, and on seeking to establish what is right rather than who is right.

Section 1. Preamble

The mobility of employment, capital, products, and technology is making business increasingly global in its transaction and its effects.

Laws and market forces are necessary but insufficient guides for conduct.

Responsibility for the policies and actions of business and respect for the dignity and interests of its stakeholders are fundamental.

Shared values, including a commitment to shared prosperity, are as important for a global community as for communities of smaller scale.

For these reasons, and because business can be a powerful agent of positive social change, we offer the following principles as a foundation for dialogue and action by business leaders in search of business responsibility. In so doing, we affirm the necessity for moral values in business decision making. Without them, stable business relationships and a sustainable world community are impossible.

Section 2. General principles

Principle 1. The responsibilities of business: beyond shareholders toward stakeholders.

Principle 2. The economic and social impact of business: towards innovation, justice and world community.

Principle 3. Business behavior: beyond the letter of law, towards a spirit of trust.

Principle 4. Respect for rules.

Principle 5. Support for multilateral trade.

Principle 6. Respect for the environment.

Principle 7. Avoidance of illicit operations.

Section 3. Stakeholder principles

Customers

We believe in treating all customers with dignity, irrespective of whether they purchase our products and services directly from us or otherwise acquire them in the market. We therefore have a responsibility to:

- Provide our customers with the highest-quality products and services consistent with their requirements;
- Treat our customers fairly in all aspects of our business transactions, including a high level of service and remedies for their dissatisfaction;
- Make every effort to ensure that the health and safety of our customers, as well as the quality of their environment, will be sustained or enhanced by our products and service;
- Assure respect for human dignity in products offered, marketing, and advertising; and
- Respect the integrity of the culture of our customers.

Employees

We believe in the dignity of every employee and in taking employee interests seriously. We therefore have a responsibility to:

- Provide jobs and compensation that improve workers' living conditions;
- Provide working conditions that respect each employee's health and dignity;

- Be honest in communications with employees and open in sharing information, limited only by legal and competitive constraints;
- Listen to and, where possible, act on employee suggestions, ideas, requests, and complaints;
- Engage in good-faith negotiations when conflict arises;
- Avoid discriminatory practices and guarantee equal treatment and opportunity in areas such as gender, age, race, and religion;
- Promote in the business itself the employment of differently abled people in places of work where they can be genuinely useful;
- Protect employees from avoidable injury and illness in the workplace;
- Encourage and assist employees in developing relevant and transferable skills and knowledge; and
- Be sensitive to the serious unemployment problems frequently associated with business decision, and work with governments, employee groups, other agencies, and each other in addressing these dislocations.

Owners/investors

We believe in honoring the trust our investors place in us. We therefore have a responsibility to:

- Apply professional and diligent management in order to secure a fair and competitive return on our owners' investment;
- Disclose relevant information to owners/investors subject only to legal requirements and competitive constraints;
- Conserve, protect, and increase the owners'/investors' assets; and
- Respect owners'/investors' requests, suggestions, complaints, and formal resolutions.

Suppliers

Our relationship with suppliers and subcontractors must be based on mutual respect. We therefore have a responsibility to:

- Seek fairness and truthfulness in all our activities, including pricing, licensing, and rights to sell;
- Ensure that our business activities are free from coercion and unnecessary litigation;
- Foster long-term stability in the supplier relationship in return for value, quality, competitiveness, and reliability;
- Share information with suppliers and integrate them into our planning processes;
- Pay suppliers on time and in accordance with agreed terms of trade; and

- Seek, encourage, and prefer suppliers and subcontractors whose employment practices respect human dignity.

Competitors

We believe that fair economic competition is one of the basic requirements for increasing the wealth of nations and ultimately for making possible the just distribution of goods and services. We therefore have a responsibility to:

- Foster open markets for trade and investment;
- Promote competitive behavior that is socially and environmentally beneficial and demonstrates mutual respect among competitors;
- Refrain from either seeking or participating in questionable payments or favors to secure competitive advantages;
- Respect both tangible and intellectual property rights; and
- Refuse to acquire commercial information by dishonest or unethical means, such as industrial espionage.

Communities

We believe that as global corporate citizens we can contribute to such forces of reform and human rights as we are at work in the communities in which we operate. We therefore have a responsibility in the communities to:

- Support peace, security, diversity, and social integration;
- Respect the integrity of local cultures; and
- Be a good corporate citizen through charitable donations, educational and cultural contributions, and employee participation in community and civic affairs.[91]

Dealing with globalization

When Caux staffer Michael Olson ran into health problems, Wallin asked Young if he would help organize a planning meeting — and Young, with connections in the East, suggested that the meeting be held in Singapore. Young comments,

> [The meeting in Singapore] laid out a whole range of problems about where does capitalism go? What do business people want? It raises the problem, which is not widely recognized or acted upon, I think, in scholarship, that business people and capitalism run on risk aversion. The whole talk is about the entrepreneur and that is part of the system. If you studied business from the perspective of financial analysts, everything would be about reducing risk. Business people do risk–return trade-offs. If you want somebody to take some risk you really have to pay for it. If you deal with venture capitalists, not

only do you have to pay for risk in terms of the return, but they're always after you to lower the risk: Can you guarantee me my 25% return on the investment? Can you make sure the mayor gives us a sole source contract? Or they demand intellectual property rights.

Young details how business leaders in the Caux group think about the principles,

> Related to risk aversion is a phenomenon that Adam Smith noted, and people don't give the man credit for it, that business people in their heart of hearts don't like competition! Because competition is risk! So why would I want to do something where other people can come in and do a little better job and get the customers? Smith had that famous line about there never being a social gathering of business people where the conversation does not turn to how to create monopolies and cartels and harm the public.[92] So poor countries tend to be high-risk environments and you get a logical, rational circle of capitalism, which leads to the conclusion of the left that the rich get richer and the poor stay poor. And that's a fact. So what do we do about it? That's one of the challenges of the Caux Round Table.

Young talks about his own vision as it fits into what the Caux Round Table tries to accomplish, as influenced by his youth in Asia:

> Part of my sense of vision for people is that we should have a calling. We should have a mission. That is part of being fully human, and therefore having a calling and having a sense of mission means you need to step up to responsibilities, and you need to step up to social roles. The process of relying on intuition is rather intriguing and influenced by two concepts. One is the *trung dung*, which in Vietnamese is the golden mean, the concept of the mean. The mean is not the middle between two extremes. The mean could be an extreme position under certain circumstances.
>
> [*Trung dung* means] allowing ourselves to be guided by some intuitive appreciation of something else and trying to be ourselves, but at the same time having a sense of limitation and not trying to impose ourselves too much. Which raises an issue of constant awareness and alertness of Am I pushing too hard? If I'm getting resistance does that mean I give up?
>
> The second part of the vision is the sense of the social — the cultural, the interconnectedness, whether it's to the environment, other people or parents or previous generations or future generations [which has become an important element of sustainability discussions].

Moving the Caux Principles forward

Young elaborates how the Caux Round Table is moving the principles into a new stage, now that they have been around for a while,

> When you start from principles that are universal, think about the human condition, and think about a better world, [these seven Caux Round Table Principles for Business] go everywhere. So you're already thinking about how you implement them and how you get people on board the environment, lack of corruption, free trade, customers, employees, investors, suppliers, competitors and community. So we're evolving, I think, from the intuition of these guys who came up with the principles, into a kind of think-tank, conditioned by experienced business people from different cultures, particularly Japan, Europe and the United States, but we're adding more.

Notably, this evolution is quite similar to the one that Ceres is undergoing.

The recognition that principles standing alone are not enough characterizes the development of the Caux Round Table and, as we shall see below, also the even broader UN Global Compact principles. Young emphasizes,

> It's a think-tank of people who have experience in business but some extra dimension, dimension X, which is either a worry or a moral basis. A lot of these men — not that many women have been involved — have religious [inclinations] and they also have an interest in the right-brain, intuitive cast of their minds, I've noticed. Or they tend to jump to conclusions, which then makes it hard for them to backtrack and do the written documentation, the implementation. Still, they have tended to be executives coming out of successful product structures, where you make a product and the product moves. You're a finance guy. You've got a lot of money people who come to you. The notion of proselytizing is uncomfortable for them.

Given this background and the need to ensure that the principles are implemented, the Caux Round Table has taken on new challenges, as Young relates:

> One of the things I've been trying to work with in the Caux Round Table is to add fellows, add dialogue, discussions, relationships, papers, things, so that you take the core, the vision, and the principles, and you have ways of putting it all into frameworks and discourses and comfort levels which other people can relate to. We've developed an implementation guide based on the Baldrige National Quality Award implementation process for managers. We have a feeling that corporate boards are the black hole of capitalism, especially American capitalism. So how do you build up boards to perform the functions they were given in law, which is to be the stewards and the guides and the conscience of the entity, right? So we're pioneering a certifi-

cate training program for corporate directors in Minnesota, based on concepts of fiduciary law and stewardship.

Principles for Responsible Globalization

Over time, the Caux Round Table has developed numerous new initiatives to foster better implementation of the principles. One of these initiatives involves creating dialogues for senior business leaders, thought leaders, and opinion leaders on issues of global poverty, legal and regulatory challenges in developing nations, and improving investment environments in selected developing countries. To enhance this effort, the Caux Round Table has drafted a set of Principles for Government as part of a larger set of Principles for Responsible Globalization,[93] and more recently a set of Principles for NGOs.[94] This broad set of principles recognizes the important roles that all three sectors, business, government, and NGOs, play in the globalization process — and that entities in each sector need to behave responsibly to ensure a secure and healthy future.

The Principles for Responsible Government, which are supplemented by a handbook, *Moral Government*, argue that "public power is held in trust for the community," as a fundamental principle, and set forth eight general principles, with attendant explanations (see Box 5.4).

Box 5.4 **The Caux Round Table Principles for Responsible Government**

1. Discourse ethics should guide application of public power
2. The Civic Order shall serve all those who accept the responsibilities of citizenship
3. Public Servants shall refrain from abuse of office, corruption and shall demonstrate high levels of personal integrity
4. Security of persons, individual liberty and ownership of property are the foundation for individual justice
5. Justice shall be provided
6. General welfare contemplates improving the well-being of individual citizens
7. Transparency of government ensures accountability
8. Global cooperation advances national welfare[95]

Because many NGOs claim to represent the public interest or take a moral stand in their work, and because of its fundamental belief in *kyosei* — together-living —

Caux believes that NGOs also need to live up to principles that make integrity and cooperation possible. The fundamental principle for NGOs is that an NGO should not "adversely affect the peoples, communities, or natural resources that it touches" and that they live up to and be transparent about their service, mission and objectives, governance, actions, and the means chosen to achieve objectives.[96] Caux also gives a set of "derived principles" to which it believes NGOs should adhere: independence, representation, participation, respect for law, care, integrity, and accountability.[97]

Toward what end?

Young argues that the need for an entity like the Caux Round Table is twofold, but not necessarily widely accepted, particularly in US culture today:

> The whole justification for the American way of business is short term, seek profit, determine what the short-term dollar return is, maximize shareholder returns. And that's the moral norm. But nobody is saying anything about what the *shareholders* should be doing or thinking. Do the owners of property have any moral responsibilities to go to their financial advisors and say, "Don't get me 10% next year, I can live on a 3% return. What I want you to do is put the money in companies that are really going to clean up the environment" or something like that? Are there any financial advisors who have a sense of fiduciary relationship where they should ask their clients these kinds of questions?

There are numerous obstacles, of course, to fully achieving the Caux vision, just as the rest of the difference makers have faced obstacles in achieving their visions. Young comments,

> We're up against a culture of the times. We live in a time of basically cynicism, disbelief, nihilism, and selfishness. I have two thoughts about that. One is the old thing that they used to say about Eleanor Roosevelt: better to light a candle than curse the darkness. But a tiny candle doesn't necessarily dispel the arguments. One thing is to light the candle. But you've got to get a lot of candles.

That lighting of many candles may help to explain the rapid proliferation of codes of conduct and sets of principles that have evolved in the years since the earliest ones were drawn up. The final section of this chapter will focus on what is probably the best-known set of principles today, the UN Global Compact's ten principles, drafted for then UN Secretary-General Kofi Annan by John Ruggie and implemented by Georg Kell.

■ John Ruggie

John Ruggie, Evron and Jeane Kirkpatrick Professor of International Affairs and director of the Mossavar-Rahmani Center for Business and Government at Harvard University's Kennedy School of Government Center for Business and Government, considers himself a bimodal person. In addition to his role at Harvard, he also serves as the UN secretary-general's special representative for business and human rights, appointed by then Secretary-General Kofi Annan. He had previously served as assistant secretary-general and chief adviser for strategic planning to the secretary-general. Prior to joining Harvard, he had served as dean of Columbia University's School of International and Public Affairs and for many years before that as a faculty member at Columbia, where his theoretical work on international relations was widely acclaimed. His academic work deals with the impact of globalization on global rule making and the evolving global political order. He has published six books (and dozens of articles), including *Winning the Peace: America and World Order in the New Era* and *Constructing the World Polity*.

But it is the practical side of his work where his impact on the responsibility assurance infrastructure is prominent and which makes Ruggie a real difference maker. From 1999 he designed and managed the earliest days of the UN Global Compact, which has since become the world's largest corporate citizenship initiative with, at the time of writing (2008), nearly 5,000 participants, including over 3,700 businesses, and which is now run by another of our difference makers, Georg Kell. In addition to Ruggie's critical role as the special representative to the UN on business and human rights, where he is responsible for drafting a set of human rights principles, Ruggie was the idea person behind the UN Millennium Development Goals and played a lead role in the associated UN Millennium Summit in 2000.

Born into a poor family in Austria in 1944, Ruggie learned early about how challenging life can be. When he entered graduate school he became interested in the study of change and transformation, or, as he puts it,

> Economic crises, social classes, and inequality. How do things improve? How does one make things improve? Those were just part and parcel of my early life. Then when I got to graduate school I discovered that there is actually a way to study this [subject] in an organized fashion. So I became a political scientist doing just that. I've always had this sort of bimodal professional existence. Most of my academic work has been highly theoretical, and the influence that it has had on the discipline has been because of the theoretical contributions. But I've also always had an interest in making things happen — sort of the plumbing side. Once we [Ruggie and his wife of more than 40 years] moved to New York, which was in 1978, I started interacting more and more with the UN.

In 1997, Ruggie was dean of the School of International Affairs at Columbia when Kofi Annan was elected as secretary-general of the United Nations. Ruggie recalls,

> I had met him before, and a number of mutual friends had suggested that it might be interesting for me and useful for him if we could work out some sort of relationship. So he invited me to lunch and he asked me on the spot to come and work for him full-time. I asked, "What's my job description?" He replied, "Don't get swallowed up by the in-box." That became the basis of what is now a regular position of assistant secretary-general for strategic planning. We made it up as we went along. Part of that was to begin to develop more systematic relationships and better relationships between the UN, the business community, and civil society. That was how we gradually moved toward creation of the Global Compact and [several] other things.

The UN Global Compact

The UN Global Compact originated in a speech given by Kofi Annan at the World Economic Forum in January 1999 and has since become the world's largest corporate citizenship initiative. The Global Compact consists of ten (originally nine) principles around human rights, labor rights, the natural environment, and anti-corruption, and is based on internationally agreed documents.

The Global Compact's website gave in 2007 the following goal for the compact and its objectives:

> Through the power of collective action, the Global Compact seeks to promote responsible corporate citizenship so that business can be part of the solution to the challenges of globalization. In this way, the private sector — in partnership with other social actors — can help realize the Secretary-General's vision: a more sustainable and inclusive global economy.[98]

It is a voluntary initiative to which companies and other organizations can sign up if they agree to uphold the ten principles. The Global Compact has two objectives:

- To mainstream the ten principles in business activities around the world

- To catalyze actions in support of UN goals[99]

Because the Global Compact is a voluntary initiative and its goals are aspirational, it lacks enforcement mechanisms or capacity, other than delisting companies that are not actively engaging the principles and reporting as required. It operates through other voluntary mechanisms to leverage the moral persuasion of the UN. Among these mechanisms are policy dialogues, learning forums, including conferences and other convenings, actively engaged country and regional networks, and a wide range of partnership projects.

Ruggie recalls the fortuitous way that the Global Compact began — or rather almost didn't begin:

> The Global Compact was an accidental program. We knew we needed to establish better relationships with the business community, and it was obvious that foreign investment far overshadowed official development assistance to developing countries. If developing countries were going to make any progress in economic development and poverty alleviation, and if the UN was going to meet its own objectives in the areas of development, environment, human rights, and a host of other areas, we needed to work with the corporate sector because it had enormous reach and capacity. So we encouraged the secretary-general to accept invitations to Davos, for example, to get out there and to engage more. He was invited to come to the Davos [World Economic Forum] meeting in January of 1999. He had been the year before just to say "Hello, I'm the new secretary-general," and he wasn't sure he wanted to go back for a second year running, unless there was something specific that he could propose. As he put it, "If we can put a challenge before the business leaders, I'll consider going. But otherwise I think I'll skip this year."
>
> My junior colleague Georg Kell and I had been thinking about how to frame the [UN's] engagement with business, so it wasn't a total fluke, and it didn't come out of the blue, but we didn't have a lot of time to prepare the speech itself. It contained the elements of what became the Global Compact, except it wasn't intended as a program. It was intended as a challenge to the business community, and then we were all going to go home and get on with other things.

Ruggie grins wryly as he observes, "The reception was so positive that in a sense we had to turn [the speech] into a program, so we spent the next 18 months, turning it into a program. Then we rolled it out on July 26, 2000." What Ruggie and Georg Kell, now executive head of the UN Global Compact, rolled out was originally a set of nine principles drawn from UN documents, with the tenth anticorruption principle added at the Global Compact Leaders Summit, in June 2004, which was enabled by broad international endorsement of the UN Convention against Corruption, on October 31, 2003.

Box 5.5 **The Global Compact's Ten Principles**

Human Rights

Principle 1: Businesses should support and respect the protection of internationally proclaimed human rights; and

Principle 2: make sure that they are not complicit in human rights abuses.

Labor Standards

Principle 3: Businesses should uphold the freedom of association and the effective recognition of the right to collective bargaining;

Principle 4: the elimination of all forms of forced and compulsory labor;

Principle 5: the effective abolition of child labor; and

Principle 6: the elimination of discrimination in respect of employment and occupation.

Environment

Principle 7: Businesses should support a precautionary approach to environmental challenges;

Principle 8: undertake initiatives to promote greater environmental responsibility; and

Principle 9: encourage the development and diffusion of environmentally friendly technologies.

Anticorruption

Principle 10: Businesses should work against corruption in all its forms, including extortion and bribery.[100]

■ Georg Kell

Georg Kell was born in post-World War II Germany in what he characterizes as a "very brutal environment" and "fairly modest conditions." Lucky enough to be encouraged by several good teachers, and attracted more to sciences such as math and physics than to social sciences, he studied engineering and economics at the Technical University in Berlin and began a PhD, never completed, at the Fraunhofer Institute. Thus, he became involved as a very young man by what he calls the hippie revolution in Germany, in which younger people forced their elders to come to grips with Germany's past, which triggered a sense that a "broader vision of peaceful coexistence and understanding is the most important asset we have in life and the most precious one." Then he made a life-changing decision to move to Tanzania, in East Africa, at the age of 31, where he worked on development issues for four years with the UN. There he learned to "question many assumptions I had from my education, and about economic principles of efficiencies," and, as he comments, "I was drawn to the UN early on. Already in these years I saw in the UN the embodiment of hope for many. So that is really where my love affair with the UN started."

After four years as a financial analyst, he basically started his career over, joining the UN in Geneva doing research on trade and investment in the macroeconomy. In Geneva, he began working for the United Nations Conference on Trade and Development (UNCTAD), learned about politics, and developed what he calls an

> obsession to look at the world in pragmatic terms, in non-ideological terms. I always regretted that ideology and sometimes religion can be a hindrance to cooperation. The idea of pragmatism trumping ideology — I carried it in me from the beginning and am a strong believer in productivity and efficiency as a means to organizing economic life. I saw enormous opportunities in the UN to advance that thinking.

The emerging notion of a Global Compact between business and society was therefore attractive to Kell, who provides more background on the compact's origins:

> Prior to the Global Compact speech, I had already been working on the subject of the UN and business extensively, and we came up with policy statements with the International Chamber of Commerce. I convinced the secretary-general and John Ruggie, who fully understood this approach and supported it, that business and the UN had much more in common than was articulated in their joint undertakings. That it was time to overcome the idolatries of the past. That, as there is more and more interdependence between nations and cultures, there was a premium for supportive services, and the UN indeed offered many of these services, whether it's on poverty, environ-

ment, security. And that indeed a strong UN should actually be in the interest of the business world to reduce externalities, negative externalities, insecurity, and provide a little bit more credibility.

The Global Compact

Prior to the 1999 World Economic Forum, Kell had helped to write other speeches for the secretary-general and had also done several studies on related topics, which served as excellent background for understanding which activities the UN might become involved in that would support and help stabilize markets and create the conditions for wealth creation in developing nations. Kell illustrates the connections that he, Ruggie, and Kofi Annan were making:

> The Global Compact speech was a kind of logical extension of these arguments, but a lot of research was invested into this particular speech, six months to be precise. We knew we would hit the feeling of the day then, one year before Seattle [antiglobalization demonstrations]. The backlash against globalization was in the making. The need for a constructive engagement became apparent and the strength of the UN in offering in principle part of the solution was right before our eyes. Then it was just a question of putting it together in a manner that was appealing and would get through to CEOs.

The outcome was certainly not a foregone conclusion, though, as Kell recalls:

> When Kofi Annan delivered the speech, for an hour before I was nervous like never in my life before, because I knew we would hit the mark. It was pretty obvious. But the question was: would the message be understood in this way? It was probably the greatest excitement of my life when I could feel in the plenary [session of the World Economic Forum] how Kofi Annan's words, as he delivered the statement, were actually felt in the room, and how you could almost *feel* how the words set into motion reflective thinking, which presumably laid a foundation for the willingness to engage on a long-term basis in the Compact.

John Ruggie also points out how the stars aligned to make the moment right for Annan's speech, and points to some of his earlier academic work:

> There were a number of issues that came together. One of them was a direct outgrowth of some academic work I'd done. Back in the 1980s, I published [articles] on the concept of embedded liberalism, which looked back at how the industrialized countries responded to the collapse of the Victorian era of globalization after World War I, and the failure of trying to reconstruct a *laissez-faire* international economic system in the 1930s. [They learned] the lesson that you need to reconcile markets with shared social values and

safety nets and social investments and all the rest of it. Social democracy or the social market economy or the New Deal in the United States, whatever it was called, did reconcile those forces more effectively than had been done before.

But the premise of all of those innovations had been that markets were essentially national, with external interactions among the national markets, but not that they were globally integrated. Once markets began to be globally integrated, those sorts of social compromises or social bargains, if you will, began to get frayed. The challenge, as we defined it, was that we needed to do at the global level what the industrialized world had learned to do at the national level — except that was going to be infinitely harder because there is no central government at the global level. Anyway, that was one major stream that went into the thinking of the Global Compact.

The other [major stream] was the sheer capacity of the business community to help meet UN objectives, including in relation to poverty and the environment and human rights. In the beginning there were just the two of us, and Georg [Kell] was working for the deputy secretary-general as a junior economics officer, until he and I conspired to steal him from her, which eventually we did formally. I worked part-time on the Global Compact, but Georg began to work full-time on operationalizing this thing, pulling together the various stakeholders, labor, the NGOs, the internal articulation of the effort with the UN agencies, which typically is the hardest part, because everyone else cooperates but not the UN itself. Those things all worked out over the course of 18 months with a lot of trial and error. Then we went public in July 2000, with [apparently] 50 companies but that was a lie. It was actually 47 including Nike, and we caught a lot of crap for that. The people at Nike still remember that we were at a press briefing and somebody asked Kofi words to the effect of: "So you don't mind doing business with the devil?" His response, without batting an eyelash, was "There's no need to convert the angels."

Coalitions and partnerships

In many ways the UN Global Compact is a unique institution: for instance, in its aspirational qualities. But, in a very real sense, it also played an important role in linking typically separate UN agencies because the principles themselves encompassed arenas typically emphasized by different agencies. Today, six UN agencies are engaged with the Global Compact, which is run out of the secretary-general's office in an effort to avoid some of the bureaucracy of UN agencies. The six agencies are the Office of the High Commissioner on Human Rights (OHCHR), the International Labour Organization (ILO), the UN Environment Program (UNEP), the UN

Office on Drugs and Crime (UNODC), the UN Development Program (UNDP), and the UN Industrial Development Organization (UNIDO).

Georg Kell reflects on the evolution of the Compact:

> The evolution of the Compact was quite exciting and still is. The problem came in really building something up in an organization that is basically hostile towards innovation, which still in many quarters regarded business as something alien, something that doesn't really belong here. So there was enormous resistance here within the house. Building up the initiative then over the next five or six years was really tough work and required a lot of determination. There were many, many serious obstacles.

The whole enterprise was built on a shoestring because, as Kell points out, it had not been planned as a program:

> The reaction to the speech was so overwhelming, because CEOs wrote the secretary-general and ambassadors here in New York; the UK and Swiss ambassadors especially, said: "These are great words. It's exactly what we need. But now, Secretary-General, please do more than just speeches. Translate this into an operational context." We had no funding, no money. The secretary-general gave me $20,000 out of his own trust fund and asked, "Can you do something with this?" [he chuckles wryly] The money proved sufficient to build a website and rally, initially, four UN agencies around the effort, the ILO, UNIDO, UNEP, and the OHCHR.

It wasn't easy going, despite the support from Annan, CEOs, and UN agencies. Kell recollects,

> We started off quite naive because, while at the rhetorical macro-level we knew what we were talking about, when it then came to firm, specific rationales as to why and what and how, we discovered that engaging on a sustained basis was easier said than done. The multi-stakeholder tensions at that point in time were enormous with labor, with civil society. I visited global labor. I made some gross mistakes initially. I had to do some quick learning on global justice and the labor agenda and the politics behind them. The same with the environmental NGOs, with the human rights NGOs and the developmental NGOs. But it all more or less fell into place because the idea of the Global Compact was appealing to many of them. The operational concepts that one could work out on a scalable level, while not clear, were early on recognized as having to do with dialogue, learning, and partnership projects. So these conceptual elements then were thrashed out in multi-stakeholder dialogue sessions, until we had sufficient initial corporate buy-in to stage a launch event here in New York in 2000 with initially only 47 CEOs, labor, and about a dozen NGO leaders.

Dialogue and learning at the core

Understanding that learning and dialogue would be the key to successful implementation of a global compact without any enforcement powers, Kell and his small staff of associates have developed extensive networks globally. He remembers that, right after the launch in 2000,

> Basically we were saying the idea is now born as an operational thing, and all we know at this point is that we have to build up support structures for learning, for dialogue, and for partnership projects. If you want to make this scalable, we need to embed it in the local context, but we also need to nurture the idea globally. These ideas were in essence the big building blocks from the beginning. Ever since then we have worked with this kind of framework. And the beauty of the thing is that the idea is self-sustained because the idea is also extremely appealing to CEOs from emerging economies [as well as developed economies].

In addition to the 3,700 businesses that had joined the Compact by 2007, it also had linkages with the UN agencies noted above, business associations around the world, labor and trade unions globally, numerous local and global NGOs, governments, and a worldwide academic network. To ground its work in dialogue and learning, the Global Compact offers a series of action-oriented meetings annually, which it calls multi-sector Global Policy Dialogues. The Global Compact has also established or encouraged the development of local networks at the country and regional levels, which support the implementation of the ten principles, mutual learning, and information exchange by convening their own meetings on issues related to globalization and related matters.

Since learning is also an integral part of the Compact, all participating companies are invited – and expected – to share examples of their Compact-related best practices. In addition, the compact encourages development of in-depth case studies and related analyses that can be disseminated to various instructional resources. The other important element of the Compact's evolving strategy encompasses partnerships between participating companies and UN agencies and civil society organizations, particularly around implementation of UN goals.

Kell reflects,

> It has been a tremendously rewarding experience in terms of growth, but the thing that has always been fascinating is that the idea itself remains; that's the beauty of it. Every country's different. Every story is different. The politics play out differently. But the bottom line is always the same. Pragmatism – practical solutions – *can* trump politics. They can trump political ideology, and hopefully they can also trump at some point fanaticism and religious ideology. It's a simple belief system in that you can do better if you focus on the

essential problem-solving component of it. It's almost like looking at problems in the world, not from an ideological or religious perspective, but from a purely pragmatic angle. And I'm quite aware that this approach can be accused of being naive because of *realpolitik*, so to speak. History again and again shows that other forces are more dominant, yet I like to believe that, if one has to believe in something, with what human beings are capable of, it also must be in the collective ability to find pragmatic solutions in a non-ideological manner.

Principles for Responsible Investment

Another piece of the Global Compact's work has been to tackle the dominant economic logic of shareholder capitalism. In what becomes a familiar pattern among the institutions building the responsibility assurance infrastructure, the Global Compact has branched out and in April 2006 launched the Principles for Responsible Investment with the collaboration, involvement, and commitment of the heads of financial institutions from 16 countries. By mid-2007 the group of signatories represented more than US$8 trillion in assets. These principles recognize the importance of a long-term perspective on investments, rather than the notoriously short-term outlook favored by many analysts and institutional investors (see Box 5.6).

Principles for Responsible Management Education

Another recent innovation is a set of Principles for Responsible Management Education presented at the July 2007 World Leaders Forum in Geneva, Switzerland (see Box 5.7).

Practical solutions to difficult problems associated with globalization have been what many difference makers have focused on. After birthing the initial idea for the Global Compact with Georg Kell, John Ruggie focused on some of the other UN goals — and generated what have become known as the Millennium Development Goals.

Box 5.6 **Principles for Responsible Investment**

As institutional investors, we have a duty to act in the best long-term interests of our beneficiaries. In this fiduciary role, we believe that environmental, social, and corporate governance (ESG) issues can affect the performance of investment portfolios (to varying degrees across companies, sectors, regions, asset classes and through time). We also recognise that applying these Principles may better align investors with broader objectives of society. Therefore, where consistent with our fiduciary responsibilities, we commit to the following:

1. We will incorporate ESG issues into investment analysis and decision-making processes.

2. We will be active owners and incorporate ESG issues into our ownership policies and practices.

3. We will seek appropriate disclosure on ESG issues by the entities in which we invest.

4. We will promote acceptance and implementation of the Principles within the investment industry.

5. We will work together to enhance our effectiveness in implementing the Principles.

6. We will each report on our activities and progress towards implementing the Principles.

In signing the Principles, we as investors publicly commit to adopt and implement them, where consistent with our fiduciary responsibilities. We also commit to evaluate the effectiveness and improve the content of the Principles over time. We believe this will improve our ability to meet commitments to beneficiaries as well as better align our investment activities with the broader interests of society.

We encourage other investors to adopt the Principles.[101]

Box 5.7 **Principles for Responsible Management Education**

As institutions of higher learning involved in the education of current and future managers we are voluntarily committed to engaging in a continuous process of improvement in the application of the following Principles, reporting on progress to all our stakeholders and exchanging effective practices with other academic institutions:

Principle 1. Purpose: We will develop the capabilities of students to be future generators of sustainable value for business and society at large and to work for an inclusive and sustainable global economy.

Principle 2. Values: We will incorporate into our academic activities and curricula the values of global social responsibility as portrayed in international initiatives such as the United Nations Global Compact.

Principle 3. Method: We will create educational frameworks, materials, processes and environments that enable effective learning experiences for responsible leadership.

Principle 4. Research: We will engage in conceptual and empirical research that advances our understanding about the role, dynamics, and impact of corporations in the creation of sustainable social, environmental and economic value.

Principle 5. Partnership: We will interact with managers of business corporations to extend our knowledge of their challenges in meeting social and environmental responsibilities and to explore jointly effective approaches to meeting these challenges.

Principle 6. Dialog: We will facilitate and support dialog and debate among educators, business, government, consumers, media, civil society organizations and other interested groups and stakeholders on critical issues related to global social responsibility and sustainability.

We understand that our own organizational practices should serve as example of the values and attitudes we convey to our students.

We encourage other academic institutions, associations and accrediting bodies to adopt and support these Principles.[102]

■ John Ruggie: broadening scope

Millennium Development Goals

About the time the Global Compact was being launched, John Ruggie was involved in other efforts to create new standards in the world. As he puts it, "I then went on to – I don't know what the right verb is, I guess – 'invent' the Millennium Development Goals." In September 2000, the heads of state of 189 countries had gathered in New York and adopted the Millennium Declaration, which was then signed by 147 heads of state and government.

The Millennium Declaration recognized their "collective responsibility to uphold the principles of human dignity, equality and equity at the global level."[103] The Declaration argued that the "central challenge we face today is to ensure that globalization becomes a positive force for all the world's people,"[104] and that freedom, security, equality, solidarity, tolerance, respect for nature, and shared responsibility are essential components and goals of international relations in the 21st century. In addition to arguing for peace, security, and disarmament, the Millennium Declaration went on to argue that poverty eradication and economic development were essential aspects of achieving the fundamental goals. The Declaration articulated specific goals and targets related to poverty reduction and development, environmental protection, human rights, democracy, good governance, and protecting the vulnerable, particularly meeting the needs of Africa

While the Millennium Declaration articulated specific goals and targets, it was John Ruggie, once again, who articulated these goals in the way that caught public attention – as the Millennium Development Goals (see Box 5.8). Ruggie explains their genesis:

> The UN has been involved in target setting of one sort or another for a long time. The opportunity of the Millennium Summit was just too good not to exploit. We knew, or at least we hoped, we were going to have heads of state, heads of government from at least 150 countries come. From the beginning we wanted to make sure that [the Summit] wasn't simply a celebratory event, as the 50th anniversary had been, but that we could actually mobilize their presence in support of something important. So I was given the job of producing the secretary-general's report for the Summit. Andy Mack, an innovative and irreverent Australian whom I hired worked with me very closely on that, and we had a small team. The report was very well received. It was called "We The Peoples: The United Nations in the 21st Century." It was in part an empirical analysis of dominant trends. And then it became a more normative statement of: "Given that these are the dominant trends, how do we best meet UN objectives and what kind of approaches can we articulate and have the Summit endorse?"

Box 5.8 **The Millennium Development Goals**

1. Eradicate extreme poverty and hunger
  - Reduce by half the proportion of people living on less than one US dollar a day.
  - Reduce by half the proportion of people who suffer from hunger.
  - Increase the amount of food for those who suffer from hunger.

2. Achieve universal primary education
  - Ensure that all boys and girls complete a full course of primary schooling.
  - Increased enrollment must be accompanied by efforts to ensure that all children remain in school and receive a high-quality education.

3. Promote gender equality and empower women
  - Eliminate gender disparity in primary and secondary education preferably by 2005, and at all levels by 2015.

4. Reduce child mortality
  - Reduce the mortality rate among children under five by two thirds.

5. Improve maternal health
  - Reduce by three quarters the maternal mortality ratio.

6. Combat HIV/Aids, malaria, and other diseases
  - Halt and begin to reverse the spread of HIV/Aids.
  - Halt and begin to reverse the incidence of malaria and other major diseases.

7. Ensure environmental sustainability
  - Integrate the principles of sustainable development into country policies and programmes; reverse loss of environmental resources.
  - Reduce by half the proportion of people without sustainable access to safe drinking water (for more information see the entry on water supply).
  - Achieve significant improvement in lives of at least 100 million slum dwellers, by 2020.

8. Develop a global partnership for development
  - Develop further an open trading and financial system that is rule-based, predictable and non-discriminatory. Includes a commitment to good governance, development and poverty reduction — nationally and internationally.
  - Address the least developed countries' special needs. This includes tariff- and quota-free access for their exports; enhanced debt relief for

(continued over)

heavily indebted poor countries; cancellation of official bilateral debt; and more generous official development assistance for countries committed to poverty reduction.

- Address the special needs of landlocked and small island developing States.
- Deal comprehensively with developing countries' debt problems through national and international measures to make debt sustainable in the long term.
- In cooperation with the developing countries, develop decent and productive work for youth.
- In cooperation with pharmaceutical companies, provide access to affordable essential drugs in developing countries.
- In cooperation with the private sector, make available the benefits of new technologies — especially information and communications technologies.[105]

So the Millennium Development Goals, which were baked into the Declaration of the Summit, and which I drafted, stipulated that the Summit endorse [the Declaration] at the highest political level that is possible in the world. It had a number of goals with regard to poverty reduction, girls' education, health, and so on. It went through with only minor objections. The following year came the test of operationalizing all of this and trying to get the entire UN system involved. I was on my way out by then, but the fact that you had the endorsement of fairly concrete targets like this by the heads of state made it much easier to go to the World Bank, or WHO, or whoever and say, "Look, the presidents and prime ministers of the whole world signed on to this — it was not just a general assembly resolution — these are *your* bosses, too, and they expect us to work together." So it got traction inside the system as a whole.

Ruggie comments on other important facets of the way the Millennium Development Goals were designed:

This kind of an approach is something that appeals to business. You've got measurable objectives. You can see who is contributing what and who is falling short. That made it very useful as a business engagement tool. [Then,] and I didn't quite know how this would happen, but I remember saying in interviews at the time that the Millennium Development Goals would become part of political processes, too. Recently during the parliamentary Ugandan election, somebody sent me a clipping about a candidate running against an incumbent complaining that not enough had been done to meet the Millennium Development Goals and so "throw the bums out and elect me." [Ruggie chuckles] So we thought about it in all of these ways: in terms of mobilizing the UN system and the Bretton Woods institutions behind a common set of objectives that belong to everybody, business engagement, and then broadly social mobilization. I think that it's worked remarkably well in all of those respects. Obviously, it hasn't solved all the world's problems, but no single thing does.

Human rights

Always ready for a new challenge, Ruggie accepted Kofi Annan's invitation in July 2005 to serve as his special assistant to the secretary-general for human rights — a part-time pro bono assignment that became an all-consuming effort. Ruggie notes wryly,

> Well, in some ways that's the hardest assignment I've had. It has a history. The Geneva process, the Sub-Commission on Human Rights, at about the same time that the Global Compact was getting going, drafted a set of "norms" for business and human rights, and the two had been evolving in parallel. The norms process initially started out to clearly articulate the standards that business ought to respect with regard to human rights. That is a perfectly straightforward and sensible question to ask, but it got carried away, claiming, for example, that certain human rights standards that states hadn't even accepted for themselves now had "non-voluntary" effects on companies worldwide. The company lawyers were saying, 'How did this happen? Where were we?' And I asked, "What does this do to governance? Companies are not democratic public interest institutions. They serve particular economic functions." [The original process] made the argument that essentially the only thing that differed between states and companies is their sphere of influence, that within their respective spheres of influence the obligations of states and companies for human rights were basically identical. Well, the world doesn't work that way, and it shouldn't.

The politics made the situation that Ruggie entered difficult, as he recollects:

> You had business on one side, NGOs on the other, and governments not sure of what to do. In 2003 the sub-commission endorsed the norms and sent them up to its parent body, the Commission on Human Rights. But the Commission didn't know what to do with it. They didn't want it. It was too radioactive. So they called for another year of consultation, adopted a resolution saying that they didn't request this, thank you very much, and don't do

anything until you hear further. So one year went by and they still hadn't fig-
ured out what to do with it [set of norms]. The votes were there to defeat it,
but a number of countries didn't want the issue of business and human
rights itself to fall off the table. They wanted the legal excesses to go away
but they wanted to advance the agenda.

The choice between a counterproductive legalistic approach favored by NGOs
and an entirely voluntary approach favored by business put the UN on the horns of
a dilemma. That's where Ruggie comes into the picture:

The compromise was to ask the secretary-general to appoint a special representative with a two-year mandate initially to produce greater clarity about
exactly what are the standards of corporate responsibility and accountability
with regard to human rights. What are some best practices that companies
should follow? What is the current state of play in international law with
regard to complicity? Sphere of influence? What can be done to advance
tools with regard to human rights impact assessments? And where do we go
from here with regard to legal standards? So that was my mandate.

Ruggie grins,

I guess I knew that it was going to be difficult. The minute I was appointed, I
got a flood of letters from the human rights community asking me to endorse
the norms. At that point I started looking at the document seriously, and
parts of it are very useful. But the excessive and mistaken legal baggage that
[the sub-commission had] managed to drag into [the norms], and the potentially perverse effects they would have produced on the ground, put me in
the unhappy position of either going along with something that I didn't
believe in, or telling it like it was and hoping for the best. Well I chose the latter. I remember coming out of a meeting in Geneva early on in my mandate.
It was a meeting on the extractive sector that we had organized, and it was a
complete replay between business and the NGOs of the norms debate. I
walked out of there and I said to my High Commissioner's Office colleagues,
"We're not going to make any progress with this mandate if this continues.
The only solution I see is to drive the stake through the heart of the norms,
but to do it in such a way as not to lose the NGOs entirely." That was hard. I
spent a good part of the first year doing that and I think we've salvaged a
reasonable space. And the NGOs have slowly come around to saying, "We
understand that the 'norms' effort as such is dead, but let's see if we can't
work together to address some of the substantial challenges." And that's fine.
That's where I want to be.

Ruggie interprets the secretary-general's mandate this way:

> I present a picture of what I think the current state of play is, both with
> regard to legal issues and non-legal issues, and within the legal basket differ-
> entiating criminal behavior from non-criminal. Here's the current state of
> play. Here are the trends. Here are the gaps. Here are some options one can
> take to try to bridge the gaps, and here is what I think you, the Human Rights
> Council, ought to do. I'm treating it not as a traditional human rights stan-
> dard-setting exercise but as a policy analysis and recommendation exercise.
> I'm not going to draft new standards. That's what we have the machinery in
> Geneva for. But I will propose principles for effective action, based on how
> best to move forward.

At the time of writing, an interim report has been issued, which describes the
evolution of the global context and emergence of essentially stateless multinational
corporations with extended supply chains and the need for principles on human
rights to be clearly articulated for businesses. The report also looks at the drivers
behind increased attention on multinationals with respect to human rights: the
accumulated power of transnational corporations, the fact that some corporate
behaviors have resulted in serious human rights, labor standards, environmental,
and societal abuses, and the reality of many corporations' global reach. The interim
report also identifies significant trends that are important to the ongoing conversation about human rights: the pattern of abuses is most associated with extractive
industries, followed in a distant second by food and beverages, and third by apparel
and footwear industries. Further, most of the reported abuses occur in low-income
nations that have recently emerged from conflict and have weak governance mechanisms in place.

Rather than revisit the 2003 norms, which were riddled with political problems,
Ruggie's draft report[106] focused on what he termed "principled pragmatism" and
basically outlined the strategic direction for next steps. Although no formal principles were given in the Interim Report, it was clear that, ultimately, the document
would be based, like the Global Compact, on a set of principles and standards of
behavior rather than embedded in an overly legalistic framework.

The difference makers discussed in this chapter have made noted innovations in
establishing clear standards that businesses are increasingly expected to live up to.
But finding out whether companies are living up to those standards requires a
wholly different set of institutions that concentrate on the issue of transparency.
That will be the focus of the institution building in the responsibility assurance
infrastructure we look at in the next chapter.

6

Transparency and common reporting

In 1995, very few companies were issuing social or sustainability reports. But, less than ten years later, virtually every large company in the public eye, as well as many smaller companies, was doing some sort of social or environmental reporting beyond financial statements in an effort to demonstrate transparency. These documents had many names: social reports, environmental reports, sustainability reports, triple-bottom-line reports, people, planet, and profits reports, or some other name, but whatever they were called they had become part of the corporate landscape — after several earlier efforts to engender social reporting had failed rather dramatically. Indeed, many, if not most "companies and accountants alike were passionately opposed to pretty much any discussion of environmental or social issues in a business or reporting context," prior to 1990, according to one knowledgeable source.[107] Transparency in such reports had not yet become an issue and, though there were demands from the NGO and activist communities, few companies were paying attention. That was about to change as demands for transparency — and consistency — in reporting began to grow.

The situation began to shift because of the confluence of a number of factors and pressures and the emergence of new institutions that made greater transparency possible — and seemingly necessary. Social investors were beginning to become more sophisticated and demand information on a greater array of topics than the simple negative screening of the 1990s. NGOs and other activist groups were growing in importance, particularly after use of the World Wide Web exploded from about 1995, making global connectivity — and organizing — feasible.

In fact, the history goes back a bit further. In 1987, the World Commission on Environment and Development produced the now famous report *Our Common Future* (popularly known as the Brundtland Report), presenting it to the United Nations General Assembly. This report used the term *sustainable development*, defining it as "development that meets the needs of the present without compromising the ability of future generations to meet their own needs." It served as a clarion call to action on the state of the natural environment, highlighting businesses' roles in both the problems and possible solutions. The Brundtland Report was followed, in 1992, by the first-ever Earth Summit held by the United Nations in Rio de Janeiro, Brazil. The Earth Summit called attention to issues of environmental sustainability in a wholly new way, and was followed ten years later in 2002, by the World Summit on Sustainable Development in Johannesburg, South Africa.

All of these developments, and many more, of course, placed considerable attention on the contribution of businesses, particularly large businesses, to the deterioration of the global natural environment. Combined with growing recognition of the labor and human rights problems of extended supply chains, and increasing attention on issues of corruption with the establishment in 1995 of Transparency International, the need for greater corporate transparency was becoming obvious, even if not desired by the business community. Simultaneously, businesses began feeling greater pressure to show what they were doing about their environmental and social responsibilities.

As we have already seen, in the United States organizations such as the CEP were already pointing to problematic business practices in widely available publications such as *Shopping for a Better World*. These pressures spread to Europe in the late 1980s when difference maker John Elkington (with Julia Hailes) published a UK counterpart *The Green Consumer Guide*. By 1997, when Elkington published his *Cannibals with Forks*, a book that popularized the term that he had coined, "the triple bottom line," reporting on social, environmental, and economic issues became much more of an imperative — and much more possible — than it had previously been. Notably, in 1997, Royal Dutch Shell became one of the first multinational companies to issue a triple-bottom-line report, which it called "People, Planet, Profits" (and now calls its "Sustainability Report").

John Elkington

John Elkington is founder and chief entrepreneur of SustainAbility, one of the earliest consulting firms in the area of corporate responsibility and responsibility assurance. SustainAbility's mission is specifically associated with responsibility assurance:

> Established in 1987, SustainAbility advises clients on the risks and opportunities associated with corporate responsibility and sustainable development. Working at the interface between market forces and societal expectations, we seek solutions to social and environmental challenges that deliver long term value. We understand business and what society expects of it.[108]

It is exactly this proposition of working at the "interface between market forces and societal expectations" that sets Elkington's organization apart from traditional consulting firms and also makes the company part of the growing responsibility infrastructure that difference makers have constructed. Working collaboratively across sectors — that is, with businesses, NGOs, and other "influencers" — SustainAbility attempts to "put a challenging frame around our client work, helping ensure tangible progress."[109]

John Elkington, never one to shy away from a challenge, gained a sense of passion for the natural environment as a young child when he had a profound — indeed, a life-changing — experience that connected him deeply to the natural world and has guided the nature of his work over the years. He relates the tale:

> I'm afraid the story starts relatively early because my family traveled a lot when I was a child. When I was in Northern Ireland as a five- or six-year-old, something happened to me which switched me on to the natural world. It wasn't planned, and it was just simply being out one night very late on my own, walking back from a farm laborer's cottage to my parent's home with no moon. It was completely dark. And suddenly finding myself completely surrounded by elvers or baby eels on their way either to the nearby river or to ponds, which were also in the fields I was walking through. It was just one of those transformative moments.

It was a moment whose implications — how deeply connected humans are to nature — has stayed with Elkington, as he notes:

> A whole bunch of things spooled out from that. We traveled to places like Cyprus and Israel and so on, and I came back from all of that feeling slightly removed from Britain, though I studied here. I went to a school that was extraordinarily liberal; it was like a campus-based university. Even from when you were about 12 or 13, it gave you quite a high proportion of your time to structure yourself. So I did that. When I left and finally went to the university, which I didn't particularly expect to do, I initially went into economics [in 1967]. I gave [university] up after a year because 1968 happened. The university that I accidentally ended up at, Essex University, which was one of the

very new ones, again, very much a campus-based university, just blew up. It was *the* one in England, which like Bonn, and to some extent the Sorbonne in France, went incandescent with the student protests.

In another early incident, the extremely shy 11-year-old Elkington suddenly found himself standing up in front of his schoolmates

and asking all of the students for what we would call pocket money for two weeks and donating it to WWF (then called the World Wildlife Fund), which was founded that year. I simply couldn't remember afterwards what had made me do that. Then in 1978, I set up a company with two people, one of whom was one of the founders of WWF: Max Nicholson. He asked me how I got involved in this area. I told him the story about raising the money, and he said, "I know exactly what switched you on. We got 24 pages into a major tabloid newspaper on World Wildlife Fund." As soon as he said that I could remember going to the school library and finding the newspaper on a read-ing stand, and reading it, and just feeling electrified, and feeling I had to do something, and going off and doing it.

Elkington continues,

It wasn't until the late 1960s, which is when I was at university [bachelor's in sociology and social psychology, University of Essex, 1970; master's in urban and regional planning, University College London, 1974], that groups like Friends of the Earth started to embryonically form in California, and then spread to other parts of the world. I started to find a form of environmental-ism that I really strongly connected with. I've never worked for an NGO, though I've worked alongside them and worked with them in many different ways. I'm a trustee of a number of NGOs and even a chairman of one. But I've never worked directly in that space, though I've always had a *huge* affec-tion for the people who do what Friends of the Earth, Greenpeace, Amnesty, Human Rights Watch and so on, do.

Things were not always as clear for Elkington as they seem to be today. He recalls,

I came out of my first degree with not a clue in the world as to what I would do, so I traveled and then I did all sorts of odd jobs. I became very interested in cities and architecture and how urban settlements evolved. That's what really pulled me into planning, and then when I came out of the MPhil, the postgraduate degree, literally a week from the end of that course I knew what I *didn't* want to do. I didn't want to be an economist, I didn't want to be a sociologist, and I didn't want to be a planner. But I came out very luckily. I had chosen a really weird tutor at [University College London], who just hap-pened to be approached a week from the end of term by a small environmental consultancy in London, and I got a job with them. There were only about six people, but they were doing spectacularly interesting work — early environmental impact assessments in countries like Egypt — and this was from 1974 onwards.

The decision proved seminal, as Elkington notes,

Something happened as a result of that [job], which wasn't planned, but which was absolutely fundamental in what happened later on in what I've done in this career. I was running a small team of environmental scientists in Egypt for the UNDP, probably in almost its first year. We had an 80,000-square-mile territory to look after. We were looking specifically at things like impact on the environment, the spread of parasitic diseases, oil pollution, but the issue that got my interest was that there were three different studies, each of which had been allocated a third of the biggest Nile Delta lake: Manzana.

I was the first person to put all of those three projects together and realize that, while what they were severally doing was intelligent at the local level, the plan would wreak environmental havoc if implemented. If you had a third of the lake, you could probably get away with draining that part of the lake for agriculture, because you'd assume that the other two-thirds would still be there. But if you went across to the other two-thirds you'd find one was going to have a motorway put right through, which would mean that you no longer had a flow of water. It's hard to exaggerate the scale of this lake. It is vast and it's absolutely vital for the Mediterranean offshore fisheries. It's a nursery. But it's also hugely important for migrating birds and for traditional extensive lake fisheries. I just realized the whole thing was going to be destroyed. It was no part of our brief to look at that and it was no part of our brief to do anything about it.

Going public once

Undaunted by the fact that it was not within his purview to address the environmental disaster he saw brewing — and was contrary to the clients' interests — Elkington was galvanized into action:

I thought I couldn't not, so I went and visited something like 17 ministries and government agencies. They all without exception either said, "Don't worry your head: Manzana is a ditch, its average depth is a meter and, if development means we sacrifice an area like that, so be it." Or they would say, "Trust us: when we ruined the Nile with the Aswan Dam, we were being helped by the Russians. Now we're being helped by the Americans so everything will be all right."

Elkington comments wryly,

> Well, I came out of [those conversations] not remotely reassured, came back to London, and had one of these very tough decisions to make. I felt this was a disaster in the making and if I left it (I know it sounds arrogant), that it wouldn't be picked up and things would start to go very seriously wrong. So I asked, "Well what do I do?" As a consultant, you don't go public. You don't speak in public about the work that you've done for a client. [But] I thought, I have no choice *but* to go public. We have a magazine here, *New Scientist* so I rang them up and said, "Look, there's a problem and I'd like to talk about it." They gave me four pages and I wrote the piece, and it should have destroyed what I sometimes laughingly call a career. But it reframed a whole series of projects. The UN came back and did a full ecosystem study, which ended up with a very different set of results. That was the environmental outcome. The unintended consequence for me was that I then wrote in *New Scientist* for about four or five years, a feature every month.

In 1978, Elkington and Max Nicholson set up a new company (with David Layton) called Environmental Data Services (ENDS), where Elkington stayed for five years, gaining experience that was to prove instrumental in his later role as founder and CEO of SustainAbility. He comments,

> What we did, at a time when it wasn't done, was to not only look at where environmental policy and regulation was going and the implications for business, but actually go inside companies and see how they saw the environmental challenge, how they were responding in terms of technology, or investment or stakeholder engagement. We didn't use that term then but that was again one of the themes. It took me nine months to get through the door of the first company, because basically they didn't want to talk to people who were interested in the environment. They saw that as just a damn nuisance. This was despite the fact that we had a parent company that in Britain is the leading supplier of information to companies on industrial relations. But, once we got into some of these companies, by 1981 I was helping, for example, BP and ICI write their first written environmental policy statements.
>
> That was why after about five years I decided I wanted to go back and work directly with companies rather than reporting on what they were doing. It was an extraordinary experience, because it meant that I visited something like 300–400 companies around the world to talk about what they were doing on the environmental front, which was absolutely fascinating.

So, in 1987, Elkington went on to establish his own consultancy, SustainAbility.

SustainAbility

Elkington actually founded SustainAbility after Earthlife, a foundation he had been working with, imploded, as a way of fulfilling responsibilities associated with projects in that foundation. He points out,

> I was going to do these projects with a very young woman, Julia Hailes. We decided we would set up SustainAbility as an organization to do the projects, but we would do it as a limited company to try to give ourselves some financial protection. It was a complete accident that we set it up as a business, but in the work that we've subsequently done it's been one of the strongest assets that we've had. Even companies of the size of Procter & Gamble have seen the fact that we are a for-profit limited business as very reassuring and a symbol of the fact that we not only sympathize with, but understand, busi-

---

Box 6.1 **SustainAbility's Rules of Engagement**

Our Rules of Engagement guide our relationships with clients and partners. They ensure that our work reflects our mission and does not compromise our values. They are the basis for building a shared understanding both of what we do and what we are working towards. They are essential to our independence and integrity.

Here are the basics:

1. **Only serious players**

We only work with clients and partners we believe are genuinely serious, both in their intent and in their capacity to contribute to sustainable development through changes in their policies and practices.

2. **Guardians of our mission**

It's essential that we are accountable to our staff, Board and Council for the work that we do and for meeting our mission. We provide frequent opportunities for our staff to both examine client programmes and voice any concerns and ideas.

3. **Independence non-negotiable**

We are professional, but not neutral — and our independence is central to the roles we play. We strive to ensure that we are never compromised in our actions and in what we can say to clients and partners. Our integrity and independence are fundamental to achieving our mission and providing real value to our clients.[110]

ness and operate a business, which I think in the early days was a bit spurious, but that's another story.

SustainAbility defines itself as a strategy consultancy and independent think-tank. It specializes in the business risks and market opportunities of corporate responsibility and sustainable development. Founded on Elkington's own philosophy, the company states on its website that it believes not only that profitable business must be socially and environmentally responsible, but further that social and environmental innovation is key to the new market opportunities of the future.[111] The company's socially oriented mission is clearly stated: "to help business contribute to a world that future generations want to inherit."[112]

SustainAbility is distinguished by its Rules of Engagement for clients (see Box 6.1), rules that, Elkington points out, have served the company well under certain difficult circumstances.

Going public twice: The Green Consumer Guide

Elkington continues the SustainAbility story:

> Having set this company up in 1987, in 1988 we did a book called *The Green Consumer Guide,* which I think was my seventh, which to our absolute bewilderment sold a million copies in 18 months with 20 foreign editions. We had just hit what we see as a second wave of societal pressure on both government and particularly now business. The ozone depletion issue and a whole bunch of other things helped drive all of that. It was insane in the same way as with Egypt. I should have been dropped like a hot potato as a consultant because we named names and I had broken confidences, but that didn't happen with this book. We said, "We're not just going to talk about environmental issues. We're going to talk about which companies and which brands are most closely associated with particular problems. We're going to tell you, the consumer, how you can choose between those products, those brands, on the basis of their environmental performance." It sent absolute shockwaves through the world of business. There were a lot of other things going on at the same time, which were pushing in the same direction but this was absolutely the right product at the right time.

Notably, *The Green Consumer Guide* was published shortly after Alice Tepper Marlin and Steve Lydenberg with coauthors published *Rating America's Corporate Conscience* and about the time that *Shopping for a Better World* was published in the United States — publications that also named names and provided data and insight into companies' social performance for the first time. In an ironic twist, Elkington notes that several of the companies, including McDonald's, which had been "named" in *The Green Consumer Guide* sued SustainAbility initially, though

> None of the suits were brought to court because our research was pretty thorough. But we had all of that going on. The McDonald's thing went on for months and we were very fearful of losing the company because they threw everything they had at us. But in the end they asked if we would work with them.

The consulting company continued to grow as interest in sustainability and responsibility issues grew and other companies took notice. But, in all the frenzy, there were some companies that Elkington refused to work with: "We said, no, we wouldn't [work with McDonald's]. Actually, the Environmental Defense Fund [now Environmental Defense] within about six months started working with them on recycling and things like that, and I'm glad that happened."

Changing expectations and rules of engagement

Expectations began to shift, as Elkington recalls:

> From 1988, from *The Green Consumer Guide* period, everything changed, at least it did for us. Companies were really interested in understanding the market trends that we were helping to drive, but they didn't, and they wanted to really open up some of their new product ideas and strategic thinking, and so it did become competitive. In the past what we had done in helping companies on environment had been non-competitive so I could work with ICI and Monsanto at the same time, BP and Shell at the same time and nobody cared a hoot. But now it was competitive. We couldn't work with a Unilever *and* a Procter & Gamble at the same time. So that was again not something we had planned. One competitor said, "I cannot understand how Sustain-Ability, on the one hand, is extraordinarily rude about business, very challenging about business's role in society — in some cases you even name and shame your own clients — yet at the same time you have an extraordinary list of blue-chip clients, who are also extraordinary loyal." And he knew this because they had been trying to get these clients to work with them rather than us and finding it almost impossible. I explained, "It's an accident. We didn't set out to create that business environment. But by the very way in which we have operated we've almost set up a natural selection process, where the companies who choose to come to us." (And much of the work at that stage still largely did come to us.) "That natural selection process is tending to filter out the ones who aren't serious, and self-select the ones who probably on balance are more likely to stick with the stuff."

In part, this seriousness goes back to SustainAbility's own Rules of Engagement for clients, which demand "only serious players": that is, companies that are serious about wanting to deal with the environmental and social issues facing them. Elkington himself is guided by a number of core values, which he details on his personal home page and which are also reflected in the way that SustainAbility operates:

- **Evolution.** Real change happens over generations

- **Sustainability.** Future generations as stakeholders today

- **Diversity.** Evolution feeds on difference

- **Transparency.** Sustainable economies are see-through

- **Conversation.** Wellspring of insight

- **Memory.** Capture lessons of experience

- **Intuition.** Facts only get you so far

- **Serendipity.** Learn from mistakes and fortunate accidents[113]

A balancing act

SustainAbility has always attempted to stick closely to its mission, which has sometimes been a delicate balancing act. Its success, as Elkington notes, has not always been the result of strict strategic planning: "A lot of what has turned out to work well for us has been a result of somewhat wild experimentation and a willingness to try a bunch of stuff and have a proportion of that fail." An early book by Elkington called *The Green Capitalists* [with coauthor Tom Burke] foreshadowed Elkington's role as a trend spotter:

> The book basically said, "Unless and until the environmental movement learns to work with business and through markets, most of what we want to see happen in the world won't. And capitalism is the future." So it was a little bit ahead of the trend, and it was seen by many people in the green movement as profoundly provocative, because we were putting green and capitalism together, which they really didn't like a bit. Green consumerism was no better. But I suppose we were relatively early in getting companies to think very seriously and strategically about the environmental challenge and how they responded.

Elkington's vision for SustainAbility has guided the company's work through the years, as he notes:

> The vision has been, in part, that we wouldn't choose capitalism, but, as Churchill said of democracy, it's the least worst option that we have. It does experiment. Out of those experiments new stuff mutates and evolves. We wanted to work *only* with business. My view was that we'd be much better

off, if we wanted to try changing the world, working with the private sector
and particularly with selective companies [rather than government].

It is in the relationships that SustainAbility has with NGOs that the delicate balancing act comes in, as Elkington points out:

> The vision, insofar as there was one, had to do with being seen to be and
> being very much part of the wider NGO movement. So we didn't want to
> become a consultancy where we lost contact with and lost the respect of
> campaigners. A few years back Greenpeace described us as a for-profit NGO.
> I still find that difficult to process, but these sorts of commentaries by people
> in the NGO world are reassuring, because I think, if we don't have their trust,
> if we don't have their respect, we don't have the sort of business that certainly I would want to have. It doesn't mean that they're always right. In fact,
> they're often wrong. But they are representative of a public sentiment and
> you know we would betray that at our peril.

The vision is even more complicated, as Elkington observes:

> I think another part of the vision was that we would largely work in the OECD
> countries, the rich world, because that's where the biggest opportunities
> were, where the biggest potential to leverage change was, we felt. At least my
> experience, and I'd done a lot of work in the developing world before setting
> up SustainAbility and a bit after we started, was that, if you worked in countries like South Africa or Malaysia or wherever it happened to be, you generally ended up working with aid agencies or development agencies. The same
> problem [occurred]: things didn't happen as fast as we felt that they might.
> We also ruled out the entire central and eastern European domain for the
> same reasons: you'd end up working with the European Bank for Reconstruction and Development or people like that. So with all of those countries we
> just said, "Look, if you want information, if you want our products, if you
> want our advice we'll give it to you for free, but we're not going to work in
> those parts of the world."

Things change

Despite the consistency of SustainAbility's approach to businesses, things do
change, as Elkington recounts, because the pressure began to come from clients:

> [In the late 1990s], something started to happen that began a process of
> change, which was that our corporate clients started to take us into some of
> those countries because they had issues which they wanted our help with.
> [Then], two colleagues, one Indian, one Canadian, particularly started to

whack me around the head and say, "Look, we're ignoring the countries where the biggest changes are going to happen, because of demographics, trends and so on. We've got to be in there." So SustainAbility said to them, "Well, fine, we'll take a look at that area." Over a period of some years we worked with the International Finance Corporation and some other partners and clients in that sort of area and gradually narrowed down the focus.

Still, the evolution is problematic because, despite its visibility in the global corporate responsibility scene, as Elkington notes, SustainAbility has chosen to remain small:

> We are a tiny organization. There are 25 of us. We're in four locations; two of those are just one person: Zurich and San Francisco. London is the biggest office and Washington, DC, is the second largest. But we've tried to strangle our own growth through the 19 years that we've operated. The reason for that has largely been because we don't want to market. We would infinitely prefer to be in a position where the work comes to us and we can then set terms and conditions.

Not neutral

Part of the reason also has to do with naming names and being highly selective about the "seriousness" of clients and a desire always to push toward real results. Elkington states,

> For example, we resigned a client publicly. We've done it several times — in '97, '98, we resigned Monsanto. We had been brought into that company by their then CEO Bob Shapiro to help them understand public sentiment internationally, but particularly in Europe, to genetically modified [GM] foods. At the end of that process we had done a whole lot of stakeholder work among other things, and we concluded that Monsanto were headed for a brick wall. I flew across to St. Louis to see Bob Shapiro. Unfortunately, on the day I arrived, he had to fly to New York because one of their big mergers had collapsed. I to some degree got fobbed off onto the head of international foods, who knew nothing about the issues we were working on, [but] who was a brilliantly intelligent man. He's now chairman of the company.
>
> But the net result of that conversation was that I came out feeling it would be a betrayal if we stayed or were seen to stay in this company, because they either cannot understand or cannot afford to understand what we're telling them, because the market is putting such high multiples on the biotechnology side of their business that they can't afford not to bulldoze GM foods into Europe. Well, anyway, we publicly resigned that contract, and nine

months later they ran headlong into that brick wall. Subsequently, I've talked both to Bob Shapiro and to Hugh Grant, who was then head of the foods business and they have both said that we were right to resign. They both wish we'd stayed in longer or made even more noise when we came out. But neither of them think that we would have actually been able to change Monsanto's direction.

Having the courage to stand up for principles stood SustainAbility and Elkington in good stead, as he comments,

The reason I've gone through that story is because, again, it was suicidal in many ways to have done that. Many of our competitors looked at what we'd done and thought we were just insane, not only to resign the work, which they would have gladly have had, but to do so in public. But six months later, Bill Ford, who was then the chairman of Ford, invited us in and the second question he asked me pretty much was: "If you had a relationship with Ford, what would it take to get you to the point where you'd resign that relationship?" He knew about the Monsanto story, but he was actually quite intrigued about it, because he didn't see us as straightforward consultants just prepared to do whatever the client wanted, but having an agenda of our own. We've often said — I said it first because I was trying to articulate what it is that we feel is important in all of this — that we try very hard to be objective and professional, but we are absolutely not neutral. We're probably neutral if we're successful 15 to 20 years into the future. Sometimes when things go fast maybe it's five years. But we're trying to push an agenda that for many of our clients doesn't make too much sense in the market conditions of today, but we're trying to drive them towards a different set of outcomes.

The demand for transparency and reporting consistency

John Elkington's work in "naming names" in the United Kingdom and the parallel work of Alice Tepper Marlin and colleagues in the United States highlighted a new need for corporate transparency. By the mid-1990s, it had become clear that, if companies were going to issue social, sustainability, or what have come to be called, after Elkington, triple-bottom-line reports, there needed to be some consistent ways of doing so. But, of course, reporting about social and environmental performance, as social investors and the difference makers who founded KLD Research & Analytics had already discovered in trying to assess companies along those dimensions, was not as straightforward as for financial reporting.

Complicated enough in itself, financial reporting covers only a few aspects of the broader set of risks associated with social issues, sustainability, and governance. To be effective at all, the emerging accountability infrastructure needed to provide key new tools and mechanisms so that corporate managers would know where to turn for advice and what to do when they actually wanted to develop reporting related to accountability and transparency. One such tool was clearly the need for the development of a standardized reporting mechanism comparable to generally accepted accounting principles (GAAP). Today, this need has been satisfied by the Global Reporting Initiative, which is the collective brainchild of Allen White and Bob Massie, with Joan Bavaria and numerous others.

■ Allen White

Allen White is vice president at Boston's Tellus Institute, which has the mission of "advancing the transition to a sustainable, equitable, and humane global civilization."[114] As part of its multilevel approach to systemic change, Tellus has worked at the global, regional, national, local, and enterprise levels of development, and has provided in-depth work on what it calls its Great Transition Initiative, headed by Tellus's Paul Raskin, which builds networks for large-scale system change, develops futures scenarios to help people envision another way of living on the planet, and emphasizes outreach and dissemination of those ideas. Another core aspect of Tellus's work, which Allen White heads, is the Corporate Redesign project, because it has become clear from the work of the Great Transition project that a sustainable, equitable, and human global civilization cannot be achieved without a shift in the nature and purposes of the corporation.

But White's involvement in creating the emerging accountability infrastructure goes back way before Corporate Redesign, and the resulting project Corporation 20/20 (see Chapter 8) became realities. Joan Bavaria was co-chair of Ceres when, as she puts it,

> Allen White and Bob Massie thought up the GRI [Global Reporting Initiative].
> Ceres basically knew that there were a lot of "challenging" disclosure efforts.
> From the very beginning over and over again, industry would try to copy
> Ceres in one way or another. They would try to grab control of something by
> putting up an initiative that looked and acted like ours but didn't have the
> accountability.

Bavaria downplays her own role in establishing the GRI by emphasizing that she was merely chair of Ceres at the time and Massie's boss, but clearly her vision of inclusiveness and diversity and the orientation toward environmental sustainability have influenced the direction of the initiative as well as its two main founders, Allen White and Bob Massie.

Allen White was trained as a geographer, but he has worked for more than 25 years in diverse areas of corporate responsibility. He has advised numerous multilateral organizations, companies, and NGOs, after beginning his career as a faculty member and researcher at the University of Connecticut, Clark University, and Battelle Laboratories. He was a former Fulbright Scholar in Peru and Peace Corps volunteer in Nicaragua. Much of his work has focused on strategic issues associated with corporate responsibility, including governance, accountability, and the integration of environmental issues into corporate strategies.

From Ceres to the Global Reporting Initiative

White was deeply involved not only in the formation of the GRI, but also in the early years of Ceres, as that organization struggled to figure out how to measure the environmental impacts of companies. His own perspective on the evolution of Ceres, as backdrop to the GRI, and his knowledge of measurement, which resulted in part from his background as a scientist (geologist), is informative,[115]

> The first phase [of White's involvement in the accountability infrastructure] was work in reporting that started in the early 1990s. At that time, reporting on non-financial [performance] was essentially unheard of; it was not an idea whose time had come — it had no currency. There was no understanding of its scope, content, or metrics on my part and, I would say, on the part of others who were beginning to explore the field. But I did have the sense that there was something very important taking shape, still nascent but potentially powerful. The world was changing fast. Environmentalism was two decades old. But the notion that companies ought to be accountable through some kind of mechanism, some kind of high-quality credible disclosure framework, seemed like an idea ready to emerge. The triggering event for my involvement was the *Exxon Valdez* accident, which gave birth to Ceres and to the Valdez Principles for corporate environmental conduct, soon to be renamed the Ceres Principles.
>
> Basically I was called one day by the director and founder, Joan Bavaria. She said, "Someone told me you understand measurement." And I said, "Well, I can tell you my belt size if that helps." She said, "I had something a little different in mind. You see, we're in this conundrum. We've now put forward these principles, but we now understand they'll be meaningless unless there's an accountability mechanism behind them. We have to develop this accountability framework, but nobody has a clue how to do it. Do you think you can help us out?" I said, "Well, I'll be happy to try." That was the fateful call that led to about five years of essentially pro bono work for Ceres, leading to some pioneering work on environmental reporting.

There were no models for White and Bavaria to follow in creating a reporting framework for Ceres, as he recollects:

> We were learning by doing. There was no precedent. A few companies had dabbled in environmental reporting, but there was nothing standardized, nothing robust, nothing credible. The few reports in the market were as much public relations as substance. So Ceres was out there on a limb, watching other initiatives, particularly business-led initiatives, challenge the work it was doing. In the business community, considerable anxiety was directed at the possibility that the Valdez Principles and a future Ceres reporting framework would morph into a generally accepted standard. For many companies that would be a most unwelcome development. Others, however, could see the future and said, "You know, this actually is not a bad idea if we can get it right and get it reasonable." A level playing field in a newly emerging area would be a positive thing in the eyes of those companies who chose to keep an open mind. So there were different views within the corporate community. Meanwhile, Ceres plodded ahead. I played the role of architect of the very early versions of the Ceres reporting framework, which went through *multiple* generations in the early to mid-1990s.

Genesis of GRI

White explains how the work with Ceres resulted, eventually, in the development of the GRI:

> The Ceres reporting work was the seedling for GRI. By 1996, Ceres had secured full-time leadership in the person of Bob Massie. By 1997, the Ceres reporting work was at a crossroads. It wasn't clear that an environmental-only, North America-only framework would achieve the objective of creating a generally accepted framework. The number of adopting companies was increasing, but very slowly, numbering perhaps two or three dozen.

Frustration proved fruitful, as White makes clear:

> We had the feeling there was something bigger on the horizon, but what was it? It took an unsuccessful meeting in Chicago with a couple of companies to gain clarity on what this big prize was. With the help of a few beers, we [Allen White, Bob Massie, and Judy Kuszewski (at the time of writing at SustainAbility)] realized we didn't want to spend the next ten years pursuing the unsatisfactory trajectory of the previous six or seven years. We were distressed by the sluggishness of the pace of uptake by companies, even as the quality of reporting was gradually increasing. We were operating in a market, namely the US, which simply was not receptive to non-financial reporting.

For every reporting enthusiast, there were hundreds of skeptics. The US was very defensive, and very litigious. In many sectors, the appetite for collaboration between companies and a small NGO like Ceres in developing a reporting framework was extremely limited or outright absent. Our conclusion: the US is and always will be a critical market. But it is a big, globalizing world, and it was time to look beyond borders of the US for markets that were more receptive to the idea of a generally accepted framework. In short, it was time for a "global reporting initiative."

With that insight, White joined with Bob Massie to really begin the development of what became the GRI. As he notes,

Thus began a journey that accelerated and expanded at a rate we never dreamed possible. We began outreach to key stakeholders. Reactions ranged from instant enthusiasm to profound doubts that we — or anybody else — could put in motion a process that would lead to a global reporting framework acceptable to a broad spectrum of stakeholders. We talked to some Ceres companies that we thought would be receptive. These were global companies that, we believed, would be drawn to a standard framework, thereby avoiding the real threat of dozens of competing frameworks across countries and business sectors. And we talked to some NGOs with international reach, like WWF, Greenpeace, Transparency International, and Oxfam. Further, we engaged with some trade unions including the international office of the AFL–CIO [American Federation of Labor and Congress of Industrial Organizations] and the International Confederation of Free Trade Unions (ICFTU) in Brussels. We talked to accountants, business schools, and every other group that we believed might be interested in participating in a global initiative.

Bob Massie has his own way of framing the origins of the GRI:

One of the little stories about how GRI succeeded the way it did was that we understood early and, well, intuitively — it wasn't like we had a strategic plan — that the Internet made possible a different kind of conversation and an extremely rapid ability to reach consensus on documents. So, we could meet in a country for two days, get 70% of the way there, then under the old way things got done, you would have to mail things back and forth, and the next stage would have taken three years. We literally did it in three weeks. Somebody would say, "I'll draft this and people put in their comments by next week." It wasn't perfect, but it went from 70% to 98% in three weeks instead of what in the past would have been three years.

Just to put this in perspective, GRI got off the ground and started planning and working in 1996, particularly 1997. Amazon only went online in 1995, but people were just starting to use email by then. Certainly for NGOs there were new potential elements of global governance and possibilities for collaboration; there was a big difference between 1995 and 1998 and 2001.

Allen White reflects on the GRI's progress and gives credit to what he calls "creating a big tent," in inclusive outreach to anyone interested in the process of developing a global reporting initiative – globally accepted standards for what has come to be called sustainability reporting. He remembers,

> Our intensive outreach, stressing inclusiveness and diversity of participation, paid off. To be sure, skepticism that we could succeed with such a bold idea was heard even among those inclined to join the process. But the idea of building a process and product that would be the environmental equivalent of a financial reporting framework was exciting enough to overcome all but the most resistant disbelievers. Our confidence increased. We came around to the view that if not now, then when? And if not us, then who?
>
> A vacuum existed, and we believed we were as capable as any party of filling it. That was the situation in late 1997. And the rest is history. Upon reflection, it is clear that the experience in conceiving and catalyzing GRI was not an act of genius. It was about timing, seeing a need and an opportunity, and aggressively reaching out to individuals and organizations essential to the success of the venture. We knew if we were going to succeed, however, significant financial resources would be required, at least a few million dollars. We also knew that we needed a world-class process – credible, legitimate, transparent – to create a world-class reporting framework. Without such a process, even the best technical products would not be widely accepted.

As White points out, however, there were several crucial moments in the early history of the GRI:

> By 1997, the reporting initiatives were proliferating, led by business, by government and civil society groups. But still missing was a high-credibility global process in which all stakeholders were welcome and engaged. This commitment to process, to what amounts to a "stakeholder governance" process would become the signature of GRI in the ensuing years. We formed a steering committee, began identifying the first working groups, and did so always with an eye toward multi-stakeholder engagement.

Two other critical moments occurred in early 1998. White continues,

> The first, in April, was when we received one of the most critical pieces of advice that ever reached GRI, in this case from John Elkington, who was a steering committee member. In his usual understated delivery, John observed, "If this initiative remains environmental only, you will be history

before you get the first guidelines completed. Time will have passed you by. You've got to do more than the environment." He would be proven absolutely right in the years ahead. From that moment on, GRI became a sustainability reporting framework, retaining its environmental content, of course, but expanding its purview to include issues such as labor standards, governance, and anticorruption policies.

But that was not the end of the complexities, as White notes:

The future would be more complex — more stakeholders, more metrics, and more differences to resolve. We knew the technical challenges were formidable, but we firmly believed that, if we had created and maintained a process with high integrity and inclusiveness, we could overcome any obstacles that would emerge.

There was one other important challenge, as White recalls:

The second critical moment related to resource requirements. We were running on a shoestring at the same time the initiative showed every sign of moving into rapid take-off. Interest intensified each month owing to a combination of our outreach plus individuals and organizations on their own proactively seeking to participate in the process. There were times when my email box received 200–300 GRI-related messages per day. Each and every one deserved a response. This avalanche of interest confirmed our premise that a need and opportunity were present, and that we were filling a leadership vacuum that was even more pressing than we originally thought. How, then, would we address the resource need? This was the moment where Bob Massie's extraordinary powers of intellect and persuasion were deployed. Through his contact with a long-time friend, he visited a family foundation in Florida. Meeting with the former businessman-turned-philanthropist, Bob explained the grand idea we had developed. We believed at this early stage, only foundation money would protect the neutrality that would enable GRI to attract a broad spectrum of stakeholders. Corporate money at this juncture would jeopardize credibility among civil society and labor, and government money might color the process with the appearance of a new regulatory program.

Bob Massie relates the story of how that seed money came to be directed at Ceres for the development of the GRI,

I was starting to get the idea about how this would work, and Judy Kuszewski [then] of Ceres and I wrote a short proposal for our friend Ralph Taylor, whose family came from Brookline [and has] their own Olin Foundation, and Ralph said, "I'd like you to come down and meet my parents and talk to them about this project." I had just had a knee replacement in February of 1997; this was in April, so I was still on crutches. I flew down to Palm Beach and went to Ralph's parents' house, where I spent the next day or two with them, and laid out this deal. I remember we were having cocktails at the country club at Palm Beach, a place I'd never been, so there were lots of cultural adjustments for me. So Ralph's dad, who was the former CEO of a modest-sized company and a military type, in his gruffness and his directness says, "So, Bob, let me get this straight. You are telling me that you are going to set up a system that is going to alter how companies are going to disclose on their economic, and social, and labor, and environmental impacts, and you're going to do this on a global basis over the next couple of years. And you're going to do it with a hundred thousand dollars?" I looked at him, and the crutches were leaning against the couch, and I said, "Yes, that's what I'm telling you. I think your hundred thousand dollars is going to trigger another hundred thousand dollars and then that's going to trigger several million dollars, and then we're going to be able to do it. Of course, it's going to depend on a lot of people being willing to participate. But you would be the first."

Allen White provides further insight into the seed money:

Bob explained the rationale behind GRI [to the eventual donor], and the great contribution it would make to corporate accountability and sustainable development. The sale was not easy because the idea, by any measure, was grandiose and its prospects for success highly uncertain. Building a global framework equivalent to an international financial reporting framework was a high mountain to climb. But the combination of Bob's enthusiasm and intelligence, mixed with the irresistible quality of a big idea and a compelling story, carried the day. Soon afterwards, the first ever check arrived, paving the way for several million dollars more that would follow in the next four years.

The importance of process

Bob Massie explains how the processes used to establish the GRI led to its ability to draw in key stakeholders:

I had witnessed the evolution of Ceres, which I did not start, watched Joan Bavaria establish the culture and mission of Ceres, gradually redirecting the institutional investors who'd been interested in a range of other issues, including South Africa, which I knew well, into the environmental field. And then we gradually went from this question of "We believe that disclosure is a critical component of driving internal and external behavior and change overall, but there are certain impediments to achieving disclosure. How are we going to address those impediments?"

One of the biggest impediments was that everybody had their own mechanisms. Everyone had a "mine's better than yours" attitude. There was a lot of competitive behavior, a lot of pairing up. What I always say is every NGO had their pet company; every company had their pet NGO. So you come into a situation that's highly competitive, where people's resources and institutional leadership depends on differentiating themselves from others, and proving that their version is slightly better than someone else's version of something, and locking in their base of supporters. How do you turn that into a situation where you get everyone to participate and do something? That's an interesting problem, which I think we solved, which when I'm sitting here all day by myself, I think, "Hey, we solved that one."

White has a similar reflection,

By the time GRI was launched in April 2002 at the UN, it was a new global institution with an independent board of directors and a partnership with the UN. GRI became what is known as a collaborating center of UNEP. To reach this level of profile in such a short time vastly exceeded our expectations and the expectations of most people involved in the process. It would not have been possible without the social venture capital of our original donor, and the generosity and foresight of the many others — including the United Nations Foundation, the GM [General Motors] Foundation, the World Bank and dozens of others who shared our vision.

There is an important lesson for would-be difference makers in how the GRI was established, as one of White's comments indicates:

The challenge of GRI and, I would argue, similar initiatives in innovative global governance is to mobilize people with seemingly disparate interests around a public good. The key challenge is to adhere to a policy of inclusiveness and to find a place for each and every person who seeks to, or should, contribute. This is the path to both legitimacy as well as innovation. It is the power of the collective mind of diverse individuals that was, and remains, the soul of GRI.

The Global Reporting Initiative

The GRI is creating a common framework for sustainability reporting, becoming the GAAP for social and environmental reporting. Its vision is to ensure that "reporting on economic, environmental, and social performance by all organizations becomes as routine and comparable as financial reporting."[116] By 1999, UNEP had joined as a collaborator, and a draft framework was being circulated, with the first Sustainability Guidelines issued in 2000. Ceres spun GRI off as an independent institution with its own mission and board in 2002.

By 2006, GRI had issued its G3, or third draft, set of guidelines for broad circulation and comment, and more than 850 organizations were reporting using the guidelines as a reporting framework.[117]

The GRI reporting framework consists of a number of different elements.[118] The G3 Guidelines provide an overview and general framework for companies in all industries, sectors, and locations, and of all sizes. The guidelines specify what should be reported and how it should be reported, including the report content and quality. Four criteria define appropriate content for the report in general terms: materiality (what are the enterprises' significant social, economic, and environmental impacts?), stakeholder inclusiveness (who are relevant stakeholders and what are their concerns and interests?), sustainability context (how does the organization contribute to or impact future sustainability?), and completeness (are all relevant indicators and topics included?).[119] Quality of reporting is assessed using six criteria: reliability, clarity, balance, comparability, accuracy, and timeliness.[120]

The guidelines also establish boundaries for what does and what does not have to be reported. In addition, they provide an overall context or profile for understanding organizational performance around issues such as strategy and governance, seek disclosures on the management approach to different relevant topical areas so that a company's performance can be understood, and provide performance indicators on economic, environmental, and social performance of the company. In reporting, companies are asked to indicate key areas of their impacts, risks, and opportunities, with particular emphasis on issues related to sustainability.

Disclosures on a company's management approach are categorized into several areas: economic, environmental, and social (including labor practices and decent work, human rights, society, and product responsibility). In addition, in recognition of the complexities facing companies in different industry sectors, the GRI has developed a series of what it calls sector supplements and protocols to deal with the particulars of different industries, including financial services, logistics and transportation, mining and metals, public agencies, tour operators, telecommunications, and automotive sectors.

From code to transparency

In a relatively short time, the GRI has taken center-stage as the most important sustainability reporting initiative in the world. It deliberately provides a common platform for reporting, despite the complexities of doing that successfully.

Certainly, it has been helped by the fact that innovations in transparency are often undertaken by the largest and most public brand-name companies, whose activities come under the most frequent fire from activists and NGOs, and it is those companies who have taken up the mantle of the GRI as well as other initiatives aimed at demonstrating their responsibility.

These responses have raised the bar for companies, particularly brand-name companies, but, if the institutionalization process continues, will eventually do so for other types of companies as well. For example, in 2006, Levi Strauss, a code of conduct pioneer in 1991, found itself following the transparency lead of other clothing retailers, such as Gap Inc. and Nike, in publishing a list of its active suppliers. In 2004, Gap Inc., in a major innovation, had taken a critical step towards transparency as a corporation by issuing an innovative social report that detailed not just the good things that the company was doing, but also some of the problems in its supply chain. Highlighting the cutting edge of integrating issues of corporate responsibility into the business model, Gap Inc. claimed that "To us, being socially responsible means striving to incorporate our values and ethics into everything we do – from how we run our business, to how we treat our employees, to how we impact the communities where we live and work."[121] Not to be outdone, Nike soon followed suit and in 2005 published on its website a list of all of its active suppliers, complete with names and addresses. Clearly, for these large and highly visible companies, greater transparency about supply chain matters had become an imperative as had the need to be seen as a leader and not a laggard in an increasingly fast-moving agenda.

Signs that more companies were becoming involved in this infrastructure were also apparent. For example, Ceres notes on its website two other important examples that it helped to foster. Insurance giant American International Group (AIG) began in May 2006 to try to deal with the financial issues associated with global warming – a first for a US insurance company. The next month, computer manufacturer Dell began supporting German-style take-back legislation that would require electronic product recycling and take-back programs.

A key question that our difference makers raised, however, was whether or not it would be feasible to have all companies, whether they were in the public spotlight or not, eventually enter into the accountability, responsibility, and transparency movement. For that to happen, a different part of the emerging accountability infrastructure – the networks – was needed. Some of the central networks in the infrastructure and the difference makers who established them will be the subject of the next chapter.

7

Networking

In assessing the social movement associated with building the emerging account-ability assurance infrastructure so far, we have been considering the efforts of those difference makers who saw a gap in the existing institutional arrangements and built new institutions and organizations to bridge that space. This type of activity is what social movement theorists call tapping into opportunity structures. Of course, the early efforts of difference makers also involved the framing processes of defining relevant issues and the landscape for responsibility, accountability, and transparency. As the movement developed, a third element of social movements became apparent – the building of mobilizing structures: in this case, networks of actors with similar interests in changing the way that businesses interacted with society. It is to these difference makers – the networkers – whose primary activities have been in building various and interlinked networks of actors to potentially mobilize action, that we now turn.

▪ Laury Hammel

Laury Hammel is an example of how the founder of a relatively small business can make a big impact on the world through networking and institution building. Hammel is owner, president, and tennis professional of the Longfellow Clubs, a group of four health and recreation clubs established in 1972 and now located in Wayland,

Sudbury, Natick, and Franklin, Massachusetts. These four clubs now serve more than 10,000 members and were founded with the express purpose of making a contribution to the health of all life on earth.

Hammel's contribution to the emerging accountability infrastructure, however, goes far beyond his work at the Longfellow Clubs. He is responsible (sometimes with others, but as a primary leader in all cases) for founding four different and now important associations that are leading today's charge toward a different – more accountable and responsible – corporate world. First, New England Businesses for Social Responsibility (NEBSR), which he founded in 1988 and then went on to serve as president. Three years later, he founded the national organization Business for Social Responsibility (BSR), which is now one of the world's largest business membership organizations focused on accountability and responsibility, and which was subsequently led by difference maker Bob Dunn. Later, in 1998 Hammel initiated the International Symposium on Business and Spirituality, where he still serves as chair. Not yet finished with his entrepreneurial activities, Hammel turned his attention to regionalization and healthy small businesses in 2001, when he cofounded the Business Alliance for Local Living Economies (BALLE). He serves, at the time of writing, as its co-chair, and also as co-chair of the regional affiliate in the Greater Boston area, the Responsible Business Association, which grew out of the divested local chapter of the national BSR organization. Further, thinking about being local in a small business spurred Hammel to publish (with Gun Denhart) his first book, *Growing Local Value*, in 2007.

Hammel's social consciousness began to develop at a young age, as he relates:

> My social conscience was developed through my parents who have – we were in Salt Lake City, Utah, at that time – very progressive views and are very concerned about humanity and fairness in the world and against racism, so I was brought up on those values. Also, my mother was a founder and a leader of a church, the United Church of Christ, which is a liberal Protestant denomination. It was one of the two United Church of Christ churches in Utah then and *the* most radical church in the state. The pastor was the first public clergy person to protest the war in Vietnam. We were active in the civil rights movement, so part of existing in my community and in my church and family was really burned into my heart and soul – a commitment to changing the world. I remember when I was six, seven, or eight seeing a slide show on Albert Schweitzer or some missionary in Africa (I remember him as Albert Schweitzer but who knows who it was) and at that point deciding I wanted to spend the rest of my life dedicated to serving humanity and God. So that has pretty much guided all my decisions there on out. My parents were both teachers and both tennis pros and both in the Tennis Hall of Fame in Utah. So when I came to Boston I was a radical in the '60s and came to work with

other people who were committed to fighting against the war in Vietnam and fighting against racism.

After majoring in political science and math education at the University of Utah (and founding the local university chapter of the activist organization Students for a Democratic Society during the Vietnam War era), Hammel migrated to Boston to seek a teaching job during the early 1970s when teaching jobs were scarce. He ended up teaching tennis for eight years, and in 1980 cofounded the Longfellow Clubs as indoor tennis clubs (now expanded to full service health clubs), with a mission "To build a world where everyone's basic needs are met, and people experience love, happiness, and fulfillment. To create a model organization, through the development of successful health and recreation clubs, that works toward the attainment of our global vision."[122]

Part of building any social movement, including the accountability infrastructure, involves connecting with others who have similar ideals, insights, and values. Recognizing this need, Hammel began trying to find like-minded people early on:

> From the very beginning we were looking around for other businesses that shared those values. In those days, in 1980, even doing a mission statement was radical, let alone a mission statement that included other stakeholders than just customers or owners. Most mission statements focused on making the customer happy and that meant being profitable, and we expanded that to trying to change the world, to taking care of the environment, taking care of our staff, taking care of vendors, and contributing to the community in any way we could. So we went about that for a few years.
>
> We were looking for businesses that shared these values to talk with them and figure out ways to do it together. We started hearing about Ben & Jerry's[123] in '85 and then went to a conference and heard Ben Cohen speak and talked to him about it. The idea of radical or innovative entrepreneurs coming together and organizing themselves to change the world is sort of a paradoxical notion because entrepreneurs are about as independent people as you get. If you overlay that with radical ex-hippie or '60s graduates who were trying to change the world you've got a whole other overlay of complicated personalities that makes it difficult to organize. But, nonetheless, it needed to be done. I was clear, having been involved in organizations since I was 14, not to mention my church at an early age. We needed to have an organization. Then in 1988 I organized a group of businesses that committed to that [type of vision] and we formed New England Businesses for Social Responsibility. And that included Tom's of Maine,[124] it included Stonyfield Farm,[125] it included Ben & Jerry's, it included Stride Rite.[126]

The businesses that joined in NEBSR were those whose leaders had publicly committed their companies to a mission of responsibility or a multiple-bottom-line orientation, but, as Hammel recalls,

> There was willingness to participate, but there wasn't a lot of leadership. There weren't that many socially responsible businesses around in 1988. So at that time it was a very small group, but I knew that [an association] needed to happen, and we had the founding meeting in that room right there [pointing to a room across the hall from where we were sitting at the Longfellow Club in Natick, Massachusetts] in September 1988. We had very few people show up, but we started it and got it going. It kept growing and growing, though it had its ups and downs.

Hammel continues the story,

> In 1991 we founded the national BSR and that really got some traction. Then in 1993 we held our first national conference in Washington, DC. We got President Clinton, Senator Bill Bradley, and Paul Fireman, chairman of Reebok, to speak. We had James Rouse, the legendary socially responsible developer, speak. We had Robert Reich, the secretary of labor [in the Clinton administration] speak. There were some pretty heavy hitters. So we became a factor at that point. The term "social responsibility" was a term that had been used in the '90s around the nuclear-weapons-freeze movement. One of the leaders of that whole movement was [a group] called Physicians for Social Responsibility, so somebody started talking about Businesses for Social Responsibility, and it started catching on.

Business for Social Responsibility

Three years later, Hammel with colleagues, realizing that larger businesses were being attracted to the idea of NEBSR, founded what is now the national association BSR. He recounts the story of what happened next, highlighting some of the complexities of operating in the domain of a social movement:

> All the small businesses were striving to be big businesses, and we've always felt a little bit like we had an inferiority complex because it was the big businesses that really had an impact. We didn't feel we had much of an impact other than "our community." I put that in quotes because that was, "Well, that's nice to be local, but it really doesn't change the world," so by about 1999 or so BSR had been taken over by big business, basically. In 1999 they let go of all the local initiatives and all the small businesses and so we were left hanging and trying to figure out what we were going to do next.

■ Bob Dunn and the evolution of BSR

During the early 1990s when Hammel and his collaborators gave BSR its start, Bob Dunn was still working at Levi Strauss, which had just recently developed its innovative supplier code of conduct. Dunn recalls what happened next:

> In 1992 or '93 I was approached by a group of business leaders who had the idea of creating an entity in Washington, DC, that would serve as a counterbalance to the established business organizations by bringing business leaders to Washington to advocate for progressive public policy. This was an initiative that was started by leaders of companies like Tom's of Maine, Patagonia, The Body Shop and Ben & Jerry's, and I told them that I wasn't the right person to lead that organization and that I had reservations about whether they would be successful, because they were undercapitalized and for the most part represented a collection of small businesses. I worried that people wouldn't pay attention because they weren't major campaign contributors and because they didn't speak for thousands of companies and because they didn't have the resources to build that kind of a membership.

Despite Dunn initially turning down the opportunity to lead BSR, the group persisted and established a small presence in Washington, working in conjunction with the Clinton administration. But, after about a year, as Dunn recalls,

> It was then clear to the board of directors that the original concept wasn't going to be as impactful as they had hoped. They needed to step back, reflect, and either find a different way to be successful pursuing that strategy or modify the mission of the organization or close down the organization. So some of the people who had originally approached me about possibly leading the organization asked if I would join that discussion, because one of the frustrations had been that they had not been able to attract large companies and that a company like Levi Strauss was not a member. I agreed because I cared about these people and what they were trying to do and spent a weekend at Cape Cod with the board of directors. They said, "Well, you have argued against what we set out to do, what would you advocate instead?"

This question, of course, put Dunn on the spot. He remembers his response:

> I said that I thought that they had taken on a difficult assignment and that, as someone who was trying to advance the agenda they cared about inside a company, I was more worried about the decisions that were taken every day inside the company than I was about the decisions that were being made in Washington.

Dunn also pointed out that

> When Levi Strauss had tried to be a leader, whenever we sought to work on an issue or a problem, I had been struck by the fact that there was no place to turn for guidance or help. That there was no one who knew the players or who could map the field or who had their hands on the best practices, and so forth. That, if BSR became an organization that really sought to work with companies of all sizes and sectors, and help make it easier for them to implement more responsible policies and practices, then I thought there was a real need for that.
>
> After a lot of discussion, the board basically embraced that as a new mission and asked if I would serve as a co-chair and asked if Levi Strauss would join. I said that, with this new charter, Levi Strauss would be very comfortable as a member and that I was happy to serve as a co-chair, along with Arnold Hyatt, who was then the CEO of Stride Rite, and Helen Mills, who was the first franchisee for The Body Shop in the United States. So we were tri-chairs.

Other shifts for BSR were in the works, since BSR's initial executive director had signed on to do public policy work, not to focus on internal company activities, operations, and impacts, and decided to leave. The BSR board began searching for a replacement. Dunn smiles as he recalls what happened next:

> So we began a search process and saw a lot of good people and interviewed them, but no one was satisfied and time was passing. We finally resolved that we probably needed to go out and pay a search firm a fee and get help even though we didn't have money. After that meeting I went back to my room — it was in Washington, DC — and Arnold Hyatt asked if he could stop by and just chat a bit, and I said sure. He said that after the meeting had formally adjourned the other members of the search committee had been talking. They felt that this had been *my* idea and that I should lead it and make it happen. And I told him that it was a very nice offer, but that I was pretty happy where I was, and didn't really feel that I could do that.

Remembering Hyatt's persuasive abilities, Dunn continues,

> He's amazing. He's such a smart man, and such a kind man. So he said, "Well, here's what I think you should do. You know, we're co-chairs of a young organization that's fragile. Somehow we have to convince members of this board to make a real commitment. If you just say no, that's going to be modeling the wrong behavior. So why don't you just go back to San Francisco and write me a letter and say, 'You know, Arnold, I would really love to do this, and here's the set of problems for me that would have to be overcome.' " So I went back to San Francisco, wrote this letter, and said, "I'm not

willing to move to Washington and I wouldn't want to take this on and spend the whole year just trying to raise my own salary. There would have to be an assurance of pledges from board members, and it would be imperative for me that the organization would be an open organization and that we not set ourselves up to sit in judgment as to who's virtuous and who's not. I'd rather just say we're going to make everyone *more* virtuous and not worry about it." I knew that was a very contentious issue in the organization. I wrote probably seven or eight things, and said that I again appreciated the offer and was sorry that it wouldn't work.

But Hyatt was not one to take no for an answer easily, as Dunn remembers:

I think two days later Arnold called and said, "You know, Bob, I have wonderful news for you. The board's been talking and we've agreed to all of your conditions. So now there's no reason at all why you can't say yes!" He's just masterful. So I went in and had a long talk with the chairman and CEO of Levi Strauss [Robert Haas] and said this had all happened very unexpectedly without my solicitation, and I said I found that I wanted to think about this, because it was the work that I was most passionate about and cared about most deeply. So [Haas] said, 'You have to follow your heart on some of this. I'm happy to be a talking partner.' "

In an odd way, the timing was right. Dunn's father had recently passed away and he had spent time taking care of him, giving him time to contemplate the purpose of his own life. As he states, "This opportunity struck me as a way in which I could capitalize on everything I had done and use it to really good advantage."

Several issues arose as Dunn began to try to move the new version of BSR forward: local chapters were not charging membership fees, meaning that they were composed mainly of small businesses, while he and other members of the board believed that the greatest impacts would come from involving large businesses. Some of the early members of BSR were interested more in the political agenda and pushing larger companies to change, or in other political processes such as the peace movement, rather than wanting to focus internally on companies.

Once the purposes of the new BSR were sorted out, it began to rapidly expand. After starting in Dunn's own home, as Dunn recalls,

BSR moved from the house to an unheated garage space that was at least arguably in a commercial district, but not anywhere near downtown. It began to grow and attract companies. It began to develop products and services, monitor news and trends and developments in the field, an annual conference, workshops and trainings, working groups of people who had a common interest in an issue or who were aligned by sector. As we started working with larger companies, it became clear that we had to be able to work beyond the boundaries of the United States and that led to a commitment on our part to support the creation of organizations initially throughout the hemisphere which ultimately became the Empresa Alliance. We opened an office in Europe for BSR and helped to create a group in Israel and supported organizations in places like the Philippians and South Africa and Japan. Then eventually we opened an office in China, as well as starting to do more and more supply chain work with member companies.

BSR ultimately decided to focus away from the smaller local networks in favor of attracting and retaining larger businesses, a decision guided at least partially by available resources, as Dunn relates:

You know, if we were 25 or 30 people, and even if we were going to double or triple in size, we came to believe that we would have the greatest impact if we were working with the large global companies, and that we could influence smaller companies by using the larger companies to apply standards to their supply chain partners. When we stepped back and looked at our work over the first five or six years, it seemed to everyone that that was the best way to get the highest return on the assets that we had. We never excluded smaller businesses, but we began to tailor our offerings so that they were of greater value to larger companies and recognize that what did happen would happen. Namely, that the smaller businesses would begin to opt out and look for alternative ways to meet some of their needs. BSR has evolved into an organization that's primarily an organization of large global companies, and over time BSR has also sought to establish its core competencies in certain sectors where either there seems to be the greatest impact on society and the environment like mining and extractive industries, or industries where there seems to be the greatest pressure for change, which might be companies like consumer-branded companies, and those who seem to have the greatest impact on others like the information technology sector or the financial sector.

BSR[127] today is one of the global leaders in helping businesses navigate the complexities of the global economy from an ethical, social, and ecologically responsible stance. The stated mission is that "Business for Social Responsibility seeks to create a just and sustainable world by working with companies to promote more responsible business practices, innovation and collaboration."[128] Headquartered in San Francisco, BSR serves its 250 members and other Global 1000 enterprises, and focuses on helping members address a diverse array of issues, including ethics, environment, community investment, governance and accountability, human rights, market and workplace issues, and mission, vision, and values. BSR promotes multi-sector collaboration, attempts to research and analyze the business case for better responsibility, and works in alliance with numerous related organizations throughout the globe. Its annual conference brings together more than 1,000 leaders from around the world to discuss issues relevant to corporate responsibility.

Developed along the lines that Dunn noted, BSR also offers advisory services to companies in specific industries that have particular issues associated with corporate citizenship, notably consumer goods, information and communications technology, extractive industries, pharmaceuticals and biotechnology, food and agriculture, and transportation. BSR offers tools and methodologies to help with responsibility reporting, implementation, stakeholder engagement, supply chain management, and developing strategies for responsibility strategy and structure, assessment, and policy. In addition, true to its original intent of providing resources to companies, BSR offers numerous online tools and guidelines on relevant topics and generally serves as an opinion leader on issues related to responsibility management and accountability.

Laury Hammel moves on

Business and spirituality

Laury Hammel did not stop creating networks and alliances with the founding and reorientation of BSR toward large companies. In 1997, he got together with other interested parties and started the first-ever Symposium on Business and Spirituality, now an annual international event that draws together people interested in integrating the values of building a better world directly into businesses. The International Symposium on Business and Spirituality states the following goals for participants:

- Make a positive impact on the local and global community, and actively contribute to the greater good

- Create corporate cultures that engage all stakeholders in open-hearted dialogue embracing the diversity of ideas, beliefs, faiths, and backgrounds

- Foster integrity and honesty by modeling congruent and principled leadership

- Rejoice in the beauty of the moment, revel in life, celebrate growth and learning, reflect on discoveries, rise to challenges, and appreciate fun and humor[129]

Hammel recalls the start of the Business and Spirituality conference,

> In 1997 I got together some people from Andover-Newton Theological Semi-
> nary and some business leaders involved in BSR New England, and we
> wanted to set up a symposium that would deal specifically with what the
> philosophical, emotional, and spiritual foundation was for the running of
> business.

That germ of an idea became in 1998 the Symposium on Spirituality and Business, which has been run every year since that time.

Engaging local networks

After it became clear that BSR was gong to be oriented toward multinational corporations rather than small local businesses, Hammel started thinking about the ways in which smaller businesses could contribute to society. He remembers,

> [After BSR divested the local chapters,] we ran into people like Michael Shu-
> man, who was working on going local. If you want to talk about socially
> responsible business, his two books are mandatory reading. One is called
> *Going Local*, and another one is called *The Small-Mart Revolution*. He and
> David Korten[130] started talking to us about the importance of small business
> in changing the world. They noted that the fact that we are local and small is
> actually good and not something to feel inferior about, or a situation where
> we were thinking, "Well, if someday we could grow up, we'll be able to be in
> big business."

The insight about the importance of local businesses in sustaining healthy communities became the impetus for the formation of another network, as Hammel points out,

> At that point, it was around the same time that the protests were happening
> in Seattle against the WTO [World Trade Organization], and it became
> apparent that big businesses not only didn't have necessarily the same inter-
> ests as small businesses, but they were actually the main contributors to
> destroying our planet. BSR recognized before we did that there was a big dif-
> ference between us and them, so in 2001 we organized another group called
> the Business Alliance for Local Living Economies [BALLE] and that board
> includes David Korten, Michael Shuman and Judy Wicks and now Paul Sagi-
> naw.

BALLE seems to have struck a chord around rootedness and community with a lot of people, as Hammel notes,

Five years [after starting BALLE] there were almost 50 local networks around North America, and there are thousands and thousands of businesses involved. So we feel that being local is really, really important to keeping a deep connection with the community. When you have these chains and big-box stores, by their very structure they are oriented to profitability, as opposed to providing a unique service that meets the needs and wants of the people in the community. So we think local's critical; we think being small is important. We think being locally owned is important. We think that being independent and not having to be publicly held is an important issue. When you take on the model about multiple stakeholders, it's all about how you can contribute to the local community by working with various stakeholders. And that's what my book[131] is about, which is how businesses can contribute to the community through all the various stakeholders.

Business Alliance for Local Living Economies

BALLE catalyzes, strengthens, and connects the local networks and alliances that comprise its membership.[132] Using a flexible definition, BALLE argues that the definition of local is "really the area that people in the community consider to be local. Is your region defined by natural landscape features, or historic boundaries? Rural communities may define themselves by county, or by multiple counties."[133] In developing its networks, which are loosely linked to the national organization, BALLE has developed a definition of a local living economy and specific principles associated with it (see Box 7.1).

Hammel explains the rationale behind the formation of BALLE. Referring to the typical business strategy of growing as big as possible, he notes,

> The BALLE movement really rejects that notion that the "bigger is better" model is good. We think aesthetically and lifestyle-wise that having a Starbucks and a McDonald's on every corner of every city in the world is really not a very pretty picture; we think that there's a character of community issue. There's an issue of uniqueness and there's an issue of connecting with a local owner who's got a particular style of running a business, which is very important to who we are as human beings; and the desire to have the exact same flavor of coffee in Starbucks in Boston as you have in San Francisco — that desire is certainly legitimate but we find that to be less important than the ability to have a unique flavor that represents the particular community and the person who is the entrepreneur.

Reflecting on the earlier split of the local groups from BSR, Hammel comments,

> At that point in time we [BSR] thought that being big was the only way to do it. As time went on what happened was we didn't stop thinking that way. We

Box 7.1 **BALLE's Living Economy Principles**

A Living Economy ensures that economic power resides locally, sustaining healthy community life and natural life as well as long-term economic viability. A Living Economy is guided by the following principles:

- Living economy communities produce and exchange locally as many products needed by their citizens as they reasonably can, while reaching out to other communities to trade in those products they cannot reasonably produce at home. These communities value their unique character and encourage cultural exchange and cooperation.

- Living economy **public policies** support decentralized ownership of businesses and farms, fair wages, taxes, and budget allocations, trade policies benefiting local economies, and stewardship of the natural environment.

- Living economy **citizens** appreciate the benefits of buying from living economy businesses and, if necessary, are willing to pay a price premium to secure those personal and community benefits.

- Living economy **investors** value businesses that are community stewards and as such accept a "living return" on their financial investments rather than a maximum return, recognizing the value derived from enjoying a healthy and vibrant community and sustainable global economy.

- Living economy **media** provide sources of news independent of corporate control, so that citizens can make informed decisions in the best interests of their communities and natural environment.

- Living economy **businesses** are primarily independent and locally owned, and value the needs and interests of all stakeholders, while building long-term profitability.

They strive to:

- Source products from businesses with similar values, with a preference for local procurement
- Provide employees a healthy workplace with meaningful living-wage jobs
- Offer customers personal service and useful safe, quality products
- Work with suppliers to establish a fair exchange
- Cooperate with other businesses in ways that balance their self-interest with their obligation to the community and future generations
- Use their business practices to support an inclusive and healthy community, and to protect our natural environment
- Yield a "living return" to owners and investors[134]

just kept getting shunted to the side because we didn't have any money and BSR was focusing its time and energy with people who had all the money, which were big businesses. In fact, I ran BSR for two years out of my office, and after we organized a formal board and one of the people who was making this whole thing happen called me up at one point and said, "Now that the board has been formed, I think a couple of other people who are small-business people have resigned and I think it's probably time for you to resign." I asked, "Why is that?" He said, "Well here's the deal, Laury, we're looking for people who either have money or stature and you don't have either."

Despite wondering about whether spending the time and energy to build another entity was worthwhile, Hammel found himself being drawn toward a new organization. He elaborates,

You've worked so hard for 12 years to make [BSR] happen and it was actually doing a pretty good job. I really didn't want to start this thing over. You know, get people together again. Raise the money. Talk to the people. I actually never take a penny; it's just a cost center for me and the business. Then what happened was that, little by little, through conversations with [board members of] the Social Venture Network, I started realizing that our vision of the future and our vision of what was really possible for our communities was really in direct opposition to what these big businesses were doing. Even though we knew there were a lot of businesses we didn't really like being involved with, we sort of said they were like bad apples. But then we started reading David Korten's work and realizing that it's just the other way around. There is almost no publicly held company that was really doing a good job of practicing social responsible business.

The trigger point — and major difference between Hammel's thinking and Bob Dunn's — for Hammel's shifting of his energy towards local economies came after recognizing that the new emphasis at BSR would be on multinational corporations, even if they were considered to be poor performers with respect to their responsibilities. He recalls some of his thinking at that time:

I went [to the BSR conference in about 2001] to see what was going on and maybe recruit some new members because there were still some small businesses that were involved at the conference at that point. There were people sitting around; four people had name tags with Philip Morris Company. I thought it was maybe Philip/Morris, like an advertising agency or something. "You guys aren't from the cigarette company are you?" They responded, "Yeah." I said, "You are? Because, well, what do you do that's socially responsible?" They got up and left when I said that.

But that was my nightmare, because when we were starting people would say, "Are you going to let Philip Morris in? You're going to let RJR in? Are you going to let Exxon in?" We said, "We don't think they want to join." Well, what happened was: companies like that did join. Part of their reason was that management was legitimately interested in trying to improve their business practice. But a large part of it was trying to improve their image. So I was like, "Whoa!" It was a great juxtaposition for why I was leaving that organization and going to start another one. Then it became clear that we had more that was different than we had in common. BSR recognized that before we [BALLE] did.

The differences that emerged reflect a different attitude toward big businesses on the part of BSR and the members of BALLE. Hammel explains some of the logic:

[For example], Wal-Mart was tossing tons of businesses into bankruptcy, and CVS was pushing out pharmacies. Home Depot was pushing out hardware stores and lumber yards that were independent, local. At the beginning we embraced BSR and embraced Home Depot because they did some good things. But the bottom line is that their role towards developing a diverse economy and supporting entrepreneurship was just devastating. As time went along we started realizing that there was a philosophical basis for [the split] that they understood better than we did. Intuitively, anyway.

So we started organizing around local living economies, and there was a huge interest in making that happen, and we were in the middle now of this major wave of people who wanted to either build socially responsible small businesses or wanted to support them. It was an interesting transition. We still work with BSR. We're looking at this as evolution not revolution. A revolution implies bad guys and that we're going to get together and kick the bad guys out. What we're really talking about is an evolutionary process where, even though we're focusing on small and mid-size companies, we know that there will be a lot of big corporations around for many years. If people are working to improve them, we say great. But we think the most important way to improve them is — in many cases — to support them downsizing, breaking up, and do what the trust busters did back in the days of Theodore Roosevelt. So we're not saying that the big businesses are the bad guys and we're the good guys, because there are a lot of bad small businesses in the world. What we are saying is that the structure of small businesses in the world economy and, in particular, local economies is crucial to successful local economies. We would like to encourage people to support local small businesses voluntarily. We're trying to develop sort of a cultural mandate where people want to support that even more than they already do.

Social Venture Network

Hammel notes that he has worked with Social Venture Network (SVN), a network organization that has spawned a number of corporate responsibility initiatives, including BALLE. SVN was founded in 1987 by a group of leaders focused on responsible entrepreneurship and investment. SVN serves as a non-profit network "that transforms the way the world does business by leveraging its members' collective strengths of leadership, knowledge, and enterprise for a more just and sustainable economy."[135] SVN's mission, as listed in 2007, is presented in Box 7.2.

Box 7.2 **Social Venture Network's Mission**

SVN inspires a community of business and social leaders to build a just economy and sustainable planet. SVN works to achieve this mission by:

- Providing forums, information, and initiatives that enable leaders to work together to transform the way the world does business
- Sharing best practices and resources that help companies generate healthy profits and serve the common good
- Supporting a diverse community of leaders who can effect positive social change through business
- Creating a vibrant community that nourishes deep and lasting friendships
- Producing unique conferences that promote the exchange of ideas and encourage the development of relationships and partnerships
- Offering programs that support the spiritual, professional, and personal development of our members[136]

In addition to helping Hammel form BALLE, the SVN has fostered numerous other initiatives over the years, including a book partnership with Berrett-Koehler Publishers, the Social Impact Leadership Coalition (a network of networks consisting of 14 national non-profits focused on responsible enterprise), and the Social Venture Institute to mentor and support entrepreneurs. SVN has also been involved in creating SVN's Standard on Corporate Social Responsibility for entrepreneurs and a Carbon Neutral Initiative designed to fight global warming.

David Grayson

The institution-building process of a global social movement needs people who have the foresight to build new networks of like-minded people and create new organizations – and the capacity to frame things in novel ways that help people see what they could not see before. One of the people who has done both of these things for many years is David Grayson, CBE (Commander of the British Empire, one of the highest honors the UK gives to individuals). Grayson is now director of the Doughty Centre for Corporate Responsibility and holder of the Doughty Chair of Corporate Responsibility at Cranfield University. Author of *Business-Led Corporate Responsibility Coalitions: Learning from the Example of Business in the Community in the UK*, Grayson has been a director of Business in the Community (BITC), which is a unique movement of over 700 of the UK's major companies. BITC companies commit themselves to improving their positive impact on society. Grayson has been with BITC since 1987, where he has held central positions, including joint managing director of BITC and managing director of the Business Strategy Group. He also serves as the founder and principal of the UK's first virtual corporate university, BLU, which is designed for individuals who are designing policy and delivering services for small business enterprises. Grayson holds masters' degrees from Cambridge and Brussels Universities; and an MBA from Newcastle University.

Grayson explains how he initially got involved in the work that ultimately led him to BITC:

> At the end of my master's [1978], I went to work in Newcastle in the northeast of England for Procter & Gamble in marketing management [from 1978 to 1980]. I suddenly found myself living in a region of the country that was going to experience in practice all of the things I had just been studying theoretically, just as Margaret Thatcher came to power in 1979, because it's a region with coal mining, ship building, steel making, basic chemical manufacturing, etc. I started to get interested and began talking to people in local political parties in the region, in local government, the trade unions, and the business organizations and found, at that stage, very little thinking going on about where the new jobs, the new business, were going to come from apart from a rather touching belief that we'd all be OK.

He continues, illustrating how these insights shaped his actions as an entrepreneur:

> With a friend of mine I started a non-profit organization called Project North East in the summer of 1980 with absolutely nothing, frankly. We rather bravely or madly quit our jobs at the time just to start this not-for-profit. That organization, I'm pleased to say, is still going strong now 26 years [later as PNE Group working] in about 40 countries around the world. What we

started off doing in 1980 was to develop some new approaches to job and enterprise generation, by doing some demonstration projects that we could then write up and share with others so they might become new models. We started some variously identified projects that helped young people to find employment by starting their own businesses. I think that we ran promotional campaigns around the idea of creating a great job, which was quite new at that stage and particularly in that part of the country. We became quite well known as a result of a lot our hands-on activities. We had started what would now be called a microcredit enterprise, which provides low-interest, low-security baseline-scale loans to help young people start their own businesses. That came to the attention of various people nationally, who were setting up something very similar on a national basis. We worked to start what became known as the Prince's Youth Business Trust in the UK, which is a fund that helps young people start their own business.

Business in the Community

Grayson recalls his next move:

> From there I moved over very quickly to BITC, which had been going at that point for about three or four years, initially very much concerned with small-business development. Of course, now BITC is more than 25 years old and is very active in forming ideas of corporate social responsibility overall — responsible business practice. Over time, we made the evolution from an emphasis on what a big company could contribute to the community to recognizing that, while that was important and a useful contribution, it was very limited by contrast to how a business operates within its core operations in terms of how it treats its own employees, its supply chain, its customers, as well as its wide impact on the environment and society.

The recognition of where company impacts were actually most important grew out of a series of insights, according to Grayson, that over time shifted BITC's emphasis:

> We had the recognition that company contributions into the community would always have to be constrained by 1% of pre-tax properties or 5% or what have you. Whereas if you could get companies to think not just "We're responsible because we're sponsoring some school projects or some training initiatives" but [to recognize they're] not really thinking about how they are handling their own employees' learning and training opportunities, and recognizing that, if you could get a company which had been doing some projects to help disabled people get into employment, not just to sponsor those

external activities, but to then start to think about how they themselves recruited and developed disabled employees, that would have a much, much bigger impact.

BITC describes itself as "a unique movement of over 800 of the UK's top companies committed to improving their positive impact on society."[137] Celebrating its 25th anniversary in 2007, BITC is one of the longest-running initiatives anywhere in which businesses concerned about their social and environmental impacts attempt to create a greater emphasis on responsibility and accountability. Member companies are expected to measure and report their societal impacts, and the initiatives that they have take to produce positive change on society and the natural environment. Established in 1982 by a small group of companies that wanted to take action against the same backdrop of youth unemployment that Grayson was dealing with in the northeast of England, BITC has benefited from the active involvement of its president the Prince of Wales since 1985.

Perhaps most notable among BITC's programs is the Prince's Seeing is Believing program, which tries to develop inspirational leadership by taking senior business leaders into rural and inner cities areas to see for themselves the ways that businesses can help, and are helping, to improve conditions. Seeing is Believing was founded in 1990 by the Prince of Wales with the belief that a direct experience of disadvantaged urban and rural conditions would be a powerful motivator for change leadership among business executives.

In addition, BITC provides benchmarking tools for established businesses so that they can measure their social and environmental impacts – and report progress. In 1996, BITC established an environmental index, which was expanded into the Corporate Responsibility Index at the request of member companies in 2002 to encompass social as well as environmental impacts. Participating companies complete a survey and then get feedback on their progress from BITC, based on the results and comparisons with other companies. Results of the CR Index are published in *The Sunday Times* "Companies That Count" supplement each May, providing visibility and transparency around issues of corporate responsibility. BITC also supports companies in developing and implementing volunteer programs.

Grayson reflects on the changes that have taken place in BITC and elsewhere in the world of corporate responsibility since he has been involved:

> Over the years at various crucial points in our history, we have had some quite major conversations, trying to develop a forward agenda. We have consciously tried to push the bar higher rather than just waiting for it to be pushed higher by outsiders. So, for example, after the third Thatcher general election victory in 1987, we set up a series of leadership teams that would look at the role business might play in many different aspects of urban regeneration, which was a major social and political issue in the UK at the end of the 1980s. In 1990–91 I personally led a program called "Directions for the

'90s", which tried to foresee what the priorities for businesses would be in the next decade in terms of their role in society and in the community. In the mid-1990s, we looked at how businesses might measure their impacts in terms of environment and social reporting.

More recently, in 2002, we launched the Corporate Responsibility Index, which we do now each year, and we publish that with one of our leading newspapers, *The Sunday Times*. We also produce an annual supplement with them which describes the results of our Corporate Responsibility Index. And we continue to try and evolve the agenda.

In evolving this agenda, BITC obviously faced numerous obstacles and challenges, as have all the other institutions discussed earlier. Grayson highlights some of them:

I think there are continuing obstacles in terms of getting air time for the issue. I think by comparison with 5, 10, or certainly 15 years ago, the seriousness with which the mainstream media, with which the political world, the business media, the business schools, and so on, treat this issue has increased dramatically, so there's much, much more attention. In a speech I made the point that if you Google "corporate social responsibility" now, you'll get over 42 million references. So this is much more of a serious issue than it was even a few years ago. But it's still, I think, a constant battle to get quality boardroom attention for the issues.

International Business Leaders Forum

BITC also spawned another important institution dealing with corporate responsibility, the International Business Leaders Forum (IBLF). Grayson relates a brief history:

In February 1990, we held an international meeting in Charleston, South Carolina, with about 140 business leaders from 13 or 14 different countries, but principally from the US and the UK, to talk about what might be the role of business in this drastically changing world. That was just a few weeks after the Berlin Wall had come down, of course, and that was the origin of the International Business Leaders Forum, which has now been going for over 15 years as an independent organization, based and successfully operating in some 50 or more countries around the world since then.

The IBLF claims that it is "at the heart of sustainable business. IBLF promotes responsible business leadership and partnerships for international development."[138] According to the website, the IBLF "works with business, government and civil society to enhance the contribution that companies can make to sustainable development."[139] The organization comprises the chief executives of more than 100 global corporations and private investors, and focuses on business's role in achieving the UN's Millennium Development Goals (see Chapter 5), reducing global poverty, and promoting economic stability. IBLF now works with governments, NGOs, and businesses in more than 60 countries around the world. IBLF focuses on multi-sector collaborations and partnerships, enhancing visionary leadership, and creative solutions to economic development.

Small Business Journey

Much as Laury Hammel has focused on the role of smaller businesses in fostering economic health and promulgating ethical business, David Grayson has also worked on the responsibility of small and medium-sized enterprises (SMEs), having founded the Small Business Consortium and created a set of tools designed to help small businesses behave responsibly.[140] The Small Business Journey provides a set of guidelines and tools that show people in small businesses how to behave responsibly – and make a profit – focusing on multiple bottom lines, stakeholders, and generally responsible business practice.

Grayson explains the evolution of this newer entity:

> Here in the UK a number of different organizations have come together, some of them representing small firms, like the British Chamber of Commerce, and the Institute for Directors, and the Federation for Small Businesses, together with Business in the Community. We formed the Small Business Consortium, which I am chairman of, and we developed something called the Small Business Journey. We're now talking with other countries in the European Union to see if they would be interested in doing something similar. I very much hope that we can do more to encourage small firms. Indeed, we can learn from small firms in terms of responsible business, because I think in the next few years the responsible business agenda will be developing faster amongst small firms rather than amongst the international companies.

Small businesses are not only the major source of new jobs in the world, but, as Grayson points out,

> I think small firms that really get to this [responsibility] agenda, *really* understand it, find it much easier to integrate it throughout their business because typically the owner-manager, the person running the business, will know personally everyone in the business. They probably are seeing each other day in and day out. It's much easier for them to really understand what this means in practice for their business. So if an owner-manager of a small business really understands and believes in this agenda, I think they'll probably be able

to make faster progress than some huge multinational that's operating in 150 different countries or more, maybe with several hundred thousand employees, whom you have to try and engage and convince.

Focus on multinationals

In the emerging infrastructure around corporate accountability and responsibility, it is large corporations that have been the predominant focus, as their impacts are the most notable. We have already seen how BSR shifted its focus toward multinationals, creating some tensions with the philosophy of its founders. Clearly, there is a need to recognize the role that both multinational companies and SMEs play in fostering a climate of accountability, responsibility, and transparency. The work of the next difference maker, Brad Googins, emphasizes bringing the responsibility agenda to multinationals.

Bradley K. (Brad) Googins

Bradley K. (Brad) Googins is the executive director of the Boston College Center for Corporate Citizenship (CCC), which is a company membership organization focused on helping businesses enhance their corporate responsibility. It has a membership of more than 320 companies. Googins earlier founded the Center for Work and Family, now housed at Boston College, in 1990 at Boston University. Googins holds a bachelor's degree and a master's in social work from Boston College and gained a PhD in social policy from the Heller Graduate School at Brandeis University, Massachusetts.

Googins was on the path to becoming a Jesuit priest when he

> stumbled across this field of practice called social work and thought this sounded interesting. It took almost two years of asking within the Jesuits if I could go and get a master's in social work — they were not happy about that. They wanted me to go and teach English. But they finally relented if I would go to Boston College.

He relates what happened next as he tried to figure out what work made the most sense:

> I got my master's in social work, but had no idea what I was doing. In fact, I went up to Worcester the summer before to do some case work — it was all

new to me, and I sort of liked it but — and this is important — as much as I liked it, it was much too limiting for me. It was great helping this person, but all I could see were all of the systemic issues behind it, so when I went to the School of Social Work, they said, "It sounds like you want to major in community organizing." I said, "What's that?" and they said, "You want to talk to this guy Ed Burke, who's just come to the school and is starting a new program." So I stumbled my way into this sort of macro practice of social work at a very interesting time.

As Googins remembers it, there was a constellation of key academics around urban and city planning and community planning, who were new to the School of Social Work at the time. One of them was Edmund Burke, who in 1985 became the founder at Boston College of the Center for Corporate Community Relations, which is now the Center for Corporate Citizenship, headed by Googins. His path to the Center, however, has been far from straightforward.

A new direction emerged rather suddenly as Googins, after receiving his master's from Boston College, struggled with what to do next.

I wanted to focus, but had no idea on what. About four months later, I got a letter from the School of Social Work at Boston University saying that someone had recommended my name for a new position that they were creating for a grant that was going to develop some curriculum initiatives around alcoholism and community organizing. I was curious enough to go interview. I said, " I know something about community organizing, but quite honestly, alcoholism isn't something I know a lot about, other than helping to start a halfway house over in Malden."

It turns out that in the whole city of Boston — and this is quite amazing to me — in 1969, there were two social workers focused on alcoholism. So I said, "Hey, it wouldn't have been anything I would have chosen, but I liked the fact that it provided a focus." A couple of things happened. One is that I got really interested in the whole issue of alcoholism. What intrigued me about it was how pervasive it was, yet how little attention it would get within professional disciplines like medicine or social work. So I'd go down to the family service agency in Boston, and I'd say, "What percentage of your caseload does alcoholism factor in?" They'd say, "Oh, probably about 85%, 90% maybe." I'd ask, "Well, who here knows anything about alcoholism?" Nobody! So it was never touched upon, brought up, dealt with, even though it was the most basic problem.

The other thing that happened was that Googins was invited to participate in a seminar on case teaching taught by Harvard Business School's case teaching guru C. Roland (Chris) Christensen, a course that transformed his teaching.

From there, Googins was recruited to the Graduate School of Social Work at Boston College, which was starting a new program on alcoholism in industry. He recalls,

> I said, "Now I know something about alcoholism, but I don't know a thing about alcoholism in the workplace." They said, "Well, neither does anybody else." So off I trudged to Boston College and this experience opened up a whole new world: basically, the world of work.

With some pressure from the dean, Googins worked on his doctorate at Brandeis on a part-time basis and finished it, and then went to work at Boston University doing research on occupational alcoholism and, ultimately, became involved with the emerging field of employee assistance programs. He notes,

> It was an exciting time for me, because it was where I like to be. I like to be on the edge of something. I get bored if it gets too formalized, too set. This was the case with employee assistance, which was opening up all sorts of new and very interesting issues. Why should companies get involved in this? What are the boundaries between personal life and home life? So, as this was going on, a couple of interesting things began to happen.

From employee assistance Googins began becoming involved with the broader issue of work and family, in part because he and his wife had just had their first child, and he once again found himself on the cusp of a new field:

> I went and spent a year at Polaroid, where I knew people, and I wound up working with the vice president who put a committee together on single-parent issues, and that quickly broadened, as people said, "You know it's not just single parents, it's all parents. We're all struggling with these issues." I wanted to study this, so I wound up doing what turned out to be the first work-based study of work–family stress. It was a really interesting process, both doing the research, but even more so — it's one of those things that you hope for in your academic life, where it gets all sorts of attention because it is the first.

As this topic began to take shape, Googins started the Center for Work and Family (CWF) at Boston University in 1990. About that time, he also was awarded a Kellogg Fellowship, which gave him the freedom to spend about a quarter of his time exploring the world. He recounts what happened:

> It's an interesting program that takes about 30 or 40 people a year and for three years immerses them in a model of leadership training that is quite unique. It basically believes that people are much too narrowly focused and they want to expand your horizons so they send you out to the world by yourself or together with others in the group to explore the world. Not acad-

emically, not rigorously, but just go out and explore the world, related to anything but what you are currently interested in. They really want to stretch
you.

He went to see his dean at Boston University and got permission to do both the
CWF and the fellowship, which, with now two young children at home, created as
he puts it, "quite a furor."

Center for Work and Family

The CWF, now at Boston College, helps "organizations create effective workplaces
that support and develop healthy and productive employees."[141] CWF's vision is
"that companies and communities will work together to ensure their mutual prosperity and the well being of employees and their families."[142] CWF works with
human resources professionals in major companies to link academic work and corporate practice and emphasizes organizational change processes designed to produce better-balanced workplaces that are healthier for all workers and their families.

Moving to corporate citizenship

About ten years into running the CWF, Googins had another knock on his door —
this time from Boston College, where his former mentor Ed Burke had begun
another center — as founder and director of what was then the Center for Corporate
Community Relations (CCR). As with the CWF, this center had focused on field
building, in the CCR's case on building up the profession of corporate community
relations officers, a function within many large firms that focused on the interface
between a business and its local communities, with a particular emphasis on philanthropic activities. Burke was retiring and the CCR was seeking a new director.
Googins remembers the transition:

> I was interested professionally because the more I got into the work–life fam-
> ily [issues] the more I came up against the limits of corporations, because, no
> matter what they did in terms of flextime, childcare centers, and so on, it
> never even came close to meeting the real needs. Even then it was only a few
> people in a few privileged companies, so it bumped up against [the ques-
> tions of] what do communities do? What do governments do? What do col-
> leges do? So here was a very interesting proposition of a center at Boston
> College that focused on an area I was interested in, which had a membership
> model, which the CWF didn't, and had a very strong education model, which
> the CWF didn't. On the other hand, the CWF had been known for research,
> which the CCR wasn't.

For the CCR, which had its roots deeply in the narrower functional arena of cor-porate–community relations, the transition to the broader corporate citizenship agenda was not easy, as Googins recounts:

> Whether it was the employee assistance or work and family, I was at the right place at the right time. Here was the CCR, which was sort of a backwater of foundations and volunteering, and all of a sudden, after two or three years, the world started changing. Globalization was taking root more and more, and the whole notion of the role of corporations in society began to change. It was so clear to me that this center had to move, and it had to move in a broader context. It took me two years of really tough organizational struggle to make that happen. I was determined that the sustainability and success of the center depended on it moving with the times, so we chose the term Cen-ter for Corporate Citizenship (CCC) [in 2001], with the notion that it became a much broader umbrella to address a much broader set of issues. Corpo-rate citizenship became a much more profound set of issues in the board-room, as opposed to a function within the company, which is what the CCR was doing.

Building on his experience with the CWF, Googins also recognized that, in addi-tion to the CCC's existing strengths in the executive education of corporate–com-munity relations specialists, research needed to be a priority. He remembers his thinking:

> I decided that I wanted to really invest in research. The field of corporate citi-zenship in the US had almost no research. There was no one else doing what the center did in education. So with a lot of help from the Ford Foundation, we were able to incrementally start adding some research, some projects, and we built that up over the years, so that the move to corporate citizenship brought in all sorts of dimensions, a much more profound research compo-nent. It brought in a big globalization component because now the center is really operating globally and really tying in to things globally. The center also began to really look at moving from a model that focused on individual prac-titioners to how can the organization, the company itself, change.

Googins brings a broad perspective to the work of the CCC, stating,

> What I really love, and also worry about, is will this area become fossilized and put in a box and captured say by social reports or something like that? But right now the field is really filled with challenges; it's really up against a fundamental set of issues, which is the role of business in society, writ large and writ small. Yet to me the role of companies is really a fundamental part of how society operates.

Boston College Center for Corporate Citizenship

The BCCCC has a mission to engage "with companies to redefine business success as creating measurable gains for business and society. The Center achieves results through the power of research, education and member engagement" with a vision of having business "use its assets to help assure economic prosperity and a just and sustainable world."[143] Part of that mission is accomplished by bringing together the corporate responsibility leaders in the CCC's member companies annually, by developing and sharing research, and through the CCC's educational programs.

The center views itself as a think-tank and educational resource, particularly with the heightened emphasis on research that Googins brought to it. Recent activities have included the creation of influential networks of companies that have made a commitment to corporate citizenship through forums where they can engage in hands-on learning and knowledge sharing, convenings of all sorts, and practice-based research. The center has created a set of standards of excellence for corporate–community involvement and a diagnostic toolkit that companies can use to assess their own stage of development,[144] plus a wide variety of member services and member-only initiatives.

Among the types of activities CCC gets involved in[145] are: the Global Leadership Network, which is a collaboration of ten leading companies attempting to establish best-practice standards for aligning company strategies, practices, and corporate citizenship;[146] the Going Global Project, which addresses the ways in which US multinational companies integrate triple-bottom-line dimensions into global operations;[147] and numerous other research and educational projects designed to advance the field.

Emerging professional networks — someone to consult to

One sign of the maturation of this industry is the evolution of new professional organizations, in addition to the Boston College Center for Corporate Citizenship, which attempt to professionalize the plethora of activities related to responsible business practice.

The Corporate Responsibility Officer Association (CRO),[148] joins the Boston College Center for Corporate Citizenship and an earlier organization, the Ethics and Compliance Officer Association in attempting to build professional standards, networking opportunities, and educational programming for its members.

The CRO offers a set of publications, including CRO magazine and newsletters, as well a variety of convenings, including a series of conferences, to its members. CRO is intended to reach individuals with a wide variety of functional responsibilities associated with better responsibility in companies, among them, general counsel, compliance, ethics, HR, auditing, environment, sustainability, philanthropy, communications, investor relations, corporate social responsibility, socially responsible investing, chairman, chief executive officer, and chief financial officer.

The Ethics and Compliance Officer Association is a membership organization for companies' ethics and compliance officers, which provides a network for individuals in those capacities within their organizations, and numerous member services. It focuses on being the "recognized authority on business ethics, compliance, and corporate integrity."[149]

Global action networks: a new approach to global governance

Entrepreneurial and a consummate networker, difference maker Laury Hammel served as a founding business partner for an innovative leadership development program at Boston College called Leadership for Change, which was initiated by difference maker Steve Waddell in the early 1990s. Waddell, who could be called a networker's networker, is similarly focused on building and understanding the networks that create and sustain the emerging accountability infrastructure through a new entity that he has established which focuses on what he calls global action networks (GANs).

Steve Waddell

Before starting his innovative network of networks — Global Action Network Net (GAN-Net) — where he is now chief learning steward and founding executive director — Steve Waddell had done a wide variety of things in the 1980s and early 1990s. Born in Canada, Waddell graduated from the University of British Columbia in international relations and economics, after which he worked in a variety of positions, including freelance journalism, as director of communications for a labor organization, and managing his own property development company. He became involved in labor issues and then served as a director on the board of Van City Savings Credit Union — the world's largest community-based credit union. He relates some of his history:

> In the late '80s I started asking myself, well, given the scale of global challenges around poverty and equity and environmental degradation, what would make sense for me to think about for the rest of my life? I was 35 then. So I decided that I wanted to go to the United States, because the United States was having increasing influence in Canada.

Attracted to the PhD in sociology and MBA programs at Boston College because of a book called *Beyond the Market and State* by sociologist Severyn Bruyn (a visionary thinker, whose seminal work on social investing was discussed in Chapter 3), Waddell recalls,

> I went with two different things in mind. One was that I wanted to credential myself there and learn more about how to learn. The other was around starting something that I was at that time thinking about as an institute in business in society.

In the course of studying for the degrees, Waddell was determined to bring faculty from the management program and the sociology department together to see what they might do together. The result of this cross-departmental collaboration was an innovative work-based learning Friday–Saturday program, still running today, called Leadership for Change.[150] Waddell became the first director of the program, and when he finished his doctorate he left to work for the Institute for Development Research (IDR)[151] for several years before starting out on his own.

Even in these earlier activities, we can see how the networker operates, bringing together people who might not ordinarily come into contact with each other for purposes that are sometimes not entirely clear at the outset of the engagement. Waddell points out that, after leaving IDR, through his work at that organization, he had gained a novel expertise in intersectoral partnerships and collaboration, which was just beginning to be a hot topic. Waddell recalls,

> My title at IDR was director of intersectoral services, so the work emerged into that. So I moved from [focusing on] business and civil society to business, civil society, and government, and thinking about the intersectoral — intraorganizational — spaces that were pretty clear by about 1997–98.

He was approached by the relief agency USAID to help with intersectoral relationships after leaving IDR. He remembers,

> There was a fellow at USAID who was very interested in this intersector collaboration work. He was a senior VP named Wolfgang Reinicke, who was writing an important report [with F.M. Deng] called *Critical Choices: The United Nations, Networks, and the Future of Global Governance*, and saw intersectoral relationships as being critical to this new evolving model of global governance that he used as a framework. He was from the Brookings Institution, was German and was pretty well placed. He used the term "global public policy networks." So I said to him, "Isn't anyone doing anything more about this?" He said, "No." I said, "Well I think it's a critical global idea you are emerging here." So he offered to be on an advisory group as an attractor for others. I put together a very illustrious advisory group in something called the Global Public Policy Network Research Group, with some money from Ralph Taylor,[152] who has been my great patron.

The ideas about newly emerging global governance structures that had little to do with traditional governmental governance mechanisms emerged relatively rapidly. Waddell notes,

> The global perspective on this was really emerging in 1999–2000 when I did this work for the World Bank. The perspective of these things we were observing being a global network really grew out of what I call action research development methodology. [We developed] a case conference type of methodology working with the organizations to deepen their understanding and realized that they were asking similar questions.

The questions that Waddell and his collaborators were dealing with were relatively new, since the kinds of organization they were dealing with were also new, as Waddell comments:

> The questions were: How do you organize networks? How do you build relationships between very different parties? The case study work I did at IDR really was useful for that, too. Then I continued to work further in South Africa around water and sanitation issues, which started me thinking: What is the evolutionary model here? How did you start these networks? How do you *do* these things? I come from a business management perspective, saying, How do you do the strategic planning? Well, business management strategic planning — I don't want to say it is totally irrelevant, there's some useful stuff there, but when you're working in these complex interorganizational spaces, when there's great diversity and opinion even about what you're aiming for, it's a totally different ball game. I realized that the questions that management would ask were good, but the tools that they developed weren't particularly useful.

Waddell continues,

> So we did some work around formulating more clearly the concepts of what these entities we were observing were about and then that shifted to something that we now call the Global Action Network Net. It grew out of a critical perspective that these things that we're looking at didn't think of themselves as policy networks. They thought of themselves as changing the world. The fact is that the political science traditions, while useful, were very limited for them to understand the development challenge and help them move forward. It was more the case that concepts of social development and organization network development types of change were more useful for them.

GAN-Net has now become a formal entity.[153] Its mission is

> to strengthen the capacity of multi-sector, global networks to address urgent sustainability issues — social, economic, and environmental.

> Our strategy is to do this by coordinating events that connect leaders in the field and promote learning, innovation, and attention to what GANs are accomplishing worldwide on a range of crucial issues. GAN-Net works with GANs to increase their legitimacy, improve their results and build their capacity.[154]

GAN-Net changed its name from the Global Public Policy Network Research Group in response to recognition that, although these networks have implications for public policy and bridge their activities into public policy spaces, they are not actually formally creating public policy.

The GAN-Net group, headed by Waddell and the other co-lead steward Janjeev Khagram, has identified many GANs working in multiple sectors including: anti-corruption, provision of water, climate change, corporate reporting and performance standards, corporate performance, sustainable fishing, youth employment, nutrition, HIV/Aids, tuberculosis and malaria, and microenterprise.[155] By 2007, GAN-Net had identified more than 40 GANs in the world, some of which were listed on its website, including some directly linked to the emerging responsibility and accountability infrastructure. Among entities related to responsibility, account-ability, and transparency that have been identified as GANs are the Ethical Trading Initiative,[156] the Fair Labor Association,[157] the Forest Stewardship Council,[158] the UN Global Compact,[159] the Global Reporting Initiative,[160] the International Centre for Trade and Sustainable Development,[161] IFAT: the global network of Fair Trade Organizations,[162] the Microcredit Summit Campaign,[163] Social Accountability International,[164] and Transparency International,[165] among others.

A definition of GANs can be found in Box 7.3.

GAN-Net

Because GANs were new, they had not been studied much and little was known about how they operate, evolve, or become effective in achieving their goals. That was the impetus behind the formation of GAN-Net. According to Waddell,

> We were finding that people in the networks were continually their own sub-stantive area experts while trying to do the organizing, too; for example, somebody who knows a lot about environment, or who knows about forests or health, or a physician, [having to be] the head of one of these global net-works. Well, these people were coming to me with discoveries they had made about the development of these networks and processes. I'd say, "Oh yeah, well that's interesting. I mean, we knew this about 15 years ago. It's funny you've never connected with anyone who knew that." So I began think-ing what a waste of time this was. They were continually reinventing the wheel. Why didn't we get people talking to each other? I was always very much more an action-oriented person, and I didn't perceive myself as know-

Box 7.3 **GANs: a definition**

GANs are distinguished from traditional NGOs and intergovernmental and business organizations because they are formed by diverse stakeholders who are interested in a common issue, and who agree to work together to achieve extraordinary results. The critical contribution that they can provide to global issues is their ability to create consensual knowledge and action among diverse stakeholders. GANs are defined by five key characteristics. GANs are:

- Global
- Focused on issues for the public good (not profit-seeking)
- Integrating systems-building agents that foster linkages among diverse organizations and projects that share common goals
- Boundary-crossing — North/South, rich/poor, policy-makers, techno-scientists, funders, global institutions, professional disciplines, and cultures
- Intersectoral structures that promote fundamental changes by engaging business, government, and civil society (non-profit) organizations collaboratively[166]

ing the answers to the questions they would ask, and they were the experts in actually *knowing* what they were doing.

Waddell explains how linking people to share ideas actually works in practice:

> I had this great example of an experience of going down to the Forest Stewardship Council, who asked me to help them think through some stuff they'd been doing, and I asked them these questions about how they were organizing themselves. Each of them was always just astonished to discover what I knew about the organization that *they* didn't know. For example, there was the global network: they have a national node, a US node, a Canadian node. I knew something about how they were organized, but *they* didn't know internally how it was organized. So I said, "Well, you've got organizing experiments happening right here. You've got to talk to each other to be able to surface what the experiments are and understand how to move the enterprise forward. You're doing the doing, and you need to learn from that doing." That's the image behind GAN-Net: these people learning from one another in a very profound way. I'm audacious enough to suggest to them that they have something in common, but they've never thought that they had anything in common with similar networks. They acknowledge that they

have something in common but to think of actually talking to each other to learn how to do things? This is a new idea for them.

Waddell has studied and written extensively about multi-sector collaboration and, more recently, the evolution of GANs, so he has some perspective that he attempts to share with GAN-Networkers, as he points out:

> All of these GANs operate in different domains. So for me to say, "'You have these five characteristics in common and you're facing similar management challenges. And that means that the management challenges, the development challenges, you have in common are common in this type of organization; they are ones that no one knows how to *do*. You could go to a [consultant] and they'll pretend that they know the answer, but the fact is they don't." So I would suggest that they really should change the way they think about organizing the GAN, because a critical need for the world is that we learn differently.

■ A broad base of networks

The work of GAN-Net is to study how global action networks grow, evolve, and are effective in their work of changing the world for the better. But, as we have already seen, the institutions created by many of the other difference makers and their activities have generated numerous other networks and associations that bring like-mind people together around issues of importance to the world. For example, Bavaria and Massie's Ceres played an instrumental role in bringing together more than 500 investors, Wall Street and European financial institutions, and corporate leaders, to work on a ten-point action plan on issues of climate change. Ceres also launched and directs the Investor Network on Climate Risk, which includes more than 50 leading institutional investors holding assets of more than US$3 trillion.

Steve Lydenberg's efforts to establish the Institute for Responsible Investment has generated numerous new networking opportunities around specific topic areas, such as the social and environmental risks associated with mergers and acquisitions, a new emphasis on evaluating bonds in terms of their environmental, social, and governance issues, and real-estate investment trusts as well. A group called the Social Investment Research Analyst Network (SIRAN) was also formed and complements other networks engaged in the SRI arena, including the Social Investment Forum and the Social Venture Network.

The next step beyond simple networking is engagement on multiple levels; and it is to that subject that we now turn.

8

Engagement and dialogue
Changing the fundamentals

The difference makers in this chapter have played differing roles in the building of the accountability infrastructure, but they are roles that highlight overall the changes that have taken place and, in some respects, forecast changes that will continue to evolve. Social movements, such as the accountability, responsibility, and transparency movement addressed in this book, are complex and have many different elements, with each distinctive part evolving in its own unique way.

In this chapter we will look at the role that David Logan, like John Elkington, played in establishing one of the first consultancies directly geared to helping companies establish better corporate citizenship. We will look at how Malcolm McIntosh, an academic (mostly), has worked on issues of global peace and security — with implications for social as well as environmental sustainability — through to his work to build an academic center on corporate citizenship that in its heyday drew many diverse actors together in conversation, established a journal to focus academic attention on issues of corporate citizenship, and more recently turned his attention toward system change. We will witness Judith Samuelson's efforts to bring pressures on existing management curricula to include issues related to business in society, and to Jane Nelson's lifelong quest for peace through prosperity through her work with the International Business Leaders Forum, at the UN and, more recently, Harvard's Kennedy School of Government. Each one of these difference makers has assumed a unique and important role in building the infrastructure and creating a global conversation about corporate responsibility.

◼ David Logan

David Logan is cofounder (with Michael Tuffrey, who had previously founded Community Affairs Briefing) and director of The Corporate Citizenship Company based in London, which at the end of 2007 merged with the Smart Company to form Corporate Citizenship. The Corporate Citizenship Company specialized in corporate responsibility. Logan holds a master's in philosophy and an Advanced Diploma in Education from the University of London and is senior visiting fellow in corporate responsibility at the University of Manchester's Business School and the City University Graduate School Center for the Study of Philanthropy in New York. Logan was coauthor of one of the first important studies of corporate citizenship, the 1997 Hitachi Foundation Report entitled *Global Corporate Citizenship: Rationale and Strategies*, as well as the first report of the London Benchmarking Group and associated follow-up studies with Corporate Citizenship's cofounder Michael Tuffrey. He also served as Levi Strauss & Co.'s director of special programs before establishing his own consulting firm.

Logan chuckles when he thinks about his early socialist leanings and his early work with the British Trades Union Congress, recalling,

> I spent seven years there writing papers as a researcher on policy for the Trades Union Congress. We were anticapitalists. I was anticapitalist. But, after seven years, I realized that we were in a really big "D" dead end intellectually and practically, with that kind of socialistic answer. The idea that you could run a society without a private sector had to me become un-credible. If you think about the vast majority of the people in the world who were then living under social systems where the private sector was forbidden — China, Russia, large swaths of the developing world were communistic. The whole essence of all that thinking was that private profit is immoral and wrong and must be stopped. I just came to the conclusion that this was madness and that we had to have a for-profit sector. But it needed to be a responsible one.

That insight was the beginning of a major shift in Logan's work and thinking. In a story that in some respects parallels David Grayson's, Logan recalls,

> I left the trade unions at the height of the massive restructuring in Britain of the Thatcher years [starting in 1979], where large numbers of blue-collar workers were laid off and we had a massive youth unemployment problem. So I went to work with unemployed youth for three years. Then I took a further step in my thinking because we were running government make-work programs for these kids. You know, you come and dig a hole and another bunch of kids come and fill it in. It kept them off the streets but it was completely unconstructive. I got involved in a community-owned business that provided real jobs for these kids, providing a socially useful project, which

was sports and recreation in the heart of inner-city London. We made a profit. So I learned that making a profit wasn't a bad thing. In helping to run this community project for unemployed kids — this urban renewal project — we blended private-sector entrepreneurialism with public-sector social aims and created a social business that actually, once the capital costs, which was the property, were taken out of the equation, we had to make a profit on a recurrent annual basis or the government wouldn't pay our salaries. [In effect] the people coming to use the facility paid our salary.

The introduction to market incentives as a basis of social change proved fruitful, Logan believes, because of the insights he gained about how businesses actually work:

We got terrific support from companies like Marks & Spencer, CitiCorp, BP, Shell, Sainsbury's. They backed us. I met all these guys who worked for these companies — all these capitalists — who were much more friendly, much more helpful than anybody in the public sector. After, there was a great crisis in the organization. The government tried to close us down and we won the fight to stay open. They wanted to take the property back and knock it down and build an office block. We saved the building. It's still there today. It's still a highly successful community-owned business. It's now cloned itself into two or three other similar businesses around London. Once the battle to save it was won, I began to look around.

Logan struggled with his former anticapitalist beliefs as he considered whether to accept the next opportunity that presented itself:

Then along came Levi Strauss and Company who said to me, "Would you like to run our community programs just like the programs at CitiCorp, just the like the programs at Marks & Spencer?" I interviewed. They offered me the job. I actually turned them down. The guy who was interviewing me said he was a Californian. He had a certain acuity about psychology. He said to me, "You're having a crisis of confidence. Why don't you take the job, try it for six months, and if you don't like it, leave?" I was thinking, "Yeah, but my friends will know I sold out." He said, "If you don't take the job, I'll take the next best guy, and this will be a mistake for both of us. I'll give you 24 hours to think about it." I spent 24 hours pacing up and down the banks of the River Thames wondering whether I could sell my soul to capitalism and join Levi Strauss and Company.

This conversation took place in 1980 in the early days of companies becoming actively engaged with their communities. Logan relates what happened next:

> So I went into the capitalist machine and worked as a community affairs manager in Europe. The reason I could *do* that was because I had done my research. I had read up on Levi Strauss and Company and I *knew* that in the late '40s and early '50s the company had created racially integrated workplaces in Virginia, Alabama, Arkansas, Georgia, and Tennessee. I thought, "I can learn something from these guys." So I took the risk and in 1980 became one of the first-ever professional corporate community affairs managers outside of the United States working for a US company, and one of the very, very few people in Europe who did this kind of work.

The experience with Levi Strauss proved seminal to the rest of Logan's career. He comments wryly,

> I had come to the view that capitalism was for real. It wasn't going to go away. It was a fantasy to believe you could run society without the for-profit sector, and that what we needed was a positive, creative, and responsible for-profit sector to play its role within the mix of public, not-for-profit and private-sector institutions that make up a modern liberal democratic society. I knew that there were models out there. We had a firm I now work with a lot, Cadbury, and also Unilever. There were lots of great firms in Britain that had been responsible, but some of them had been swept away in the tidal wave of socialism that engulfed both eastern and western Europe in post-war years. So for me it wasn't just a career change; it was quite a fundamental world-view change.

The work at Levi Strauss was focused mainly on what we would today call community involvement rather than the broader corporate responsibility agenda, as Logan recalls:

> I was asked to implement in Europe an American approach to community relations. It wasn't easy because of Levi's one-size-fits-all community relations. "Here's the one-size package, David, sell it to the Europeans." It was really hard, and I didn't have a lot of latitude to change the rules. I had to try and sell it into a European culture that was either indifferent or suspicious, or it didn't fit. Getting blue-collar women, who ran a home and did eight to ten hours at work a day, to do volunteering wasn't easy in a culture where *nobody* did volunteering, because the government did it all. I had two or three years of doing that. It was hard work but it was worthwhile.

Then crisis struck Levi Strauss, as business began to decline, and Logan unexpectedly found himself at the center of a plant-closing situation. He relates the story:

> I was going up to the North Shields plant to talk about their latest fund-raising drive for a local project. The head of HR [human resources] called me in and said, "David, I hear you're going up to North Shields. There's something I need to tell you in absolute confidence" (because I wasn't part of the management team). He said, "You need to cancel this trip, because we're going to close the factory in six weeks' time." I said, "Leo, why didn't you tell me before?" He said, "Well, it's very confidential." Everybody in that European business had a job to make money for Levi Strauss. I was the one guy who gave money away. People would meet me in the lift and say, "Hi. How much money are you giving away today?" By implication: "I've been out there making it and what kind of job have you got?'"

He continues,

> I said to this guy, "Leo, you need me there. I should be involved." Remember, this is the ex-union guy. I spent half an hour talking to him about all the contacts I had in the community. All the training schemes I knew. We'd just set up a computer-training scheme for unemployed kids in that very community, 200 yards from the plant. It was the only public computer-training scheme open to unqualified kids. Most of our women were unqualified. I said, "We've got to get these women into a new technology. They've got to learn how to use computers instead of sewing machines." After half an hour, he took me down the corridor to talk to the president of Europe, a man called Robin Dow, who listened to me for five minutes. He said, "How much money do you need?" I said, "Well how about £50,000? I mean £75,000." He said, "I'll give you a hundred [thousand]. Get up there, do what the hell you can to help these people."

Logan's intervention proved useful both for the company and the community, and also gained him a great deal of credibility around issues of responsible practice. He illustrates what happened next:

> I went up and sat through all the negotiations with the union, where the union was beaten down. There was nothing they could do. I drove the union representative from that plant back from the negotiations in Scotland, over the mountains down to North Shields. It took about three hours. She cried every moment of the way down there. We went in the next morning and we made the announcement. I was on the platform when the announcement was made: "We're closing you. Not because you aren't good people, not because you don't do a good job, but there are five plants here. We're going down to four. You're the guys who are going." It was horrendous. People were sick, people were crying; they hated us. But over the next six weeks, we put a package together to really help those people and help the community.

> We set up a sewing cooperative, led by the union convener. We set up train-
> ing. We got people into college. We got people into high school. We got
> about 70% into other jobs around the town. We gave a large grant to expand
> the computer-training workshop. We did everything we could to help the
> town recover from the loss of these jobs.
>
> When the plant finally closed, there was a party and we were invited. The
> management were invited. I met with the mayor of that town; and he said,
> "I've seen dozens and dozens and dozens of closures in this town, and I've
> never seen a company do for their people and for the community what you
> and Levi's have done. You can be proud of that."

Levi's innovative community relations program in the UK proved useful as the
company continued its retrenchment strategy around the world, and Logan
became the front man for numerous other plant closures. Logan continues, "I was
yanked out to San Francisco and given a plant closure budget that operated in
Arkansas, Argentina, China, Belgium, all over the world. I was the man who did
plant closures for quite a while."

Logan left Levi Strauss in 1988, recalling,

> By the end of my time at Levi's, I was working with Bob Dunn, whom I learnt
> a lot from on all aspects of corporate responsibility. So I went from being the
> charity man to being part of a small team that advised the senior manage-
> ment of the company on everything from sex in advertising to child labor,
> water pollution from stonewashing and whitewashing jeans, bribery and cor-
> ruption. We did the works. Disinvestment from South Africa; what do we do
> about HIV/Aids? We were a small team of people whose job was to help the
> senior management of the company and the directors manage the social
> dimension of the business. I was doing the kind of thinking and research
> work for them that I used to do for the leadership of the trade unions. We
> were policy guys, but we were also practical. So, when a problem came up, I
> had to go and sit with the head of childrenswear, while we talked through the
> fact that we couldn't get childrenswear out of US plants at the price we
> needed to get it, and we had to start looking at outsourcing overseas. So
> how did we manage running down the childrenswear plants? It wasn't just
> theoretical, although I was very interested in the theory; it was intensely prac-
> tical.

Logan faced a kind of life crisis as he had to make a determination whether to stay
in the United States or return to the United Kingdom, and start his own consulting
business. He remembers the tension he faced:

> What kind of work was I going to do? I had worked for the government as a
> teacher. I'd worked for the labour unions. I'd worked three years in the not-

for-profit sector, and I'd had between seven and eight years in the for-profit sector. I decided that the only thing I hadn't done was run my own business. I started consulting on corporate social responsibility. I've been doing that now for nearly 20 years. We've built a business around that theme.

Logan had a certain type of vision in mind, given his varied background:

I saw that the kind of society we have in the West — we don't just have a conflict relationship between workers and capital, we have a symbiotic relationship. Conflicts arise. But, fundamentally, you need a creative, vigorous for-profit sector. My vision was that the for-profit sector is a key player in the future of humanity. How can we work around the tremendous creativity of this sector to deal with the negative aspects of its impact and improve the positive, inclusive, engagement aspects of its creativity? Rather than trying to replace the private sector, I guess I was trying to humanize it.

He elaborates his vision:

I feel in the debate about corporate responsibility that I have a fundamental weakness in some respects because I actually admire what marketing managers, plant managers, distribution managers, procurement managers, and senior executives accomplish. I just want to help them accomplish it in a more environmentally friendly, socially responsible manner, because I know they're a very important part of the social mix of our society. So for me it's a vision about an inclusive, liberal, democratic, free-market society, in which all three sectors [economic, governmental, and civil society] have an appropriate role and they're able to get on together and make the whole better than the parts for the people who live in our society.

Corporate Citizenship

Founded in 1997 by David Logan and Michael Tuffrey, The Corporate Citizenship Company, now simply "Corporate Citizenship"[167] and part of Smart Company, emphasizes research and consulting, as well as publications, that are aimed at helping businesses become better corporate citizens in a fast-paced and dramatically changing world. The consulting firm emphasizes benchmarking, assessment of social and economic impact, international issues management, evaluation of corporate–community relations programs, and news briefings.

Corporate Citizenship's mission is "to help companies succeed as commercial entities by being active corporate citizens, so meeting the aspirations of their diverse stakeholders and the wider society of which they are a part."[168] The work includes social auditing and reporting, using a comprehensive approach developed by Logan and colleagues, which helps companies self-assess and manage their triple-bottom-line (social, environmental, and economic) impacts on their stakeholders. The company also helps clients with benchmarking their corporate–community impacts and contributions using a method developed jointly by Logan and his partner Tuffrey, which is called the London Benchmarking Group methodology.[169] The consulting firm is also involved in helping companies understand the impact of community involvement on employees through its human resources programs and publishes a number of newsletters that help clients stay up to date on issues of corporate responsibility.

Corporate Citizenship is one of the pioneer consulting firms on the issues of corporate responsibility. Today it stands as a leader among what has today become an industry of consulting firms that attempt to help organizations with various aspects of their stakeholder and environmental practices.

■ Malcolm McIntosh

Some individuals use their networking skills to create different types of initiatives that bring people together around the theme of corporate responsibility. One of these individuals is Malcolm McIntosh, coauthor of one of the earliest books explicitly focused on corporate citizenship, founder of the *Journal of Corporate Citizenship*, and now professor and director of the Applied Research Centre in Human Security at Coventry University, the first transdisciplinary center of its kind in the UK. Prior to coming to Coventry in 2006, McIntosh, who is also professor extraordinary in the School of Public Management and Planning at Stellenbosch University, had served as the director of the Corporate Citizenship Unit at the University of Warwick Business School in the UK and European director of the New York-based CEP. He holds masters' and doctoral degrees from the Department of Peace Studies at the University of Bradford in England and is a Fellow of the Royal Society of Arts, Manufacture and Commerce (RSA).

McIntosh has always built bridges between academia and practice, in part because he started with a very broad understanding of what he wanted the focus of his work to be. He explains,

> This area [corporate responsibility/citizenship] most definitely for me is about peace and social justice. That's the first point. The second point is it's most definitely about seeing the planet as one space. It's about connecting economic, social, and environmental issues and impact and performance around the idea that we share one planetary space connected back to the human world of people, making the world a peaceful and socially just place for everybody. That's absolutely fundamental.

Brought up in a family imbued with the values of the Society of Friends (Quakers), McIntosh's roots (like Logan's) are deep in labor and socialism, as well as pacifism. He explains the implications of this background for him:

> The notion of social justice, of bringing everybody with you, and collectivism was very much part of the way I think and feel, the way I was brought up. That does not make me a Communist in the way in which some Americans seem to have a paranoid view of anybody who says they're a socialist. By socialist, I mean that the means of production could be private, public, or civil, which is regulated by the public. I believe in enterprise and entrepreneurialism. I've been a social private entrepreneur for the whole of my life and I think very successfully. It doesn't make me anticapitalist in any way. It means that you redistribute wealth, and it means you provide for those in need in a way in which most social democracies in Europe do. These are the core values that have guided me whether I've been in business, in civil society, or in academia. I was a BBC [British Broadcasting Company] television journalist and producer for ten years. I was in business for ten years. I was a peace researcher for five years and I've been doing this stuff since 1983 now.

McIntosh continues, explaining the roots of his philosophy:

> Two other things pervade my thinking. One is the difference between people who work *in* organizations and the organizations themselves. I have not met too many evil people in business. I've met some, but not many. I've met some terribly evil organizations, though. I've met some organizations that do evil in the way they act. But I haven't met too many people who are like that. The greatest point of intellectual learning for me was actually when I did my master's degree in peace studies, when I read every single book, word, newspaper article, academic article, anything I could lay hands on, about the bombing of Hiroshima and Nagasaki. My master's dissertation was subsequently published as a book called *Japan Re-Armed*. It was about post-war Japanese defense policy under American management. That taught me about the relationship between scientific thinking and the development of technology: in other words, the bombs, the role of politics and militarism in that, and then the role of business [in relation] to those other variables. That interrelationship, I suppose, taught me more intellectually than anything else I've ever done.
>
> The second part of it is the moral argument. It is immoral for a third of the planet to live on less than US$2 a day, for 500,000 women a year to die in childbirth or near childbirth. One could keep on quoting the figures, so I feel impassioned about that.

McIntosh started his career teaching English in Japan, and, in true entrepreneurial style, then moved to Australia, where he founded a language school that is still running today. That stint was followed by his master's and ultimately doctoral work on peace studies. This expertise landed him a reporting job with the BBC when, as he explains: "BBC television in Britain wanted to make a major series on defense decision-making. I got a call through the networks saying would I like to do the work on it so I absolutely leapt at it." Becoming a television producer, McIntosh then landed a post with the Natural History Unit in Bristol, where in the mid-1980s, as he recalls, "I convinced them to make a program about corporate social responsibility. So the BBC basically paid for my initial training or background in corporate social responsibility, and I became hooked on that and [on] environmental management."

Talking about how he does his networking, McIntosh notes, "I'm a social entrepreneur at heart. I make things happen, put people and things together in a way that most people don't see or don't want to do. I'm a risk taker and a change agent." One of the most noted of McIntosh's activities as change agent was his tenure as the first hired director of the University of Warwick's Corporate Citizenship Unit, one of the first academic units so focused. McIntosh explains how he came to hold that position:

> I pioneered a whole lot of stuff in environmental management and started to talk to people back at the end of the '80s, beginning of the '90s, about corporate responsibility. People still said, "What's that, Malcolm?" So you'd have long conversations with people of what it was about and the issues, which are largely all the same issues as now. Then — I was the only person teaching it — I started teaching it at Bristol University at that time. But it was something that I don't think was really happening much anywhere else. Then I got the job as the European director of what was then the Council on Economic Priorities and now Social Accountability International, based in London working for Alice Tepper Marlin.
>
>   This job came up at the University of Warwick in the business school in the Corporate Citizenship Unit, and it was being run at the time by [its founder] Chris [Christopher] Marsden, who is in charge of the Amnesty International business section now. Chris had been the BP community affairs manager for 15 years then he'd gone to Warwick to set up this research and teaching unit, but he needed to leave because he was being paid by BP. Anyway, I applied and said to them, "Please don't call it the BP Corporate Citizenship Unit, otherwise I won't come. Just call it the Corporate Citizenship Unit."

McIntosh continues, speaking about the late 1990s and early 2000s:

> I went there and there was immediately an explosion in the sense that Chris Marsden had three or four companies sponsoring it, and we ended up with

about ten. The staff increased from about three part-time people plus me to — well, in the end there were 30 people being paid, but there were about 13 people working there full-time. We were very successful in running conferences, starting the journal [*Journal of Corporate Citizenship*], attracting money, attracting interest. It just went bananas. I got invited to speak all over the world. I ended up doing the [academic side of the] Global Compact as well.

Corporate Citizenship Unit, University of Warwick

The Corporate Citizenship Unit at the University of Warwick became well known for its innovative conference on corporate citizenship, which brought together academics, practitioners, and NGO representatives into dialogue sessions during McIntosh's tenure. The unit states as its mission today,

> The Corporate Citizenship Unit (CCU) aims to become a globally recognised centre of excellence in the area of research and teaching in corporate citizenship by bringing together diverse people from business, government, and civil society organisations to examine changes in the relationship between corporations, states and communities. We recognise that the role, scope and purpose of business is changing rapidly as the global economy develops and that management priorities and business responsibilities are under scrutiny as never before.[170]

McIntosh ended up leaving the CCU in the early 2000s in the midst of some political and personal turmoil which he recalls: "I burnt myself out. Basically, it was just too much to do." Still, he believes,

> What I did at Warwick was to get corporate responsibility into a very highly rated, mainstream, globally rated business school and build on Chris Marsden's beginnings. We also got buy-in from the governments of the UK, Norway and others as well as attracting research students at a time when the area was still regarded skeptically. We were also able to affect the corporate responsibility debates around the world through our work for the UN, the newly elected Labour government and others, and the *Journal of Corporate Citizenship* started.

Journal of Corporate Citizenship

The *Journal of Corporate Citizenship* (JCC) focuses explicitly on integrating theory about corporate citizenship with management practice. Thus, the journal provides a forum in which the tensions and practical realities of making corporate citizenship real are addressed in a reader-friendly, yet conceptually and empirically rigorous format.[171] Aimed at making the link between practice and theory, the journal publishes articles on issues related to corporate citizenship from around the globe, as well as updates on what has been happening the world of corporate citizenship, opinion and idea pieces, and reviews.

JCC is one example of the proliferation of new outlets related to issues of corporate responsibility generally, some of which, like JCC have a mixed academic–practitioner audience, others of which are more academic in their orientation (e.g., *Business and Society*, *Business Ethics Quarterly*, the *Journal of Business Ethics*, *Organizations and the Natural Environment*), and others of which, print and electronic, are more practice-based (e.g., *GreenBiz*, *CSRwire*, *Business Respect*, *Ethical Corporation*). Website details for these and other journals and magazines are given in Box 2.15 on page 56.

Applied Research Centre in Human Security, Coventry University

The Applied Research Centre in Human Security (ARCHS), Coventry University, is McIntosh's passion at the time of writing. In taking this position in 2006 as the center's first director, after leaving Warwick about four years earlier to continue his work as a free agent, McIntosh has returned to his roots in global peace and security as a foundation for corporate responsibility. See Box 8.1 for ARCHS's fundamental approach.

Box 8.1 **Applied Research Centre in Human Security**

Human security is a people-centred approach to global security which recognises that lasting peace and social justice cannot be achieved unless people are protected from threats to basic needs and rights. Among the main threats to people's security are climate change, an inequitable global economic system, bad governance, corruption, abuse of human rights and violence.

We work in collaborative partnerships with business, government, civil society and individuals and their communities to find solutions to the problems that people face in their everyday lives. The solutions to these problems will come through understanding planetary ecosystems, through collecting and collating evidence on good practice that produces peaceful and socially just outcomes for people and communities, and on developing systems, policies and strategies for the future that involve the active participation of all stakeholders.[172]

To accomplish its mission, ARCHS has a number of initiatives under way, including a conference called "The Next Great Transformation: The Role of Business in a

Sustainable World," an active seminar series, consultation services, newsletters, and related activities. McIntosh believes it is necessary to return to fundamental issues so that peace and security — and business's role in establishing and maintaining peace and security — can be achieved. As he comments,

> We do not understand and we have not got a hold of what I call STCs — supra-territorial corporations. We have created something that *could* be beneficial and *can* be beneficial to humankind, but can also be terribly destructive, and I'm sure in many cases is out of control. Most of the literature is not dealing with that. Most of the literature in our field is dealing with peripheral stuff like: How do we get them to report better? How do we put in another governance committee here, there and everywhere, rather than standing back and looking at the animal we have created and say, "What is this thing? Is it a state? Is it a community organization? Is it a flying pig? What is it?" I don't think we've done enough of that, frankly. I think we've created a monster.

Thinking about how to control these entities — multinational or transnational corporations — McIntosh remarks,

> There are three things, actually, which I keep banging on about when I talk about this in public. One is: we go back to October 1856 and look at the first incorporation act [the Companies Act] in the British parliament, on which most other incorporation acts around the world are based. We created limited liability — the ability to invest in some vehicle that would increase profitability, increase your income by its activity somewhere else — because it was about raising money in order that British companies could invest in commodities from around the world.
>
> We haven't gone back to 1856 and said, "What is this thing?" I know there's a movement in North America and various other attempts, but most of the attempts around the world have been about increasing reporting and transparency in governance and ethics and stuff like that. They haven't actually gone back and said, "What is it that we've created here? How can we separate this from our discussion of business, per se, or enterprise, per se, which everybody would agree with?" I sell you eggs; you sell me bread. That's fine. You know, that's business. [But now] we're talking about supra-territorial organizations.

McIntosh continues,

> The second one is: going back and reading people like [Karl] Polanyi and looking at the great transformation. What caused the Great Depression? What caused the First World War, then effectively caused the Second World War?, For instance, Winston Churchill, as I've been re-looking at him, said

the Second World War was entirely avoidable. The model of capitalism that we had caused it: that allowed Hitler to come to power. This is Churchill basically saying exactly what my *father* said to me as a pacifist when I was growing up. So I find that conjunction quite interesting. So then you've got 1945, when we did have a chance to sit down and reform things. We did. We put the social and the environmental into the agenda to a certain extent. In 1948 we had the Universal Declaration of Human Rights, a fantastic advance.

Thinking about what is needed, McIntosh, adds his third point:

We *have* to have another great transformation now on a similar scale, which says, "Hang on a minute. We've done quite well but we need to do much more to measure wealth around the world in ways other than just by the financial performance of corporation." So 1856, 1945 . . . 1989, of course, because it's the fall of the Berlin Wall and the notion of the end of the cold war, I think is another interesting turning point. We've got to get through the next one before the Indian and Chinese economies take off without any regard for the fate of the planet, which is happening at the moment. But this will only happen if the United States shows leadership and says, *"We* must change first," because they are still the world's largest resource users and polluters.

◼ Jane Nelson

Other difference makers agree that the world must change in significant ways. One of them, Jane Nelson, has worked for years with the UN and other important institutions to eradicate poverty and violence through better business practices.

Jane Nelson's name appears on most conference programs of global importance that have anything to do with business involvement in zones of conflict, business and peace, corporate responsibility, accountability, and sustainable development, but her path to that recognition differs from that of many of the other difference makers. At the time of writing, Nelson is senior fellow and director of the Corporate Social Responsibility Initiative (CSRI) at the Kennedy School of Government, Harvard University.[173] She also serves as director, business leadership and strategy, for the Prince of Wales International Business Leaders Forum (IBLF),[174] which she joined in 1993, and a senior fellow at the Brookings Institution.

Nelson's activities over the years have included producing significant reports for the UN. For example, during 2001, she worked for then Secretary-General Kofi Annan developing a report for the General Assembly on collaboration between the UN and business. This report became the basis of a UN resolution on cooperation between the UN and the private sector. Nelson had previously served as a vice president at Citibank and head of marketing for its Worldwide Securities Services in Asia Pacific. She has lectured in economics at the University of Natal in South Africa, and worked as a consultant for the World Business Council for Sustainable Development, FUNDES (Fundación para Desarrollo Sostenible) in Latin America, and UNEP, among other things. She serves on numerous boards and has written several books related to corporate responsibility and multiple reports on corporate citizenship for the World Economic Forum. She holds a master's in politics, philosophy and economics from Oxford University and a bachelor's in agricultural economics from the University of Natal, South Africa.

Nelson's background set her on her present path, as she indicates:

> My background is a fairly peripatetic mixed life, I guess, in that I was born in Zimbabwe and have since lived and worked on four other continents in a variety of corporate, NGO, academic, and UN-related jobs. I think that growing up as a white African in a very difficult environment, really a civil war, has had a big impact on my life. My father was chairman of the Centre Party, a multiracial opposition party to the white Rhodesian Front government. So I had a confusing childhood in many ways, because both my parents were very actively involved politically in advocating for equality and yet I went to an all-white school. It was a government school; my parents couldn't afford to send me to a mixed-race private school. A lot of the white kids' parents suggested that our parents were communists and all sorts of other ghastly things, so at one level I resented my parents' activism and, at another level, from an early age I think they tried to instill in us some sense of the importance of human dignity, the importance of humanity, and cherishing people regardless of race or background or color or religion.

She continues, elaborating the deep roots of her activism around issues of peace, non-violence, and sustainability,

> So I had that orientation since birth through my parents, and yet desperately wanted to belong as a child. It required, at quite an early stage, a lot of working through what matters and what one's principles and values are. From the age of 12, I lived through a civil war; friends were killed; our next-door neighbors were killed. So all the tension and loss of going through that made me realize and appreciate very deeply the futility of war and bloodshed and violence and that it didn't solve anything. That was my childhood until I was about 18. Then I went to America for a year in high school, followed by the University of Natal in South Africa and again, was hit with the implications of inequality. There was segregation and a lot of bigotry and racial intolerance in Zimbabwe, but it was even worse when I got to South Africa and even more institutionalized. So I got involved with student politics there and had

the tensions of being a foreign student in the country, but quite actively involved with the student council. So I think my early years, living in a segregated and unjust society, and discovering what justice, human dignity, and human rights actually meant in practice, were very much linked to the kind of work I do now.

The interest in issues related to poverty also began early, as Nelson explains:

I grew up on a farm surrounded by severe rural poverty, and always thought I was going to go into rural development and agriculture and community-based development. I studied agriculture at university, which was unusual. I think there were about a dozen or so women in the class of several hundred guys. I also got involved in trying to do other things that women weren't supposed to do, so I was the first woman to serve as the secretary of the university sports union, which was very much a male endeavor.

Nelson had another important formative experience when she went to work in rural South Africa as part of her university experience. She details the insights she gained:

Originally, I was convinced I was going to stay in rural development and work with small-scale farmers in Africa. I did research in some of the poorest rural communities in the Province of Natal in South Africa. That was probably one of *the* most valuable learning experiences of my life. It was my final year of a four-year degree working with these very poor, rural farming communities in a remote part of the country. I was just so humbled by the acceptance, and the welcome I received as a white African in an all-black farming community. I realized that the poorest people in terms of income often have an incredible generosity of spirit, even though they lack a lot materially and they also have major problem-solving and entrepreneurial skills. I had no concept of social entrepreneurship in those days, but that was my first exposure to how people who had almost nothing, and had all the institutional odds stacked against them, somehow survived. It went beyond just survival. Somehow they managed to eke out a living, managed to do the best they could to improve the lives of their children. Cared *passionately* about giving their children things they hadn't had.

Nelson became a Rhodes scholar, then came to the United States and ended up traveling around the world, landing in Japan, where by luck of circumstance she began working for Citibank and talking "to private banks, insurance companies, and fund managers, who were investing in Japan at a time that the Japanese market skyrocketed and so this business became really big business in Citibank" during the heyday of the boom market of the mid-1980s. Later, Nelson began traveling throughout Asia, during a time of great economic and political change, as she recalls:

> Citibank decided that they wanted to provide similar services in other emerging markets in Asia, from India to Indonesia. I can remember sitting in Jakarta on one steamy day helping sign bond certificates before the stock exchanges were automated. I was based in Hong Kong, and I started my job in June 1989, a week after Tiananmen Square. Everyone was in shock. Many of my Hong Kong Chinese colleagues at Citibank were looking for ways to leave, as they knew that Hong Kong was going to be handed back in '97 to China and the future was very uncertain. The Chinese government's backlash against students was therefore another sudden wake-up call about injustice and human rights abuses. Yet I was in this very exciting, very entrepreneurial part of a great business and focused on revenue growth and markets – so was constantly trying to reconcile the complex links between political and economic transformation.

Another chance meeting got Nelson involved as an advisor to the International Association of Students of Economics and Commerce (AIESEC), the world's largest student-run organization – an involvement she continues to this day – where she became involved in environmental activism in Hong Kong. A taxi ride in Tokyo with Hugh Faulkner, who had just been asked by Swiss industrialist Stephan Schmidheiny to lead the Business Council for Sustainable Development (BCSD), now the World Business Council for Sustainable Development (WBCSD), introduced Nelson to the 1992 Earth Summit in Rio. She ended up back in her boss's office with a request, as she recalls:

> At the end of the taxi ride, I went into my office in Japan, and I said to my boss, "Can I take a sabbatical? I have to go and work on this thing called the Rio Earth Summit." To his credit, he didn't bat an eyelid. We discussed it a lot, and he said, 'Yes.'

Nelson recounts what happened next:

> So I took a sabbatical from Citibank and went to work for the BCSD. I had the great privilege of researching and co-writing their report for Africa, and I actually got to go back home to Africa, base myself with my dad in Zimbabwe and traveled all over the continent for six months, preparing a report on business and sustainable development in Africa. Suddenly all these different parts of my life just came together and I realized I'd found an absolute purpose and passion. It was an epiphany. I was flying up to Kenya one day to do some interviews and just had this vision of the financial trading floor in Tokyo, which I got to know well at Citibank . . . and these small-scale farmers

— the farm communities that I'd worked with when I was doing my research in South Africa — and both of them were entrepreneurial, both of them were focused on problem-solving, and yet they might as well have been on different planets. I started to think about the innovative ways that one could make connections between these different worlds and actually use business and the market to address the type of development challenges I'd seen in these very poor rural communities. After doing the research for BCSD, where I was interviewing everyone from small-scale farmers to the CEOs of big African companies to government ministers, and NGOs, all looking at business and sustainable development, I realized that poverty was often the biggest environmental degrader, not just industrialization.

Nelson's background also informed her work in Africa for BCSD, as she explains:

Just through experiential learning, not any great intuition or insight on my part, I realized that poverty, the environment, and economic growth were all integrally linked and needed to be looked at together as a whole if you were going to solve any one of them. So I became more interested in and focused on the poverty and social development side of sustainable development, rather than only the environmental side.

World Business Council for Sustainable Development

The WBCSD provides "business leadership as a catalyst for change toward sustainable development, and to support the business license to operate, innovate and grow in a world increasingly shaped by sustainable development issues."[175] The WBCSD is a CEO-only organization comprising about 190 of the world's largest corporations from some 35 countries and 20 different industry sectors. It is focused on issues related to business and sustainable development, providing its members with a "platform for companies to explore sustainable development, share knowledge, experiences and best practices, and to advocate business positions on these issues in a variety of forums, working with governments, non-governmental and intergovernmental organizations."[176] Its objectives are shown in Box 8.2.

To achieve its objectives, the WBCSD focuses on environment and development, and business roles in achieving both of the former, through its global organization as well as a regional network that works more locally and regionally. At the time of writing, it had projects on climate change, economic development, water, ecosystems, and capacity building and has several sector-specific projects as well, in the cement, electric utilities, forest products, mining and minerals, and mobility industries.

Jane Nelson's adventure in sustainable development continued after she attended the Earth Summit in Rio de Janeiro, as she recalls,

---

Box 8.2 **WBCSD objectives for members**

- Be a **leading business advocate** on sustainable development
- Participate in **policy development** to create the right framework conditions for business to make an effective contribution to sustainable human progress
- Develop and promote the **business case for sustainable development**
- **Demonstrate the business contribution** to sustainable development solutions and share leading edge practices among members
- Contribute to a **sustainable future** for developing nations and nations in transition[177]

I just had this wonderful exposure to how integrated this all was and became convinced that we needed to look at it in a more holistic, systemic way. Rio was critical, one of the most amazing experiences of my life. Stephan Schmidheiny, who founded the Business Council for Sustainable Development, also had a foundation in Latin America helping fund small-scale business — with loan guarantees — FUNDES. He said to me one day that, if you can learn enough Spanish to do interviews, we would like you to help us research and write a book on small business and sustainable development in Latin America, as you did in Africa. So I took this immersion Spanish course in Costa Rica — I think I was there for a month and a half and lived, spoke, ate, dreamed, and sniffed Spanish — and then I traveled all over Latin America: again, a wonderful opportunity, interviewing everyone from women selling fruit on the side of the street to entrepreneurs who had one-million or two-million-dollar turnover, mostly small to medium-sized businesses.

The project turned into a coauthored book called *The Cutting Edge: Small Business and Progress*[178] after Nelson went back to some of her interviewees with a photographer. Though technically still on leave from Citibank, Nelson suddenly knew her life's work lay in this new field,

I realized that, having done this work in Africa and then doing this project in Latin America, that it was this link between large companies and small business and NGOs and government trying to solve development challenges that was my passion and my calling. The wealth-creating, entrepreneurial problem-solving capacity of business, if it's geared toward some of the big global challenges — whether it's climate change, whether it's poverty, whether it's nutrition, whether it's water access, whether it is energy access — can really play a role.

The International Business Leaders Forum

In 1990, His Royal Highness the Prince of Wales established a new business leaders' forum to promote sustainable development and responsible business practices in the emerging markets of Central and Eastern Europe, Asia, Africa, Latin America, and the Middle East. Nelson joined his International Business Leaders Forum (IBLF) in 1993, and has worked there for 15 years as a director covering a variety of roles from policy and research, to business leadership and strategy. As she explains,

> At the onset most of the work in corporate citizenship was addressed from a community engagement and philanthropy perspective, but very quickly the IBLF started focusing on the mainstream operations and investment role of business in developing countries. Most of my work has been on developing the intellectual and conceptual frameworks for what we do and understanding the business impact on development. I have also focused on building alliances between companies and the international development agencies like the UN, the World Bank, and some of the big international NGOs. I did a lot of work with the World Bank as they were thinking through how to engage with business, and with various parts of the UN and the World Economic Forum, all trying to explore new models of development that harness the resources, capacities, and networks of the private sector.

Corporate Social Responsibility Initiative, Harvard Kennedy School of Government

Since 2004, Nelson has been heading the CSRI at the Mossavar-Rahmani Center for Business and Government at Harvard's Kennedy School of Government. In a sense, her work is a continuation of past initiatives, with a slightly different focus, as she makes clear: "At Harvard we are trying to identify and study practical ways that businesses can get engaged and address international development challenges in a more systemic and scalable manner than one-off community projects." In particular, the CSRI has turned its attention to the ways business can support the Millennium Development Goals and respect human rights.

She further comments,

> A lot of people say, "Why isn't this CSR Initiative at the Harvard Business School?" Right from the beginning John Ruggie and I had the vision that what we're really looking at is the interface between business, government, and civil society in finding solutions to complex public problems, and the

negotiating of appropriate boundaries, roles, and responsibilities between these different actors, rather than how companies are managing CSR internally. The Business School is starting to do that, which is great, and there is growing demand from students in both schools. At the CSR Initiative we've got two key strands of work: one focuses on governance and accountability mechanisms, looking at voluntary business and multi-stakeholder initiatives in areas such as the environment and human rights and doing research on how effective these new mechanisms are. Are they a temporary stage or are they actually new alternatives to government regulations? The other strand of work is focused on business and development. Here we're looking at the new business models, alliances, and institutions that can mobilize private and public resources to address complex development challenges, ranging from small enterprise development to strengthening health systems.

The CSRI's purpose and approach is shown in Box 8.3.

Box 8.3 **Corporate Social Responsibility Initiative**

The CSRI says that it is a:

multi-disciplinary and multi-stakeholder program that seeks to study and enhance the public role of the private enterprise. It explores the intersection of corporate responsibility, corporate governance, public policy, and international development. It bridges theory and practice, builds leadership skills, and supports constructive dialogue and collaboration among business, government, civil society and academics.[179]

The CSRI has an approach to corporate responsibility that mirrors what other difference makers have developed:

We define corporate social responsibility strategically. Corporate social responsibility encompasses not only what companies do with their profits, but also how they make them. It goes beyond philanthropy and compliance and addresses how companies manage their economic, social, and environmental impacts, as well as their relationships in all key spheres of influence: the workplace, the marketplace, the supply chain, the community, and the public policy realm.[180]

The CSRI has an active student group and offers numerous seminars and discussions throughout the year, in addition to the ongoing research agenda. It also reaches out to other schools to foster greater insight and attention to corporate responsibility. It brings students together with company representatives to discuss in-depth issues related to the company's responsibility performance, and offers a variety of other initiatives and programs.

Jane Nelson comments on how her own vision has shaped CSRI:

> My vision is that the private sector can really make a difference, particularly in partnership with other groups. We should not see the private sector as the panacea, however, which it isn't by any stretch of the imagination. Often CSR is a response to governance gaps and failures, and helping to build effective public-sector institutions and capacities is also essential. Equally, I believe that there's an increasingly essential role for social entrepreneurs to serve as bridge builders between large companies, foundations, governments, and communities in tackling social problems. There is a new kind of leadership required that is not right out there charging in front, but is rather the ability to act as a boundary spanner or connector between these different groups and these different possibilities. A new kind of leader who can understand and interpret the varied motivations, languages, perspectives, and capacities of companies, NGOs, and organizations like the UN, and who can help to build effective and scalable alliances between them. We have to be able to demonstrate that there is a link between companies achieving their own strategic objectives and risk management targets and at the same time helping to achieve key international development goals. We need to move beyond simply making the operational "business case," to show why these issues are strategically important to long-term corporate success, and also important from a leadership perspective.

The key point for the CSRI at Harvard, however, is its presence and visibility at one of the world's most prestigious universities, as well as the influence that it will have on the views and practices of future leaders in multiple sectors. It is exactly on this latter point — influencing the education of future leaders in business and other sectors — that Judith Samuelson has focused.

Judith Samuelson

Judith (Judy) Samuelson is the founder and executive director of the Aspen Institute's Business and Society Program, which she founded in 1998. Prior to this, Samuelson had worked at the Ford Foundation from 1989 to 1996, where she led Ford's Office of Program Related Investments, especially the Corporate Involvement Initiative, which focused on encouraging public–private partnerships and developing businesses that have social benefits — businesses that today would be called social enterprises.

The Business and Society Program has a number of important initiatives all associated with changing management education to incorporate issues of sustainability and corporate responsibility, including Beyond Grey Pinstripes (a business school sustainability and corporate responsibility rating), CasePlace.org (teaching resources for management educators), and the Corporate Values Strategy Group (a forum for business leaders to promote change in policy and business practice). Samuelson holds a bachelor's degree from the University of California, Los Angeles, and master's from the Yale School of Management, is on the board of ACCIÓN-New York, a domestic microfinance organization, and is chair emeritus of Net Impact, a network of business students.

After leaving Yale in 1982, Samuelson worked in banking for about seven years, and eventually migrated to the Ford Foundation, where, as she puts it, she

> became more immersed in thinking about the role that business has to play in tackling big complex problems and its ability to deliver big results. We did a lot of partnering. I ran the soft loan window at Ford, the program in the economic development investments area. We had about $150 million set aside from the Foundation's endowment to invest in projects that had a charitable purpose. We worked a lot through big intermediaries, like LISC [Local Initiatives Support Corporation], and South Shore Bank, and Grameen Bank. We helped set up and grow a lot of those entities, so we were using capital, but we were looking to leverage our ability to take big risk and leverage other sources of capital from the banks and insurance companies that were less inclined to take big risks or make substantial investments relative to their size or put real money on the table.

Several of the initiatives Samuelson's funding helped operated directly in the responsibility arena. For example, LISC helps distressed communities upgrade themselves and become healthier, more sustainable communities.[181] The South Shore Bank, now ShoreBank, is perhaps the best-known community development bank and certainly one of the first to provide needed banking services in depressed communities and help them work toward healthier environments.[182] Grameen Bank,[183] founded by Muhammad Yunus, was created as a microlender using an innovative lending strategy that provided small loans to entrepreneurs in poverty to help them grow small (micro) businesses and support themselves and their families. Grameen has expanded to offer multiple services, including phones, fisheries, and education, among other things, and now serves more than five million people with its loans. It has become the global standard bearer for a rapidly expanding microfinance industry.

The Ford Foundation's business-in-society approach

Building business involvement in economic development

One of the crucial aspects of field building is finding funding for innovative initiatives that might otherwise not get off the ground. The Ford Foundation, and Samuelson in particular, played a crucial role in helping to establish the corporate responsibility infrastructure. The work of Samuelson and others at Ford provided an essential underpinning of understanding about different ways of viewing business in society, as Samuelson explains:

> That was a real bird's-eye view of the capacity of business to help garment center lenders, which is what I'd been doing. So we established a relationship with the big banks like Bank of America and Prudential, MetLife, and companies like that. But the real turning point for me was a conversation that took place at the board of the Ford Foundation. The board at that point in time had four or five of what we called the corporate types or the boy scouts — kind of big-thinking CEOs from significant firms, people who had board seats on other corporations. But they were community- and charity-minded. They thought about business and its role in society, not as a separate trough.

The conversation that took place provided some keen new insights that Samuelson was able to tap into later:

> They started asking explicitly of me as the head of the program, "'Why don't we ever talk about the business sector's participation?" The fact is that most of the Ford Foundation didn't talk about the business sector or think much about it. That was definitely true for Ford philanthropy. In fact, to a great extent, business was seen as more of a problem than part of the solution. And this was an organization that was deeply involved in areas where the business role was very germane, like economic development and community development, cultural preservation, education — big, big issues.

Of course the insight did not have a simple resolution, as Samuelson details:

> It was not immediately apparent what role business should play in economic development even if we engaged them more directly. The fact is: that decision wasn't on the table at all except in this one division that tended to co-invest. So the major areas were all grant-making areas where businesses were occasionally involved. There was an environment program, where there were some efforts to think about how to collaborate, although that was still pretty early on, and there was an area that was looking at the role of work and family issues, and they were doing some direct partnering with a few corporations. I was charged to answer, "What is our response to the board of directors?" So we launched a year-long inquiry to understand what the con-

versation should be at the Ford Foundation. But more generally to ask what would be a program that would more directly engage business as partners.

After this discussion by the board, Ford hired a consulting firm to investigate what businesses were actually doing with respect to business in society. One company that was doing a lot was Texas Instruments, which, Samuelson remembers, "had a very progressive philosophy or strategy around diversifying the workforce. And it was completely and totally rooted in the business rationale." The work identified other companies, including Bank of America, which was doing work on community reinvestment, and Levi Strauss, which, as we have already seen, had done a fair amount of work on outsourcing policies and practices.

Samuelson remembers one other conversation at this time that affected her thinking, with the chairman of the board of Reuters, who also oversaw Samuelson's Ford Foundation program. She recalls,

> He was on the board of another company, a British manufacturer of some kind that was opening a plant in Arkansas. He said he was really at sea to know how to do that well. If you wanted to do it in the best possible way, to have the best possible benefit for what was clearly one of the poorest states in the country with lots of poverty and needs, he said, it wasn't clear how you do it. He didn't feel he wanted to reinvent the wheel or be the one to figure it out. He wanted to be able to turn to some entity that would be a partner and guide him, and it wasn't clear whether or not the state was capable of doing that or how to do it.

The conclusion that Samuelson and her colleagues at Ford reached was that

> There were these incredible questions that business had when they thought about economic development, and these incredible things that they were doing. We realized we were really missing perhaps the most important anchor in the area of community and economic development, and maybe more widely. So that set us off on a two-pronged strategy; the first prong was to actually invest in some direct partnerships with business. We did one with Allstate around inner-city insurance, property and casualty insurance. It also emphasized how to work with and create relationships with community organizations to enhance the conditions and the building regulations that would make it easier to insure properties in these neighborhoods, which desperately needed redevelopment but [where] getting insurance was often a problem. So it was one of these "we win, you win, it wins" kind of things.
>
> The second prong was a strategy of providing grants to build the field of organizations in the business-in-society domain, many of which are now organizations you know well like the Boston College Center for Corporate Citizenship. We worked with Boston College as it started to grow into the

corporate citizenship arena and made a big investment in the Center. We were the first foundation to invest in BSR. Ford made a two-year grant of about half a million dollars — a big investment in that organization. Ultimately, we made a major investment in Norman Lear's [Business Enterprise Trust] organization, which unfortunately didn't last, but was doing this really extraordinary awards program at the time. Further, we were tracking the progress of all those organizations.

From this platform, under Samuelson's guidance, Ford began to play a catalytic role in advancing economic development programs that businesses were involved in, including some with Bank of America. Samuelson explains the rationale behind working with business — and doing the field development work:

There was no field here at that point. There is more of a sense of a field today, but at the time there was no sense that there was a field. There were interesting organizations that were starting up. Some were looking more at regulation and compliance or standards that had been around for quite a while. There was the whole field of social investing, which we knew well. So we looked at that field. We were interested in something that's also saying: let's work with business, not campaigners, not the investment piece per se, although we were interested in doing stuff with them and I actually worked very hard on that initially.

Corporate involvement

Samuelson highlights how Ford Foundation's grants helped to shape what is today the responsibility infrastructure in the US, noting,

We were interested in discovering if there was more of a field around what we called corporate involvement. So we created the Corporate Involvement Initiative. It had direct partnering to gain more experience and to put more examples on the table. This pool of grants tried to build the capacity of some nascent and some long-standing organizations like Boston College [Center for Corporate Citizenship], but that were clearly positioned to develop, and where there seemed to be need and some new leadership coming in. So we were trying to say, "How do we cultivate a field of organizations that would provide more of the infrastructure, thought leadership, R&D, convening power, to grow the kind of field of supporting and challenging business to be an important actor in community and economic development?" Even though we were focused on community and economic development, not all the organizations that we worked with were focused on community and economic development. Most of them had at least one piece of that but were defining it more broadly.

Another program officer was hired to do some of this work, and ultimately Ford went through reorganization. Samuelson was essentially spun off with Ford support and funding for a year to think about and prepare to start her own initiative. Engaging her network in a series of interviews with thought leaders around business-in-society issues, Samuelson ultimately focused on what she perceived as a significant need within the general domain that she had already been working in: the need to change management education to incorporate more fully what today would be called sustainability issues.

Changing management education

Samuelson gained new insights about what was needed from her interviews, as she elaborates:

> As a result of all those interviews, one of the things that was very clear was that it really mattered who was at the top of the company. The role of the CEO was critical in the work that the Ford Foundation had done on business and economic development. You really needed a leader who gave cover to whoever the champion was within the firm, the one who was doing the heavy lifting. In other words, you had champions within the firm who were making things happen but, without the cover and strong endorsement of leadership by the CEO, very little happens. And that was just absolutely clear.

She elaborates on how her thinking evolved during this period of transition:

> So I started thinking more about the leadership piece of all that and started visiting business schools, and asking what were they doing that was actually creating managers who had the capacity to think this way. I used that year at the Ford Foundation — I must have met 250 or more people to conduct these interviews. Then I guess within a few months I realized I didn't want to go work for somebody else. I was particularly interested in this idea of influencing business schools. I did a charrette [a form of dialogue] and looked at the research domain [of business in society], and did an East Coast and West Coast meeting of business faculty. Then I went out and visited probably a dozen business schools, deans, and key faculty, and a bunch of executives. I was doing a lot of going out and talking to people, just networking, and as the networking continued I got more into saying this is what I'm going to do.

Ford's support for the next step was crucial, Samuelson explains:

> I put together a proposal that Ford agreed to fund. On the advice of somebody internally, I ultimately went and asked for three years of funding, with the idea that I would go out and use that as a base and then raise money from other sources.

Ford has continued its support over the years, but Samuelson has gone on to raise funds from numerous other funders as well.

Thus, equipped with three years of funding from the Ford Foundation, Samuelson began preparing to launch what initially became the Initiative for Social Innovation through Business, and has now become the Aspen Institute's Business and Society Program. She notes the importance of linking the program to the Aspen Institute, an international organization with a mission of "fostering enlightened leadership and engaged dialogue."[184] The Aspen Institute is known for developing broadly skilled executives through its seminars, conference, and leadership development programs, with a non-partisan orientation based on what it calls timeless values. Its reputation with executives and reputation for thoughtfulness and high-level leadership development provided a central platform for the Business and Society Program.

Samuelson continues,

> The Aspen Institute was an obvious choice because there were lots of things that private foundations funded that ended up there and they had the capacity to house it. They didn't fund it at all, but they seemed to have some base capacity and more of an institutional home, than other places. They also had a brand that worked for both business people and academics, and I knew that was important. Within the first year of being there I was also being impressed by the Aspen Institute's real legacy in dialogue. So I ultimately decided to recreate a business leaders' dialogue that they had done many years before and really upgraded it. We rebuilt and reshaped it.

Aspen Institute Business and Society Program

The Business and Society Program established by Samuelson focuses on "developing leaders for a sustainable global society. Through dialogues and path-breaking research, we create opportunities for executives and educators to explore new pathways to sustainability and values-based leadership."[185] Over the years the program has established numerous initiatives and multiple surveys, as well as various convenings that bring thought leaders together. The two most prominent activities are CasePlace, a web-based resource for teaching materials related to business in society and, in conjunction with the World Resources Institute, the Beyond Grey Pinstripes project, which has multiple aspects, the most important of which is a ranking of business schools along social and environmental criteria. One other program of note is the Faculty Pioneers Program, which recognizes academic leaders in the broadly defined field of business.

CasePlace

Samuelson views CasePlace as an important tool for faculty who wish to develop curriculum in the business-in-society arena. CasePlace provides online access to information about case studies, course syllabi, and related innovative teaching materials in a wide variety of arenas related to sustainability, governance, and corporate responsibility. Topics covered by cases span the scope of the corporate responsibility movement and the emerging infrastructure, including business–government relations, community and economic development, corporate responsibility/citizenship, governance and accountability, crisis management, diversity, environment, transnational issues, poverty alleviation, technological change, and numerous others. CasePlace also provides listings of (and sometimes links to) other resources, including articles and books related to business in society topics, and sets of what it calls teaching modules that bring readings and exercises on key topics together in one place.

Partnership with the World Resources Institute

Samuelson remembers that the collaboration with the World Resources Institute (WRI) on what became the Beyond Grey Pinstripes project began even before she left Ford. WRI is a think-tank that attempts to combine environmental issues and economic development. Its stated mission is "to move human society to live in ways that protect Earth's environment and its capacity to provide for the needs and aspirations of current and future generations."[186] WRI attempts to reverse deterioration of ecosystems and ensure their capacity to support human life and needs, guarantee public access to environmental information, protect the global climate system from further harm by humans, and use markets and businesses to protect nature and expand opportunities.[187]

According to Samuelson, WRI already had an interest in shifting the rating systems that apply to business schools when she approached them; thus there was good congruence of interests. She recalls,

> [WRI was] having these conversations and trying to influence the ranking business. They were meeting with *Business Week* and *US News*. They gave up on being able to influence them and I endorsed their idea of creating an alternative ranking. First, we were going to do a kind of green guide to business schools. Actually, that was sort of what happened: they went ahead and did it that first year just focusing on the environment, and then once I opened doors with them we did it again the next year but broadened the scope and did the first of what's now more rounded and focused on the environment, society, and social issues.

Beyond Grey Pinstripes

Beyond Grey Pinstripes is a biennial survey and ranking originally produced jointly by the Business and Society Program of the Aspen Institute and the WRI (since 2007 administered only by Aspen BSP). The survey ranks the extent to which business schools are integrating social and environmental issues into their curricula. Beyond Grey Pinstripes claims that "These schools are preparing students for the reality of tomorrow's markets by equipping them with the social, environmental, and economic perspectives required for business success in a competitive fast changing world."[188] The goals of Beyond Grey Pinstripes are shown in Box 8.4.

Box 8.4 **Goals of the Beyond Grey Pinstripes program**

1. **Promote and celebrate innovation** in business education. The School Rankings[189] call attention to places and people that do this work well

2. Inform **prospective students** about environmental and social impact management programs

3. Raise the bar by challenging business schools to incorporate social and environmental impact management topics into their curricula

4. **Inform corporate recruiters** of business schools that are providing training in social and environmental skills as part of business decision making

5. **Disseminate best practices in teaching, research, and extracurricular activities**. The Search function on the website provides access to detailed information — often including syllabi — on thousands of courses, journal articles, and more

6. **Facilitate conversation**. Real change only comes after students, faculty, administrators and business leaders begin to discuss these issues.[190]

The Beyond Grey Pinstripes program invites 600 full-time MBA programs to participate in its evaluation every other year and celebrates the top 100 among those programs with respect to their social and environmental programming. Unlike other business school rankings, which focus on ratings by deans, placement rates and salaries, student evaluations, and similar criteria, the Beyond Grey Pinstripes program fosters attention to social-environmental issues by ranking schools on what the program calls student opportunity or the number of courses with environmental and social content, student exposure or the percentage of course time devoted to those topics, content, which reflects the degree to which courses value integrating social-environmental issues, and research, which focuses attention on faculty research output in these arenas. The goal is to foster greater attention on these issues by celebrating schools that are doing a good job of integrating them into the curriculum.

This initiative is supported by another initiative, the Faculty Pioneer Awards, which bring attention to individual faculty members who have been doing outstanding work in these areas.

Faculty Pioneer Awards

The Faculty Pioneer Awards "recognize exceptional faculty that are leaders in integrating social and environmental issues into their research and teaching both on as well as off campus."[191] Each year awards are given to pioneering faculty members for lifetime achievement in the business-in-society domain, for academic leadership generally, for institutional leadership, for external impact, as well as to rising stars: that is, faculty members whose early careers show promise of impact in the business-in-society arena. In addition, starting in 2006, in cooperation with EABIS, Grey Pinstripes gave a European Award as well.

Samuelson reflects on the overall route that her initiatives have taken:

> I had a lot of experience with the Ford Foundation about how you actually make a difference or a change. I had done lots of interviews. I knew in my gut that we were talking about something that was *really* important and different, that we were going to need to try lots of things, and that it made sense to have both push and pull type strategies. I think a lot of that stuff just evolved naturally because I realized there was not one strategy. It was about a lot of things. It was about finding internal champions. It was about bringing pressure. It was about creating consortia. It was about getting people to talk together. But I knew we were up against entrenched systems. The faculty basically were incentivized, and paid, and committed in terms of the life choices that they had made to be academics to begin with. There was nothing wrong from where they sat. There was no market for what we were trying to do. The market was external and disconnected from the academic reality of how people succeed in their careers, what makes them personally happy, what benefit could this change bring.

The initiatives that Samuelson created, like those of other difference makers, have been about creating a movement for change toward a vision of a world that would be different in significant ways than the world we have today. Just what those visions might be — what this different world might look like — is the focus of a new organization attempting to articulate a future view of the purpose of the corporation.

EABIS: the European Academy of Business in Society

In the European Union, issues related to changing management education to incorporate sustainability and ESG issues have also received considerable attention, particularly from EABIS, the European Academy of Business in Society. EABIS states its mission as being "a unique alliance of companies, business schools and academic institutions that is, with the support of the European Commission, committed to integrating business in society issues into the heart of business theory and practice in Europe."[192]

EABIS was founded in 2002 by company CEOs and business school deans concerned with developing managers and leaders better prepared for the 21st century than those produced by traditional management education. The mission of EABIS is to:

- Shape and enhance the quality of debate on the role of business-in-society in Europe

- Equip current and future business leaders with the mind-set and capacity to put business-in-society at the heart of the way companies are run by integrating the changing role of business-in-society into the mainstream of business research, education, and training

- Transform the way that business leaders, academics, policy-makers, and others interact and communicate on business-in-society issues among themselves and with a wider audience

- Inform policy-making on issues of business-in-society[193]

To accomplish these objectives, EABIS focuses on interdisciplinary and relevant management research, helping business schools place business-in-society issues at the heart of management education, and building a multi-stakeholder learning network to support training management professionals in understanding the social impacts of their decisions. A big part of how EABIS works is through fostering significant research on the role of business in society: for example, through what it calls its RESPONSE project, which is looking at corporate responsibility at the organizational and individual behavior levels, focusing on stakeholder expectations facing companies and how they can be better handled, and why there is a gap between stakeholders' expectations of companies and companies' understanding of their own responsibilities to society. EABIS also sponsors what it calls its CSR Platform, which attempts to provide a means of dialogue among academic institutions, businesses, policy-makers, and actors in civil society around CSR and an appropriate going-forward research agenda. EABIS also sponsors major research projects that can help shed light on the fundamental questions: for example, stakeholder relationships, the business case for corporate responsibility, social entrepreneurship, the role of government, bottom-of-the-pyramid strategies, and management education.

■ Tomorrow's dream: changing the nature of the corporation

Allen White, who cofounded the Global Reporting Initiative with Bob Massie, has embarked on a new venture aimed at changing the fundamentals of the corporation with Marjorie Kelly (now of Tellus Institute, but earlier editor of *Business Ethics* magazine). The new initiative is called Corporation 20/20 and is aimed at nothing less than changing the core purpose of the modern corporation to incorporate social and environmental issues.

White recalls how the idea for Corporation 20/20 germinated during his tenure as CEO of the GRI:

> In the time since I left the GRI, I have come to understand the inherent limitations of GRI-type programs. Here we had a sterling example of a grand idea, the emergence of a critical public good — corporate accountability — *within* the rules of the game. In the end, we had great success in incremental change. But would such change, even multiplied many times over, be enough to direct corporations toward a level of social performance congruent with 21st-century needs and expectations? As the most powerful institution operating in the world today, can such incremental progress be enough to optimize the corporate contribution to the urgent social and environmental problems facing humanity now and in the coming decades?[194]

White continues,

> My answer to this question, after much contemplation, is a decisive "no." I have come to believe that corporations (and the capital markets on which they depend) contain certain design flaws that restrict their capacity to serve societal needs at a level commensurate with their unparalleled resources, know-how, and capacity to innovate. We, as a society, have both the right and the obligation to rethink the received wisdom and prevailing definition of corporate purpose and obligations in light of 21st-century realities. If we do so, I believe we will come to the conclusion that the corporation as we know it, while possessing many attributes worthy of retaining, must be transformed from within and from without if it is going to deliver the level of social value needed in the coming decades. The joint stock, publicly traded corporation has grown so large, so complex, and so influential that traditional policies of containment of harm rather than maximization of good are no longer capable of meeting societal needs. We see attempts to reform governance structures for organizations with a quarter of a trillion dollars in turnover and operating in a hundred countries and employing 300,000 people. But these reforms are simply not up to the task. Our concepts of corporate governance

at the company level, national level, and international level have not kept pace with the scale of modern global enterprise. No amount of incremental reform in corporate reporting, or any other aspect of corporate management, will correct this growing "governance deficit."

It was this view that spawned Corporation 20/20, an initiative that now consumes most of my mental and physical energy. Its goal is to build visions and prototypes of future corporations that have social purpose deeply and irreversibly embedded in their "genetic structure." In the spirit of GRI, it operates in multi-stakeholder mode, seeking to engage all those with something to contribute to the definition and attainment of new corporate forms. Its method is backcasting: that is, creating normative models of high-performing corporations and then asking, "How do we get from the present to the preferred future?" Launched in 2004, it is moving steadily toward assuming a leadership role in catalyzing and shaping changes in corporate purpose, directors' duties, shareholder primacy, capital structure, internal rewards and incentives, and all other core aspects of the corporation.

Corporation 20/20

Corporation 20/20 asks a foundational set of questions about the nature of today's corporation in its mission statement:

> What would a corporation look like that was designed to seamlessly integrate both social and financial purpose? Corporation 20/20 is a new multi-stakeholder initiative that seeks to answer this question. Its goal is to develop and disseminate corporate designs where social purpose moves from the periphery to the heart of future organizations.[195]

Rather than focusing on improving the current structure and purpose of the corporation, Corporation 20/20 focuses on what its founders term "system redesign": that is, a rethinking of the nature and fundamental purposes of the firm in society. The rationale for redesign is in the flaws that can be found in the modern corporation, as the website details:

> Corporation 20/20 posits a third path: *system redesign*. This path is grounded in recognition that the existing corporate form — directors duties, capitalization, liability, accountability — are in urgent need of redefinition. While the corporate responsibility and governance movements have achieved some notable progress, a more systemic, integrated transformation is both needed and plausible at this moment in history. Redesign aims at such transformation by shifting

the focus from the "what" and "how" of wealth creation to the nature and purpose of the corporation itself.[196]

To achieve this vision, Corporation 20/20 posits that future corporations will need to be designed around an entirely different set of assumptions and principles than the current corporation. White and his multi-stakeholder-network collaborators have set forth a set of Principles for Corporate Redesign that attempt to offset the current focus on maximization of shareholder wealth (see Box 8.5).

Box 8.5 **Corporation 20/20 Principles of Corporate Redesign**

1. The purpose of the corporation is to harness private interests to serve the public interest

2. Corporations shall accrue fair returns for shareholders, but not at the expense of the legitimate interests of other stakeholders

3. Corporations shall operate sustainably, meeting the needs of the present generation without compromising the ability of future generations to meet their needs

4. Corporations shall distribute their wealth equitably among those who contribute to its creation

5. Corporations shall be governed in a manner that is participatory, transparent, ethical, and accountable

6. Corporations shall not infringe on the right of natural persons to govern themselves, nor infringe on other universal human rights[197]

Allen White reflects on the learning from GRI as it applies to the new initiative:

> We learned about the need to bring together parties with divergent views, keep it multi-stakeholder, keep it inclusive, because that's the way you build legitimacy as well as create the best ideas through cross-cultivation. So it's the legitimacy and the cross-cultivation [that are important]. Those are the two reasons to go this route as opposed to a room full of lawyers, as opposed to a room full of NGOs, as opposed to a room full of government people. You'd never get the product, neither the legitimacy nor the quality of the product, if you limit yourself that way. Then let it evolve slowly. So you need to create a forum, create some discussions, do some writing, all around the question of the purpose of the corporation. What is it and what should it be in the 21st century? The big prize is a consensus with enough gravitas behind it that it will stand as the benchmark kind of norm that would then

influence everything from individual company behaviors all the way to international norm-setting, say through the UN Business Norms, which are still evolving.

Despite all the work that has been done to create the responsibility assurance infrastructure, White argues that initiatives such as Corporation 20/20 are needed because a more basic shift is needed to achieve the goals that many of the difference makers seek:

> It is my view that initiatives like Corporation 20/20, ones that focus on transformative change, must be the vanguard during the next decade. This is no way diminishes the need for GRI and like-minded, issue-specific, incremental change initiatives. It does suggest, however, such initiatives, by themselves or collectively, must be viewed within the broader context of the structural and systemic change that stand beyond the reach of mainstream corporate responsibility initiatives.
>
> If you believe in these [Corporation 20/20] principles — and we think they're the right ones — here are some working examples of the shape of corporations, the form of corporations, the design of corporations in all of the various dimensions, directors, duties, liability, capitalization, the whole gamut of things. Here are some prototypes, models, of the corporate form that we offer to you, some sound benchmarks against which we invite you to take your policy and take your program and take your reform, take whatever it is you're working on and say, "Does that adhere? Does that fit? Is that harmonious with this prototype and those principles?"

White concludes,

> The major controversies facing business today — fiduciary duties limited to shareholder interests, labor standards and supply chain management, stagnant wages and executive compensation, environmental degradation and payments to host governments, short-termism in capital markets — are symptomatic of deep-seated flaws that share a common source. This source is the purpose and character of the corporation as defined in law, practice and received wisdoms. To bring business–society relations in line with 21st-century needs and expectations, the coming decade must see far more attention to this source than the corporate responsibility movement has thus far demonstrated.

The vision thing

This book has detailed some of the key developments in the emergence of a new infrastructure around corporate responsibility, accountability, and transparency, as it has been fostered by a couple of dozen pioneering spirits. These individuals, the difference makers, together with the many, many others — partners, collaborators, and co-visionaries in all types of organizations — have put into place a new set of institutions and pressures on companies. Collectively (as well as with others), these difference makers have created a substantial social movement around issues related to corporate responsibility. Clearly, we have seen many examples of a desire to change the system, as various organizations and institutions emerged onto the corporate responsibility landscape over the past several decades — particularly since the mid-1990s when the movement began to gain real traction.

As the first half of this chapter illustrates, there has been no shortage of obstacles to achieving their vision of responsibility assurance, but there is also reason to hope that system change can indeed occur, as they also articulate in the last half of this chapter.

◼ Obstacles to achieving the vision

Each of the difference makers details the obstacles that he or she faced in establishing their institutions — and that the whole movement toward corporate responsibility, accountability, and transparency and a more equitable and sustainable system, still faces.

The fundamental issues

Some of the obstacles to system change that the difference makers pointed out are at the very core of the current system: they represent fundamental changes that are needed either in individuals, particularly leaders, or in the systems that support modern institutions if things are going to change for the better, which in the eyes of difference makers means the achievement of environmental sustainability, more equity across the peoples of the world, and greater accountability from companies. These changes go way beyond what the difference makers have yet been able to effect, though many of the institutions that they founded are working in these directions.

The ability to see what changes are needed — and act

Looking at the work of the difference makers in retrospect, it seems that what was needed to begin creating the responsibility infrastructure was obvious. But, as Steve Lydenberg points out, that is far from the case, even for individuals who, like himself, have been at the forefront of important innovations:

> I look back and it just amazes me how long it's taken me to see what seems to be obvious to me now. Seeing with the kind of clarity that I had when working on my book,[198] I thought when I started the process that I could say what I wanted to say because it was relatively simple. In the end I did sort of say it, but in the process I just had to look, and understand what I was looking at in a different way, in order to articulate it in a reasonably lengthy form. So the process of seeing, in and of itself, is a real challenge — and a challenge to all of us. It's very hard. It's easy to look in retrospect and see what the challenges have been, but when you're in the middle of something that's going on it's very hard to see them. The advances in technologies and the sheer number of people in the world have put into people's hands the ability not only to do a lot of good but also to do tremendous harm. Ozone depletion is just one example of the incalculable harm that can be done very easily. So it's very important to be able to see correctly.

Of course, seeing what changes might be needed is not enough, as Lydenberg comments:

> The second [obstacle] for me in particular is learning how, even if you see a problem and see what the solution is, to make it happen, to act politically, to act effectively. In fact, I'd say one of the weaknesses of social investors in gen-

eral is that we're very good at seeing problems, but aren't particularly good at seeing the solutions, so that's the other real challenge.

Bob Massie experienced a similar need to create a "seeing" among the executives he was trying to introduce to the risks of climate change back in the early 2000s:

> This was in April 2002, five years after Kyoto. Why is some guy named Bob Massie, or anybody else, explaining the obvious to people who are paid hundreds of millions of dollars to supposedly be aware of what's happening in the future. There was that deep resistance to paying attention to the obvious because it was inconvenient. I am a huge opponent of the idea that we are barred from making a better world because it's inconvenient, because, well, no, we haven't ever done that before, and it would be complicated to do it so we're not going to try. I'm an enormous believer in the ability of systems to change, and one of the advantages of getting a little older is that I can now rack up 25 examples of things that have been completely transformed since the moment I was born, three or four of which I've been directly involved in, and I can tell you about the point when it was completely laughed at and everyone thought it was absurd. And now we've reached the point where real differences are being made.

The risk of system failure

One risk that some of the difference makers see, particularly John Elkington, is of system collapse. He comments,

> I think increasingly we're building a global footprint, which risks bringing a much larger set of systems down. That could take a thousand years. It could happen in 50. I wouldn't want to put a time-scale on it. To some degree, it may actually happen far faster and have much more to do with climate change processes, which we are influencing but are not totally responsible for, but are totally unable to adapt to in time.
>
> You then come down to the level of capitalism and I think we're going to see capitalism mutating into many different forms as it already has done. I think Chinese variants of capitalism are going to be quite different. I'm *very* optimistic that, as Tom Friedman[199] says, China may well become an incubator of green technologies because it will have no choice but to become so.

Elkington goes on to talk about corruption in some countries as a huge obstacle, and the fact that, despite his optimism about China, some practices — for example, the nation's fishing practices — are potentially environmentally disastrous, commenting, "So you've got this weird paradox where on the one hand China may go up a green track and at the same time it's actually helping bring down the global ecosystem."

A global system built on nations

John Ruggie sees a similar set of risks from the perspective of his work at the UN, as well as from his directorship of the Mossavar-Rahmani Center for Business and Government at Harvard's Kennedy School of Government, which educates many of tomorrow's political and NGO leaders. Ruggie comments,

> The fundamental problem that we face at the global level obviously is the fact that the scope of problems far outreaches the scope of organized interests of a political nature in favor of dealing with the problems. We've got this increasingly dynamic and integrated global economic system. We've got a transforming environment from which you can't exempt yourself, and yet the political mechanisms through which we have to work are territorially based. Within those territorial configurations, you've got a variety of interests at play, none of which encompass the whole. They're all partial views and the challenge, especially when you're sitting at the UN, is how do you build mechanisms that allow the notion of national interest to be stretched horizontally to encompass more people and temporally to encompass a longer time-frame than is the norm? That's almost a trivial thing to say but that's the fundamental problem in how we govern ourselves globally.
>
> Beyond that you've got the obvious constraints of lack of capacity, or lack of will, on the part of many governments to govern effectively even *within* their territory. I did a project on how to engage the business sector more effectively as a social partner in developing the capacity to respond to Aids. And you hear horror stories of officials allowing drugs to rot on the docks because they hadn't been bribed. Apart from these macro-structural constraints, there are these all-too-human constraints of incapable, ineffective, or corrupt governments that contribute to some of the worse things that we see on the face of the planet. You've got all sorts of things going on in between, so there's no end to identifying impediments.

Lack of global governance mechanisms

Picking up on this theme, John Elkington points to the fact that the initiatives established by the difference makers are all voluntary, and that the voluntary nature has arisen in the face of lack of workable *global* governance mechanisms. As Elkington points out,

> I think capitalism red in tooth and claw is a major barrier because we do not have the global governance mechanisms to really regulate capitalism as it is currently practiced. Even the above-board forms of capitalism are destructive. But if you look at the drug industry, human trafficking, the sex trade, you look at the trade norms, and these sorts of things [are all] around the world.

The vacuum at the global governance level I think is a massive and a much underestimated barrier.

The leadership gap

Peter Kinder says that one of the major obstacles to achieving some of the needed changes is the "lack of people with the wherewithal to move the process forward. It's a huge impediment. My hope is that it's not insuperable," he comments, focusing in particular on problems in the US educational system as a major root of that problem. The issue is finding leaders with a broad enough vision to see the problem from a global perspective rather than a territorial or company-based one — and finding a willingness to act on that vision.

Steve Waddell concludes that the same problem is a major obstacle to change for two reasons: "Number one: people giving time for vision, and letting it develop and realize something. Number two is being open to innovation and thinking about things differently." To accomplish these goals, Waddell believes, "We need places for people to understand how to create those dynamics and build those different mental models about how to be together with one another." Focusing on using networks to create new ways of thinking about the world, Waddell comments,

> We need a space that will help us understand how to build these networks. Networks are fundamentally about relationships, and, unless you can appreciate our relationships differently, you aren't going to create different types of networks. We're still going to have these ones that we've had that don't work very well.

Brad Googins similarly points to this critically important factor: the leadership gap at the top of organizations today. He comments,

> There is a huge absence of leadership right now, which I worry about on all levels. The political structure has become almost pathetic in some ways, so that almost everybody's given up on it. But I look at something more germane to what I do, for example, business leadership. The Boston College Center for Corporate Citizenship did a series of interviews with CEOs, and it's clear to me that the leadership is not what it was, and is probably not going to be again, because of the narrowing of perspective. So I think we're in the midst of a cycle, and maybe after we pass along there'll be a new vision of society, and they'll go through their struggles.

Jane Nelson concurs and adds an important point: business cannot be expected to completely fill the gaps left by other sectors. She comments,

> The vision is also about companies not being as powerful as a lot of people think they are. But certain business leaders do have power and are influen-

tial. It is about individual business leaders being influential, and having a leadership responsibility to make a difference in the world and to develop that ethos of public service through private enterprising.

Short-termism

A number of the difference makers focused on the short-term orientation of modern business and financial markets as major barriers to change. According to John Elkington,

> You get into financial markets and the shortsightedness that prevails there. It isn't that [for example] the reinsurers and so on aren't waking up to issues like climate change. They are. Even Wal-Mart and companies like General Electric are now responding in ways that would have seemed inconceivable a few years back. But nonetheless the financial markets are brutally short-sighted. We're dealing with a life form [the corporation] that is able to look a couple of quarters out if you're lucky. There are exceptions to every rule, I know, and there are institutions that are looking very considerably further out into the field, including some hedge funds, but others as well. But I look at financial markets and I think we have a major problem, Houston.

Allen White states the problem baldly:

> The problem of impatient capital is *huge*. It's just huge. It's poisonous, and you can see the damage that it wreaks. Thinking about the transformation of capital markets is crucial and I'd love to see somebody step forward and work on that. I think there are huge numbers of business leaders who won't say it or don't have time to think about it: people in business who live under the stress of capital markets, who neither should do so nor, if given an alternative, would choose to do so. They'd still make handsome salaries, yet the corrosive effects of the capital market intermediaries, including the whole pool of people, everything from the investment bankers to the asset managers, give us a system that really is socially corrosive, socially damaging.

Georg Kell agrees that the short-term orientation is problematic — not just in business but in other contexts as well:

> There's the time-horizon issue. It's maddening to see the short-term obsession of so many business people and of politicians, for that matter. I think it's one of the basic problems we have in governance whether it's public or private. Politicians are elected for a short cycle and it often looks like they couldn't care less about what happens after them. Human beings' vision about time and history is very, very short-term. People not only forget about the past (and it's one of our tragedies that we don't seem to be able to learn

even from mistakes), but it's also in anticipating the future. We don't seem to have the mental capacity collectively to really apply more rational thinking together. There seems to be a race to the short-term viewpoint because incentive structures are still so perverse that often the short-term actors are rewarded more than the long-term thinkers. I think that's the most maddening [thing]. It's the time dimension in all decision-making that's fundamental.

Redefining democracy

Bob Dunn points out that some of the issues facing businesses are quite fundamental, For example:

> Our institutions aren't working the way we want them to. I think democracy is under siege because it's not delivering what it has promised. I think that there are great concerns that the private sector is not acting in an ethical and responsible way, and the NGO community has also been tarnished by evidence of the failure of its own standards with respect to issues like governance, transparency, and accountability. So there's dissatisfaction with the institutions that we have. There's a way in which I think society is still struggling to try to redefine the role of these institutions and to ensure that they serve a common purpose.
>
> I'm not saying that corporate social responsibility or some of these issues are going to go away, but they're going to transform and come back at companies in very different and often quite challenging ways that drive these sorts of priorities deep into the heart of business.

Other obstacles

The list of fundamental issues above represents core elements related to obstacles to system change that difference makers identify. Other obstacles arise from turf divisions, from lack of vision, or from an inability to even see the need for change, as the difference makers discuss below.

Turf: whose domain is this?

Alice Tepper Marlin of SAI notes,

> In broad terms the major obstacle was the resistance of the national standard-setting bodies and national accreditation agencies to doing this [standard setting] on a global basis, and to doing it as a civil society exercise as opposed to an intergovernmental exercise. So the formation of SAI raised questions like: Is this an invasion of sovereignty? Are we on the turf of what are essentially national monopolies? So that's the major challenge to the system as a whole.

These obstacles are carried over institutionally, according to Bob Dunn:

> At the institutional level, we're really challenged because we're shifting from old models with clearly defined and separated functions for the major institutions of our society — government, business, and NGOs — to a time when roles are more ambiguous and seem to overlap, where there's more permeability among the sectors. So you've got NGOs doing R&D for corporations, and corporations providing functions that have historically been part of the domain of the public sector, and you've got places where the public sector is taking initiatives like wiring communities that might have been a function in the past of the private sector.

Business as usual

When asked "What are the obstacles to achieving the central vision of accountability that ties companies together (apart from the fact that the opposition is so much better funded)?" Tim Smith responded,

> The major obstacles are that the rules of the road generally for global corporations are primarily to make a profit, and even though we're talking about changing them so that these other issues become part of their formula, profits are still primary. On an issue like climate change it's really a debate whether we're going to be able to be successful. Some huge changes are going to occur, whether it's the increase in the gap between the rich and the poor, using up our energy sources, climate change, which we just may not be able to impact in time.

Fear, insecurity, lack of hope — and entrenched interests

Bob Dunn suggests that it is often individual barriers of fear, insecurity, and lack of hope that inhibit movement toward the type of world that many of the difference makers envision. He states,

> I don't think a lot about obstacles. I'm certainly mindful that there are plenty of them. So what I would say is that the obstacles start with individuals and sometimes their lack of hope and sometimes their resignation [to a belief] that it's not possible to change the world as it is. Sometimes that's affected, I think, by people's own insecurities and fears which put distance between them and others rather than viewing everyone as part of one human family.

Simon Zadek agrees, noting that the major challenges to change are

> inertia. Fear. Ignorance. Violence. It's a fairly predictable list. Let me not repeat the obvious list but maybe highlight a couple of perhaps slightly less obvious ones. I think the progressive movement, whatever that is or what its

shape is today, is terribly tied by its imagination of yesterday. Its imagination that politics is something that has to be confined to the state. Its imagination that NGOs should not be part of the structural power compact but should be outside of it lobbying in. Actually, even in the NGO community and broader civil society, an imagination that business needs to be there just for money and then we need to control it rather than business being really there for something completely different. I think we have an extraordinary failure of imagination, which has to do with our legacy and our inability to offload it. That is much more so within the progressive movement than it is within the hard right, who find it much easier to jettison ideas, being far more interested in crude versions of power than we are. I don't want to parrot Mandela, but the biggest constraint is our unbelief in ourselves. I believe that ideas make change as a part of political processes and that powerful institutions *can* be changed and have been over history, despite it seeming to be so difficult.

Laury Hammel would concur:

Fear [is the biggest obstacle to change]. I think that there are two major forces in the world. One is love and one is fear. The more you feel connected, the more you love people and the less fear you have. The more fear you have, the more hatred you have and the less connected you are to love, and the more able you are to do harmful things. If you view yourself as being connected to the terrorists in Iraq, as evil as they are, but realize they are still a part of who we are, then you bear some responsibility for why they are the way they are. That's a real challenge: how do you deal with people who are so filled with hatred and evil? How do you do that in a way that doesn't blind their whole way of being? So dealing with fear is a big, big challenge.

Bob Dunn adds one more important item to this list:

People who benefit from inequity and who have wealth, power, status, and so forth are often resistant to changes that most of us would regard as both necessary and fair. So we have to find ways to transform institutions that are clogged by a long history of institutions and individuals doing things in a particular way and in viewing the current systems as being to their own advantage.

Again, Laury Hammel is in agreement, arguing,

The other challenge is that so many people I've run into who are very, very rich spend so much of their time being afraid of losing their money. There are also the majority of people who are afraid of the fact that they don't have any money and what is going to happen if they don't have money. But the people who have it are afraid of losing it. So the way the economic structure is set up, it's really not beneficial to people, because I think that if we can set up a system that rewards people who do a good day's work, a good liveli-hood across the board, and offer jobs and opportunities and training for people so that all people could do that, then that is going to create a more equitable world, which is going to create a less fearful world. A big obstacle is: if you have equitable, fair economic systems for people who can live and feel comfortable, the ground is not very fertile for religious hatred. So I'm not saying that economics totally determines consciousness but I do think that economics does have an impact on people's consciousness.

Malcolm McIntosh also sees a similar set of issues as obstacles to change:

One [problem] is just essential greed — the tendency of being human is to be greedy and to hold onto what you've got and not give it back. So you have to create social structures that mean that things are necessarily given back and shared as the first thing. But that's on a different level from the second prob-lem. The second problem is that we've created certain sorts of organizations that do what we need in a certain sort of way. We've got to change those organizations. The third point is that those organizations now employ so many people or so many people have shares in them that it is in a *large* num-ber of people's vested interest not to change the status quo. Those people are rich and powerful and they number several million globally. Why would they want to change? If you've got shares in Shell or BP or Pfizer, why would you want to knock the system? It does very nicely, thank you. If you work in one of them, well, of course you're going to argue for that company. They pay you every day.

Brad Googins adds another dimension to this list — lack of trust, noting,

Lack of trust in institutions is probably the thing that frightens me the most. What holds for business is what holds for most institutions. We're at a stage now where there are virtually no institutions you can trust. It used to be that, well, I can trust the church, or there's an institution over here that has some credibility, like the United Way, but [now] it's like every institution is so tainted and people's perceptions of these institutions are so changed that trust is going down.

A shifting agenda — and no firm answers

As the field of corporate responsibility has evolved over the years, so have the issues that have been placed in the domain of corporate responsibility. David Grayson comments,

We don't know what all the answers are. Even if a business says, "Look, we genuinely want to be a responsible business," we can't give them a kind of Bible that gives them the Holy Word in all circumstances. One could take a number of questions, which are what I would call the frontier issues where we're continuing to evolve our understanding of what it means to be a responsible business.

Peter Kinder agrees that issues will continue to shift in the responsibility and accountability movement because it is a dialectical process. He argues,

I have a very Marxist view of how progress is made, though I'm not a Marxist, and I don't believe there is an "end." It's a dialectic. It's hard to keep going a lot of times when you have that world-view because you're not working toward a golden age, because you know damn well there isn't one and there wasn't one, so you're trying to push the pendulum. The thing that keeps me going is that there are so many things in our society that are worth preserving, fostering, nurturing, and emphasizing, and there are so many things that are out there that are going to destroy those very same things. I think that the development of corporations as, in effect, states without boundaries is a very real threat to our polity. It's the creation of, in effect, a fifth branch of government. It's really not accountable in any conventional sense. How do you integrate that, deal with that reality? It's something that has exactly the opposite set of incentives to what we might desire: for example, it's distinctly not in a corporation's interest to pay local property rates.

Kinder concludes that the key to the dilemma he sees may be

to bring the pendulum into the center and influence the direction and nature of the dialogue. Because, if you assume that there is a dialogue going on, the only way you're going to affect it (short of violent revolution, which I really don't believe in) is to participate in the conversation.

Inflated expectations around corporate responsibility

John Elkington is concerned about the current wave of activity around corporate responsibility because, in his words,

Corporate social responsibility unnerves me because I think there is much of a bubble economy about it, both in Europe and particularly in Japan where I've done quite a lot of work over the years. It isn't that bubble economies don't do good work, but they're wasteful, and there is a huge amount of collateral damage when they deflate. Bubble economies are very much part of what drives progress — I can't remember who said it — but it's often said that with new technologies in the early years we wildly overestimate what they'll give us in the short term. If you think about it, the new economy or biotechnology are examples of that, but it actually takes much longer. Quite often it is 50 or 60 years before the fruits really start to come through. Once they come through, though, they come through on a wildly different scale than we ever imagined possible.

David Grayson, too, is aware of both the shifting agenda and the time that change actually takes. He notes,

I think our understanding of what it means to be a responsible business continues to evolve over time. That is very much a result of engagement between many of the people who have been really working on these topics. So one of the very exciting and very encouraging things about our field is how much sharing and how many people have risen to advance that field. I think that the vision has been something that continues to develop and evolve very much through a lot of dialogues with a lot of the people who are really doing some of the most creative kind of frontier work in this field.

Need to get into the business DNA

John Elkington also thinks that most current corporate responsibility initiatives do not go nearly far enough, as he points out:

I look at CSR, and I see a bunch of people trying to encourage companies to be good and to be nice. I'm all for that, but actually I think companies succeed because they are predatory, they are territorial, they are competitive, and to some degree I think corporate citizenship has institutionalized itself in bits of the corporate anatomy where it really doesn't engage with business models. It doesn't engage with the guts of the DNA of the business and that's where I think we now ought to be operating.

One problem with getting into business's DNA, as Elkington further notes, is the rapid turnover of CEOs and the lack of real concern on the part of consumers and markets about these issues — at least until there is a personal stake in the issue.

The need for new types of expertise

The evolution of institutions such as SAI and AccountAbility, and the numerous other certification, monitoring, and accrediting bodies around social, ethical, and governance issues, has raised another issue: where to find individuals qualified to do the work, or, more broadly, the work of difference making in general.

Alice Tepper Marlin states clearly some of the struggles that SAI has had in finding qualified auditors:

For SA8000 in particular there are a lot of challenges. One is the difficulty of quickly finding and qualifying large numbers of auditors because social auditing is relatively new. The field of auditors has traditionally been very male-dominated, but a lot of the people you are interviewing are women, who in many cultures are not comfortable talking to men about many things, particularly sensitive things like sexual harassment, pregnancy tests, discrimination, and so on. Secondly, and more centrally, the auditors are used to things that can be objectively quantitatively measured, and it's often a real challenge both to find out how to audit in general in this area and particularly how to audit the things that are least measurable. So finding auditors who can competently do occupational safety and health is not a great leap, but finding auditors who are really good at interviewing workers, getting them to trust them, open up, understanding what they're saying, and auditors who can detect the difficult-to-detect compliances or non-compliances like discrimination or freedom of association still remains a huge challenge. The third challenge is always getting enough money to do a good job in any public service area. We started SAI with modest funds relative to the size of the job, because we were trying to do something on a global basis. We're a lot bigger than CEP was, but we're very small compared to international agencies in general and the expectations are very high.

Creating multi-stakeholder coalitions

The term "multi-stakeholder collaboration" has become very popular, because many of the responsibility initiatives realized that traditional governmental-based governance mechanisms were not adequate to deal with the complexities and reach of the global corporation. Legitimacy, however, was (and is) a significant issue for initiatives that are attempting to put pressures on companies and other institutions for reforms that, in years past, governments might have attempted through laws and regulations. One response to the legitimacy and governance issues has been the establishment of multi-stakeholder coalitions or collaborations. We have seen such coalitions, for example, in the formation of the GRI, the development of the Ceres Principles, and SAI, among others.

Alice Tepper Marlin notes that for its global scope SAI required a multi-stakeholder approach, which proved useful, but was not without problems:

> It's always a challenge working with a multi-stakeholder group. The outcome is terrific. It tends to be much better, I think, than any one sector would produce by themselves. You get very optimal outcomes but getting consensus for a multi-stakeholder group is a challenge. Then there's the challenge from companies and industry associations that want much cheaper and much easier codes and systems. So it's a struggle to keep a really credible system

going and to enable all of the stakeholders and the general public to differentiate between the more robust credible systems and ones where standards are very weak, or there isn't any real monitoring or serious capacity building.

No silver bullet

As with many social movements, once the movement has begun to take hold, individuals and groups with competing ideas enter the fray, creating competition among institutions, approaches, and frameworks. This stage has been reached at least in some areas of the movement, as Alice Tepper Marlin notes about SAI:

> Our original big idea was that we thought by taking this model we would have a global standard and that we'd move very quickly and very well. SAI's standard was pretty much the first one out there that wasn't just for one sector. But there's proved to be competition among different systems as well. In the US the Fair Labor Association was formed around a similar time, and we're moving toward cooperation in a joint project actually called the Joint Initiative on Corporate Responsibility and Worker Rights. There's been competition both from those trying to do it at a much cheaper and less robust level and also at the multi-stakeholder level from other systems, both in Europe and in the United States.

Steve Young also talks about the complexity of the current economic and political structures — and the difficulty of effecting significant changes:

> Our structures, particularly in America and some in Europe and Japan, are complex and there are many obstacles. Therefore, the response has to be complicated. There's no silver bullet and a number of players and approaches are necessary to deal with the different realms. We have the area of cultural values, perceptions, norms, loosely floating around, so then who are all the people who deal with that? There are a whole set of institutions there. In that realm I think the key process, philosophically necessary today in an era of postmodernism and nihilism, is sort of a Malcolm Gladwell[200] tipping point phenomenon. In other words, you've got to work with lots of people. You've got to find innovators, then for the early adopters at some point it tips, and a new norm is established. That also implies education, outreach, writing, talking, proselytizing, advocacy, networking, media, and all kinds of things.

◾ What needs to change: a better world

Each of the difference makers has his or her unique take on what a "better world" would be; however, as we will see by examining some of their ideas, there is general consistency and direction in their framings, a consistency that suggests an emerging collective vision of what this better world would look like.

Decision-makers' hopes for system change

New types of institutions

Serving in a role as institutional thought leader, Steve Lydenberg articulates a number of important new types of institutions that are needed if the responsibility movement is to continue to move forward successfully and effectively:

> There is a whole network of different things that we should be doing. They can be captured under certain kinds of activity, like certification and standard setting, which is an obvious way for a movement to establish itself: for example, certifying organizations who do the research work, and certifying analysts who do the investment work. There are three certification efforts bubbling up, two out of Europe. The European Social Investment Forum has issued a set of best practices for transparency by social mutual funds. The European Commission has funded the development of standards for social investment research agencies. Third is this idea of creating an actual certification process for the analysts themselves as opposed to companies or mutual funds.

Lydenberg also believes that the field could use a number of think-tanks, of which the Institute for Responsible Investment is only a seedling. For example, he comments,

> This doesn't exist, but should, and might possibly be what the Corporation 20/20 project that Allen White and Marjorie Kelly are heading up might turn into — a think-tank to just raise basic questions about what the structure and function and purpose of the publicly traded corporation should be. There is a think-tank that exists now called the Center for the Study of Fiduciary Capitalism, whose stated goal is to work with institutional investors as fiduciaries, essentially pension funds, about what the implications of social-environmental information and data are for their investment practices. That in itself is ample territory for a think-tank. I can see an institution emerging which does nothing but think about these implications for mergers and acquisitions, which has very practical implications, since more mergers or acquisitions fail than succeed, and most of those failures happen because of what is generally

described as corporate culture issues, which I take to be non-financial social and environmental issues. So having a series of these think-tanks that would work together in coordinated ways would be very useful. The Center for Business and Government at the Kennedy School [headed by John Ruggie] is a think-tank just to think about the interface between business and government — one of the most fundamental issues out there today.

Improving corporate responsibility performance

Alice Tepper Marlin is very clear about the vision that drove the initial founding of the CEP:

> The vision was to improve corporate performance, to make the idea of corporate social responsibility a broadly accepted one, through research made available to stakeholders, investors, consumers, employees, managers, and the general public. To provide incentives for companies to improve so they would compete in the way they compete for profitability or for share of market or sales volume to be competing to be the best in corporate social responsibility.

This vision was continued in the development of SAI, according to Tepper Marlin: "SAI's mission is to improve the social and environmental practices and policies of companies, but in a much more focused way, and it would do so on an international basis all through a multi-stakeholder process."

Companies helping societies

Bob Dunn also had the idea of improving corporate responsibility when he began working with BSR, combined with actually making a constructive contribution to society, as he comments:

> At BSR I had a vision of what might be possible. It was to provide what was needed to make it possible for companies to act in a more responsible and ethical way. I could imagine that if we were successful ultimately we would be dealing with some of the largest and most important companies in the world, and that the changes they implemented would have a material impact on improving the quality of life for current and future generations. The notion was that, if it were possible to demonstrate to lots of companies why it was not only a good thing to do but why it was ultimately in their own enlightened self-interest to engage in policies and practices that were more responsible, that it was possible to unleash a force that would be a major contributor to the implementation of a more just and equitable society.

A better balance and a big tent

Brad Googins believes that businesses might be quite different than they are today and still successful in economic terms, noting,

> I do think that the world could be a different place. I think that businesses don't have to be anywhere near what they are today — by most standards not very enviable institutions. They have become relatively recently focused very excessively on returning a lot [of money] to a few. They're not great environments, where people spend most of their day and they've taken a lot of the power, the feeling of power out of peoples' hands, so that employees feel they don't have any power and they don't have any voice any more. So in some ways, I think things are worse than they've ever been. But in other ways, that may be a sign that a new change period is about to approach, whether it's the changing social contract or whatever.
>
> Part of the role that I can play through the center is to really ask more questions, try to use data to raise some interesting questions. I do think that the world as I would see it would be a world in which there's much more of a balance between people's personal lives and goals, so the work–family thing still, and also [business as] an institution that can really do things that no one else can do in our society, move more flexibly, bring innovation unlike any-body else. But we haven't been able to put that together yet. I think that's because seeing is believing — people need to be able to see what this would look like, to see that companies could still make a wonderful profit — and be different.

To create better balance, there needs to be inclusivity of multiple points of views, perspectives, and opinions of people from widely divergent cultures. Allen White comments that you need

> a big tent. It's a big world — you need a big tent. If you're going to do some-thing with a global scope, you can't pick and choose and be exclusive because someone doesn't wear the right shoes, or doesn't have the right Western personality, or doesn't have the style that falls within your comfort zone. A successful change agent must be able to operate within a zone of discomfort occasioned by different cultures and languages that invariably arise in global processes.

When responsibility equals business as usual

David Grayson highlights something that many of the difference makers would probably agree with. In discussing his vision for the field, he says that the vision would be achieved when we can drop the term "responsible" before the word "business" because it is just now axiomatic that, if you want to run a business that's going to be around for anything other than the very short term, it's just how you run a good business. You do try and minimize the negative environmental and social impacts that you have and you constantly seek to try and maximize the positive environmental and social impacts. That's what I regard as being a responsible business.

I think the bar of expectations that we have of the role business plays in society both nationally and internationally is increasing.

He considers the role that Business in the Community has played, and notes,

Over the years at various crucial points in our history we have had some quite major conversations, trying to develop a forward agenda. That we have consciously tried to be ourselves pushing the bar higher while just waiting for it to be pushed higher by outsiders.

Finding ways for people to live their visions

Several of the difference makers began by listening to investment clients' desires to live their values through their investments, rather than simply making as much money as possible by any means. Joan Bavaria, for example, recalls,

It was true for a lot of people that I was talking to who had visions that they weren't exactly implementing through their investments, and they had no way to do it. But, because I was in this company and had some latitude to sell a product, I could actually do something. So that was the origin of it all.

But she adds, modestly,

I don't think anything that I have done I would ever say was my own personal vision. What I think I do is synthesize and bring people together. I catch something. I have a dream. Other people have been totally necessary in helping me develop it. I just love facilitating, both thinking and working through a problem. So I wouldn't ever think or say it [Ceres, GRI, the Investor Network on Climate Risk, the Social Investment Forum, all of which she founded or was central in the founding of] was my vision.

As Joan Bavaria notes, give people a worthy cause and something to believe in and they will respond:

These people put in hours and hours of time and often their own time voluntarily [to build these institutions] and didn't get paid to do that. I'm always amazed that people will do so much for a cause. So [for example] Ceres was started with a very open kind of mission around environmental concerns, the environment and investment people looking at capital. It then evolved into something where we decided to create some principles, and we've gone on from there.

Amy Domini sees the tension between acting at the global level and creating a new global governance structure, while simultaneously understanding that simple acts at the individual level matter a great deal in creating responsible institutions and companies:

> The United States does not yet acknowledge that there's a need for a world court or pay much attention to the United Nations. But, as we go to this new era, we're alone in the world in believing that. If you go to *any* other nation, the United Nations is an important component in day-to-day life. I think that, to the extent that there is any global infrastructure for protective mechanisms, for disaster response, for holding dictators accountable, the United Nations is functioning in that role. In Europe, particularly old Europe, there's a gradually dying-off but still-alive memory of World War II, and virtually every person in Europe has a story, a legacy story, around World War II; and virtually all of them will tell you a story about how their fathers, themselves, grandmothers would be dead were it not for the kindness of a stranger. They know at a visceral level the importance of the kind act of a stranger. So they are not letting go of the social safety nets as eagerly as the US did . . . I think, in the future, we're going to have a far greater respect for international norms, and some important economic institutions that have assumptions that society comes first, before corporate profits, so that profits are there to support society's needs.

Jim Post, too, reflects on how people can learn to step forward and take action on issues that matter:

> There are some issues that you have no idea are going to appear. But then they are there and need something to be done about them. And then, step by step, you do what you can do. And, if you *do* that, that really does take your values and translate them into action. And it gives a purpose to something. The costs are there. They're real. They drive a lot of other things out of your life, but what *really* matters is being able to look in the mirror and say, "Did I stand up for something that really matters?"

Envisioning a different world: core values

John Ruggie articulates a set of personal core values that echo what many of the difference makers believe:

I believe firmly in the basic principles of fairness and equity but not in a coherent ideological frame. I'm appalled when I see unnecessary human suffering or underutilized potential and I want to do something about it, but it's not a vision in the sense of a program that emerges out of a deductive set of axiomatic principles. It's a way of envisioning a better world, but tempered, I think, by a deep appreciation of the realities of power and how power works — both economic and political power. I think realizing that to achieve things, or to live in the kind of world that we [want to] live in, it's necessary to find ways of identifying allies and coalitions, and they have to include people from all parts of the spectrum. When I presented my first report on business and human rights, I referred to this approach as "principled pragmatism" — to the horror of the activist community.

Allen White and Bob Massie, of course, used a multi-stakeholder-coalition approach to building the GRI. Applying the learning from this experience to his new venture, Corporation 20/20, Allen White highlights the fact that envisioning a different future involves an exercise of imagination:

This is something more amorphous, more ungainly, more unwieldy, but in some sense a lot more important. That's what the vision is here: to create what we're calling the Principles of Corporate Design. These principles provide a compass for constructing prototypes of corporations of the future.

Working from within the system

Bob Massie reflects on the development of the GRI and Ceres over time and the importance of understanding the imperatives faced by corporations today — and working incrementally to change those incentives:

I had a set of ideas about how we could engage investors, because for me the solution, the vision, taken down a notch from the grand vision, is that, viewed historically, corporations have, through no particular fault of their own, become institutions that are no longer well integrated with the accomplishment of broad human purpose. They could be wired very well into the accomplishment of broad human purpose, but, because they have become players in the political process that determines what broad political purpose *is*, what humanity wants to achieve, and they are very powerful players, they tend to create structures that perpetuate whatever it is they want to do. They're a little bit like robots to whom we've given the vote, and we shouldn't be surprised that these robots follow their original programs and just keep relentlessly pursuing the things that they think they're supposed to do.

I actually believe that, viewed historically against 500 years of democracy, we're in a stage where the whole idea of government by the people and for the people is under challenge, and has at some very basic level become corrupted. Now there are ways in which you can change that by changing the political system. I endorse and support those ways, including getting people elected. It does matter who you have in office and it does matter what our laws are and so forth. However, I also believe that you need to construct parallel systems of accountability, because these very large entities, which have very smart people and very good people associated with them, are trapped in these institutional logarithms that force certain kinds of outputs. Well, you need to change the logarithms that people are facing. So the question that has gripped me for some time, and that has found expression in GRI and Ceres, is: How do you adjust capital market structures so that capital markets become instruments of accountability, in a sense of the stewardship of the future? If government has been subject to large-scale corporate capture, and government no longer fully accepts the responsibility to determine what is best for us as human beings living collectively on this planet — in some cases has abandoned that responsibility — is it possible to rebalance the signals and behaviors in the capital markets so that capital markets perform this function?

Massie concludes,

In an ideal world you'd have the capital markets doing this because they would see, understand, reward, and punish appropriate behaviors that lead to real prosperity or non-prosperity — they would punish those things that were damaging. You'd have governments making critical investments and putting dollars on the table to create markets that are ready to be launched but just need a certain level of economy of scale. And you'd have local communities doing these things, and you could actually achieve the kind of fair and beautiful world that I continue to dream of.

Jane Nelson also reflects on links between markets and governments:

To achieve that "better world" requires two fundamental things. One is good government. The more I have focused on the role of the private sector in areas such as climate change, poverty, and international development, the more I realize how incredibly important good government is. It is not about big government but about effective government that enables rather than obstructs the rights and opportunities of citizens. It is about responsible government, non-corrupt government that really listens to the needs and hopes of people, whether it is in the United States or Zimbabwe. This requires better mechanisms for holding governments and public agencies to account, and more creative ways to strengthen public institutions. Second, more than ever before, we need entrepreneurship.

Reframing

Tim Smith highlights an important set of developments around corporate responsibility assurance — that of reframing — noting,

> Certainly there is a reframing of how the concept [of corporate responsibility] is seen. In the Social Investment Forum, we're having quite a debate about the language. We're *not* going to be able to bring in the mainstream if we sound like social crusaders, and it's not just changing the spots on the leopard — it is actually saying we're doing these things for different reasons now, but there will be a tension between that perspective and those who do want to be in a social crusade to work on justice, or poverty, or the like. The new language is that of fiduciary responsibility.

Accordingly, in the first decade of the 21st century, the language in the social investment movement in general has shifted toward risk and fiduciary responsibility as related to the very material risk posed by social, environmental, and governance issues faced by large businesses today. Smith elaborates,

> Get rid of the word "social" in everything we say. Just like when Ceres or ICCR members now are filing a resolution or soliciting votes, they make the business case, instead of just making the social and moral case.

Changing the purpose of the corporation

Allen White argues that the corporation itself needs to change:

> Where's the vision for this thing? It evolved over a couple of hundred years in a very incremental, disjointed fashion. Certainly in all the Western countries and in the industrial countries, the corporation as we know it had its origin 200 years ago. But, as powerful and influential as it is today, we actually have no broad-based consensus on its obligations and its rights. We have no consensus on its purpose. It's actually astonishing but true that the purpose and form of the corporation never has been a matter of broad-based public discourse at the level of associated critical issues such as global security, universal health, and minimum labor standards. The joint stock corporation, then the publicly traded corporation, has grown to be so large, so influential, so multifaceted, so complex that they overextend current nationally based governance structures. From a public-interest perspective as well as an internal organizational perspective, how do we govern organizations with a quarter of a trillion dollars in turnover, operating in a hundred countries and employing three hundred thousand people? That is core challenge that lies ahead.

Global governance: authority structures and sources

Thinking about what is needed to move forward, Alice Tepper Marlin comments,

> What you most need is to internationalize or globalize many of the functions
> of national governments. SAI, for example, is a totally voluntary system.
> These voluntary systems can be very effective with the leaders, the best-prac-
> tice companies that have a very high stake in protecting their reputation and
> the value of their brand names. They need to minimize their risk of any
> exposés. But it doesn't really get at the vast number of employers, the slack-
> ers at the bottom, who aren't directly or through their supply chain selling to
> consumers and therefore exposed with brand-name products. So where is
> the incentive system for the ones who will cut corners and go for the very
> lowest prices? Or, even if they're not going for the lowest prices, will consis-
> tently violate laws and international standards.
>
> So you get a two-track system. One [track] is more pressure on this [issue]
> in some cases from the export sectors, and the other is, within any country,
> you have your competition to be among the best and to be recognized for
> that. For that, the voluntary systems can work very well, but it's a lot harder
> to get the bottom feeders, because we can't force anybody into our system.
> We have no authority whatsoever to force anybody into our system. So you
> need some kind of *actual* authority that can enforce against the worst viola-
> tors.

John Ruggie adds another important set of points on the need for global governance mechanisms:

> I'm not a believer in world government. I'm not a world federalist or anything
> of that nature. In fact, I'm frightened by that vision. But it's clear that we need
> more robust capacity at the global level to respond to some of these chal-
> lenges. If you leave it only to the dynamics of the intergovernmental arena,
> what you get is a replay of the [UN] Security Council reform debate: "Why
> would we want to dilute our power to give permanent seats to somebody
> else?" I don't know exactly what this looks like in terms of architecture, but in
> the long run the only solution that I see is one that allows for a multi-stake-
> holder form of collaboration, including states, of course, within a set of
> shared norms. But one that doesn't aim at sapping capacity from the units
> but rather building capacity within common frameworks.

Ruggie explains,

> This may be a bad analogy, but in medieval Europe you had a phenomenal
> fragmentation of political entities, but more or less within a common moral
> and legal framework. So, you didn't need the legal doctrine of extraterritorial-

ity to protect emissaries, for example, because the law that was applied at the municipal level was a common body of law. So what you had was the distinct identities of social groups and political organization, highly decentralized, but within a shared, normative legal and moral framework. Somehow, something like that needs to be constructed at the global level, and we're a long way from that. Europe is getting there. But we're undergoing a very different kind of transformation at the global level today with the emergence of new powers — China, India, Brazil — which share some of these objectives but not others. So it's going to be slow going, but that, in the very long term, is the direction, so that the units in a sense become agents for the implementation of shared norms and aims to a greater extent than now. Now, the commons is an accidental byproduct of the interests of the units. Flipping that around is the kind of transformation that I would see at the global level, but we're a long way from achieving that.

Global why, local how

Georg Kell also recognizes the importance of understanding the context — and the realities — of the system that already exists as the work of making a difference continues:

> You need a very practical and pragmatic relation back to the organization — so you can actually translate the idea into it. In other words, it's easy to dream when you watch the river flow by. I guess everybody has beautiful dreams, or should have, but the real challenge is to find a way to give them practical meaning. That's why the institutional embeddedness [of, for example, the UN Global Compact in the United Nations], and the tactical argument that the Global Compact is good for the organization because it positions the organization as part of the solution in contemporary issues, was ultimately, I think, an essential part of the whole puzzle.

Kell continues,

> We are experimenting now with different thought concepts. What we are doing at the global level is that we are driving the advocacy campaign. We are giving the global "why." But the "how" is always local. So one way of looking at it is — global why, local how.

Jane Nelson also recognizes the tension between the global and the local, suggesting that the macro-structures around globalization influence what happens at the individual level, arguing,

> The simplest way to describe the vision is for no child to die an avoidable death because his or her parents can't get access to the absolute basic essen-

tials needed for survival. Obviously, the practical and policy obstacles to achieving this vision are numerous and complex, but essentially it comes down to protecting and respecting people's human rights and giving them access to opportunity. It is about every person being treated with dignity, but also about people having access to the basic enablers — education, health, clean water, energy, technology, credit, justice, property rights — the basic building blocks that enable people to determine their own futures.

Collaboration within and between sectors

One of the critical needs that Georg Kell sees going forward is that public institutions be able to collaborate more effectively — both with each other and with other types of institutions. He argues,

> At the end of the day what matters really is that policy-making in all countries is not only attuned to and supportive of, but is fully redefining the business–society angle to achieve maximum social benefits. Unfortunately, we're still far away from that and we could start now, country by country — whether it's in emerging economies or least-developed countries where the nexus between business and public institutions is quite often destructive, counterproductive.

He elaborates,

> In some countries, the notion of entrepreneurship is still not recognized as the source of wealth creation and it's next to impossible to set up small-scale business, and the costs for doing so are very high. The incentive structure is not yet in such a way that long-term investment in entrepreneurship is fairly rewarded. There is still an emphasis on short-term rent seeking. So there is still a long way to go to create what generally we refer to as the so-called enabling environment and the nexus between business and society.

But unrestrained entrepreneurship is not the answer either, according to Kell, who points out,

> On the other extreme of the pendulum, if you just go for unleashing entrepreneurship solving all the problems . . . Wrong! History tells us again and again that extreme inequality is not only the seed of future destruction of society, but it's also unjust to individuals who are marginalized. You will soon see that you also need a helping and supportive public framework that is at least striving for some notion of equity and protects the vulnerable and the weak. Above all, it needs to ensure that there is some kind of equal access to opportunities, be it for education or health.
>
> So you need healthy public and healthy private actors and the two need to work together in harmony.

Integrated leadership

Judy Samuelson points out that the whole purpose of the Aspen Institute's Business and Society Program is to generate a new type of leader who can understand concepts such as global governance, inequity, and what Georg Kell calls the "global why, local how." Samuelson comments that "the founding vision of the Aspen Business and Society Program was producing managers and leaders who could integrate — who could really integrate into their management principles and values — the context in which business operates, and the impact of it on the wider world."

Steve Young concurs, noting, "I do believe on the optimistic side that given time a small group of people who can speak with moral authority and clarity and skill can make a difference."

Resources in a shifting context

A critical element in building the accountability infrastructure has been and is likely to continue to be the availability of resources that support initiatives and institutions like the GRI, Ceres, and SAI. Traditional business and NGO models of funding do not necessarily work, so finding ways to support these budding institutions over the long term is essential. As Alice Tepper Marlin points out,

> You just need better ways of resourcing more adequately this new phenomenon of global civil society organizations. Though it's not brand new, as some large development agencies have been around for a long time, you're getting civil society operating at a global level in many other fields, and there are not equivalent global funders, global civil society funders, around.

Balance

Malcolm McIntosh talks a lot these days about "one planet living" — a WWF program — or much better balance in the world for long-term sustainability. Amy Domini has a similar vision, framed a little differently:

> I think you're going to have quite a few checks and balances. You're going to have a far greater respect for international norms, and you're going to have some important economic members that have presumptions that society comes first and that corporate profits and things are there to support society's needs. Those would be my hopes. I guess one more, bizarre as it may seem, is with regard to the global climate change; that's another hopeful thing because it's the kind of a crisis that forces the planet to act in conjunction — [like] the tsunami — and that this is a long-term struggle for the survival of billions.

The issue of better-balanced sectors frames much of Steve Lydenberg's view of what is needed in the future, too:

For a variety of historical reasons, corporations have come to play an incredibly powerful role in society now. Their size and influence in many senses is much bigger than it's ever been, though you could certainly argue that at the end of the 19th century they were certainly as big and influential as today, but not as pervasive as they are now. The whole history of the last 100 or 150 years has been to try to figure out the proper balance between government and corporations with very dramatically different solutions being proposed by different companies, countries, and cultures around the world. That's the fact, the world we're born into, a world of big companies, big governments, and a lot of little people. What I would like to see emerge from the work that social investors have done is a world in which the actors on this stage, to go back to the drama metaphor, are empowered to influence both governments and corporations because they have enough information at their disposal to make active choices, whether it's consuming, investing, or where they work, to put real pressure on governments and corporations to change their policies. This isn't just about companies, not just about governments. Sometimes government works and companies don't; sometimes companies work and government doesn't. Finding tools that will allow the right pressures to be put on the right parties in different places will hopefully contribute to the resolution of a problem that's been with us for 150 years and we're still struggling with it.

Another aspect of "one planet living" is expressed by Laury Hammel, who talks about the benefits of what he calls local living economies:

There was a *New York Times* article where I was quoted saying that I felt that "local" was one of the most beautiful words in the English language and that building community is something that many of us in the United States have lost — a sense of community — that there are people who live in the city or the suburbs and don't know their neighbors. Don't talk to their neighbors. Don't have conversations with anybody they know who runs a business. They basically live in almost an isolated world where they watch television, they do computer work, they talk on the cell phone, but they have very little human interaction. I think human interaction is the essence of being alive and being a real person, and to have positive and supportive and loving and friendly human interactions with your fellow human beings is what community is all about. So my vision of the future is to have local communities being very strong and vibrant and vital and have people being empowered to create the type of communities that sit and support the lives of all people in that community.

Localizing as much as possible, rather than simply accepting that globalization is inevitable, is critical, according to Laury Hammel, who points out,

> I think that [a radically] decentralized organization of business leaders that are caring about the community needs to exist in every community in the world. That's one institution that needs to happen — an organization of businesses that believe in the multiple-stakeholder model of running a business as independent, locally owned, and they want to change the world.

Framing much the same issue another way, in terms of capitalism, David Logan comments,

> I think we have learned that capitalism, liberal capitalism, allied to democracy, is capable of being inclusive in a way that the Marxists said it never could be. What we're now also learning is that it's very possible that the environmental cost of that inclusivity is unacceptable and too threatening. The left said, "Capitalism can never give economic and social justice to people. It has to go." I think we've learned that a pragmatic liberal democratic capitalism actually, probably, is important for social justice, but it may be that capitalism can pay the social price that the capitalism of 1900 found difficult to pay, but it can't pay the environmental price.

Logan continues his commentary on capitalism:

> There's a wonderful book called *The Seven Cultures of Capitalism*.[201] I always recommend it to my audiences when I speak. I think there's a Muslim variant of capitalism. There's a Swiss variant. There's an American variant. There's a Japanese variant. Capitalism is impacted by the cultures of these peoples. And capitalism is flexible enough for everybody to participate on terms that work for them. There are systemic problems. Monopoly is an issue. The strength of multinationals in weak countries is an issue. These are all issues. But capitalism is not monolithic. There are many facets to it and people can find a home in it, and people who deal with capitalism at the level of theory I don't think ever saw that.

Creating new leadership

The theme of living in balance and harmony with others and with nature recurs in the thinking of many of the difference makers. To get there, Jane Nelson argues, requires new types of leadership not just in businesses but also in the public and civil society sectors:

> I do think there is a strategic leadership case for leaders to think beyond how these directly affect their bottom line. Good governance and political leadership are essential, but certain business leaders also have power and influ-

ence. Increasingly, they need to work in partnership with leaders from other sectors to tackle complex public problems and to demonstrate how the public good can also be served through responsible and innovative private enterprise and markets. You can go to work in government or civil society organizations to make a difference, but you can also achieve a public service ethos through working in the private sector and mobilizing the activities, competences, and networks of business to help solve public challenges. So the opportunity is how to develop leaders in all sectors who can think across traditional boundaries and work effectively with each other — especially in developing countries where resources and local capacity are often weak, and the environmental and poverty alleviation challenges are substantial.

New language, new ideas, repeating patterns

Pointing out that language is indeed very important in framing the debate, John Elkington comments,

> I think sustainability is grotesquely unhelpful as language for most ordinary people. We've got to get infinitely sexier ways of articulating what it is that we want to see happen in the world. We can't simply talk about the problems the whole time because that shuts people down. We've got to talk about the opportunities.

David Logan, like Peter Kinder and John Elkington, sees the advance of corporate responsibility in a long-term evolutionary context replete with repeating patterns and new ways of expressing what is happening. Logan comments,

> I'm a great history buff, and I believe that history is to the human race what psychoanalysis is to the individual: that one of the key things to look for is these repeating patterns and try and understand what's happening. We had a global economy which the British led and dominated until it was killed off by World War I, the Russian Revolution, and the stock market collapse. Since World War II, with the existence of communism in two or three of the largest states and deep socialism in India, the vast majority of the world's population was locked up in socialism. We've been moving back to a mixed model of society. We're getting the world that for us in our lifetimes is pretty much inevitable, and most societies now conform to it. It's a world in which everybody has a for-profit sector, a not-for-profit sector, and a public sector. They are the three formal groupings which synthesize the informal sector of society. Only North Korea and Cuba are really outside of this model. So the question is: What are the roles of the three sectors? How do they work together? I think in my lifetime the private sector's moved back to center-stage and we're still working out what its role is in society and the future.

Logan believes that corporate responsibility is being reinvented today, to encompass but go well beyond its roots in philanthropy, to being more integrated into business purpose. He comments,

> As I learned with Levi's, if I was to make the case to my business colleagues, I had to talk their language. The language of business people all over the world is numbers. The language of business is numbers. The language of too many social groups is social need. Whereas with the business guys, you need to be able to talk to them in a language they can understand, which is: "If you give me a hundred thousand pounds, this is what I'll deliver for you in that community when you close that plant."

Regionalized initiatives

One of the things that is needed, according to David Grayson, is regionalized initiatives that can help companies deal with the particulars of their locations, cultures, and economies. Grayson comments,

> There are at least 60 initiatives needed, by my calculation, at least 60 business coalitions in countries around the world, promoting the idea of responsible business for starters. As well as a number of international ones that already exist like the World Business Council for Sustainable Development. The fact now is that many business schools are incorporating ideas of responsible business into their research programs. You've got the existence of things like the European Academy of Business and Society [EABIS], which is supporting business schools across Europe, getting CSR both into the teaching of executive and MBA programs as well as into research. You've got Aspen Institute's Business and Society Program in the States. EABIS has helped to develop an Asian Institute for Business in Society in the last few months. So there is a whole series of different groupings, which are championing ideas of responsible business.

The UN Global Compact, although obviously a global organization, has also made it a point to emphasize its regional networks, as Georg Kell articulates:

> So we made a deliberate effort to plant the idea in these critical countries where delegates here in New York theoretically have the means to propel the idea from future growth. But the local network growth is amazing. It continues to grow. It's probably organizationally the biggest challenge we have at hand, because in every society there are different codes for organizations. In some countries there's a heavy bureaucracy that is being advanced. Coming to grips with the organizational dimensions of network formation is a true challenge. Because it always connects back to the political, cultural condi-

tions that prevail in each country and places in the world are very different. It's not just the different languages, but it's also the deeply cultural sense of how you organize yourself.

Getting consumers into the responsibility act

Consumers have been remarkably absent from the corporate responsibility front since *Shopping for a Better World* and *The Green Consumer Guide* went out of print. But, as David Grayson points out, technology may provide new ways in the future for consumers to shop for their values:

> I think one of the other areas is obviously how consumers get more information about responsible business. I think that there are probably many more consumers who would be interested to act if they knew more information about responsible business, if it's easily accessible at the point where they're making their consumer decisions. You can't really take several volumes of information around the supermarket at night when you do your shopping. So I think one of the interesting, exciting developments might be when it's possible for you to go around with your mobile phone and just swipe it over the bar codes of different goods in supermarkets. I think it will be able to tell you whether that is a good rating or a bad rating against a list of products that you've previously chosen. That might be a list produced for you by a national consumers' association or it might be an environmental organization, because you're a member of Greenpeace or what have you.

◼ A better world?

Perhaps the words of Bob Massie summarize the work that many of the individuals discussed in this book have done:

> I'm an idealist in the sense expressed in the very last sentence of my book[202] after I've laid everything out, that we become what we believe. So what we believe matters, and if we believe this about human nature, or that about markets, or that about justice, or this about diversity, or this about what the purpose of life is, that because of the nature of the human species, that those beliefs become reified into very physical structures. Into walls and bullets and machine guns and amusement parks and whatever it is. So that our convictions establish the physical reality in which people live. And, therefore, it matters a lot what those convictions are.

What is this thing called making a difference?

The difference makers whose individual and institutional stories are told in this book are, of course, only a few of the many thousands of visionary individuals in all sectors whose work is attempting to move businesses and the societies in which they exist toward a more balanced and ecologically sustainable world. But these difference makers have chosen the particular realm of corporate accountability, responsibility, and transparency in which to do their work — and, though it appears that none of them quite planned it that way, have collectively moved questions about the proper role of business in society forward significantly.

Generally guided by strong values, positive beliefs about the ability of humanity to achieve noble purposes, and a desire to leave the world better off than they found it, the difference makers have taken the best of what already exists and worked with that to create new institutions that foster greater balance, greater transparency, and, ultimately, more awareness of our interdependence with each other in this interconnected world. Mostly beginning with few resources, the difference makers have served the world as entrepreneurs, institution builders, collaborators, and networkers, slowly but surely building awareness that a different way for companies to behave is possible and ultimately desirable. Their examples — and those of the thousands of others who have worked alongside of these 23 individuals — serve as exemplars for all of us, illustrating how simple actions, insights, and initiatives can really make a difference in the structure and shape of our world and in what we believe is possible.

Bob Massie is correct: "We become what we believe." And, if we believe that a better world is possible, then we can collectively work to create that better world, just as these difference makers have done. The shamans of South America tell us that we dream our world into existence — that is exactly what the difference makers have done and what we all must do to ensure our grandchildren's children's future.

References

Anderson, S., and J. Cavanagh (2000) "The Rise of Corporate Global Power," Institute for Policy Studies; www.corpwatch.org/article.php?id=377, accessed February 19, 2008.

Annan, K. (2000) "We The Peoples: The United Nations in the 21st Century. Millennium Report of the UN Secretary General"; www.un.org/millennium/sg/report/full.htm, accessed February 12, 2008.

Barkstrom, J. (2000) "An Empire of Spices," in *Poverty, Wealth, Dictatorship, Democracy: Resource Scarcity and the Origins of Dictatorship* (Golden, CO: Pericles Press; www.periclespress.com/Dutch_tulip.html, accessed February 19, 2008).

Brugger, E.A., J. Nelson, L. Timberlake, and M. Edwards (1994) *The Cutting Edge: Small Business and Progress* (New York: McGraw-Hill).

Bruyn, S.T. (1987) *The Field of Social Investment* (New York: Cambridge University Press).

Carson, R. (1962) *Silent Spring* (Boston, MA: Houghton Mifflin).

Cavanagh, J., *et al.* (eds.) (2004) *Alternatives to Economic Globalization: A Better Way is Possible* (San Francisco: Berrett-Koehler, 2nd edn).

Crofts, M.S., and T.H. Smith (2002) "A Review of Prakash Sethi's and Oliver Williams' *Economic Imperatives and Ethical Values in Global Business*," *Business and Society Review* 107.2, pp. 275-82.

Davies, J.B., S. Sandstrom, A. Shorrocks, and E.N. Wolff (2006) "The World Distribution of Household Wealth," United Nations University World Institute for Development Economics Research (UNU-WIDER); www.wider.unu.edu/publications/working-papers/discussion-papers/2008/en_GB/dp2008-03, accessed March 31, 2008.

Derber, C. (1998) *Corporation Nation: How Corporations Are Taking Over Our Lives and What We Can Do About It* (New York: St. Martin's Press).

—— (2002) *People Before Profit: The New Globalization in an Era of Terror, Big Money, and Economic Crisis* (New York: St. Martin's Press).

Domini, A., and P. Kinder (1984) *Ethical Investing* (Reading, MA: Addison-Wesley).

Elkington, J. (1997) *Cannibals with Forks: The Triple Bottom Line of 21st Century Business* (Oxford, UK: Capstone Publishing).

— and T. Burke (1987) *The Green Capitalists: Industry's Search for Environmental Excellence* (London: Gollancz).

— and J. Hailes (1988) *The Green Consumer Guide: From Shampoo to Champagne – High-Street Shopping for a Better Environment* (London: Gollancz).

Frederick, W.C. (1995) *Values, Nature, and Culture in the American Corporation* (New York: Oxford University Press).

Freeman, R.E. (1984) *Strategic Management: A Stakeholder Approach* (Boston, MA: Pitman).

—, E.J. Harrison, and A. Wicks (2007) *Managing for Stakeholders: Business in the 21st Century* (New Haven, CT: Yale University Press).

Friedman, T. (2007) *The World is Flat: A Brief History of the Twenty-first Century* (London: Picador, 3rd edn).

Gap Inc. (2004) "Social Report," www.gapinc.com/public/SocialResponsibility/socialres. shtml, accessed February 19, 2008.

Gladwell, M. (2000) *The Tipping Point: How Little Things Can Make a Big Difference* (Boston, MA: Little Brown).

Gray, R., and M.J. Milne (2002) "Sustainability Reporting: Who's Kidding Whom?" *Chartered Accountants Journal of New Zealand,* www.accaglobal.com/pdfs/environment/ newsletter/gray_milne.pdf, accessed February 19, 2008.

Grayson, D. (2007) *Business-Led Corporate Responsibility Coalitions: Learning from the Example of Business in the Community in the UK. An Insider's Perspective* (Doughty Centre for Corporate Responsibility, Cranfield School of Management and the Fellows of Harvard College; available at Harvard Kennedy School of Government Corporate Social Responsibility Initiative website: www.hks.harvard.edu/m-rcbg/CSRI/publications/ report_26_GraysonBus-LedCRCoalitions.pdf, accessed March 14, 2008).

Greider, W. (1998) *One World, Ready or Not: The Manic Logic of Global Capitalism* (New York: Touchstone Books).

Hammel, L., and G. Denhart (2007) *Growing Local Value: How to Build a Values-Driven Business that Strengthens your Community* (San Francisco: Berrett-Koehler).

Hampden-Turner, C., and F. Trompenaars (1995) *The Seven Cultures of Capitalism* (London: Piatkus Books, 2nd edn).

Hargrave T.J., and A.H. Van de Ven (2006) "A Collective Action Model of Institutional Innovation," *Academy of Management Review* 31.4, pp. 864-88.

Harvard Business School Bulletin (2002) "Profile: The Invisible Hand – Robert Massie and God's Green Earth," *Harvard Business School Bulletin,* June 2002, www.alumni.hbs.edu/ bulletin/2002/june/profile.html, accessed February 11, 2008.

Heilbruner, R.L. (1987) "Integrity: You Can Get It Retail," *New York Times,* January 18, 1987.

Isaacs, W.N. (1996) "The Process and Potential of Dialogue in Social Change," *Educational Technology,* January–February 1996, pp. 20-30.

Kolk, A., M. van der Veen, J. Pinkse, and F. Fortanier (2005) KPMG *International Survey of Corporate Responsibility Reporting* (Amsterdam: KPMG International).

Korten, D. (1995) *When Corporations Rule the World* (San Francisco: Berrett-Koehler).

— (2006) *The Great Turning: From Empire to Earth Community* (San Francisco: Berrett-Koehler).

Kuhn, T.H. (1962) *The Structure of Scientific Revolutions* (Chicago: University of Chicago Press, 1996 repr.).

Logan, D., D. Roy, and L. Regelbruge (1997) *Global Corporate Citizenship: Rationale and Strategies* (Washington, DC: Hitachi Foundation).

Lydenberg, S.D. (2005) *Corporations and the Public Interest: Guiding the Invisible Hand* (San Francisco: Berrett-Koehler).

—, A. Tepper Marlin, and S.O. Strub (1986) *Rating America's Corporate Conscience: A Provocative Guide to the Companies behind the Products You Buy Every Day* (Reading, MA: Addison-Wesley).

Massie, R.K. (1997) *Loosing the Bonds: The United States and South Africa in the Apartheid Years* (New York: Talese/Doubleday).

McAdam, D., J.D. McCarthy, and M.N. Zald (1996) "Introduction: Opportunities, Mobilizing Structures, and Framing Processes — Toward a Synthetic Comparative Perspective on Social Movements," in D. McAdam, J.D. McCarthy, and M.N. Zald (eds.), *Comparative Perspectives on Social Movements: Political Opportunities, Mobilizing Structures, and Cultural Framings* (New York: Cambridge University Press): 1-20.

McGann, J., and M. Johnstone (2006) "The Power Shift and the NGO Credibility Crisis," *The International Journal of Not-for-Profit Law* 8.2 (www.icnl.org/knowledge/ijnl/vol8iss2/art_4.htm, accessed February 7, 2008).

McIntosh, M. (1986) *Japan Re-armed* (London: Pinter).

Muller, M. (1974) *The Baby Killer: A War on Want Investigation into the Promotion and Sale of Powdered Baby Milks in the Third World* (London: War on Want).

Nader, R. (1965) *Unsafe at Any Speed: The Designed-In Dangers of the American Automobile* (New York: Grossman).

Newton, L.H. (1999) "Truth is the Daughter of Time: The Real Story of the Nestlé Case," *Business and Society Review* 104.4, pp. 367-95.

North, D.C. (1990) *Institutions, Institutional Change, and Economic Performance* (New York: Cambridge University Press).

Perkins, J. (2004) *Confessions of an Economic Hit Man* (San Francisco: Berrett-Koehler).

Polanyi, K. (2001) *The Great Transformation: The Political and Economic Origins of our Times* (Boston, MA: Beacon Press).

Post, J.E. (1978) *Corporate Behavior and Social Change* (Reston, VA: Reston Publishing).

—, L.E. Preston, and S. Sachs (2002) *Redefining the Corporation* (New York: Oxford University Press).

Powell, W.W., and P.J. DiMaggio (1991) *The New Institutionalism in Organizational Analysis* (Chicago: University of Chicago Press).

Preston, L.E., and J.E. Post (1975) *Private Management and Public Policy* (New York: Prentice-Hall).

Reinicke, W.H., and F.M. Deng (2000) *Critical Choices: The United Nations, Networks, and the Future of Global Governance* (Toronto: International Development Research Council).

Rifkin, J., and T. Howard (1977) *Who Should Play God? The Artificial Creation of Life and What it Means for the Future of the Human* (New York: Dell).

Ruggie, J. (1996) *Winning the Peace: America and World Order in the New Era* (New York: Columbia University Press).

— (1998) *Constructing the World Polity: Essays on International Institutionalization* (London: Routledge).

Savitz, A.W., with K. Weber (2006) *The Triple Bottom Line: How Today's Best-Run Companies Are Achieving Economic, Social, and Environmental Success — And How You Can Too* (New York: John Wiley).

Schwartz, D.E. (1971) "The Public Interest Proxy Contest: Reflections on Campaign GM," *Michigan Law Review* 69.3, pp. 419-38.

Scott, W.R. (2001) *Institutions and Organizations* (New York: Free Press, 2nd edn).

Senge, P. (1990) *The Fifth Discipline: The Art and Practice of the Learning Organization* (New York: Doubleday).

Shuman, M.H. (2000) *Going Local: Creating Self-reliant Communities in a Global Age* (London: Routledge).

— (2006) *The Small-Mart Revolution: How Local Businesses Are Beating the Global Competition* (San Francisco: Berrett-Koehler).

Smith, A. (1776) *The Wealth of Nations*.

Social Investment Forum (2007) *2007 Report on Socially Responsible Investing Trends in the United States: Executive Summary* (Washington, DC: Social Investment Forum; www.socialinvest.org/pdf/SRI_Trends_ExecSummary_2007.pdf).

Tapscott, D., and D. Ticoll (2003) *The Naked Corporation: How the Age of Transparency Will Revolutionize Business* (New York: Free Press).

Tepper Marlin, A., *et al.* (1988) *Shopping for a Better World* (New York: Ballantine Books).

— *et al.* (1993) *Student Shopping for a Better World* (New York: Ballantine Books).

UN (United Nations) (2000) "Resolution adopted by the UN General Assembly, 55/2 United Nations Millennium Declaration; www.un.org/millennium/declaration/ares552e.htm, accessed February 12, 2008.

— (2006) "Promotion and Protection of Human Rights? Interim Report of the Special Representative of the Secretary General," February 2006; www.globalpolicy.org/reform/business/2006/02srsgreport.htm, accessed February 12, 2008.

Van de Ven, A.H., and T.J. Hargrave (2004) "Social, Technical, and Institutional Change: A Literature Review and Synthesis," in M.S. Poole and A.H. Van de Ven (eds.), *Handbook of Organizational Change and Innovation* (New York: Oxford University Press), pp. 259-303.

—, D.E. Polley, R. Garud, and S. Venkataraman (1999) *The Innovation Journey* (Oxford, UK: Oxford University Press).

Waddock, S. (2005) "Corporate Responsibility, Accountability, and Stakeholder Relationships: Will Voluntary Action Suffice?" in J.P. Doh and S.A. Stumpf (eds.), *Handbook on Responsible Leadership and Governance in Global Business* (Cheltenham, UK: Edward Elgar), pp. 180-194.

— (2006) "Building the Institutional Infrastructure for Corporate Responsibility," paper presented at the Inter-Continental Dialogue on Corporate Social Responsibility, University of Quebec, Montreal, October 2006, and the Harvard Kennedy School of Government, Cambridge, MA, November 2006.

— (2006) *Leading Corporate Citizens: Vision, Values, Value-Added* (New York: McGraw-Hill, 2nd edn).

— (2006) "What Will it Take to Create a Tipping Point for Corporate Responsibility?" in M. Epstein and K.O. Hanson (eds.), *The Accountable Corporation* (Greenfield, CT: Praeger), pp. 75-96.

— (2007) "On Ceres, the GRI and Corporation 20/20 (Interview). Sandra Waddock talks to Allen White," *Journal of Corporate Citizenship* 26, pp. 38-42.

— and C. Bodwell (2004) "Managing Responsibility: What Can Be Learned from the Quality Movement?" *California Management Review* 47.1 (Fall 2004), pp. 25-37.

— and C. Bodwell (2002) "From TQM to TRM: The Emerging Evolution of Total Responsibility Management (TRM) Systems," *Journal of Corporate Citizenship* 7, pp. 113-26.

— and C. Bodwell (2007) *Total Responsibility Management: The Manual* (Sheffield, UK: Greenleaf Publishing).

—, C. Bodwell, and S.B. Graves (2002) "Responsibility: The New Business Imperative," *Academy of Management Executive* 16.2, pp. 132-48.

WCED (World Commission on Environment and Development) (1987) *Our Common Future: Report of the World Commission on Environment and Development* (known as the Brundtland Report; Oxford, UK: Oxford University Press; www.un.org/documents/ga/res/42/ares42-187.htm, accessed February 15, 2008).

Zadek, S. (1993) *An Economics of Utopia: Democratising Scarcity* (Aldershot, UK: Ashgate).

Endnotes

Introduction

1 McGann and Johnstone, "The Power Shift and the NGO Credibility Crisis."

Chapter 1

2 How social or institutional entrepreneurs effect a dialectical process of institutional change is discussed at length in Hargrave and Van de Ven, "A Collective Action Model of Institutional Innovation."

3 See Van de Ven and Hargrave, "Social, Technical, and Institutional Change."

4 E.g., Van de Ven *et al.*, *The Innovation Journey*.

5 I have discussed this emerging responsibility infrastructure in several papers: Waddock, "What Will It Take to Create a Tipping Point for Corporate Responsibility?", "Corporate Responsibility, Accountability, and Stakeholder Relationships", and "Building the Institutional Infrastructure for Corporate Responsibility."

6 Some of this history is documented in Korten, *The Great Turning*. See also Derber, *Corporation Nation*.

7 Derber, *People Before Profit*.

8 Encyclopedia Britannica entry on "Dutch East India Company," from *Encyclopedia Britannica* (1911) 8: 717 at Online Encyclopedia, encyclopedia.jrank.org/DRO_ECG/DUTCH_EAST_INDIA_COMPANY_THE_Oo.html, accessed February 19, 2008.

9 Barkstrom, "An Empire of Spices."

10 Cavanagh and Mander, *Alternatives to Economic Globalization*.

11 Savitz with Weber, *The Triple Bottom Line*.

12 Cavanagh and Mander, *Alternatives to Economic Globalization*; also Perkins, *Confessions of an Economic Hit Man*, and Korten, *The Great Turning*.

13 Anderson and Cavanagh, "The Rise of Corporate Global Power."

14 Korten, *When Corporations Rule the World*; Greider, *One World, Ready or Not*.

15 Davies *et al.*, "The World Distribution of Household Wealth".

16 Ibid.

Chapter 2

17 For a succinct look at a broad sweep of the responsibility assurance infrastructure, see Waddock, "Building the Institutional Infrastructure for Corporate Responsibility." Lists of institutions and portions of this chapter are excerpted from this paper.

18 Savitz with Weber, *The Triple Bottom Line*.

19 Here I am following Hargrave and Van de Ven, "A Collective Action Model of Institutional Innovation", p. 866, who define institutions as "the humanly devised schemas, norms, and regulations that enable and constrain the behavior of social actors and that make life predictable and meaningful (North, 1990; Powell & DiMaggio, 1991; Scott, 2001)."

20 William C. Frederick called this motivation "economizing" in his important book *Values, Nature, and Culture in the American Corporation*; see also Corporation 20/20, www. corporation2020.org, accessed February 19, 2008.

21 Kolk *et al.*, "KPMG International Survey of Corporate Responsibility Reporting."

22 Charles Bodwell and I have written extensively about what we called total responsibility management systems in Waddock and Bodwell, "From TQM to TRM" and "Managing Responsibility"; and Waddock *et al.*, "Responsibility: The New Business Imperative." See also Waddock and Bodwell, *Total Responsibility Management*.

23 Polanyi, *The Great Transformation*.

24 See Waddock, *Leading Corporate Citizens*.

25 See www.icaew.co.uk/index.cfm?route=112326, accessed February 19, 2008.

26 This point is forcefully and cogently argued by Korten in *The Great Turning* and Cavanagh and Mander in *Alternatives to Economic Globalization*.

27 Risk Metrics took over, and continue to further the work of, the Investor Responsibility Research Center (IRRC).

28 See ENDS Directory: www.endsdirectory.com/index.cfm?action=search.listings& specialist=4&view=names, accessed February 19, 2008.

29 www.ethicalperformance.com, accessed February 19, 2008.

30 ethicalperformance.co.uk/csrdirectory, accessed February 19, 2008.

31 See, e.g., Reputation Institute's research and publications page, www.reputationinstitute. com/main/index.php?pg=pub&box=articles_by_ri, accessed February 19, 2008, or the journal *Reputation Management*.

32 See BSR website: www.bsr.org/CSRResources/IssueBriefDetail.cfm?DocumentID=48813, accessed February 19, 2008. The classic definition of stakeholder, given here, is from Freeman, *Strategic Management*.

33 AccountAbility website, www.accountability21.net/publications.aspx?id=384, accessed March 17, 2008.

34 BSR website, www.bsr.org/CSRResources/IssueBriefDetail.cfm?DocumentID=48813, accessed February 19, 2008.

35 Isaacs, "The Process and Potential of Dialogue in Social Change."

36 Business in the Community mission statement at: www.bitc.org.uk/index.html, accessed February 19, 2008.

37 See www.gan-net.net/about/examples_of_gans.html, accessed February 19, 2008.

38 Cavanagh *et al.*, *Alternatives to Economic Globalization*.

Chapter 3

39 McAdam *et al.*, "Introduction: Opportunities, Mobilizing Structures, and Framing Processes."

40 Hargrave and Van de Ven, "A Collective Action Model of Institutional Innovation."

41 Ibid.

42 Details of this process as discussed in this section are explicated in Hargrave and Van de Ven, "A Collective Action Model of Institutional Innovation."

43 US sociologist and four-time senator, who was author of the 1965 "Moynihan Report," *The Negro Family: The Case for National Action*, and numerous other books on the problems of the urban poor.

44 Perhaps the seminal documentation of the social investment movement which provides these facts is Bruyn, *The Field of Social Investment.*

45 Bruyn, *The Field of Social Investment.*

46 Ibid, p. 2.

47 Ibid, p. 2.

48 www.trilliuminvest.com/pages/about/about_home.asp, accessed February 19, 2008.

49 Ibid.

50 www.trilliuminvest.com/pages/about/about_mission.asp, accessed February 19, 2008.

51 The history of Campaign GM is detailed in Schwartz, "The Public Interest Proxy Contest."

52 Details from Schwartz, "The Public Interest Proxy Contest."

53 Crofts and Smith, "A Review of *Economic Imperatives and Ethical Values in Global Business.*"

54 Detailed in Schwartz, "The Public Interest Proxy Contest", pp. 423-25.

55 Ibid., p. 197.

56 From www.iccr.org, accessed February 19, 2008.

57 From www.iccr.org/about, accessed March 11, 2008.

58 Ibid.

59 See Global Sullivan Principles website, www.globalsullivanprinciples.org/principles.htm, accessed February 19, 2008.

60 Crofts and Smith, "A Review of *Economic Imperatives and Ethical Values in Global Business*", pp. 277-78.

61 Smith's term as SIF president ended in 2007 and he was succeeded by Cheryl Smith (no relation) of Trillium Asset Management.

62 *Maquiladoras* (or *maquilas*) are factories, originally found on the border between the US and Mexico, but now spread throughout Latin America. The factories from the developing world typically use tariff- and duty-free imports to manufacture and assemble goods for larger companies in the developed world, which then reimport them back to the original company. *Maquilas* are often accused of poor labor standards, sweatshop working conditions, and environmental abuses. The term is being used here as a synonym for factories in the developing world that have larger companies from the developed world as customers.

63 With all the advances that have been made, it is still not clear that the financial community has much interest in what is today called ESG — ecological, social, and governance information — albeit the pressures from a wider and wider array of investors keep mounting based in part on the work of difference makers.

Chapter 4

64 Heilbruner, "Integrity: You Can Get It Retail."

65 By Alice Tepper Marlin *et al.*

66 Annual reports required of US companies by the Securities and Exchange Commission.

67 *Business Ethics* became CRO magazine (Corporate Responsibility Officer) and has since changed the methodology.

68 See www.kld.com, accessed February 19, 2008.

69 www.siricompany.com/partners.shtml, accessed February 19, 2008.

70 From the Institute for Responsible Investment website, www.bcccc.net/index.cfm?fuseaction=Page.viewPage&pageId=884&parentID=883, accessed February 10, 2008.

71 From Institute for Responsible Investment website: "Our Goals," www.bcccc.net/index.cfm?fuseaction=Page.viewPage&pageId=1162&parentID=883, accessed February 10, 2008.

72 Bob Dunn was involved with the development of this code, and will be discussed in the next chapter.

73 www.iso.org/iso/en/ISOOnline.frontpage, accessed February 10, 2008.

74 From SAI website, www.sa-intl.org/index.cfm?fuseaction=Page.viewPage&pageId=472, accessed February 10, 2008.

75 www.accountability21.net, accessed February 10, 2008.

76 Details about the infant formula scandal are from Newton, "Truth is the Daughter of Time."

77 By Mike Muller.

78 Thomas Kuhn, whose important book on paradigm shifts has guided many scholars. See Kuhn, *The Structure of Scientific Revolutions.*

Chapter 5

79 From Ceres website: www.ceres.org/ceres, accessed February 11, 2008.

80 From www.ceres.org/NETCOMMUNITY/Page.aspx?pid=416&srcid=415, accessed February 11, 2008.

81 *Harvard Business School Bulletin,* "Profile: The Invisible Hand."

82 Massie's father, also Robert K. Massie, is the acclaimed author of *Nicholas and Alexandra.*

83 Green is a politician, public-interest lawyer, and author who worked with political activist Nader at the latter's Public Citizen.

84 Levi Strauss's Global Sourcing and Operating Guidelines can be found at: www.levistrauss.com/Citizenship/ProductSourcing.aspx, accessed February 11, 2008.

85 See FLA website: www.fairlabor.org/index.html, accessed February 11, 2008.

86 From the FLA Workplace Code of Conduct website: www.fairlabor.org/all/code/index.html, accessed February 11, 2008.

87 Some of this history can be found at LEAP's website: www.usleap.org/node/407, accessed February 19, 2008.

88 Starbucks' Supplier Code and a link to the Sourcing Guidelines can be found at: www.starbucks.com/aboutus/supplier_code.asp, accessed February 19, 2008.

89 See the Caux Round Table's history at www.cauxroundtable.org/history.html, accessed February 11, 2008.

90 In 1984 R. Edward Freeman published the book that popularized stakeholder thinking, *Strategic Management: A Stakeholder Approach*. Freeman has continued to develop his ideas and with others has published an updated version of the original book: *Managing for Stakeholders*.

91 Source: Caux Roundtable website, "Principles": www.cauxroundtable.org/documents/ Principles%20for%20Business.PDF, accessed March 12, 2008. Note that explanations of the principles have been omitted.

92 "People of the same trade seldom meet together, even for merriment or diversion, but the conversation ends in a conspiracy," in Smith, *The Wealth of Nations*.

93 Principles for Responsible Globalization, drafted in 2002, can be found at: www. cauxroundtable.org/documents/PRINCIPLESFORGLOBALIZATION2.doc, accessed February 11, 2008.

94 Principles for NGOs can be found at: www.cauxroundtable.org/documents/ PrinciplesforNGOs11-03.pdf, accessed February 11, 2008.

95 From Principles for Responsible Government embedded in Principles for Responsible Globalization, at: www.cauxroundtable.org/principles.html, accessed March 31, 2008.

96 From Caux Round Table, Principles for NGOs: www.cauxroundtable.org/documents/ PrinciplesforNGOs11-03.pdf, accessed February 11, 2008.

97 Ibid.

98 From the Global Compact website, available at: unglobalcompact.org/NewsAndEvents/ news_archives/2007_07_05d.html, accessed March 17, 2008.

99 From UN Global Compact website: unglobalcompact.org/AboutTheGC/index.html, accessed 12 February, 2008.

100 From UN Global Compact Principles website at: unglobalcompact.org/AboutTheGC/ TheTenPrinciples/index.html, accessed February 12, 2008.

101 The Principles for Responsible Investment, along with suggested possible actions, can be found at: www.unpri.org/principles, accessed February 12, 2008.

102 Information on Principles of Responsible Management Education Final Draft Principles can be found at www.unglobalcompact.org/HowToParticipate/academic_network/ index.html, accessed February 12, 2008.

103 UN, "Resolution adopted by the UN General Assembly, 55/2 United Nations Millennium Declaration."

104 Ibid.

105 From the UN Millennium Goals website: www.un.org/millenniumgoals, accessed February 12, 2008.

106 UN, "Promotion and Protection of Human Rights?"

Chapter 6

107 Gray and Milne, "Sustainability Reporting," p. 2.

108 www.sustainability.com, accessed February 19, 2008.

109 www.sustainability.com/about/index.asp, accessed February 19, 2008.

110 www.sustainability.com/about/rules-of-engagement.asp, accessed February 14, 2008.

111 SustainAbility, "Overview," at: www.sustainability.com/about/overview.asp, accessed February 19, 2008.

112 Sustainability, "Governance," posted at: www.sustainability.com/about/governance.asp, accessed March 1, 2007.

113 From John Elkington's website, johnelkington.com/babelfish.htm, accessed February 14, 2008.

114 www.tellus.org/institute/#, accessed February 19, 2008.

115 Portions of the Allen White interview are published in Waddock, "On Ceres, the GRI, and Corporation 20/20."

116 See www.globalreporting.org/Home, accessed February 15, 2008.

117 These and other details of the history of the GRI can be found at: www.globalreporting.org/AboutGRI/WhatWeDo/OurHistory, accessed February 19, 2008.

118 Details of the GRI framework and the specific guidelines can be found at: www.globalreporting.org, accessed February 19, 2008, and www.globalreporting.org/ReportingFramework, accessed February 19, 2008.

119 See www.globalreporting.org/ReportingFramework/G3Online/DefiningReportContent, accessed February 19, 2008.

120 See www.globalreporting.org/ReportingFramework/G3Online/DefiningReportQuality, accessed February 19, 2008.

121 Gap Inc., "Social Report" (2004).

Chapter 7

122 See www.longfellowclubs.com, accessed February 19, 2008.

123 Ben & Jerry's Ice Cream, founded by Ben Cohen and Jerry Greenfield in 1978 in Burlington, VT, was one of the first companies to operate with what would today be called the triple bottom line. Now owned by multinational consumer giant Unilever, the company operated independently with this mission for many years and was one of the early business leaders of the responsibility movement. For background and information, see the Ben & Jerry's website: www.benjerry.com, particularly the history page: www.benjerry.com/our_company/our_history, accessed February 19, 2008.

124 See www.tomsofmaine.com, accessed March 28, 2008.

125 Information about Stonyfield Farm, now owned by the French company, Danone, can be found at: www.stonyfield.com, accessed February 19, 2008.

126 For information on Stride Rite, see www.striderite.com, accessed February 19, 2008. For all the companies mentioned in this paragraph, numerous changes have occurred over the years, including acquisitions and dramatic business shifts. Nonetheless, all were considered leaders in corporate responsibility during the era that Hammel is discussing.

127 www.bsr.org, accessed February 15, 2008.

128 www.bsr.org/Meta/about/Mission.cfm, accessed February 15, 2008.

129 The 2007 International Symposium on Business and Spirituality was posted on the Babson College website: www3.babson.edu/Events/spiritualityandbusiness. The goals are at: www3.babson.edu/Events/spiritualityandbusiness/Event-Overview.cfm, accessed February 15, 2008.

130 David Korten is a well-known activist and author of *When Corporations Rule the World* and *The Great Turning.*

131 Hammel and Denhart, *Growing Local Value.*

132 BALLE's website: www.livingeconomies.org. See also www.livingeconomies.org/aboutus, accessed February 15, 2008..

133 From www.livingeconomies.org/aboutus/defininglocal, accessed February 19, 2008.

134 www.livingeconomies.org/aboutus/mission-and-principles-1, accessed February 15, 2008.

135 Social Venture Network website, "Who We Are": www.svn.org/index.cfm?fuseaction= page.viewPage&pageid=482, accessed March 17, 2008.

136 Social Venture Network website: www.svn.org/organization.html, viewed March 26, 2007.

137 BITC website: www.bitc.org.uk/#story1, accessed February 15, 2008.

138 IBLF website: www.iblf.org, accessed February 15, 2008.

139 www.iblf.org/about_us.jsp, accessed March 14, 2008.

140 For information on the Small Business Consortium and the tools, see www.smallbusinessjourney.com, accessed February 15, 2008.

141 www.bc.edu/centers/cwf, accessed February 15, 2008.

142 www.bc.edu/centers/cwf/about.html, accessed February 15, 2008.

143 www.bcccc.net/index.cfm?fuseaction=Page.viewPage&pageId=490, accessed February 15, 2008.

144 The model for standards of excellence can be found at: www.bcccc.net/index.cfm? fuseaction=Page.viewPage&pageID=707, accessed February 15, 2008, and the toolkit can be downloaded at: www.bcccc.net/_uploads/documents/live/diag_tool_2.pdf, accessed February 15, 2008

145 Current activities of the CCC are listed at: www.bcccc.net/index.cfm?fuseaction=Page. viewPage&pageId=569&nodeID=1&parentID=490, accessed February 15, 2008.

146 www.bcccc.net/index.cfm?fuseaction=Page.viewPage&pageID=1100, accessed February 15, 2008.

147 www.bcccc.net/index.cfm?fuseaction=Page.viewPage&pageId=1082&grandparentID=490 &parentID=569, accessed February 15, 2008.

148 www.thecro.com/index.php, accessed February 15, 2008.

149 The Ethics and Compliance Officer Association website: www.theecoa.org//AM/Template. cfm?Section=Home. The vision statement is at: www.theecoa.org/AM/Template.cfm? Section=Mission&Template=/CM/HTMLDisplay.cfm&ContentID=1278, both accessed February 15, 2008.

150 www.bc.edu/schools/csom/leadership/lfc, accessed February 15, 2008.

151 Founded by Harvard Kennedy School of Government professor L. David Brown and Jane Covey, an organization that worked with and resourced large-scale social change, mostly in developing nations. It is no longer in operation.

152 Ralph Taylor is the same person whose family foundation funded the start-up of the GRI.

153 gan-net.net, accessed February 15, 2008.

154 www.gan-net.net/institutions_people, accessed February 15, 2008.

155 This list is from the GAN-Net website, which can be checked for updates and elaboration at: gan-net.net/about, accessed February 15, 2008.

156 www.ethicaltrade.org, accessed February 19, 2008.

157 www.fairlabor.org, accessed February 19, 2008.

158 www.fsc.org, accessed February 19, 2008.

159 www.unglobalcompact.org, accessed February 19, 2008.

160 www.globalreporting.org, accessed February 19, 2008.

161 www.ictsd.org, accessed February 15, 2008.

162 www.ifat.org, accessed February 19, 2008.

163 www.microcreditsummit.org, accessed February 19, 2008.

164 www.sa-intl.org, accessed February 19, 2008.

165 www.transparency.org, accessed February 19, 2008.

166 gan-net.net/about, accessed February 15, 2008.

Chapter 8

167 Corporate Citizenship's website is: www.corporate-citizenship.com, accessed February 15, 2008.

168 Corporate Citizenship, "What We Do": www.corporate-citizenship.co.uk/what-we-do, accessed March 17, 2008.

169 Details about the London Benchmarking Group can be found at: www.lbg-online.net, accessed February 15, 2008.

170 www2.warwick.ac.uk/fac/soc/wbs/research/ccu, accessed February 15, 2008.

171 This language is from the *Journal of Corporate Citizenship*'s website: www.greenleaf-publishing.com/jcc, accessed February 19, 2008. Disclosure: I served as the second editor of JCC, following Malcolm McIntosh's first term as editor.

172 www.coventry.ac.uk/researchnet/d/176/a/492, accessed February 15, 2008.

173 www.ksg.harvard.edu/m-rcbg/CSRI/home.html, accessed February 15, 2008. Note that difference maker John Ruggie, discussed in Chapter 5, heads the Mossavar-Rahmani Center for Business and Government, which houses the CSRI.

174 The IBLF, discussed in Chapter 7 in the context of David Grayson's difference making, can be found at: www.iblf.org, accessed February 15, 2008.

175 The WBCSD's website is: www.wbcsd.ch and its mission statement can be found at: www.wbcsd.ch → "About the WBCSD," accessed February 15, 2008.

176 Ibid.

177 Ibid.

178 Brugger *et al.*

179 www.ksg.harvard.edu/m-rcbg/CSRI, accessed February 15, 2008.

180 www.ksg.harvard.edu/m-rcbg/CSRI/init_define.html, accessed February 15, 2008.

181 www.lisc.org, accessed February 19, 2008.

182 www.sbk.com, accessed February 19, 2008.

183 www.grameen-info.org, accessed February 19, 2008.

184 The Aspen Institute's website is: www.aspeninstitute.org, and the mission statement can be found at: www.aspeninstitute.org → "About the Aspen Institute," accessed February 19, 2008.

185 www.aspeninstitute.org → "Our Policy Work" → "Business & Society," accessed February 19, 2008.

186 www.wri.org/about, accessed February 15, 2008.

187 Ibid.

188 www.beyondgreypinstripes.org/about, accessed February 15, 2008.

189 Current rankings can be found at: www.beyondgreypinstripes.org/rankings/top30.cfm, accessed February 15, 2008.

190 www.beyondgreypinstripes.org/about, accessed February 15, 2008.

191 www.aspencbe.org/awards/pioneers, accessed February 15, 2008. Disclosure: I was awarded the 2005 Faculty Pioneer Award for External Impact.

192 www.eabis.org, accessed March 28, 2008.

193 "About EABIS": www.eabis.org/about, accessed March 17, 2008.

194 Portions of this interview were published in Waddock, "On Ceres, the GRI, and Corporation 20/20."

195 www.corporation2020.org, accessed February 15, 2008.

196 Ibid.

197 Ibid.

Chapter 9

198 *Corporations and the Public Interest.*

199 *New York Times* columnist and author of *The World is Flat.*

200 Gladwell, *The Tipping Point.*

201 By C. Hampden-Turner and A. Trompenaars.

202 *Loosing the Bonds.*

Abbreviations and acronyms

AS	Assurance Standard
AFL–CIO	American Federation of Labor and Congress of Industrial Organizations
AIESEC	International Association of Students of Economics and Commerce
AIG	American International Group
ARCHS	Applied Research Centre in Human Security (Coventry University)
BALLE	Business Alliance for Local Living Economies.
BBC	British Broadcasting Corporation
BCSD	Business Council for Sustainable Development
BITC	Business in the Community
BSR	Business for Social Responsibility
CCC	Center for Corporate Citizenship (Boston College)
CCU	Corporate Citizenship Unit
CEO	chief executive officer
CEP	Council on Economic Priorities
CSR	corporate social responsibility
CSRI	Corporate Social Responsibility Initiative (Harvard University)
CWF	Center for Work and Family (Boston University)
DSI	Domini Social Index
EBEN	European Business Ethics Network
EABIS	European Academy of Business in Society
ENDS	Environmental Data Services
ESG	environmental, social, and governance
ETI	Ethical Trading Initiative
FLA	Fair Labor Association
FUNDES	Fundación para Desarrollo Sostenible
GAAP	generally accepted accounting principles
GAN	global action network
GAN-Net	Global Action Network Net
GE	General Electric
GEMI	Global Environmental Management Initiative
GM	General Motors; genetically modified

GRI	Global Reporting Initiative
IBLF	International Business Leaders Forum
ICCR	Interfaith Center on Corporate Responsibility
ICFTU	International Confederation of Free Trade Unions
IDR	Institute for Development Research
ILO	International Labour Organization
IRI	Institute for Responsible Investment
ISO	International Organization for Standardization
JCC	*Journal of Corporate Citizenship*
LEAP	Labor Education in the Americas Project
LISC	Local Initiatives Support Corporation
MFA	Multi-Fiber Agreement
NEBSR	New England Businesses for Social Responsibility
NEF	New Economics Foundation
NGO	non-governmental organization
OECD	Organization for Economic Cooperation and Development
OHCHR	Office of the High Commissioner on Human Rights
RSA	Royal Society of Arts, Manufacture & Commerce
S&P	Standard & Poor's
SAI	Social Accountability International
SES	Stakeholder Engagement Standard
SIRAN	Social Investment Research Analysts Network
SiRi	Sustainable Investment Research International
SME	small or medium-sized enterprise
SRI	socially responsible investing
SVN	Social Venture Network
TIAA-CREF	Teachers Insurance and Annuity Association and College Retirement Equities Fund
TQM	total quality management
TRM	total responsibility management
UN	United Nations
UNCTAD	United Nations Conference on Trade and Development
UNDP	United Nations Development Program
UNEP	United Nations Environment Program
UNESCO	United Nations Educational, Scientific, and Cultural Organization
UNIDO	United Nations Industrial Development Organization
UNODC	United Nations Office on Drugs and Crime
USAID	United States Agency for International Development
VOTF	Voice of the Faithful
WBCSD	World Business Council for Sustainable Development
WCED	World Commission on Environment and Development
WHO	World Health Organization
WIDER	World Institute for Development Economics Research
WRI	World Resources Institute
WTO	World Trade Organization

Index of organizations

principles • publications • awards • funds • indexes

50 Best Companies for Minorities (*Fortune*)
49
100 Best Companies for Working Mothers
49
100 Best Companies to Work For (*Fortune*)
49

Academy of Management
Organizations and the Natural Environment
57
Social Issues in Management 57
AccountAbility 26, 44, 106-14, 276
AA1000 series 44, 48, 109, 112
AA1000 Assurance Standard
(AA1000AS) 44
AA1000 Stakeholder Engagement
Standard (AA1000SES) 50
Global Accountability Rating 110
Partnership, Governance, and
Accountability Framework 110
Adidas 143
AFL–CIO (American Federation of Labor and
Congress of Industrial Organizations)
190
AIESEC
see International Association of Students of
Economics and Commerce
AIG
see American International Group
Allstate 253
Altria 96
America's Corporate Conscience Award 67,
103
America's Most Admired Companies (*Fortune*)
49
**American Federation of Labor and Congress
of Industrial Organizations**
see AFL–CIO

American Home Products 117
American International Group (AIG) 196
Amnesty International 177, 238
**Analistas Internacionales en Sostenibilidad
SA** 40
Andover-Newton Theological Seminary
206
**Applied Research Centre in Human Security
(ARCHS), Coventry University** 28, 236,
240-42
Ashridge Center for Business and Society 57
Asian Institute for Business in Society 294
Aspen Institute 256
Business in Society Program 28, 55, 57,
250-51, 256, 290, 294
Faculty Pioneers Program 256, 259
see also Beyond Grey Pinstripes
Association of Sustainability Practitioners
52
AT&T 74
Avanzi SRI Research 40

Bainbridge Graduate Institute 57
Baldrige National Quality Award 153
BALLE
see Business Alliance for Local Living
Economics
Bank of America 69, 252-54
Bank of Boston 69-70
BBC 237, 238
Natural History Unit 238
BCSD
see Business Council for Sustainable
Development
Ben & Jerry's 108, 199, 201
Berrett-Koehler Publishers 211
Best 100 Corporate Citizens (*Business
Ethics/CRO*) 48-49, 98

Beyond Grey Pinstripes   250, 256-58
BITC
    see Business in the Community
BLU   212
Body Shop, The   108, 201-202
Boston College   220, 224
    Center for Corporate Citizenship (CCC)
        28, 37, 39, 51-53, 57, 90, 101, 110, 217-
        18, 221-22, 253-54, 269
    Center for Corporate Community Relations
        (CCR)   51, 218, 220-21
    Graduate School of Social Work   219
    Leadership for Change   223, 224
    see also Institute for Responsible Investment
Boston Globe   122, 125
Boston Safe Index   95
Boston University   26, 82, 115, 120, 217, 219-
    20
    Center for Work and Family (CWF)   28, 217,
        219-21
    School of Management   114
    School of Social Work   218
BP   47, 179, 182, 231, 238
Bristol University   238
Brookings Institution   224, 242
BSR
    see Business for Social Responsibility
Burnham & Co.   63-64
**Business Alliance for Local Living
    Economies (BALLE)**   27, 198, 206-208,
    210-11
**Business and Human Rights Resource
    Center**   54
Business and Society   56, 240
Business and Society Review   56
**Business Council for Sustainable
    Development (BCSD)**   245-46
Business Enterprise Trust   254
Business Ethics   56
    Best 100 Corporate Citizens   48, 98
Business Ethics Quarterly   56, 240
Business for Social Responsibility (BSR)
    27, 37, 50-53, 137-38, 198, 200-207, 209-10,
    254, 280
    BSR New England   206
    Canadian Business for Social Responsibility
        52
Business in the Community (BITC)   27, 51-
    53, 212-16, 282
    Corporate Responsibility Index   48-49,
        214-15
    Seeing is Believing   214
Business Respect   56, 240
Business Week   257

Cadbury   232
CalPERS   38

Calvert   38, 55, 84
    Calvert Social Index   39
    Calvert Social Investment Fund   66, 84
    Calvert–Henderson Quality of Life
        Indicators   55-56
Cambridge Center for Adult Education   82
Canadian Business for Social Responsibility
    52
Carbon Neutral Initiative   211
CasePlace   251, 256-57
Catholic Church   45, 114, 121-28
Caux Round Table   27, 52-53, 145-55
    Principles for Business   35-36, 147-51, 153
    Principles for NGOs   154-55
    Principles for Responsible Globalization
        154-55
    Principles for Responsible Government
        154
CBS   74
Census Bureau Data   63
Center for Business and Government
    see Harvard University
Centre for Community Enterprise (Canada)
    54
Center for Corporate Citizenship (CCC)
    see Boston College
**Center for Corporate Community Relations
    (CCR)**
    see Boston College
Center for the Study of Fiduciary Capitalism
    279
Center for Work and Family (CWF)
    see Boston University
Centre for Corporate Citizenship
    see University of South Africa
Centre Info SA   40
CEP
    see Council on Economic Priorities
Ceres   26-27, 44, 51-53, 69, 130-33, 136-38, 153,
    187-94, 196, 228, 282, 284-86, 290
    Ceres Principles   35-36, 130-32, 136, 188,
        277
Chamber of Commerce (UK)   216
Chamber of Commerce (US)
    Business Civic Leadership Center   52
Citibank   77, 243, 244-45
CitiCorp   231
Citizens Global   38
**Coalition for Environmentally Responsible
    Economies**
    see Ceres
College Retirement Equities Fund   66
Commission on Human Rights
    see UN
Commonwealth Edison   74
Companies Act (UK)   241
Conference Board, The   114, 120

Co-op America   40
Coopers & Lybrand   107
Corporate Accountability International   49
   see also INFACT
Corporate Accountability Project   48-49
Corporate Citizenship Research Unit
   see Deakin University
Corporate Citizenship Unit
   see University of Warwick
Corporate Citizenship   46, 230, 235-36
   see also Corporate Citizenship Company
Corporate Citizenship Company, The   28,
   45, 230, 235
   see also Corporate Citizenship
Corporate Predators   48-49
Corporate Responsibility Officer
   Association
   see CRO
Corporate Social Responsibility Initiative
   (CSRI)
   see Harvard University
Corporate Values Strategy Group   251
Corporate Watch   48-49
Corporation 20/20   27-28, 54-55, 187, 261-64,
   279, 284
   Principles of Corporate Design   284
Council for Responsible Public Investment
   40
Council on Economic Priorities (CEP)   26,
   63-68, 90-92, 95-96, 101-103, 106, 175, 236,
   238
   America's Corporate Conscience Awards
      67, 103
Cranfield University   212
CRO (Corporate Responsibility Officer
   Association)   45, 222
   CRO magazine   45, 56, 222
      Best 100 Corporate Citizens   49
CSR Academy   57
CSR Europe   51-53
CSR Global: Ethics and Corporate
   Responsibility Consulting   46
CSRwire   56, 240
CVS   210

Deakin University
   Corporate Citizenship Research Unit   57
Dell   196
Deloitte & Touche
   Corporate Governance and Accountability
      46
Digital Equipment   95
Directions for the '90s   214-15
Domini Social Investments   26, 38, 81, 90,
   93, 95, 99-100
   Domini 400 Social Index (DSI)   26, 38-39,
      81, 84-86, 94, 98-99

Domini EuroPacific Social Equity Fund   86
Domini European Social Equity Fund   86
Domini Money Market Account   86
Domini PacAsia Social Equity Fund   86
Domini Social Bond Fund   86
Domini Social Equity Fund   84-86
Doughty Centre for Corporate
   Responsibility   212
Dow Chemical   76
Dow Jones Sustainability Index   39
Drexel Burnham Lambert   66, 85
Dreyfus   38
   Third Century Fund   66, 84
Dubai Ethics Resource Center   52
Dutch East India Company   22
Dutch Sustainability Research BV   40

EABIS (European Academy of Business in
   Society)   57, 259-60, 294
Earth Summit, Rio de Janeiro, 1992   175,
   245-47
Earthlife   180
EBRD
   see European Bank for Reconstruction and
      Development
Empresa Alliance   204
ENDS (Environmental Data Services)   179
Enron   24, 41
Environmental Data Services
   see ENDS
Environmental Defense
   Fund/Environmental Defense   137, 182
Environmental Protection Agency (USA)   22
Episcopal Church   134
Equator Principles   35, 36
ESADE   110
Ethical Corporation   56, 240
Ethical Trading Initiative (ETI)   54, 106, 108,
   109, 226
Ethics and Compliance Officer Association
   222-23
Ethics Resource Center   52
Ethos Institute for Business and Social
   Responsibility
   see Instituto Ethos Empresas e
      Responsibilidade Social
ETI
   see Ethical Trading Initiative
European Academy of Business in Society
   see EABIS
European Bank for Reconstruction and
   Development (EBRD)   184
European Business Ethics Network   57
European Commission   279
European Partners for the Environment   54
European Policy Centre   110

Eurosif (European Social Investment Forum)   39, 72, 279
Exxon   210

Faculty Pioneer Awards   259
Fair Labor Association (FLA)   44, 108, 143, 226, 278
    Workplace Code of Conduct   143-44
Fair Pension   40
Fair Trade Labeling Organization   44
Federation for Small Businesses   216
Financial Times
    World's Most Respected Companies   48
FLA
    see Fair Labor Association
Ford   186
Ford Foundation   65, 221, 250-56, 259
    Corporate Involvement Initiative   250, 254
Foreign Corrupt Practices Act (USA)   34
Forest Stewardship Council   44, 226-28
Fortune   67
    50 Best Companies for Minorities   49
    100 Best Companies to Work For   48-49
    America's Most Admired Companies   48-49
    Global Most Admired Companies   49
Franklin Management   70
Franklin Research and Development   26, 66, 69-71, 84, 92, 95
    see also Trillium Asset Management
Friends of the Earth   177
FTSE4Good   39
Fundación Empresa y Sociedad   52
FUNDES (Fundación para Desarrollo Sostenible)   243, 247

GAAP (generally accepted accounting principles)   110-11, 187, 194
GAN-Net (Global Action Network Net)   28, 54-55, 226-28, 223, 225-26
Gap Inc.   47, 142-43, 196
GEMI (Global Environmental Management Initiative)   51-53
General Electric (GE)   74, 270
General Motors (GM)   73-74, 77
    GM Foundation   194
GES Investment Services AB   40
Global 100 Most Sustainable Corporations in the World   49
Global Action Network Net
    see GAN-Net
Global Compact   27, 35, 55, 153, 156-64, 226, 239, 288, 294
    Global Policy Dialogues   164
    Leaders Summit   158
    Principles   36, 159

Principles for Responsible Investment   35-36, 165, 166
Principles for Responsible Management Education   165, 167
Global Environmental Management Initiative
    see GEMI
Global Ethic Foundation   52
Global Exchange   49
Global Leadership Network   110, 222
Global Most Admired Companies (*Fortune*)   49
Global Public Policy Network Research Group   224, 226
Global Reporting Initiative (GRI)   27, 47, 69, 106, 111, 133, 137-38, 187-95, 226, 261-62, 277, 284-85, 290
    G3   195
    Sustainability Guidelines   194
Global Sullivan Principles   35-36, 77, 138
GM
    see General Motors
Going Global Project   222
Good Money   40, 84
Grameen Bank   88, 251
Green Century   38
Green Reporting Forum   52
GreenBiz   56, 240
Greener Management International   56
Greenpeace   177, 184, 190
GRI
    see Global Reporting Initiative
Gulf Oil   74

Hamline University School of Law   146
Harvard University
    Harvard Business School   133, 136, 248-49
    Harvard Law School   146
    Kennedy School of Government   27
        Mossavar-Rahmani Center for Business and Government   27, 106, 248, 268, 280
        Corporate Social Responsibility Initiative (CSRI)   28, 57, 242, 248-50
Herman Miller   95
Hispanic Corporate 100   49
Home Depot   210
Honeywell   74
Human Rights Advocates   49-50
Human Rights Watch   49-50, 177

IABS
    see International Association for Business in Society
IBLF
    see International Business Leaders Forum

ICC
see International Chamber of Commerce
ICCR
see Interfaith Center on Corporate
Responsibility
ICFTU
see International Confederation of Free
Trade Unions
ICI 179, 182
ICTSD
see International Center for Trade and
Sustainable Development
IDR
see Institute for Development Research
IFAT 226
IFC
see International Finance Corporation
ILO
see International Labour Organization
IMF
see International Monetary Fund
INFACT (Infant Formula Action Committee)
78
see also Corporate Accountability
International
**Initiative for Social Innovation through
Business** 256
Inner City 100 49
Innovest Strategic Value Advisors 40
Global 100 Most Sustainable Corporations
in the World 49
INSEAD 110
Institute of Chartered Accountants 37
Institute for Development Research (IDR)
224-25
Institute for Directors 216
Institute for Global Ethics 44
Institute for Responsible Investment (IRI)
26, 39-40, 90, 99-101, 228, 279
**Institute of Ethical and Social
AccountAbility**
see AccountAbility
Institute of Policy Studies 23
Institutional Shareholder Services 40
**Instituto Ethos Empresas e
Responsibilidade Social (Ethos Institute
for Business and Social Responsibility)**
54
InterAction
Private Voluntary Organization (PVO)
Standards 36
Interbrand
Most Valuable Brands 49
Interface 47
**Interfaith Center on Corporate
Responsibility (ICCR)** 26, 39-40, 72-80,
94, 117, 286

**International Association for Business in
Society (IABS)** 57
**International Association of Students of
Economics and Commerce (AIESEC)**
245
**International Business Leaders Forum
(IBLF)** 28, 51-53, 215-16, 242, 248
**International Center for Trade and
Sustainable Development (ICTSD)** 52,
226
International Chamber of Commerce (ICC)
160
**International Confederation of Free Trade
Unions (ICFTU)** 190
International Finance Corporation (IFC)
185
International Labour Organization (ILO)
34, 104-105, 162, 163
Tripartite Declaration of Principles
Concerning Multinational
Enterprises 36
International Monetary Fund (IMF) 23, 37
**International Organization for
Standardization**
see ISO
**International Physicians for the Prevention
of Nuclear War (IPPNW)** 124
**International Symposium on Business and
Spirituality** 198, 205-206
Interpraxis 46
Investor Network on Climate Risk 69, 138,
228
Investors Financial 86
IPPNW
see International Physicians for the
Prevention of Nuclear War
IRI
see Institute for Responsible Investment
**ISO (International Organization for
Standardization)** 45, 104-105
ISO 14000 104
ISO 26000 26, 105
Strategic Advisory Group on Corporate
Social Responsibility of ISO 44

Jantzi Research Inc. 40
Jesuits 217
**Joint Initiative on Corporate Responsibility
and Worker Rights** 278
Journal of Business Ethics 56, 240
Journal of Corporate Citizenship 28, 56, 236,
239-40
Joy of Movement 70
Jubilee 2000 Global Debt Campaign 109

KAYEMA Investment Research & Analysis
40

Kemper SNS/Smaller Europe Social Responsible Investment Index   39
Kennedy School of Government
see Harvard University
Kinder, Lydenberg & Domini   85, 92
KLD Research & Analytics   26, 38, 40, 65-66, 81, 84-85, 90, 92-100
   Domini 400 Social Index (DSI)
      see Domini Social Investments
   KLD Broad Market Social Index   99
   KLD Dividend Achievers Social Index   99
   KLD Global Climate 100 Index   99
   KLD Large Cap Social Index   99
   KLD Select Social Index   99
KPMG   30-31

Labor Education in the Americas Project (LEAP)   145
Levi Strauss   27, 35, 103-104, 138, 140-42, 196, 201-203, 230-34, 253
   Business Partner Terms of Engagement   142
   Country Assessment Guidelines   142
   Global Sourcing and Operating Guidelines   142
LISC (Local Initiatives Support Corporation)   251
London Benchmarking Group   230, 236
Longfellow Clubs   27, 197-99
Loring, Wolcott & Coolidge   81, 85, 92, 97

Maendeleo Consultants   107
Making Waves   54
Marks & Spencer   231
McDonald's   70, 88, 181-82, 207
MetLife   252
Microcredit Summit Campaign   226
Millennium Development Goals   54-56, 156, 168-71, 216, 248
Millennium Summit   156, 168, 170
   Millennium Declaration   168, 170
Minnesota Center for Corporate Responsibility   148
   Minnesota Principles   147-48
Monsanto   182, 185-86
Moral Re-Armament Network   146
Morrison's Cafeterias   139
Mossavar-Rahmani Center for Business and Government
see Harvard University
Multi-Fiber Agreement (MFA) Forum   110
Multinational Monitor   49

National Council of Churches   75
NEBSR
see New England Businesses for Social Responsibility

NEF
see New Economics Foundation
Nestlé   78, 114, 116-17, 119, 127-28
Nestlé Audit Commission   26, 78, 114-18
Net Impact   57
New Alternative Fund   66
New Economics Foundation (NEF)   52, 106-109, 112
New England Businesses for Social Responsibility (NEBSR)   27, 198-200
New Scientist   179
Nike   138, 143, 162, 196

OECD (Organization for Economic Cooperation and Development)   24
   Guidelines for Multinational Enterprises   36
Olin Foundation   192
Organization and Environment   56
Organizations and the Natural Environment   240
Organizations and the Natural Environment   57
OWW Responsibility Malaysia SRI Index   39
Oxfam   190

Parnassus   38
Patagonia   201
Pax World Fund   38, 66, 84
Pensions & Investment Research Consultants Ltd.
see PIRC
Philip Morris   96-97, 209-10
Physicians for Social Responsibility (PSR)   200
Pioneer Fund   66, 84
PIRC   40
PNE Group   212
Polaroid   219
PricewaterhouseCoopers   46
   World's Most Respected Companies   48
Prince of Wales International Business Leaders Forum
see International Business Leaders Forum
Prince's Youth Business Trust   28, 213
Princeton University   134
Principles for Responsible Investment   35-36, 165, 166
Procter & Gamble   180, 182, 212
Project North East   212-13
Prudential   252
PSR
see Physicians for Social Responsibility

Quakers   63, 237

Redefining Progress
    Genuine Progress Indicator   55-56
Reebok   103, 143, 200
Reputation Institute   48
Responsible Business Association   198
Responsible Business Initiative   54
Responsible Wealth   40
Reuters   253
Risk Metrics Group   40
RJR   210
Rockefeller Foundation   115
Royal Dutch Shell
    see Shell
Rugmark International   44

S&P
    see Standard & Poor's
SA8000
    see Social Accountability International
SAI
    see Social Accountability International
Sainsbury's   47, 231
Scoris GmbH   40
Shearson American Express   66
Shell   175, 182, 231
ShoreBank
    see South Shore Bank
SIF
    see Social Investment Forum
SIRAN
    see Social Investment Research Analyst
        Network
SiRi Company
    see Sustainable Investment Research
        International Ltd.
Slow Food   88
Small Business Consortium   28, 216-17
    Small Business Journey   216-17
Smart Company   235
Smith Barney   38
SmithOBrien   45-46
Social Accountability International (SAI)
    26, 44, 48, 63, 68, 91-92, 101-106, 138, 226,
    238, 271, 276-78, 280, 287, 290
    SA8000   44, 105, 277
Social Impact Leadership Coalition   211
Social Investment Forum (SIF)   26, 39, 41,
    69, 72, 78, 83, 138, 228, 286
**Social Investment Research Analyst Network
    (SIRAN)**   39, 228
Social Issues in Management   57
Social Venture Institute   211
Social Venture Network (SVN)   40, 209, 211,
    228
    Standard on Corporate Social Responsibility
        211
SocialFunds.com   40

Society for Business Ethics   57
Society of Friends
    see Quakers
South Shore Bank   86, 251
Southern Africa Committee   73
SRI in the Rockies Conference   39
SRI Index (Johannesburg)   39
Standard & Poor's   84-85, 95, 99
    S&P index   98
Starbucks   145, 207
    Framework for a Code of Conduct   145
    Sourcing Guidelines   145
    Supplier Code of Conduct   145
Stellenbosch University
    School of Public Management and Planning
        236
Stonyfield Farm   199
Stride Rite   199, 202
Sullivan Principles
    see Global Sullivan Principles
Sunday Times   214-15
SustainAbility   27, 45-46, 175-76, 179-86
    Rules of Engagement   180-82
Sustainable Business   56
Sustainable Enterprise Academy
    see York University
**Sustainable Investment Research Institute
    Pty. Ltd.**   40
**Sustainable Investment Research
    International Ltd. (SiRi Company)**   39-
    40, 99
Sustainable Value Partners   45-46
SVN
    see Social Venture Network
Sweatshop Watch   49-50
Synergos Institute   139

Tamarack   54
Teachers Insurance and Annuity Association
    66
Tellus Institute   27, 187
    Corporate Redesign   187
    Great Transition Initiative   187
Texas Instruments   253
Tom's of Maine   199, 201
Top 30 Companies for Executive Women
    49
Trades Union Congress (UK)   230
Transfair   44
Transparency International   44, 175, 190,
    226
Traveler's Corporation   66
Trillium Asset Management   26, 38, 69-72,
    84, 92, 95, 130
    see also Franklin Research and Development
Tucker Anthony   82

UK Social Investment Forum (UKSIF)   39
UN (United Nations)   28, 117, 157-58, 160,
        162-64, 168-69, 171-72, 179, 194, 239, 242,
        248, 250, 268, 283
    Business Norms   264
    Conference on Trade and Development
        (UNCTAD)   160
    Convention against Corruption   158
    Development Program (UNDP)   163, 178
    Environment Program (UNEP)   162, 194,
        243
    General Assembly   175, 242
    Industrial Development Organization
        (UNIDO)   163
    Office on Drugs and Crime (UNODC)   162-
        63
    Office of the High Commissioner on
        Human Rights (OHCHR)   162-63
        Commission on Human Rights   171-73
    Security Council   287
    UNICEF   117-18
    United Nations Foundation   194
    see also Earth Summit; Global Compact;
        Millennium Development Goals
Unilever   182, 232
Union Carbide   74
Union Theological Seminary   73
United Aircraft Corporation   74
United Auto Workers   74
United Church of Christ   73, 198
**United States Agency for International
    Development**
    see USAID
United Way   274
Universal Declaration of Human Rights
    242
University of Natal   243-44
University of South Africa
    Centre for Corporate Citizenship   57
    School of Management Sciences   106
University of Toronto   72
University of Utah   199
University of Warwick
    Corporate Citizenship Unit   28, 57, 236,
        238-39
USAID   115, 224
US News   257
US Trust   66, 84, 92
UTC   74
Utopies   46

Valdez Principles   130, 188, 189
Van City Savings Credit Union   223
Vanderbilt University   139
Verité   44
Voice of the Faithful (VOTF)   45, 119, 121-27

Walden Asset Management   26, 38, 66, 72,
        78
Wal-Mart   210, 270
WBCSD
    see World Business Council for Sustainable
        Development
WCED
    see World Commission on Environment and
        Development
Wellesley College   63
Wellington Management   86
Wesleyan University   140
WHO (World Health Organization)   116-20,
        170
WIDER
    see World Institute for Development
        Economics Research
Working Woman   67
World Bank   23, 37, 170, 194, 225, 248
**World Business Council for Sustainable
    Development (WBCSD)**   51-53, 243, 246-
        48, 294
**World Commission on Environment and
    Development (WCED)**   175
World Council for Corporate Governance
    52-53
World Economic Forum   54, 106, 157, 161,
        243, 248
    Global 100 Most Sustainable Corporations
        in the World   49
World Health Organization
    see WHO
**World Institute for Development
    Economics Research (WIDER)**   24
World Leaders Forum   165
World Resources Institute (WRI)   256-58
World Social Forum   54
**World Summit on Sustainable
    Development, Johannesburg**   175
World Trade Organization (WTO)   23, 37,
        125, 206
World's Most Respected Companies   48
WorldCom   41
WRI
    see World Resources Institute
WTO
    see World Trade Organization
WWF   177, 190

Yale Divinity School   135
York University
    Sustainable Enterprise Academy   57